palgrave advances in the modern history of sexuality

Palgrave Advances

Titles include:

H.G. Cocks and Matt Houlbrook (*editors*)
THE MODERN HISTORY OF SEXUALITY

Patrick Finney (*editor*)
INTERNATIONAL HISTORY

Jonathan Harris (*editor*)
BYZANTINE HISTORY

Marnie Hughes-Warrington (*editor*)
WORLD HISTORIES

Helen J. Nicholson (*editor*)
THE CRUSADES

Alec Ryrie (*editor*)
EUROPEAN REFORMATIONS

Jonathan Woolfson (*editor*)
RENAISSANCE HISTORIOGRAPHY

Forthcoming:

Jonathan Barry (*editor*)
WITCHCRAFT STUDIES

Katherine O'Donnell (*editor*)
IRISH HISTORY

Richard Whatmore (*editor*)
INTELLECTUAL HISTORY

Palgrave Advances
Series Standing Order ISBN 1–4039–3512–2 (Hardback) 1–4039–3513–0 (Paperback)
(*outside North America only*)

ISBN 978-1-4039-1289-3
Transferred to Digital Printing 2008

You can receive future titles in this series as they are published by placing a standing order. Please contact your bookseller or, in the case of difficulty, write to us at the address below with your name and address, the title of the series and the ISBN quoted above.

Customer Services Department, Macmillan Distribution Ltd, Houndmills, Basingstoke, Hampshire RG21 6XS, England

palgrave advances in the modern history of sexuality

edited by

h.g. cocks and matt houlbrook

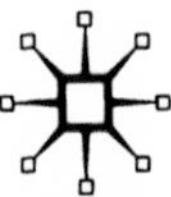

First published 2006 by
PALGRAVE MACMILLAN
Houndmills, Basingstoke, Hampshire RG21 6XS and
175 Fifth Avenue, New York, N.Y. 10010
Companies and representatives throughout the world

PALGRAVE MACMILLAN is the global academic imprint of the
Palgrave Macmillan division of St. Martin's Press, LLC and of
Palgrave Macmillan Ltd.
Macmillan® is a registered trademark in the United States,
United Kingdom and other countries. Palgrave is a registered
trademark in the European Union and other countries.

ISBN-13 978-1-4039-1289-3 hardback
ISBN-10 1-4039-1289-0 hardback
ISBN-13 978-1-4039-1290-9 paperback
ISBN-10 1-4039-1290-4 paperback

This book is printed on paper suitable for recycling and
made from fully managed and sustained forest sources.

A catalogue record for this book is available
from the British Library.

Library of Congress Cataloging-in-Publication Data
Palgrave advances in the modern history of sexuality : edited by H.G. Cocks and
Matt Houlbrook.
p. cm. — (Palgrave advances)
Includes bibliographical references and index.
ISBN 1-4039-1289-0 (cloth) — ISBN 1-4039-1290-4 (paper)
1. Sex customs—History. 2. Sex customs—United States—History. 3. Sex customs—Europe—History. I. Title: Modern history of sexuality. II. Cocks, H. G. III. Houlbrook, Matt. IV. Series.

HQ16.P35 2005
306.7'09182'1—dc22

2005051190

10 9 8 7 6 5 4 3 2 1
15 14 13 12 11 10 09 08 07 06

Transferred to Digital Printing 2008

contents

notes on contributors

Elizabeth Clement is assistant professor in U.S. Women's History at the University of Utah. Her book (forthcoming from the University of North Carolina Press) *Trick or Treat: Courting Couples, Charity Girls, and Sex Workers and the Making of Modern Heterosexuality in New York City, 1900–1945* explores how American understandings of the relationship between sexual activity and morality have changed over time.

H.G. Cocks is a lecturer in history at Birkbeck College in the University of London. His first book *Nameless Offences: Homosexual Desire in the Nineteenth Century* (London: I.B. Tauris, 2003) deals with the intersection of law, culture and homosexuality in Victorian Britain. He is working on a new book entitled *Obscene Reading: Underworlds of Print in Britain, c.1900–1965.*

Hera Cook is a New Zealander. She is a lecturer in History at the University of Birmingham. She is the author of *The Long Sexual Revolution: English Women, Sex, and Contraception, 1800–1975* (Oxford: Oxford University Press, 2004). Her current research is into the management of emotion in England from 1930 to 1980.

Matt Cook is lecturer in history at Birkbeck College, University of London, specializing in the history of sexuality. He is the author of *London and the Culture of Homosexuality, 1885–1914* (Cambridge: Cambridge University Press, 2003).

Ross Forman is a postdoctoral researcher at the Centre for Asian and African Literatures, an institute for comparative literary studies based at the School of Oriental and African Studies and University College London. A specialist in British imperialism during the Victorian and Edwardian periods, he is currently completing a book on Britain's engagement with China during the 'long' nineteenth century. He has published widely in such journals as *Victorian Studies, Victorian Literature and Culture,* and *The Journal of the History of Sexuality.* His next project, entitled *Appetites of Empire,* is a book examining how ideas about deviant diet and deviant sex coalesced in parallel to each other during the late nineteenth and early twentieth centuries.

Matt Houlbrook is a lecturer in Twentieth-Century British History at the University of Liverpool. His first book, *Queer London: Perils and Pleasures in the Sexual Metropolis, 1918–57* was published by the University of Chicago Press in 2005. He is currently working on a project called *Faking It: Modernity and Self-Fashioning in the Roaring Twenties* – about conmen, chancers and wannabes and what their lives can tell us about new forms of interiority and broader cultural anxieties in post-First World War Britain.

Louise Jackson teaches history at the University of Edinburgh. She is the author of *Child Sexual Abuse in Victorian England* (London: Routledge, 2000) and *Women Police: Gender, Welfare and Surveillance in the Twentieth Century* (Manchester: Manchester University Press, forthcoming). She is Deputy Editor of the journal *Women's History Review.*

Sarah Leonard is Assistant Professor of History at Simmons College in Boston. Her forthcoming book explores 'immoral writing' and its readers in nineteenth-century Germany.

Alison Oram is Reader in Women's Studies in the Centre for Research in Women's Studies, University College Northampton. She is the author of a number of books and articles on the history of women in the teaching profession, and, with Annmarie Turnbull, of *The Lesbian History Sourcebook* (London: Routledge, 2001). She is currently working on a book entitled *'Her Husband Was a Woman!' Women's Gender Crossing and Twentieth Century British Popular Culture* (London: Routledge, forthcoming 2007).

George Robb is Professor of History at William Paterson University of New Jersey. Author, most recently of *British Culture and the First World War* (London: Palgrave, 2002). Co-editor, with Nancy Erber, of *Disorder in the Court: Trials and Sexual Conflict at the Turn of the Century*

(London: Macmillan, 1999). Currently working on history of family law in Victorian Britain.

Chris Waters is Hans W. Gatzke '38 Professor of Modern European History at Williams College in Massachusetts. A recent director of the Williams-Exeter Programme at Oxford University, he was in 2004–05 a research fellow at the Wellcome Trust Centre for the History of Medicine at University College, London. He is the co-editor of *Moments of Modernity: Reconstructing Britain 1945–1964*, and the author of *British Socialists and the Politics of Popular Culture, 1884–1914* and some twenty articles on modern British social and cultural history. He is currently at work on a study of psychiatry, the state and the shaping of homosexual selfhood in twentieth-century Britain.

introduction

h.g. cocks and matt houlbrook

preamble

> I want you to listen to me. I'm going to say this again; I did not have sexual relations with that woman – Miss Lewinsky. I never told anybody to lie, not a single time... never. These allegations are false. And I need to go back to work for the American people. (Bill Clinton, speaking at a press conference at the White House, 26 January 1998)[1]

As far as modern day sex scandals go, this one had it all. For a start, it involved the President of the United States of America – the most powerful man in the world. Throughout 1998 and 1999, the watching world was treated to increasingly sensational and intimate revelations of Bill Clinton's sexual encounters with Monica Lewinsky, a young White House intern. When the affair culminated in impeachment proceedings, moreover, the unfolding scandal threatened to bring down Clinton's administration. For several months, the President repeatedly denied having 'sexual relations with that woman' – on one occasion while under oath before a Grand Jury. Under pressure from the Independent Counsel Kenneth Starr, with his obsessively detailed dossier of Clinton's sexual misdemeanours and accusations of perjury, obstructing the course of justice and witness tampering, Clinton finally admitted to lying about his affair with Lewinsky in August 1998. He may subsequently have been acquitted of the charges against him, but Clinton's political reputation never fully recovered.

Much of the public discussion of this scandal focused on the bodily messiness and physicality of sex – Lewinsky's thong straps or the semen stains on her blue dress, Clinton's distinction between 'sexual relations' and oral sex, what exactly the couple did with that cigar. Yet despite the prurient obsession with these details, the debates went far beyond the question of who was doing what with whom. For many observers, an individual's sexual behaviour clearly said something about their character – it was an essential component of their very self. Clinton's assumed lack of self-control and dalliances with Lewinsky thus suggested that he was unfit for the Presidency, undermining confidence in his morality, probity and trustworthiness.[2] That Clinton's conduct became, for his detractors, a matter of deep public concern in turn generated a heated debate about the proper boundaries between public and private life. The President's defence, by contrast, sought to define sex as a quintessentially private matter, with no greater import – the Lewinsky affair was, in his counsel's words 'a very personal mistake', that should not have been exposed to the public gaze.[3]

In this sense, the scandal was as much about the nature of American society and culture as it was the sexual encounters between two consenting adults. Clinton's relationship with a younger, female employee put understandings of masculinity and femininity and the politics of gender and age differences under scrutiny. The saturation of the print, visual and digital media with details of the case prompted nagging anxieties about a society obsessed with sex. Indeed, the identity of the nation itself was at stake here. Since the Second World War, at the latest, the heterosexual nuclear family – the wholesome and comfortable image of apple-pie suburban bliss – has occupied a central and foundational place in American culture. That the 'first family' could be torn apart by adultery and sexual immorality both undermined this image and, in the process, threatened the stability of the nation. Clinton and Lewinsky's 'sexual relations', it seemed, struck right to the core of what it meant to be American in the late twentieth century.[4]

It's doubtful that any of the protagonists realized it, but in raising these wider issues the Clinton–Lewinsky affair could well stand as a proxy for the growing number of historical studies of sex and sexuality in Europe and North America. If nothing else, it suggests how, in modern Western culture, sex has come to feature at the centre of many different debates – debates that, ostensibly, have very little to do with sex. From the personal to the political, from military discipline to medical knowledge, the sexual meetings between bodies are, simultaneously, meeting points for a diverse range of questions and discourses. Like many commentators on the Clinton–Lewinsky affair, at times it can seem as though historians of sexuality are writing about anything *but* sex.

In this sense, the history of sexuality has encompassed far more than simply the organization and experience of sexual behaviour in the past. Certainly, historians have explored the vexed question of who did what to whom. Rather than compile an inventory of practices and acts, however, sex has been used as a prism through which to explore wider social and cultural issues – notions of what is natural, unnatural, normal or pathological and the ways in which those categories are produced and reproduced. In short, the history of sexuality is a protean discipline that allows us to enter a world of meaning, to understand the most fundamental assumptions about everyday life that shape the social, cultural and political life of modern Western societies. It enables us to explore how these ideas worked at the most ordinary and local level: that of the individual. Rather than be content to occupy a narrow and marginal sub-discipline, historians of sexuality have had greater aspirations – aspirations to write a total history of modern Western culture.

a brief history of the history of sexuality

Although guides to moral conduct and behaviour have been a feature of every society, histories – as distinct from scientific or anthropological works – which dealt with the sexual ethics, practices and customs of past societies only began to be written in Europe in the eighteenth century. As Sarah Leonard explains in this volume, gentlemen collectors of the late eighteenth and early nineteenth century pioneered interest in sexual practices of past societies, primarily through the discovery of artefacts dating from ancient Greece and Rome and also by amassing rare books and prints – often those banned by religious authorities. In addition, Enlightenment thinkers frequently made reference to past customs in order to demonstrate the irrationality and unnatural nature of existing moral codes and social arrangements. This kind of argument – that restrictive modern morals were an artificial imposition on natural behaviour – became one of the key tenets of later nineteenth- and twentieth-century writers who wanted to liberalize sexual morals and return to the customs of the past which were invariably presented in these histories as more free and less punitive.

As the nineteenth century progressed, however, histories of sex were increasingly divided according to subject matter. Books which dealt with the laws against sexual deviance, treatises on population or marriage customs throughout the world were regarded as perfectly legitimate and circulated freely, while those which explored or described 'deviant' sexuality such as homosexual behaviour occupied a legal and cultural ghetto. These latter subjects were confined to either specialist medical texts or legally obscene underground works. Writing about sex in any form in the nineteenth century needed some justification, be it the investigation of pathological states or solving the problem of prostitution. History, which had established itself in universities as an academic discipline distinct from classics at the end of the eighteenth century, was primarily a matter of political and national history. Many histories of sex continued to circulate as illicit texts, and continued to be primarily written and read by those who set themselves against contemporary morals.

Much of the sexual science of the late nineteenth century occupied this uncertain ground between legitimate and obscene studies of sexual behaviour. As Chris Waters explains in his chapter, sexologists like the Australian doctor Henry Havelock Ellis were some of the most sophisticated historians of sexuality in the nineteenth century. As Waters explains, this historical work was a fundamental part of a more general attempt to classify various types of sexual behaviour. Writers like Ellis used an eclectic method borrowed from criminology and historical anthropology which involved listing and specifying the various forms of human sexuality and perversity. One of the first writers to classify sexuality in this way was the German doctor Karl Heinrich Ulrichs, who in 1862 invented a set of terms for the various types of homosexuality, or 'Uranism' as he called it, within which he identified lesbians 'urninds', homosexual men 'urnings' and bisexuals 'uranodionings'. An analogous method of classification was employed and much extended in the 1880s by the Austrian criminologist and psychologist Richard von Krafft-Ebing, who came across a variety of sexual types among offenders in his work with the Vienna police.[5] Sexologists like Ellis in Britain and Magnus Hirschfeld in Germany used this method of classification, along with historical and anthropological examples, to show that behaviour treated as abnormal or illegal in Europe was in fact commonly accepted in past cultures. Ellis hoped, just as his predecessors had, that this approach would lead to a more tolerant, natural and healthy sexuality that would be freed from the moral straitjacket of custom.

Ellis' major work on sexuality was, however, banned in Britain and circulated in legal form only in continental Europe. Yet the association between serious historical works and obscenity was by no means an unproductive one. By the twentieth century, dealers in obscene books were also distributing underground histories and established classics of sexual subversion. This 'illicit scholarship' remained the only purely historical treatment of sex outside sexology, although it coexisted with an increasingly large genre of social investigation, sociology and anthropology which provided legitimate grounds for investigating contemporary morals and sexual habits. In spite of the fact that from the 1890s onwards sexuality could be analysed in sociological texts, and scrutinized for signs of individual and social pathology, histories of sex did not gain any legitimacy within the European and American academy until at least the 1950s. However, the place of sex in legitimate historical scholarship was revolutionized in that decade by the advent of social history, the declared aim of which was to study ordinary life and to examine society from the ground up. All of life was now a legitimate subject for inquiry, including sex, although it wasn't until the 1960s that the study of sex in history attained any real academic respectability. There were several factors in this transformation. Most importantly, social history encouraged the study of marginalized groups who had seemingly been 'hidden from history', and stimulated the recovery of their experiences. This was often a political project, devoted to putting hitherto marginal groups like the working class, black people, women and homosexuals back into the history of the nations, economies and societies they had helped to create. Feminism played a key role in this process of recovery, and helped to place sexuality at the centre of new historical narratives. In particular, feminism directed attention to the fact that personal life has been subject to various efforts of societal, governmental and legislative control, with the result that, in the words of the feminist slogan, 'the personal is political'. Gay rights movements also suggested that their culture could be identified in the distant past and argued that the current organization of sexuality into the opposition of heterosexual/homosexual was a recent invention imposed upon a multifarious and mobile human sexuality. In short, by the early 1970s, the idea that sexuality is fundamentally social, and determined more by social priorities than by biology or 'nature' – a notion cherished by Enlightenment radicals, collectors of erotica and underground historians since the eighteenth century – had forced its way on to the agenda of academic professionals.

sexuality and theory

One feature of social history and its offshoots like women's history was the centrality of experience. The aim of rescuing those marginal and voiceless people from the past, restoring their agency and understanding their worldview made their testimony extraordinarily important. In general, social historians tended to think of individual experience recounted by ordinary people in the first person as the most authoritative, authentic and irreducible form of evidence, and to place this at the centre of their narratives. The marginalized were given their voice back and their worldview was undoubtedly better understood on their own terms. However, critics of social history have argued that one problem with this approach was that it tended to gloss over the question of how those people and groups became marginal in the first place. Instead, the recovery of marginality often slipped into a celebration of that status, and a glorying in the apparent authenticity of the excluded. Joan Scott has argued that when the experiences of the marginalized are presented in this way, as the truest form of evidence, this tends to fix those people as marginal. Their difference is naturalized. In other words, the testimony of a gay person, or a woman, or a black person or member of another historically marginalized group, is valuable evidence of how their world worked and how they lived, but tends to leave aside the question of how categories of exclusion came to exist in the first place. Scott argues that we can only understand past experience by interrogating the concepts through which we, and people in the past, grasped it. She therefore calls for us to try and understand how categories like marginal/central, normal/abnormal are made in the first place, and also how these ideas are policed and enforced.[6]

One way of doing this is to assume that people are only able to understand themselves in relation to meanings attributed to their behaviour, over which they have little control and which they inherit when they grow up in a particular culture. In other words, what it means to be a woman or a man, or gay or straight, is dictated to us, more discovered by us than created. Our experience is not outside society or pre-social, but given meaning through the language and vocabulary of our culture. In other words, if I say 'I am straight', I am invoking a variety of meanings and attributes that most people would understand went with that statement. Therefore, Scott and others have argued that instead of merely recovering the 'experience' of the marginal, historians should devote their attention to the ways that categories like woman, child, gay or straight, not to mention social forms like marriage or pornography, become historically constructed to begin with.

Scott is responding here to the work of Michel Foucault, in particular to his *History of Sexuality* vol. 1 (1978, translated into English 1984), which was one of the major interventions in the field. Foucault did not set out merely to document changes in the meanings of sexuality but to show that the very concept of sexuality itself was in fact an invention of 'modernity', that is, of the world since about 1750. For Foucault, the body has a varied capacity for sexual pleasure, only some aspects of which are emphasized at any historical moment. Our way of regulating sexual pleasure in the modern West, that is, generally around the question of which gender you have sex with, does not represent an automatic or 'natural' result of biology or physiology, he argues, but instead is merely one contingent way of organizing the body and the mind, or of 'extracting' its various capacities. Moreover, this way of organizing sexuality has a discernible historical development, and is the result not of biology, but of the various kinds of expert knowledge which have tried to define sexual 'normality'. The notion that our desires, and particularly our sexual desires, represent the core of the self and the key to the personality, is, Foucault says, *the* defining feature of sexuality in the modern age. How, he asks, did it become possible to say that we have 'a sexuality', when previously there had simply been a mass of desires and practices, licit or illicit? Although many before him going back to the eighteenth century had pointed out the historical contingency of sexual mores and identities, Foucault turned this insight into a much wider account of power in Western history. In addition, his work allowed historians to think of sexuality as more than a marginal effect of other social and economic changes, but as something important in its own right. We will deal briefly with these issues of power and sexuality here.

In general, historians since the nineteenth century have seen the history of Western Europe, which witnessed the protracted rise of democracy and the rule of law, mass leisure and eventually sexual revolution, as one of progressive liberalization on all fronts. Foucault inverts this story of progress. Instead of seeing freedom as an exponential growth, Foucault's work documents the rise of what he calls 'biopower', that is the abandonment of coercive instruments like capital punishment or coercive laws in favour of more insidious techniques of rule and control, many of which focused on sexuality, morality and reproduction. From the nineteenth century onwards, Foucault suggests, governments in Western Europe and America began to direct their attention away from the best means to maximize population, wealth and territory, and instead turned towards managing the lives and capacities of their populations in order to render them productive and amenable to the changes consequent upon the industrial revolution. The business of politics became the management of human existence as a whole and involved maintaining the quality of the population, the control of reproduction and sexuality, the safety of the family, promoting health and reducing disease, and the management of birth and death. The establishment of professional expertise in areas like crime, medicine, psychology and work was essential to this process. Statistics were compiled by learned societies, universities and governments, while forms of knowledge and investigation were established which allowed access to the capacities, desires and feelings of patients, workers, entire populations or those deemed to be socially or morally deviant. States in Europe and America adopted these techniques in order to both control their populations and provide more fully for their health and welfare. The result was that while modern people became freer from the terror of the state and its capricious authority, they nevertheless came to be endlessly calibrated, their capacities endlessly judged, their productivity endlessly rated, their normality and pathology eternally measured.[7]

For Foucault, one of the key signs of this process of measurement and control was the new attention given to sexual pathology and deviance from the mid-nineteenth century onwards. At that point, scientists, governments, academics, statisticians and experts of all kinds began to examine the factors that generated 'racial health'. As a consequence they turned their attention towards reproduction, evolutionary processes and the study of deviance, including sexual deviance. The ultimate result of this 'discursive explosion' in the study of sex was the propagation of ideas about what was normal sexual behaviour. Foucault suggests that these ideas or norms were taken up by powerful institutions like medicine and the law which encouraged individuals to examine and monitor their own desires according to these new standards. This process of 'normalization' would, in this way, also open the intimate sphere to classification, control and governance through the multiplication of, at first, legal, medical and psychological knowledge.

Starting with European criminology in the 1880s, sexual deviance was mapped and catalogued, described and specified, and new ways of identifying normality and abnormality were invented. The rise of psychology and its alliance with criminology and sexology at this time also encouraged the belief that outward acts were the sign of an inner condition. One key sign of this process was the new understanding of homosexual desire, which in turn implied a new way of thinking about heterosexuality. Psychologists, sexologists and other experts began to regard homosexuality not merely as a set of illicit or unnatural acts but as the symptom of a psychological state which governed the rest of the personality. In Foucault's famous words, the homosexual described at this time was 'a personage, a past, a case history... and a morphology, with an indiscreet anatomy and a mysterious physiology'.[8] Although this notion of homosexuality had antecedents in the eighteenth century, Foucault says that the 'invention' of this idea of homosexuality was more important as an indication that various institutions – law, medicine, the state – were making it their business to try and govern individual desires by specifying what was normal. Moreover, the homosexual and the 'pervert' were merely the first and most obvious candidates for this kind of treatment. In future heterosexuality would be similarly measured, classified and scrutinized by forces as diverse as schools, marriage guidance, consumerism, psychotherapy, the welfare state and the police, as the secret to the understanding of inner being and the mysteries of the unconscious. Ordinary people, not just 'deviants', would be asked to, and would, measure themselves against the standard of normality generated by these and similar inquiries. Sex would, in the twentieth century, be named, discussed and regulated as never before. Modern Western societies, Foucault suggests, require us to govern ourselves, to be 'free' within certain limits, and the 'invention of sexuality' has been a key technique of getting people to do this.

What we desire has become who we are, and individual experience has become the prime source of authenticity in our age. When we articulate our identities, which feels like a move towards freedom, we are in fact, Foucault says, becoming increasingly susceptible to norms which have been externally and historically established. We are therefore ever more enmeshed within systems of power and authority which seek to direct what we mistakenly regard as natural and liberatory impulses. These forms of power are all the more pervasive because on one level, they do satisfy a need, thereby ensuring that we meet them half way. Foucault describes this process as 'individualisation and totalisation'.[9] That is, the more our individual needs and wants are recognized, the more we find ourselves caught within norms, within systems of knowledge, power and control. History, then, according to Foucault, should be about trying to discern and specify how this process takes place, and how it generates particular ways of understanding, controlling and specifying sexuality.

It would be wrong to overestimate Foucault's influence on historians, however, many of whom have either passed through a phase of obligatory but unenthusiastic professional interest, or who have always ignored him altogether. Among historians of sexuality, one of the principal objections to Foucault results from his central premise – that the history of sexuality can only ever be a story of power. One implication of this method is to suggest that sexuality is a social construct, even at the level of individual desire. This principle suggests that the way in which any society describes sex has the dominant influence on how it is experienced. The job of historians then becomes to reconstruct past systems of meaning and representation as the main guide to behaviour. This idea has not been uncontested, however. John Boswell, one of Foucault's principal antagonists, argued that even though different societies described sexuality in different ways, it remained the case that behaviour was stubbornly set within certain parameters. In spite of local variation in most Western societies since the birth of Christ, Boswell suggested that three basic categories of behaviour can always be observed, described adequately by our own designations: gay, straight, bisexual. This controversy, between Foucauldian 'social constructionists' and Boswellian 'essentialists' tended to focus on the question of whether there could be said to be any homosexuals or, correspondingly, heterosexuals, in the modern sense before the term was coined and the idea of homosexual-as-separate-species entered Western culture in the nineteenth century.[10]

A way out of this impasse was suggested by the literary critic Eve Kosofsky Sedgwick, who argued that most societies live with radically incoherent and contradictory versions of sexuality, and that this can be observed by looking at the meaning of homosexuality. We should never assume, Sedgwick suggested, that actual desire is always fully subsumed by the categories that are used to describe it. There is always some excess, some part of identity and behaviour that cannot be categorized, and this realization should tell us something about the inadequacy of dominant forms of representation for fully capturing and describing the nature of individual desire. This position has come to be associated broadly with 'queer theory', a set of ideas mainly associated with literary studies, but whose main effort has been to take seriously Foucault's suggestion that resisting identity of all kinds is a virtue. As an illustration of this position, Sedgwick pointed out that modern Western societies have produced two essentially incompatible ideas of homosexuality. On the one hand, homosexual behaviour was/is thought to be the province of a special and identifiable group of people who are 'really gay', while on the other, it is usually thought possible for anyone to experience homosexual desire, or to 'become' a homosexual. A consequence of Sedgwick's 'queer' theorizing is the principle that the categories in use to describe sexuality in the past should not be taken as literal descriptions of individual desire. In other words, we should be aware of the contradictions inherent in constructing schemes of identity, sexual or otherwise, that do violence to complex forms of individuality, history and culture.[11]

This question has been only one of many raised by Foucault's work, and it is not the purpose of this book to suggest that Foucault be unquestioningly absorbed by students. However, it is necessary to demonstrate why his influence has been so large, and to describe an outline of his thought as a whole, in order to understand what historians of sexuality are doing at the moment with the problems and questions he raises. As we have suggested, much of his work has posed further questions rather than solving them, and in doing so it has suggested a research agenda which other historians have followed in different ways.

Although Foucault still informs a great deal of work in this area, the overall picture of the history of sexuality is one of diversity, as we will explain in the next section.

problems, questions, new directions

If, as this discussion suggests, Foucault's work has been far from universally accepted, the publication of his seminal *History of Sexuality* and the resurgence of interest in social history in Europe and North America has prompted a massive proliferation in empirical and theoretical studies of sexuality over the past three decades. Yet while the history of sexuality is a burgeoning field, it has also been marked by an increasing divergence in approaches. Historians remain divided by those stubborn questions that refuse to go away – what can we know? How much can we know? How can we know it? What should historians of sexuality actually study?

Rather than provide definitive answers to these questions, this book is an attempt to provide an overview of approaches, methods, recent work and major debates in the history of sexuality, drawing together a diverse range of practices and methodologies. In very different ways, our contributors examine the past, present and future of the exploration of sex, as a social, cultural and historical phenomenon. Each chapter explores what we see as a key theme in the histories of sexuality that have emerged over the past twenty-five years, seeking to address a number of key questions. How has that theme been defined and approached as a subject of historical inquiry? What have been the major debates between historians? How might the discipline move forward in future? Whilst our contributors often utilize particular examples and case studies taken from their own areas of expertise, the book as a whole aims to draw together material from North America, Britain and continental Europe in the period since the mid-eighteenth century. This chronological and geographical division is in many ways arbitrary. It has to be recognized that the idea of 'the modern West' is itself an ideological fiction, and one that often depends on severing its historical ties with European and American empires and colonial peoples. However, mainly for reasons of practicality and focus, we have maintained this division, while being aware of the imperial and racial connections that it entails – some of which are examined in Ross Forman's chapter.

The chapters which follow present a variety of methods, directions and influences, all moving beyond the research agendas provided by Foucault and others. The question of experience looms large here. For instance, one of the questions which much existing work puts to one side is whether we can ever have an accurate picture of the sexual behaviour of the majority of people. This question is complicated by the fact that before the mid-twentieth century, most people – even the literate and powerful minority – did not record any information about their intimate lives. Even in the present, with its deluge of survey data, it is difficult to tell whether reporting to such surveys is accurate, or whether most people lie even to themselves about sex. Most of the time, no record has been left in any case, so we are left to infer individual behaviour from other suggestions such as prescriptive literature, visual culture, legislation against deviance or moralizing tracts. Hera Cook argues that actual (hetero)sexual behaviour can be measured by a combination of fertility data and anecdotal evidence. In this way, she suggests, links between the demographic record of fertility and the changing experience of sexuality can be demonstrated. Changing birth rates, Cook points out, do reflect changing values, in particular the increasing prevalence of sexual restraint in late-Victorian Britain. In contrast to Foucault's idea of a 'discursive explosion' around the subject of sexuality, Cook suggests instead that there was, in fact, widespread sexual ignorance in European culture until very recently, and very little actual discussion of sex outside discourses of public health and science.

Chris Waters turns to the history of that sexual science which has been one of the key ingredients of Foucauldian histories. These narratives have tended to suggest that sexology played a formative role in making modern sexual identities, either by negatively stigmatizing certain practices or, more positively, by providing terms by which people could understand their desires in more scientific and therefore more neutral and less moralistic ways. But, Waters asks, how can we know that? Instead of berating or celebrating the sexologists, as many historians have done, Waters calls for a more specific study of how sexological ideas actually worked. To whom did they circulate, in what form, and how? That is where future inquiry should be directed, Waters argues – towards the history of individual experience, subjectivity and identity and its relationship to discourse.

Matt Cook's chapter is also about the regulatory force of a social institution – this time the law. The law has also been central to the many histories of sexuality which have tried to excavate the relationship between individual experience and societal proscription. On a simple level, Cook shows, the law defines what is right and wrong according to specific rules, and this has an enormous effect on behaviour. Again, the question is how to approach the relationship between institution and individual. Cook suggests that Foucauldian histories have tended to overemphasize the link between illegality and identity. The notion that proscription defines deviance, which is then used as the basis of deviant identity, is particularly strong in histories of homosexuality. However, one problem with this approach is that other voices, especially that of the individual 'offender', have to be mediated through the various legal rules which govern different national traditions. In short, we need to be careful about assuming that legal evidence or witness testimony is a guide to identity.

While legal history by definition explores deviance, George Robb explores the normative, ordinary version of sexuality which historically has been the most common – marital sex. He shows that since about 1750, diverse voices have used marriage as the centrepiece of their programmes for social reform. In short, marriage has been a locus of conflict which has historically been connected to much wider debates about sex and gender roles, citizenship, and the evolution of humanity and society. Robb tracks the changing views of marital sexuality in Anglo-American culture, from the anti-marriage, anti-sex views of many nineteenth-century progressives and feminists, to the pro-sex 'free love' of the early twentieth century and beyond. In particular, he shows that sexual happiness has become the essential component of marriage only recently. It was only in the 1920s that a happy sex life, rather than female obedience to a male will, came to be accepted as the *sine qua non* of marital intimacy.

Marriage was vital to society because, in the minds of both its critics and defenders, it was crucial to national and racial health. Ross Forman reminds us that race and sexuality, a relationship often seen through the prism of empire, have been inseparable for much of modern history, and have often been ignored by historians of European and American sexuality. Indeed, Forman goes further, to suggest that Western history has frequently been seen to turn on the relationship of race and sex. Sexual behaviour not only defined the hierarchy of races in which lower, less evolved races were supposed to be less moral, but also anchored a history of Western civilization in which sexual restraints were equated with more advanced societies. Miscegenation therefore threatened an entire structure of morality and belief. Forman thus demonstrates that we cannot think of Western histories in general in isolation from their racial-colonial-sexual context.

While a racial context is vital, Matt Houlbrook points out that the urban is also an indispensable component of modern sexuality. The city and sexuality have had a mutually reinforcing relationship, Houlbrook argues. The city, with its impersonality, heterogeneous spaces of leisure and its sheer size, provides a constant marketplace of sexual opportunity.

Its laws and practices define certain places and people as deviant, especially those who have historically engaged in public sex, such as prostitutes or gay men. The city, however, is not a passive backdrop against which these stories are played out, but has a role in shaping and constituting sexual identity. The relationship, however, is reciprocal. While the urban defines modern sexuality, sexual anxieties and practices have also profoundly shaped the urban landscape through the policing of spaces and deviant sexuality. More recently, though, cyberspace and the Internet have begun to replace the city as the usual location of sexual anxieties and opportunities.

While the history of modern Western sexuality has mainly been an urban history, it has also tended overwhelmingly to be the history of secularization. Foucault's legacy has encouraged historians of sexuality to write chiefly about secular institutions like medicine and the law. However, H.G. Cocks shows that religion was one of the principal influences on both modern intimacy and the emergence of modernist styles in literature and culture. In addition, religion and spiritual devotion of all kinds have historically licensed unconventional forms of sexuality, from homoerotic desire to romantic friendship between the sexes. Marital sexuality in nineteenth-century Europe and America was also widely seen as a spiritual union. This spiritual content was held to raise passionate intimacy beyond the merely sensual and to give it a 'higher' purpose. Far from being increasingly marginal, religious and occult beliefs also had a strong influence on modern culture and sexuality.

Sarah Leonard explains that pornography is also a product of modernity. While it was once seen as marginal by most historians, erotic imagery is now seen as a useful guide to areas of study apart from sexuality itself, particularly political history. Leonard shows that obscene texts collected by private individuals in the eighteenth and nineteenth century began to be regarded as a valuable historical source by sexologists looking for clues to the evolution of sexuality. These early efforts to use erotica as history were to establish a bridgehead into the academy. By the 1970s, the convergence of social history and feminist politics made porn into something with social and political resonance. In particular, erotic imagery began to be seen by historians as an important component of political history. It was discovered that the automatically subversive nature of erotic imagery made it a useful way of attacking authority throughout Enlightenment Europe. In fact, Leonard shows conclusively that links between pornography and mainstream politics remain indelible. She points out that erotic representation has repeatedly been seen to undermine secular political authority, whether in eighteenth-century France or modern Iran.

Prostitution, like pornography, often eludes precise definition, as Elizabeth Clement shows in her chapter. She demonstrates that prostitution has often been defined by male authorities who decided that a wide variety of what they saw as 'promiscuous' sexual activity on the part of women was equivalent to full-time prostitution. In this way, defining prostitution has historically been a means to police women's sexuality in general. Male prostitutes were also difficult to define, since money or gifts often changed hands as a way of distancing men from homosexual intimacy. Since sex workers and prostitutes started to speak out for themselves in the 1970s, often against feminists who saw them as passive victims, the question of whether a prostitute has any agency and in what way has been forced on to the agenda. Clement suggests that historians need to be particularly sensitive to these questions of definition and to do so by examining specific practices of commercial sex.

Many of the moralists that Clement writes about expressed particular concern for the welfare of girls. Louise Jackson also shows that anxiety surrounding childhood sexuality is not merely a contemporary concern. Jackson asks the question persistently posed by the material in this book: how can the historian recover the voice of the individual – in this case the child – from institutional histories which have obscured that individual or tried to speak for them? Just as the voice of the young person is barely heard, the idea of childhood innocence also takes away the agency of the child. Equally controversial is the question of whether childhood is socially constructed. Just as sexuality changes over time, the very idea of when childhood begins and ends is subject to similar variation. Who is a child and when? This is a question with pressing relevance when sexual desire and consent to sex are part of the equation.

Finally, Alison Oram shows how the associations between cross-dressing, transsexuality and transgender have problematized notions of gender and sexual identity. These practices have had a long history and a protean character. In the eighteenth century, for instance, passing as a member of the opposite sex was not necessarily thought of as a form of sexual deviance. It could be done simply to assume the privileges and sensibilities of the opposite sex. However, by the late nineteenth century sexologists had begun to identify such cross-gender behaviour as a symptom of sexual deviance and inner 'inversion'. However, although medical science promised to clarify various cross-gender behaviours into various syndromes and sexualities, it failed to completely disentangle cross-dressing from transsexuality, or to separate these things entirely from sexual preferences or subcultures. In the twentieth century, the feasibility of surgical gender reassignment has opened the possibility, among transgender activists and writers, of rejecting gender and sexual identity itself.

For a time the Clinton–Lewinsky affair was common currency in everyday conversation on both sides of the Atlantic – the stuff of circular emails and wisecracking talk-show hosts. A particularly enterprising company even capitalized on the public interest by marketing 'Intern Barbie' – captioned 'My Knees Bend!' As is the case with all modern day sex scandals, however, the details are slowly fading from popular cultural memory. Perhaps the strongest evidence of this is the growing number of journal articles, books and doctoral theses that obsessively scrutinize Bill and Monica's dalliances for what they can tell us about contemporary American society and culture. When the historians pick up on a story – when a scandal becomes the stuff of Serious and Important academic debate – then its time is well and truly over.[12]

In prompting us to think about the connections between intimate life and the realms of society, culture and politics, however, scandals like this embody what we see as the basic premise of all histories of modern sexuality – that those histories are about far more than sex itself. If you were to ask the contributors to this volume what the history of sexuality is actually a history of, then you might well get eleven very different answers. You might also – as the individual chapters suggest – get a very different sense of the historical practices, concepts, methodologies and sources through which the study of sex, gender and sexuality in the past can be approached. But we would also all agree that we are trying to do much more than compile an inventory of sexual behaviours and practices.

This volume is, in part, an attempt to do justice to the methodological and interpretive diversity that has characterized our discipline, while offering a set of guidelines with which those new to this area might orientate themselves. It is a starting point – an introduction that raises more questions than it provides answers. In exploring the organization and understanding of sex and sexuality in the past, we could do worse than take as our starting point the centrality of sex to questions of identity and selfhood in contemporary Western culture – demonstrated all too vividly by the Clinton–Lewinsky affair. How did sex come to be so interwoven into our everyday lives? What were the institutions and processes that fostered this fascination? What can our modern obsessions with sex tell us about the society and culture we inhabit? What can it tell us about our very selves?

notes

1. See *A Guide to the Monica Lewinsky Story*, <www.coffeeshoptimes.com/quotes.html>, accessed March 2005. 'Clinton Strongly Denies Having Sex with Intern', *Los Angeles Times*, 27 January 1998.
2. David Tipton, 'Clinton's Poor Conduct Appears Ok to Nation', *The Daily Beacon*, 4 February 1998.
3. Quoted in Mark Rowe, 'Was Justice Served in the Impeachment and Trial of President Clinton?', <www.49thparallel.bham.ac.uk/back/issue11/rowe.htm#_ednref60>.
4. For the idealization of the nuclear family in postwar American culture see, for example, Elaine Tyler May, 'Cold War – Warm Hearth: Politics and the Family in Postwar America', in Steve Fraser and Gary Gerstle (eds.), *The Rise and Fall of the New Deal Order* (Princeton, NJ: Princeton University Press, 1989), pp. 153–84. John D'Emilio and Estelle Freedman, *Intimate Matters: A History of Sexuality in America* (Chicago: Chicago University Press, 1997). For the links between national identities and notions of normative sexualities see, for example, Kevin Grant, '"Bones of Contention": The Repatriation of the Remains of Roger Casement', *Journal of British Studies*, 41, 3 (2002), 329–54. Carolyn Dean, *The Frail Social Body: Pornography, Homosexuality and Other Fantasies in Interwar France* (Berkeley: University of California Press, 2000).
5. On Ulrichs and the sexologists, see James Steakley, *The Homosexual Emancipation Movement in Germany*, 2nd edition (Salem, NH: Ayer, 1993); Harry Oosterhuis, 'Richard von Krafft-Ebing's Step-Children of Nature: Psychiatry and the Making of Homosexual Identity', in Vernon Rosario (ed.), *Science and Homosexualities* (New York: Routledge, 1997), pp. 67–88; Roy Porter and Lesley Hall, *The Facts of Life: The Creation of Sexual Knowledge in Britain 1650–1950* (London: Yale University Press, 1995), ch. 7; Robert Nye, *Sexuality* (Oxford: Oxford University Press, 1999).
6. Joan Scott, 'The Evidence of Experience', in Henry Abelove et al. (eds.), *The Gay and Lesbian Studies Reader* (New York: Routledge, 1993), pp. 397–415.
7. On this see Michel Foucault, 'Governmentality', in Graham Burchell, Colin Gordon and Peter Miller (eds.), *The Foucault Effect: Studies in Governmentality* (Hemel Hempstead: Harvester Wheatsheaf, 1991), pp. 87–104; Lois McNay, *Foucault: A Critical Introduction* (Cambridge: Polity, 1994), pp. 116–17.
8. Michel Foucault, *The History of Sexuality, Vol. 1. An Introduction*, trans. Robert Hurley (Harmondsworth: Penguin, 1990), p. 43.
9. Michel Foucault, 'The Subject and Power', in Hubert Dreyfus and Paul Rabinow, *Michel Foucault: Beyond Structuralism and Hermeneutics* (London: Harvester Wheatsheaft, 1982), pp. 208–26; McNay, *Foucault*, pp. 121–4.
10. John Boswell, 'Revolutions, Universals, and Sexual Categories', in George Chauncey, Martin Duberman, Martha Vicinus (eds.), *Hidden From History: Reclaiming the Gay and Lesbian Past* (Harmondsworth: Penguin, 1991), pp. 17–36; John Boswell, *Christianity, Social Tolerance and Homosexuality: Gay People in Europe From the Beginning of the Christian Era to the Fourteenth Century* (Chicago: University of Chicago Press, 1980); *The Marriage of Likeness: Same-Sex Unions in Pre-Modern Europe* (London: Harper Collins, 1994); Ed Stein (ed.), *Forms of Desire: Sexual Orientation and the Social Constructionist Controversy* (New York: Garland, 1990).

11. Eve Kosofsky Sedgwick, *Epistemology of the Closet* (Harmondsworth: Penguin, 1994), p. 85; Annamarie Jagose, *Queer Theory* (Carlton South: Melbourne University Press, 1996).
12. For academic discussions of the Clinton–Lewinsky affair see, for example, John Zaller, 'Monica Lewinsky's Contribution to Political Science', *PS: Political Science and Politics*, 31, 2 (1998), p. 182–9; Juliet Williams, 'The Personal Is Political: Thinking Through the Clinton/Lewinsky/Starr Affair', *PS: Political Science and Politics*, 34, 1 (2001), 93–8. A. Locke and D. Edwards, 'Bill and Monica: Memory, Emotion and Normativity in Clinton's Grand Jury Testimony', *British Journal of Social Psychology*, 42, 2 (2003), 239–56. For 'Intern Barbie' see <http://politicalhumor.about.com/library/blclintoninternbarbie.htm>.

1
demography

hera cook

Historical demography is concerned with external, measurable elements of lived experience, such as births, marriages, income, and household forms. Demography, and statistical sources more generally, offer historians new possibilities for understanding the histories of sexualities in the nineteenth and twentieth centuries. These measurable elements of people's lives both shape the context in which sexual activity takes place and are in turn shaped by the consequences of sexual activity. The most important aspect of this is the strong and enduring relationship of fertility rates with sexual behaviour. However, more than this can be inferred from demographic and other statistical findings; sexual identity and the possibilities of sexual expression available to individuals are shaped by privacy or the lack thereof, leisure or exhaustion, the extent of poverty or wealth, of disease or health, of autonomy or integration into kin or other residential groups, and the degree of societal sex segregation. Using both statistical and qualitative sources can create powerful explanations which offer new insights.

Demographic research initially became possible with the emergence of national censuses and vital registration systems. T.H. Malthus had brought the issue of population size into public prominence in 1798, when he argued that the growth of population would outstrip that of food and other resources. Research began into geographic and social differentials in mortality in the nineteenth century, and the results provided evidence of the causes of disease, and the need for public health measures. The analysis of fertility assumed growing importance from the late nineteenth century, as widespread fertility decline became evident in Western societies. Population research, the forerunner of modern demography, emerged as part of the eugenic movement in the early twentieth century.

Concerns about population change reflected existing societal structures and beliefs about class and race. In England, Francis Galton, the founder of the eugenics movement, ensured differential fertility by social class was the major concern; in the United States anxieties were aroused by the higher birth rate among immigrants and the black population; in France low fertility aroused fear of national decline following defeat in the Franco-Prussian war in 1870.

By the interwar period, the American Ford and Rockefeller Foundations had begun to fund the establishment of research centres, the Population Investigation Committee was formed in Britain in 1936, and the subject began to be taught in universities during the 1930s.[1] Following the Second World War, eugenic ideas were rejected by demographers, and the theory of the demographic transition dominated the research agenda.[2] However, during the postwar decades funding for demography departments and institutes was largely generated by Western concerns about population growth in the developing world, creating an association with neo-imperialism and racism. The scepticism these antecedents created regarding population research among the new historians of sexuality writing in the 1970s goes some way to explaining the lack of interest in the field. However, demography is a fiercely empirical discipline, largely sceptical of theory, except as a hypothesis to be tested against data.[3] This can result in socially conservative, presentist, interpretations. It is an approach which is alien to many historians of sexuality, who tend to use theory as a heuristic device and prefer to adapt speculative formulations, such as those of Foucault, rather than reject them when they do not conform to empirical findings.

The concept of a *population* is central to demography. A population consists of the persons living in a specific geographical area at a specific point in time; it is often further specified as including those with other characteristics, such as age, ethnicity or fecundity. The latter is defined as the capacity to reproduce, and usually includes women between the ages of sixteen and forty-four, or forty-nine. The term population tends to be used to refer to the aggregate characteristics of a population, which are not necessarily those descriptive of any given individual. A cohort is a group of people who are born within the same period of time, and so are exposed to the same socio-economic and historical events at each stage of their life-cycle. Demography is a statistical discipline, and interest is limited to the observable world, and to sizeable or significant definable populations, or other factors, which can be measured. Issues around the establishing of the provenance and reliability of quantifiable data are described in detail in the literature, and where available data fall short of a desirable standard, the efforts made to compensate for this are clearly explained. This specificity about the population being analysed, and the sources used makes it possible to begin establishing and analysing the complex causal links between temporal and social change and demographic phenomena.

Historical demography emerged as an autonomous field of research in the 1940s and 1950s. A series of methodological innovations resulting from the application of concepts familiar to other fields of social sciences (life tables, projections, standardized age schedules, kinship networks, techniques of indirect estimation) enabled information about population change to be obtained from sources such as parish records.[4] In particular, Louis Henry designed the method of family reconstitution that was to revolutionize the field. This enabled scholars to undertake the time-consuming task of documenting and describing the classic demographic characteristics such as population size, geographical distribution, age and sex structure and the changes produced by births, deaths and migration for historical populations. A series of studies since has enabled the reconstruction of settlement patterns and household and family structures throughout much of the ancient and modern world. The Cambridge Population Group have traced English population change from 1538 to 1837, the period covered by parish registers, leaving only a small hiatus before 1841, when the first census was taken.[5] The figures are based on a small number of parishes and there is still considerable research to be undertaken before the results can be regarded as definitive, but they provide an important resource for other historians to draw upon.

Historians have seen sexuality as something that cannot be measured, that involved private, and often hidden or forbidden experiences. Their approach to sources reflects this assumption. However, diaries, letters, court reports and so forth, tend to be produced by, or about, those whose behaviour and beliefs were unusual, and/or belonged to the elite, while the professional and institutional discourses emphasized by Foucauldian scholars stress a particular, and in many ways limited, understanding of power, rather than sexual behaviour. Demography provides convincing evidence of long-term trends in the actual behaviour of the mass of society, or of selected groups, but it is limited to aspects of experience for which records exist and which can be measured. When these different forms of evidence – that which can be measured and that which is subjective and/or individual – are placed side by side, new conclusions emerge about changing sexualities. Family history has used the findings of historical demographers in this way for decades; a major difficulty facing historians of sexuality has been to find links between measurable events and sexuality.

Sexuality still tends to be considered as if it were a first cause, from which other impulses, desires, and experiences, arose, or to which they were submitted; using demographic sources requires a reversal of this approach and a consideration of the extent to which sexuality is subject to moulding by context and circumstance.[6] John D'Emilio, for example, identified the importance of urbanization for the development of a gay identity in the US.[7] This insight is now commonplace in the history of homosexuality, and there is much research into urbanization as a process creating sexualities rather than merely as a context in which sexualities occur.[8] However, demographic, and other statistical sources, are still used only sporadically in this literature. For example, George Chauncey briefly considered household formation and kin networks in *Gay New York* (1994). He suggested that the differences between migration patterns of Italians and Jews contributed to the form taken by homosexual cultures among these ethnic groups.[9] Other statistical information that would enable evidence to be contextualized includes, for example, the sex and age structure of a population and the predominant housing types in an area.

Demographic evidence also raises questions about the interpretation of evidence. Randolph Trumbach uses English criminal records to support his argument that there was a gender revolution in England, culminating in the eighteenth century, which resulted in the repression of masculine sodomites and a restriction of the gender and sexual identities available to men and women. However, Trumbach treats Europe as a unit and feels free to draw upon Florentine history to support his claim that prior to 1700 in 'traditional European societies all males had desired both males and females'.[10] Historical demographers have found enduring differences, from as far back as the 1600s, between Northern and Southern Europe in approaches to marriage and courtship, the extent of sex-segregation and in gender relations, which casts grave doubt on the validity of such an approach.[11] These examples suggest ways in which demography raises questions and complements other sources of evidence.

Heterosexuality was, and is, the dominant sexual culture. As numerous scholars have pointed out, this term needs to be historicized in the same way as the term homosexuality. However, heterosexuality, as currently used, frequently refers to a discursive heteronormativity, which is analysed solely in terms of power.[12] This totalizing re-othering of opposite-sex sexuality limits the questions that can be asked about changing sexualities. An even greater limitation is the implicit assumption in most of this theory that we already know what heterosexuality is, what it consists of and what the practice involves.[13] For this reason, in this chapter, I refer to opposite-sex sexuality, unless explicitly referring to the hegemonic impact of heterosexuality.[14] Most, though not all, of the population engage in sexual activity. Most, though not all, restrict this activity to members of the opposite sex. Weight of numbers is not a measure of value or importance, and nor does this mean smaller groups – those who desire the same sex, those for whom both sexes are desirable, the celibate, or those to whom sexuality is not central to their identity – are never determining of sexual change. However, changes within opposite-sex sexual cultures have created major shifts in sexualities.

Reproductive sexuality is the sexuality of those whose sexual desires and experiences cannot be separated from the risk of conception. The conditions that create this sexuality are socially and culturally constructed and specific. To appreciate these conditions, it is necessary to address the question of how to situate coitus in the history of sexuality. This is of immense importance in understanding sexual change over the past two centuries. Many scholars have considerable reservations regarding any claim that implies other sexual acts such as oral or anal sex were inherently less important than coitus. Yet, in cultures without access to reliable, safe birth control, coitus is *the* reproductive act. A child is a continuing economic cost for the best part of a decade, and, in European cultures, if the biological parents cannot or will not fulfil that burden, it falls upon their community. This economic cost provides the major motivation for societal attempts to control the sexual activity of individuals. The risk of conception is nearly 90 per cent within a year for a man and woman having intercourse twice a week.[15] Reproductive sex carries the risk of greater economic and social consequences than almost any other act the majority of women – and to a lesser extent men – routinely commit in their lives. Thus coitus has a fundamentally different, and potentially greater, impact than other sexual acts.

Reproduction has been seen as a perennial, unchanging experience, but this is not correct. Rising and falling birth rates result in sharp changes in reproductive opposite-sex sexuality. Children were often highly desired and infertility was a source of intense distress, but after four or five children rates of maternal morbidity (illness and injury) and mortality rise sharply. The impact of high fertility on the individual woman varies; however, this provides many woman with an incentive, independent of society and regulation, to restrict sexuality in order to lower their fertility. Mortality rates, that is the average period of a person's life, are also relevant. The fifteen or so years that a woman who had four or five children spent caring for them, took up the prime of her life, until as late as the mid-twentieth century. This was also the case, though to a more variable and lesser extent, for a man who took responsibility for his children.[16]

It has been assumed that in the absence of safe, effective contraception or abortion, people would engage in other sexual practices rather than abstain from sexual expression. In England the evidence, albeit limited, and in part dependent upon the continuity of absences and silences in the historical record, suggests that oral, and to a lesser extent anal, sex were not part of the opposite-sex sexual repertoire until the mid-twentieth century.[17] The continuity of attitudes in English society to contraception, masturbation and the conditions under which pre-marital sex took place, suggests a similar continuity in relation to other sexual practices. In particular, the continuing silences can be compared to the continuity of evidence, albeit also fragmentary, suggesting that while courting, and before advancing to coitus, hand/genital contact was a routine substitute for coitus.[18] It is possible that this was because the existing standards of hygiene made routine mouth/genital contact unpleasant and unsafe. Cultural prohibitions that ensure food and excretion are kept separate to avoid disease vary in different cultures. Prohibitions such as the separation of toilets and kitchens, tables and chamber pots, mouths and genitals have been taken for granted in Western culture.[19] In any event, this does not mean no persons engaged in oral sex, but that only a small proportion would have done so, perhaps those whose sexuality was transgressive in other regards. There is little evidence regarding the extent of opposite-sex practice of anal sex, but that which exists, and the sexual culture, suggests it was more likely to have been used as a contraceptive substitute for coitus than oral sex.[20] It seems reasonable to conclude that for the majority of the adult population, coitus was the desirable end point of sexual activity.

Birth is one of the events for which reliable measurements exist. However, births can only provide a measure of sexual activity if there is either very little use of effective, individual, direct methods of contraception and abortion, or if the levels of use can be, and have been, measured. This is the case in England. One indirect piece of evidence showing the absence of the control over fertility provided by contraception in the nineteenth century is the absence of any norms of family size among any class. In the 1870s marriage cohort, Michael Anderson found that family sizes were widely scattered with less than 10 per cent of the population in any family size. There were more than 5 per cent of families in all sizes from zero to ten children, but more than one in ten families were of eleven or more and these families contained around one quarter of all children born.[21] The establishment of norms of family size followed, not preceded, the capacity to control fertility and did not occur until the interwar period. There is a large mass of evidence collected from throughout the world showing that efforts to control fertility have always existed, a point which is emphasized in the existing historiography.[22] This evidence proves that people were *motivated* to control their fertility, but not that the methods used were effective. There is no evidence of consistent use of effective methods for preventing conception or birth until the French fertility decline in the eighteenth century.[23]

The English evidence suggests that, aside from occasional individuals, men did not even begin to use withdrawal until the late nineteenth century.[24] Early condoms were ineffective at preventing conception and men were also unwilling to use them within marriage. Abortion techniques improved with the discovery of sepsis and antisepsis, but illegal abortion remained painful and carried a risk of serious injury until legalization in 1967. Individual accounts of contraceptive failure reinforce the argument that, regardless of experience and access to the available methods, the possibility of conception due to method failure was unavoidable until the 1960s. It is this absence of effective and direct individual birth control that results in the strong and enduring relationship of fertility rates with sexual behaviour. And it is these particular absences, of birth control, and those resulting from inhibition, regarding alternative sexual practices and sexual partners that are necessary to produce reproductive sexuality.

There was control of fertility before the late nineteenth century but this was achieved by indirect and communal control of courting, marriage, and all other sexual outlets. The historical demographer John Hajnal identified a unique pattern of late and infrequent marriage and described it as the North-West European marriage system because it occurred only in that area. He showed that within this region not only was the marriage age of plebeians late – at around twenty-six to twenty-seven or older for men, and for women at twenty-three to twenty-four – but 10 to 15 per cent of the population never married at all.[25] A rise or fall in the proportion of women who marry, and in the age at which they marry, produces a rise or fall in fertility rates. This is because a higher age at marriage means women spent fewer years married and having sexual intercourse, therefore fewer years at risk of pregnancy.

The rest of this chapter will provide two examples of the use of demographic sources. The first, birth rates, reveals that reproductive sexuality provides a radically new way to understand changes in sexuality in nineteenth-century England. Demographers measure changes in fertility in a number of different ways. The actual number of babies born each year is called the crude birth rate, but whether one woman has ten babies, or ten women have one baby each, this rate will be the same. Rates that show the average number of babies born per woman over her lifetime provide greater understanding of change. The total period fertility rate (TFR) indicates the number of children a woman would have in her reproductive lifetime if she aged through her reproductive years exposed to the age-specific rates prevailing at a given point in time. Calculating the TFR requires more information than is available for the period before 1841, and only the gross reproduction rate (GRR), which shows the number of daughters born per woman, has been obtained for the entire period from 1751 to 1976.

After rising slowly from the 1600s, the GRR began to rise sharply from 1751 (Figure 1.1). The rate peaked in 1816. In the 1820s and 1830s, there was a very sharp decline in the birth rate, but this decline then slowed down to the point where there was a slight aggregate rise from the mid-

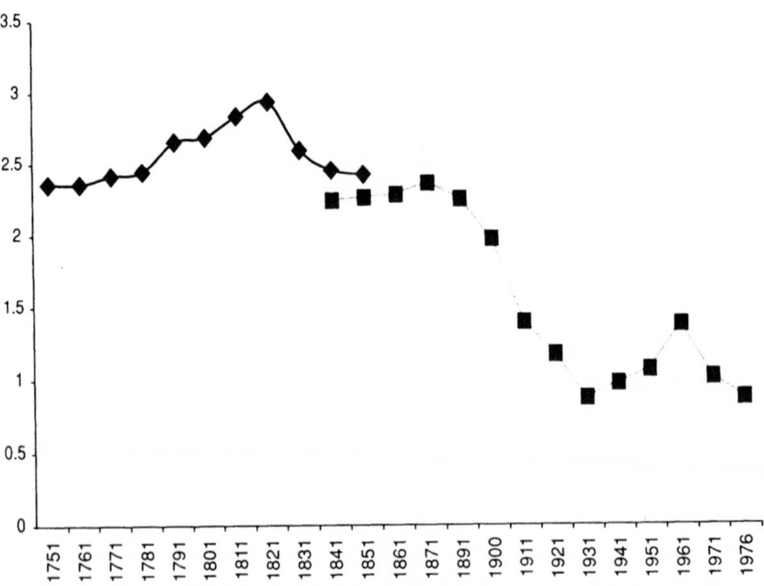

Figure 1.1 Gross Reproduction Rate 1751–1976.

Source 1751–1851, E.A. Wrigley et al., *English population history from family reconstitution 1580–1837* (1997): Table 8.7, 532. 1841–1976, *Birth statistics, Historical series of statistics from registrations of births in England and Wales, 1837–1983*, OPCS Series FM1 no.13 (1983): Table 1.4, 26.

1840s to the mid-1870s. The existing historiography of nineteenth- and twentieth-century sexuality and fertility is based on data from 1841, from which point it appeared that the aggregate decline in birth rates started from the 1870s, and on the belief that birth control was widely available but people lacked motivation to use it. Historical demographer Simon Szreter has argued that in England partial sexual abstinence, that is less frequent sexual intercourse, played the major role in bringing down the birth rate from the 1870s. He uses a range of statistical and qualitative data, and his argument is reinforced by my own research.[26] Sexual abstinence as a means of birth control both springs from, and contributes to, a culture of sexual restraint. It is probably only possible in such a culture. However, the absence of effective and widely available birth control means that throughout the nineteenth century there is a direct and close relationship between levels of sexual intercourse (controlled by access to marriage) and fertility rates. When the start of the fertility decline is taken back to the initial sharp fall from 1816, it comes into line with the growth of sexual prudery, known as Victorian sexuality.

Given these points, what do fertility rates suggest about nineteenth-century sexuality? It appears that the growing emphasis on sexual restraint and prudery coincides with, and likely results from, the efforts to control fertility. The suggestion of a causal relationship is reinforced by the early success at restraining fertility (by restraint of marriage) among the most prudish sector of society, the emerging middle classes. Fertility rates – along with marriage and illegitimacy rates – also show that the height of sexual restraint was reached around 1900 not, as much of the historiography on opposite-sex sexuality implies, in the mid-nineteenth century.[27] This has implications for the understanding of the major shifts around the turn of the twentieth century in the discursive construction of same- and opposite-sex sexualities – that is the creation of a homosexual identity and the sexological category of 'heterosexuality', which Jonathon Ned Katz argues was initially defined as an opposite-sex pleasure ethic to which procreation was irrelevant.[28] These emerging sexual identities can be understood as the result of three quarters of a century of intensifying effort to lower fertility and the increasing channelling and denial of sexual desires and experiences.

The second example also draws on qualitative evidence about the social context, as well as a variety of statistical sources. Was prostitution an important part of the sexual experience of nineteenth-century middle-class Englishmen? If it was, how should this fact be interpreted? Middle-class behaviour has been treated as particularly significant to the history of sexuality by a variety of historians, from historical demographers who noted that the English middle classes began to lower their fertility first, and assumed this meant that the working classes were led by them, to Michel Foucault, whose *History of Sexuality* focuses on bourgeois discourses. Reproductive sexuality (absence of birth control plus inhibitions) was highly gendered; men could seek extra-marital, opposite-sex sexual activity, if they could afford to pay, but the risk of pregnancy was a constant for women. Katz sees the late nineteenth-century shift away from the reproductive ideal toward a pleasure ethic as inherently desirable. However, as late as the 1950s, an English male engaging in opposite-sex sexual activity, with a partner who was not a prostitute, who thought *only* in terms of sexual pleasure, was disregarding her risk of conception – unless the couple wanted children at that time. There was therefore an incentive for men to seek paid sex.

The eighteenth century saw a sustained rise in fertility. Henry Abelove and Tim Hitchcock have both argued that this statistical evidence reveals a transition from a variety of alternative sexual practices to an emphasis on 'heterosexual', 'phallocentric', 'penetrative', 'procreative' sex, and the relegation of alternative practices to the realm of foreplay.[29] There are some problems with their arguments, of which perhaps the most important is that the historiography of opposite-sex sexuality does not provide any evidence for the earlier acceptability and practice of alternative sexual acts, aside from manual stimulation of the genitals. In the event that Trumbach provides evidence to support his claim that prior to 1700 'all males had desired both males and females', and that this had resulted in the usual expression of same-sex desire, as in Florence, this statement would have to be modified to include male same-sex sexuality, and this would shift the argument back to female sexuality. However, the examples used by Alan Bray, in support of his strong argument that the abhorrence of an abstract sodomy in Renaissance England was not associated with the actuality of male same-sex sexual acts, suggest that tolerance depended on a lack of awareness, sustainable only in the context of relative infrequency of such activity.[30]

In the absence of evidence of sexual practices, Abelove and Hitchcock's arguments are based on the assumption of a 'natural' polymorphous sexuality in which all sensations would be explored. The apparent irrationality of sexual inhibitions is perhaps an artefact of twentieth-century thought and more apparent than real in the absence of birth control. The presentation, familiar to us, of sexualities defined as medico-scientific sexual categories gives the impression that desire has a fixed object. However, there are many contexts in which the object of desire shifts, as the extensive research revealing situational heterosexuality and homosexuality among those with access only to one sex, or the other, the growing literature on bisexuality and the shifts in object choice by individuals over the lifetime which have become more visible since the 1960s reveals.[31] This more polyvalent vision of desire suggests a logic behind the rejection of the whole range of sexual desires, that is the broad based constriction or restraint of sexuality. It is at this point that the psychic forces that led to constraints upon reproductive sexuality becoming determining of the whole sexual culture become apparent. The impact of these impulses was given force because they were produced from within the dominant sexual culture, and they were tied intensely into economic life.

There is also an implied claim in Hitchcock's writing that alternative sexual practices were desired more by women, and that 'penetrative' sex necessarily implies a male-dominated agenda of desire. This assumption of the vagina as inert draws on the writings of radical feminists in the 1970s.[32] These arguments cannot be applied to the eighteenth century without contemporary qualitative evidence on women's attitude to vaginal penetration to support the interpretation of the fertility statistics. I would suggest that women also sought and found pleasure in the initial removal of constraints on marriage and sexuality, and that their retreat was not from penetrative sexual acts, but from the long-term consequences of high fertility for women and growing predatory male sexuality. The link Hitchcock makes between levels of sexual activity, changing gender relations, and socio-economic changes that were liberating for men but restrictive for women is probably valid. Abelove sees this eighteenth-century shift as the integration of sexuality into the rise of capitalist production. Michael McKeon points out that capitalism has forced individuals to choose between consumption and reproduction, not to increase the latter, as Abelove suggested. But Abelove's insistence on a connection between sexual activity and economic change remains valid.[33] These arguments can be strengthened by the examination of early to mid-nineteenth-century male sexuality. Did a male-dominated agenda of desire and practice emerge?

A culture reflects such an agenda when, as was the case in early to mid-nineteenth-century England, male recourse to prostitution is accepted but women are expected to remain sexually chaste and heavily penalized if they do not. The coarsening impact of prostitution upon unmarried men is a trope of the nineteenth-century birth control literature, as well as that on prostitution and the shortage of husbands for middle-class women. This does not mean it did not reflect much actual experience. Recent research suggests that when a man purchases a woman's consent to sex he does not learn how to arouse her desire to have intercourse or how to accept refusal. Such an unequal sexual relationship reinforces the man's perception of the woman as an object, which exists only in relation to him, in order to service his needs, demands and expectations.[34] Whilst commercial sexual relationships, especially those which endured over long periods, could be more complex and emotionally engaged than this, the essential dynamic remains.[35]

Recent historians have tended to argue that middle-class husbands were respectable and loving husbands and fathers who wielded their authority wisely and had little contact with commercial sex. In Catherine Hall and Leonore Davidoff's influential account of the provincial middle classes from 1780 to 1850, middle-class engagement with prostitution goes unmentioned, even in the guise of kept women or sexually exploited servants. John Tosh does argue that men indulged in paid sex as bachelors, but insists that once married they were faithful to their wives.[36] This contrasts with the earlier historiography of sexuality which, in keeping with the sexual ethos of the 1960s, emphasized the involvement of middle-class men with prostitution.[37] There are good reasons to consider whether middle-class men were consumers of commercial sex in this period. Historical demographers have found that during the nineteenth century the average age at marriage of men and women in the new middle classes rose sharply. By 1851, the average age at marriage of professional men was 30, and this rose further to 33.5 in 1901–06. These men were also more likely not to marry at all.[38] The rising average age at marriage of professional men resulted in a life-cycle different from that now seen as the norm. Most were single throughout much of their twenties, many remained so until considerably later in life, and a growing proportion never married.

Given the absence of birth control methods, if these men's desire to control fertility had been as high, or higher, than that of women *and* their sexual activity had been restricted to marriage, then they should have been equally committed to sexual restraint. But, by the late nineteenth century, women as a group were considerably more prudish, sexually restrained, and sexually ignorant, than men. If middle-class men had been equally committed to sexual restraint, it would be difficult to explain why a sexual culture had developed by mid-century in which women were seen as greatly lacking in sexual desire when compared to men. If men were not equally committed to sexual restraint, then they must have replaced marital sex with other sexual activity during their late teens, twenties and, often, thirties. Once accustomed to obtaining sexual relief from prostitutes during the long years they spent as bachelors, why would men choose abstinence if fertility control or their wife's physical condition made sexual restraint necessary later in their marriages? There was considerable pressure to conceal sexual matters from middle-class women and the fervently religious but there were few other societal sanctions to deter middle-class men.

There is ample evidence of recourse to female prostitutes by nineteenth-century middle-class men, single and married. A wide range of paid sexual relationships with women existed, though there is a comparative absence of casual commercial sexual encounters reported in biographies, which raises the suspicion that such brief events went unrecorded.[39] Diatribes by purity campaigners treat recourse to prostitution as an unacceptable norm and comments by mid-century visitors to London express amazement at the visibility of prostitution. Many of the men for whom there is evidence belonged to atypical groups such as writers or artists and, notwithstanding the purity campaigners, it is unclear to what extent their behaviour can be generalized to more conventional men. The question is actually one of prevalence; did married, middle-class men usually, or often, patronize prostitutes, or was this the behaviour of unusual and exceptional men? Historical research into nineteenth-century working-class women and prostitution has used institutional sources such as police reports or rescue home records.[40] These sources are biased toward women who worked on the street and are unlikely to include women who profited from wealthier men. Bracebridge Hemyng, Henry Mayhew's collaborator, noted in 1862 that 'police do not concern themselves with the higher class of prostitutes; indeed it would be impossible, and impertinent as well, were they to make the attempt'.[41]

Contemporaries agreed that prostitutes had become more visible by the mid-century, but they argued extensively as to whether their numbers were actually rising. The problems with the numerical estimates mean they are of limited use. For example, observers were counting different groups of women. The fundamental instability of the term prostitute in the first two thirds of the nineteenth century resulted in the inclusion of radically different populations of women in the varied estimates. All sexually active unmarried women, including those who were cohabiting, were frequently included in discussions of prostitution by reformers earlier in the century. Fully half the number of 'prostitutes' on the list made up by reforming magistrate Patrick Colquhoun in 1797 were in this category.[42] The gradual development of police forces and increasing respect for the new science of statistics during the middle decades of the century led to increasing reliance on police statistics. In the 1860s, however, legislators were still unable to define 'a common prostitute' for the purposes of the Contagious Diseases Acts and felt it reasonable that police suspicion should fall on any woman seen in the company of men resident within one of the subjected districts.[43] The police figures were not more accurate, rather the police categorized women as prostitutes according to different criteria. Thus the populations being counted were not equivalent.

The definition of a prostitute generally accepted since the mid-twentieth century is women who exchange sexual acts more or less directly for cash. Three measurable changes do suggest that the actual proportion of such women in the population rose. Prostitution was largely an urban phenomenon. In the middle quarters of the nineteenth century there was a massive growth in population accompanied by a substantial shift from small rural localities to the towns and cities.[44] This means that the proportion of men in the population who had easy access to prostitutes increased because the proportion of men who were town dwellers increased. Working-class women's economic position also worsened steadily, making it likely that the numbers of women undertaking sexual acts solely for financial return, as opposed to those engaging in 'immoral' sexual activity for pleasure, was likely to have increased by mid-century.[45]

However, the most convincing evidence is probably the sharply rising rates of syphilis recorded from the mid-nineteenth century. Sexually transmitted diseases cannot be caught by couples who confine their lifetime sexual activity to monogamous marriage. In the early twentieth century, the highest death rates from syphilis and parasyphilitic diseases occurred among men of the unskilled labouring class, followed by men of the middle and professional classes. The incidence of syphilis-related deaths was significantly lower among miners and textile workers and lowest of all among agricultural workers. If exposed to infection the unskilled are likely to have had a higher chance of catching the disease and dying from it, due to their already poor health, making middle-class men's relative exposure to infection in the preceding decades even greater.[46] Thus statistical evidence on the growing urban population, on working-class women's economic vulnerability and the rising rates of syphilitic diseases suggests that middle-class men were more likely to have recourse to prostitutes than had previously been the case.

There was a vociferous, and increasingly influential, minority of evangelical and dissenting Christians who preached chastity and sobriety for both men and women. There is no way of measuring the number of religious observers, though their numbers clearly grew during the course of the century.[47] They have greatly, probably overly, influenced the understanding of English middle-class male sexuality. There was a small aggregate rise in English fertility from the mid-1840s to the mid-1870s, but historian Joseph Banks used census statistics to identify a number of middle-class occupational groups in which the marital fertility rate was declining as early as the 1850s. The marital fertility rate is the numbers of children born at given durations of marriage. The earlier rates described, the GRR and TFR, are effected by age at marriage; marital fertility describes changes in levels of fertility within marriage. The range of occupations found by Banks suggests a number of strategies were being employed to lower family size. Officers of the navy and marines, painters, sculptors, artists, and army officers, are strongly associated with relaxed attitudes to sexual morality. The same is true of authors, editors and journalists, except that these men are a more heterogeneous group, and more likely to include strict religious observers. Civil and mining engineers are more likely to have been employed in mining areas where prostitution was less available, while the last category, 'Ministers of other than the established church' are almost certainly early examples of partial abstinence as a means of fertility control. The remaining occupations – accountants, physicians and solicitors – cannot be categorized in this rough fashion. Nonetheless, it appears unlikely that sexual probity – whether awakened by religious belief or desires for social status – was the only, or even the main, cause of fertility decline among most of these occupational groups.[48]

It is evident that the vast majority of nineteenth-century middle-class women were virgins until marriage. From the second quarter of the century, unmarried middle-class girls appear to have been increasingly unlikely to be permitted the privacy needed for anything other than the most limited physical sexual intimacies with young men. Undoubtedly some transgressed; there is, for example, some limited evidence concerning lower-middle-class women, who took breach of promise cases against men that revealed them to have been sexually active.[49] But by the last quarter of the century, many middle-class women appear to have had only a vague awareness that sexual acts would be expected of them after marriage and no clear knowledge of precisely what this might involve. The mid-nineteenth-century gulf between male and female sexual experience, especially before marriage, appears to have emerged with the middle classes. Pre-marital sexual intercourse had been a widely accepted stage of courting, a process which included gradually increasing sexual contact, among plebeians in small communities. The shift in sexual experience away from this goes a long way toward explaining the growing perception by the end of the nineteenth century that many, if not most middle-class Victorian women were uninterested in, or actively disliked, sexual activity.[50]

Around 1900, English sexual restraint reached a peak. Edward Fyfe Griffith, who was born in 1895, and later became a doctor and a sex reformer, said that his 'whole family exuded goodness, and religion glowed in every house I lived in and every house I visited [but] ... when one got down to realities and, in particular, to the thorny problems of sex, all this teaching and church-going seemed to be of no avail'.[51] Vera Brittain, the writer, born in 1893, wrote that information on sexual matters 'is always intensely distasteful to me.... I suppose it is the spiritual – & intellectual – development part of me that feels repugnance at being brought too closely into contact with physical "open secrets".'[52] Especially prior to 1900, there are relatively few statements such as these, directly addressing sexual feelings and inhibitions. It could be argued that those that do exist are from individuals, such as feminists, or sex reformers, who have a particular interest and may be biased. However, there is a striking absence of more relaxed and positive statements about sexuality from English women to counterbalance descriptions of discomfort and lack of knowledge.

Since the 1970s, historians in both the US and the UK have claimed that, notwithstanding such silences and the claims of the succeeding generations, the picture of the Victorians as sexually repressed is incorrect. The arguments of such historians against the stereotype of female sexual prudery and lack of interest in sexuality provide no explanation as to why major change occurred in sexual cultures over the nineteenth and twentieth centuries. Carl Degler claimed, in an oft-cited article, that a survey of US women's sexual experience undertaken by Dr Clelia Mosher in the late nineteenth century revealed that common perceptions of Victorian women as never experiencing sexual pleasure were incorrect. However, Mosher took twenty-eight years to obtain replies from only forty-five women.[53] This early statistical source is not a demonstration of relaxed sexual mores and female pleasure, but proof of a culture in which it was barely possible for women to speak of sexual experience. American demographers have analysed the rates of sexual intercourse reported by these women and their testimony actually contributes to the argument that partial sexual abstinence played a part in bringing down birth rates in the United States as well as in England.[54]

The key to much revisionist research on Victorian sexual history lies in the creation of an absolutist straw horse; any evidence of female sexual pleasure is taken to refute the claim that Victorian women never experienced sexual pleasure. That, however, is not a claim any sensitive historian would make. Any broad societal change will involve alteration in levels or averages of given behaviours, not in the absolute disappearance, or takeover by new behaviour. The pace of demographic change suggests strongly that partial sexual abstinence, while important in the US, was not as central or as enduring as was the case in England. Generally, demographic sources make it evident that there is no pan-Western sexual culture, as is implied by the citation of Mosher's survey as if it were relevant to English sexual mores, or for example, Peter Gay's history covering the US, Great Britain and Germany.[55]

Some confusion may have arisen because sexual activity is usually a private activity and so, perhaps, it does not seem necessarily disruptive of pleasure that it should be unacceptable to speak of sexuality. However, the introduction of reproductive sexuality provides a much needed reminder of the life-cycle, and the movement of individuals through varied settings over the course of their lives. The expression of an adult's sexuality can be prevented but it is extremely difficult to significantly alter his or her experience of sexual feeling. But where sexual learning in children is severely disrupted the consequences are substantial. Tightening sexual mores during the nineteenth century were made possible and effective by the denial of knowledge and experience to succeeding generations of growing children and young adults.

By the late nineteenth century, anti-masturbation fears produced efforts to prevent experience of genital pleasure in infants from a preverbal stage. As they grew children were given no opportunity to observe demonstrations of sexual affection or to hear relaxed conversations about sexuality. Girls in particular, but most boys also, were denied the opportunity to observe and enjoy the continuing changes in their own bodies and those of other children. The majority of British parents in all classes believed sexual knowledge, a category which included all embodied aspects of reproduction, was something from which children and young people, especially girls, must be protected. As a result, for example, physical events such as menstruation and, to a lesser extent, wet dreams often caused considerable anxiety, a feeling that was reinforced when adults responded as if the child was at fault, sinful or bad, for producing the event.[56] A 'norm' of treating menstruation as a disgusting event that had to be hidden obviously produces very different emotional effects than does the response to menstruation as a natural event which presages sexual maturity.

In the early twentieth century, intellectuals embraced Freud's claim for the fundamental importance of childhood sexuality in the development of the future adult's sexual behaviour. His argument that sexual drives exist, and can be discerned in children from birth, giving rise to infantile sexuality, was taken up by radical educationalists and greatly encouraged the new relaxed understanding of embodied sexuality that accompanied the behavioural change made possible by the development of contraception.[57]

Statistics offer huge rewards in terms of understanding changing sexualities, but with this comes a potential prioritizing of the majority as right, or more natural, or moral. Rejection of this claim is, and will remain, a political issue of importance for historians of sexuality. It can be counterbalanced by an awareness of the variation over time, culturally and within cultures of the social construction of sexualities and reproduction. The continued publication since the 1960s of biographies of numerous radical or literary, highly sexually active individuals, many of whom left generous diaries and letters, and of the histories of groups to whom sexuality was central has revealed the central role played by these people. Their new ideas, often disruptive behaviour and insistence on pleasure in the body, helped bring about change in twentieth-century English society and similarly elsewhere.

Demography is a fiercely empirical discipline, largely sceptical of theory, except as a hypothesis to be tested against data. This approach is quite different to that of many historians of sexuality who tend to use theory as an explanatory device to explain the data. Foucauldian theory, in particular, appears to be so elastic that there are no empirical failures that could possibly disprove the account he provided or disqualify that approach. Eric Hobsbawm, one of an older school of radical historians, recently argued that 'the point from which historians must start... is the fundamental and... absolutely central distinction between establishable fact and fiction, between historical statements based on evidence and those which are not'.[58] The transformation of attitudes to sexuality is so recent and still so hard fought that many of those who are researching and writing the history of sexuality today began their engagement with ideas about sexuality with the rejection of a supposedly objective and scientifically proven account of their own sexuality as an illness, a sign of degeneration, or a neurosis. However, it is precisely because of this that the history of sexuality must be based on a solid empirical foundation, the rejection of false claims, not the rejection of the idea that claims based on empirical evidence of material reality are possible. Engagement with other disciplines, including demography, will contribute to making this possible.

notes

1. Chris Langford, 'The Eugenics Society and the Development of Demography in Britain: The International Population Union, the British Population Society and the Population Investigation Committee', in Robert Peel (ed.), *Essays in the History of Eugenics, Proceedings of a Conference Organised by the Galton Institute, London, 1997* (London: Galton Institute, 1998), pp. 81–111.
2. G. Alter, 'Theories of Fertility Decline: A Nonspecialist's Guide to the Current Debate', in John Gillis, David Levine, and Louise Tilly (eds.), *The European Experience of Declining Fertility; A Quiet Revolution 1850–1970* (Oxford: Blackwell, 1992), pp. 13–30. Simon Szreter, 'The Idea of the Demographic Transition and the Study of Fertility Change: A Critical Intellectual History', *Population and Development Review*, 19, 4 (1993), 659–701.
3. John Caldwell, 'Demography and Social Science', *Population Studies*, 50, 3 (1996), 305–33. John Caldwell, Pat Caldwell, and B. Caldwell, 'Anthropology and Demography: The Mutual Reinforcement of Speculation and Research', *Current Anthropology*, 28, 1 (1987), 25–43.
4. David Glass and D.E. Eversley (eds.), *Population in History* (London: Edward Arnold, 1965). D.S. Reher, and R. Schofield (eds.), *Old and New Methods in Historical Demography* (Oxford: Clarendon Press, 1993). J. Dennis Willigan and Katherine Lynch, *Sources and Methods of Historical Demography* (New York/London: Academic Press, 1982).
5. E.A. Wrigley and R.S. Schofield, *The Population History of England, 1541–1871* (London: Edward Arnold, 1981). E.A. Wrigley, J.E. Oeppen, R.S. Schofield, and R.S. Davies, *English Population History from Family Reconstitution, 1580–1837* (Cambridge: Cambridge University Press, 1997).
6. See John Gagnon and W. Simon, *Sexual Conduct: The Social Sources of Human Sexuality* (London: Hutchinsons, 1974), pp. 11, 17, 26.
7. John D'Emilio, 'Capitalism and Gay Identity', in Ann Snitow, Christine Stansell, and Sharon Thompson (eds.), *Powers of Desire: The Politics of Sexuality* (London: Virago, 1983), pp. 467–76.
8. See Matt Houlbrook, 'Toward a Historical Geography of Sexuality', *Journal of Urban History*, 27, 4 (2001), 497–504.
9. George Chauncey, *Gay New York: Gender, Urban Culture and the Making of the Gay Male World, 1890–1940* (New York: Basic Books, 1994), pp. 72–6.
10. Cited in this instance from Randolph Trumbach, 'The Heterosexual Male in Eighteenth-Century London', in Katherine O'Donnell and Michael O'Rourke (eds.), *Love, Sex, Intimacy and Friendship between Men, 1550–1800* (London: Palgrave Macmillan, 2003), p. 99. See also *Sex and Gender Revolution Volume One, Heterosexuality and the Third Gender in Enlightenment London* (Chicago: University of Chicago Press, 1998).
11. J. Hajnal, 'European Marriage Patterns in Perspective', in Glass and Eversley, *Population*, pp. 101–43. See also Helmut Puff, *Sodomy in Reformation Germany and Switzerland, 1400–1600* (Chicago: University of Chicago Press, 2003), pp. 91–2, 181.
12. See Jonathon Ned Katz, *The Invention of Heterosexuality* (New York: Dutton, 1995). Judith Butler, 'Revisiting Bodies and Pleasures', *Theory Culture and Society*, 16, 2 (1999), 11–20. For the difficulties this creates, see John Kucich, 'Heterosexuality Obscured', *Victorian Studies*, 40, 3 (1997), 475.

13. See Diane Richardson (ed.), *Heterosexuality: A Feminism & Psychology Reader* (London: Sage, 1993). Stevi Jackson, 'Sexual Politics: Feminist Politics, Gay Politics and the Problem of Heterosexuality', in Terrell Carver and Veronique Mottier (eds.), *Politics of Sexuality: Identity, Gender, Citizenship* (London: Routledge, 1998). Stevi Jackson, *Heterosexuality in Question* (London: Sage, 1999). Calvin Thomas, *Straight with a Twist: Queer Theory and the Subject of Heterosexuality* (Urbana: University of Illinois, 2000).
14. Other authors have chosen to use cross-sex or different-sex. As discussion of sexualities widens to include hermaphrodites and so on, this is potentially confusing, so I have chosen to retain a familiar term, despite the consequent retention of an implied binary division into opposite and same sex.
15. This estimate is for women in the 'prime reproductive ages'. James Trussell and Kathryn Kost, 'Contraceptive Failure in the United States: A Critical Review of the Literature', *Studies in Family Planning,* 18, 5 (1987), 245.
16. Richard Titmuss, *Essays on 'The Welfare State'* (London: George Allen & Unwin, 1958), pp. 61, 92, 96. Amanda Vickery, 'Golden Age to Separate Spheres? A Review of the Categories and Chronology of English Women's History', *Historical Journal*, 36, 2 (1993), 318–19.
17. Richard Davenport-Hines, *Sex, Death and Punishment* (London: Fontana, 1991), pp. 79, 82. J.T. Noonan Jr., *Contraception: A History of its Treatment by Catholic Theologians and Canonists* (Massachusetts: Belknap/Harvard University Press, 1965). G.R. Quaife, *Wanton Wenches and Wayward Wives: Peasants and Illicit Sex in Early Seventeenth Century England* (London: Croom Helm, 1979).
18. See Tim Hitchcock, 'Sociability and Misogyny in the Life of John Cannon, 1684–1743', in Tim Hitchcock and Michele Cohen (eds.), *English Masculinities, 1660–1800* (London: Longman, 1999), pp. 25–43. See also Laura Gowing, *Common Bodies: Women, Touch, and Power in Seventeenth-Century England* (New Haven: Yale University Press, 2003), chapter 3. Quaife, *Wanton Wenches*, chapter 5.
19. Alan MacFarlane, *The Savage Wars of Peace* (Oxford: Blackwell, 1997), pp. 169–80, 251–5.
20. See Hera Cook, *The Long Sexual Revolution: English Women, Sex and Contraception, 1800–1975* (Oxford: Oxford University Press, 2004), pp. 128–30.
21. Michael Anderson, 'The Emergence of the Modern Life Cycle in Britain', *Social History*, 10 (1985), 80.
22. Linda Gordon, *Woman's Body, Woman's Right: A Social History of Birth Control in America* (New York: Grossman, 1976), p. 25. Angus McLaren, *Reproductive Rituals: the Perception of Fertility in England from the Sixteenth Century to the Nineteenth Century* (London: Methuen, 1984), p. 206. John Riddle, *Contraception and Abortion from the Ancient World to the Renaissance* (Cambridge, Mass.: Harvard University Press, 1992).
23. Angus McLaren, *Sexuality and Social Order* (London: Holmes and Meier, 1983), pp. 15, 26, 126.
24. Cook, *Long Sexual Revolution*, chapters 2 and 5.
25. Hajnal, 'European Marriage Patterns', pp. 101–43.
26. Simon Szreter, *Fertility, Class and Gender in Britain, 1860–1940* (Cambridge: Cambridge University Press, 1996).
27. K. Nield, 'Introduction', *Prostitution in the Victorian Age: Debates on the Issue from 19th-century Critical Journals* (Farnborough: Gregg, 1973). Ronald Pearsall,

The Worm in the Bud: The World of Victorian Sexuality (London: Pimlico, 1969). Eric Trudgill, *Madonnas and Magdalens: The Origins and Development of Victorian Sexual Attitudes* (London: Heinemann, 1976).
28. Katz, *Heterosexuality*, p. 19.
29. Henry Abelove, 'Some Speculations on the History of "Sexual Intercourse" During the "Long Eighteenth Century" in England', *Genders*, 6 (1989), 125–30. Tim Hitchcock, 'Redefining Sex in Eighteenth Century England', *History Workshop*, 41 (1996), 73–90.
30. Alan Bray, *Homosexuality in Renaissance England* (London: Gay Men's Press, 1982), pp. 77–80.
31. George Chauncey, 'Christian Brotherhood or Sexual Perversion? Homosexual Identities and the Construction of Sexual Boundaries in the World War I Era', in George Chauncey, Martin Duberman, and Martha Vicinus (eds.), *Hidden From History, Reclaiming the Gay and Lesbian Past* (London: New American Library, 1989), pp. 294–317. D.S. Neff, 'Bitches, Mollies and Tommies: Byron, Masculinity and the History of Sexualities', *Journal of the History of Sexuality*, 11, 3 (2002), 395–438.
32. See Cook, *Long Sexual Revolution*, chapters 4 and 11. More recent feminist debates are thoughtfully analysed in Carol Smart, 'Collusion, Collaboration and Confession: On Moving Beyond the Heterosexuality Debate', in Diane Richardson (ed.), *Theorising Heterosexuality: Telling it Straight* (Buckingham/ Philadelphia PA: Open University Press, 1996), pp. 161–77.
33. Michael McKeon, 'Historizing Patriarchy: The Emergence of Gender Difference in England, 1660–1760', *Eighteenth-Century Studies*, 28, 3 (1995), fn. 45. 318–19.
34. Julia O'Connell Davidson, 'Prostitution and the Contours of Control', in Jeffrey Weeks and Janet Holland (eds.), *Sexual Cultures, Communities, Values and Intimacy* (London: MacMillan, 1996), pp. 188–9. See also Phyllis Rose, *Parallel Lives* (London: Chatto & Windus, 1983), p. 282.
35. See, for example, the evolving relationship between essayist Samuel Butler (1835–1902) and a Madame Dumas between 1873 and 1893. P. Raby, *Samuel Butler: A Biography* (Iowa City: University of Iowa Press, 1991), pp. 141–2, 182.
36. Catherine Hall and Leonore Davidoff, *Family Fortunes: Men and Women of the English Middle Class 1780–1850* (London: Hutchinson, 1987), pp. 21, 222–3, 323–4, 403. John Tosh, *A Man's Place: Masculinity and the Middle Class Home in Victorian England* (London: Yale University Press, 1999), p. 57.
37. Steven Marcus, *The Other Victorians* (London: Weidenfeld & Nicolson, 1964).
38. S. Szreter and E. Garret, 'Reproduction, Compositional Demography and Economic Growth: Family Planning in England Long before the Fertility Decline', *Population and Development Review*, 26, 1 (2000), 66.
39. For an indication that many men did visit prostitutes or kept mistresses see, for example, J. Talbot, *The Miseries of Prostitution* (London: J. Madden, 1844), p. 42. W.E.H. Lecky, *European Morals from Augustus to Charlemagne* (London: Longmans, Green & Co, 1869), pp. 282, 284. Susan Chitty, *The Beast and the Monk* (London: Hodder and Stoughton, 1974), p. 121. W.M. Clarke, *The Secret Life of Wilkie Collins* (London: Allison & Busby, 1988). A.C. Grayling, *The Quarrel of The Age: the Life and Times of William Hazlitt* (London: Phoenix, 2001), pp. 87–8.

40. E.g. F. Finnegan, *Poverty and Prostitution: A Study of Prostitutes in Victorian York* (Cambridge: Cambridge University Press, 1979). J.R. Walkowitz, *Prostitution and Victorian Society: Women, Class and the State* (Cambridge: Cambridge University Press, 1980), p. 2.
41. Bracebridge Hemyng, 'Prostitution', in Henry Mayhew (ed.), *London Labour and the London Poor* (London: Charles Griffin, 1862), p. 215.
42. Varied estimates were made by P. Colquhoun, *A Treatise on the Police of the Metropolis* (London: Joseph Mawman, 1796), ch. vii. M. Ryan, *Prostitution in London* (London: H. Bailliere, 1839), pp. 168–9. William Bevan, *Prostitution in the Borough of Liverpool* (Liverpool: D. Marples, 1843), p. 44.
43. Report of the House of Commons Select Committee on the Contagious Diseases Act (1868–9) P.P (306), VII.
44. Szreter and Garret, 'Reproduction', 61.
45. Sarah Horrell and Jane Humphries, 'Women's Labour Force Participation and the Transition to the Male-breadwinner Family, 1790–1865', in Pamela Sharpe (ed.), *Women's work: The English Experience 1650–1914* (London: Arnold, 1998).
46. Report of the Royal Commission on Venereal Disease (1916) PP (8190), XVI.
47. See James Obelkevich, 'Religion', in F.M. Thompson (ed.), *The Cambridge Social History of Britain 1750–1950* (Cambridge: Cambridge University Press, 1990), pp. 332, 338. K.D.M. Snell and Paul S. Ell, *Rival Jerusalems: The Geography of Victorian Religion* (Cambridge: Cambridge University Press, 2000).
48. J.A. Banks, *Victorian Values: Secularism and the Size of Families* (London: Routledge and Kegan Paul, 1981), p. 40.
49. Ginger Frost, *Promises Broken: Courtship, Class, and Gender in Victorian England* (Charlottesville: University Press of Viriginia, 1995), p. 114.
50. Cook, *Long Sexual Revolution*, chapters 4 and 6.
51. Edward Griffith, *The Pioneer Spirit* (Upton Grey: Green Leaves Press, 1981), p. 23.
52. Quoted in Carol Dyhouse, 'Mothers and Daughters in the Middle-class Home, c.1870–1914', in Jane Lewis (ed.), *Labour and Love, Women's Experience of Home and Family 1850–1940* (Oxford: Blackwell, 1986).
53. C.N. Degler, 'What Ought to Be and What Was: Women's Sexuality in the 19th-Century', *American Historical Review* (1974).
54. P.A. David and W.C. Sanderson, 'Rudimentary Contraceptive Methods and the American Transition to Marital Fertility Control, 1855–1915', in S.L. Engerman and R.E. Gallman (eds.), *Long Term Factors in America's Economic Growth* (Chicago, University of Chicago Press, 1986), pp. 346–7.
55. Peter Gay, *Education of the Senses: The Bourgeois Experience, Victoria to Freud* (Oxford: Oxford University Press, 1984). *The Pleasure Wars: The Bourgeois Experience – Victoria to Freud, Vol. 5* (New York: W.W. Norton, 1998).
56. See Cook, *Long Sexual Revolution*, chapter 6.
57. For example, Susan Issacs, *Social Development in Young Children* (London: George Routledge & Sons, 1933). J. Croall, *Neill of Summerhill: The Permanent Rebel* (London: Routledge Kegan Paul, 1983). A.S. Neill, *The Problem Child* (London: Herbert Jenkins, 1900).
58. Eric Hobsbawm, *On History* (London: Weidenfeld & Nicolson, 1997), p. viii.

2
sexology

chris waters

introduction

In early twentieth-century Japan, a new, Western 'science of sexuality' began slowly to take hold, displacing understandings of sexuality derived from native intellectual traditions. Minakatu Kumagusu, an ethnographer and biologist born in 1867, was an early student of the burgeoning Western literature on sexuality and his writings bore witness to a profound shift in thinking about sexuality taking place in his society. As much as he advanced the new science, he believed that it threatened alternative ways of conceptualizing sexuality that had flourished in Japan. He argued that the Japanese were losing sight of their traditions and in one of his works he noted the existence of a Sino-Buddhist tract that identified four karmic causes that accounted for why some men desired to be sexually penetrated by other men – such as their having been guilty of committing slander or incest in a previous life. The logic of this argument may seem baffling to us today and, as Gregory Pflugfelder reminds us, it would certainly not have satisfied Western sexologists, scientists who sought the origins of human sexual behaviour in the body, not in the karma.[1] But who were those scientists who influenced Kumagusu and what was the enterprise to which they were committed? More generally, what are the origins of Western sexology? What was the 'truth' of sexuality the new science discovered? How did it establish itself as a respected discipline, coming to assert an authoritative voice on sexual matters, both in the west and beyond? How, when and by whom was that voice contested? Finally, how might we understand the relationship between sexological knowledge and the individual experience of sexuality in society? These are some of the questions this chapter seeks to address.

First and foremost, what, exactly, *is* sexology? The *Oxford English Dictionary* defines it as 'the scientific study of sex and the relations between the sexes', tracing the origins of the word to a book entitled *Sexology*, first published in 1902 by an American doctor, William Walling.[2] By this time, however, even if the term was rarely used, sexology was already well on its way to becoming an established science. A number of experts – both in Europe and the United States – had already contributed to that science, their discoveries, theories and pronouncements on sexual matters increasingly respected and more and more influential. Theirs was a science based on the growing conviction that, as the Spanish endocrinologist Gregorio Marañón put it in 1915, 'The sexual life is not something trivial or superficial, but rather the root of human biography.'[3] Writing earlier, in the 1860s, the American feminist Elizabeth Willard had anticipated Marañón's assertion in a book which, like Walling's, was entitled *Sexology*. Her own understanding of the term, however, had much less to do with sexuality than with what we would term gender, with the relationship between the sexes. She argued that there were essential differences between men and women, that these were part of 'natural sexual law', and that, armed with 'true scientific knowledge' of that law, we might bring the relations between the sexes into harmony.[4] Willard's ideas were not new; indeed, many nineteenth-century feminists grounded their arguments in natural law, even if they did not use the term sexology to describe the science of reforming society in accord with that law. Nevertheless, although Willard was much more concerned with gender than she was with sexuality, central to her project was the belief – shared by subsequent sexologists – that the organization of sexual relations had become an important scientific project. In his own 1902 study, Walling stressed that importance when he argued that in a rapidly industrializing society Americans were woefully ignorant of the laws of nature, self and sex, in need of the 'revelations of science', which would provide them with the sexual knowledge they required to lead happy and healthy lives as husbands, wives and citizens.[5]

By the early 1900s, individuals in various fields – including anthropology, biology, history, psychiatry and the medical sciences – had all contributed to this emergent project, leading historian Paul Robinson to argue thirty years ago that 'thinking about sex became explicit and systematic, giving rise to a new intellectual type, the sexologist'.[6] Moreover, by the outbreak of the First World War thinking about sex had also given rise to an increasingly well-defined intellectual field, a system of knowledge consolidated and disseminated through a panoply of journals, conferences and professional bodies. Early in the century it was given intellectual coherence by Iwan Bloch (1872–1922), who coined the term 'sexual science' in 1906 and who, in *The Sexual Life of Our Time*, provided 'a complete encyclopædia of the sexual sciences', bringing together everything he took to be of value 'since the beginning of the truly scientific study of the subject'.[7] His compatriot, Magnus Hirschfeld (1868–1935), founded the first journal devoted to sexology in 1908. In 1919 he established the Institute for Sexual Science in Berlin, dedicated to the acquisition of scientific knowledge about human sexuality and to the use of that knowledge for the improvement of society. Hirschfeld keenly stressed the social benefits to be derived from the sexological project, like others conceiving of a therapeutic role for sexology in society. In the 1930s, a decade in which the therapeutic functions of sexology became entrenched in a number of Western nations, Norman Haire (1892–1952) was one of many optimists who insisted that the fruits of modern sexual science would dispel ignorance and bring enlightenment – both to individuals suffering from sexual problems and to a society burdened by outdated conventions.[8]

Such rhetoric was widespread by the 1930s and flourished in the 1950s; moreover, it was accepted at face value by historians when they began to write the history of sexology. This is no longer the case: as Jeffrey Weeks has argued, it 'is impossible to understand the impact of sexology if we simply accept its own evaluation of its history'.[9] While claiming to be scientists of desire who would merely reveal the hidden keys to our identity, sexologists have actually shaped the meanings and experience of sexuality – sometimes in dubious ways. As Roy Porter and Mikuláš Teich remind us, we therefore need to ask what sexology reveals about the wider ideological and practical ends that sexual science has served.[10] This chapter will address their question, first by offering a brief history of sexology, then by exploring the ways in which historians have understood the sexological project, and finally by turning to recent debates about the role played by sexology in the history of sexuality more generally.

sexology: a brief historical narrative

In the nineteenth century, particularly in the wake of rapid urban and industrial growth in Western Europe, legislators and doctors related the health of the individual body to that of the social body, conceiving of the nation's life in organic terms, increasingly to be regulated by experts. The work of Thomas Malthus (1766–1834) and Charles Darwin (1809–1882) was central to this project. For Malthus, uncontrolled procreation would result in overpopulation, the consequence of which was poverty, disease, famine and war. As a result of his work, the question of birth control would soon become a pressing social issue. Darwin's interest in the role played by sexual selection in evolution fuelled the growth of eugenics, the science that held that the nation's health depended on the well-being of its populace, guaranteed through the encouragement of the selective breeding of the fittest. In the wake of the Malthusian and Darwinian revolutions, new social conventions, new practices of self-control, new sanitary prescriptions and new policies of sex education were all put forward as means of controlling what were increasingly mapped as the unruly forces of sexuality that threatened to dissolve crucial social bonds and impede the advance of civilization. In short, good sexual conduct, especially amongst the lower social orders, became crucial to the nation's health. The study of that conduct gave rise to new biomedical knowledge; moreover, because that knowledge was useful to various governmental agencies, the experts who developed it gained more and more authority to pronounce on sexual matters, their stature in society greatly enhanced in the process.[11]

As the century progressed, cities were increasingly defined by their critics as spaces in which customary moral restraints were being eroded. Against the backdrop of this anxiety, doctors, psychiatrists, criminologists, jurists and others carefully mapped those spaces and the so-called aberrant behaviours they discovered in them, developing the classificatory and diagnostic tools necessary for the regulation and control of those who troubled the guardians of society. In so doing, they gradually came to articulate what Arnold Davidson terms a 'new psychiatric style of reasoning'. In the earlier part of the century, aberrant sexual behaviour was often viewed as a result of a simple lapse of the moral will, or conceptualized through what Davidson views as an 'anatomo-pathological style of reasoning' in which the source of that behaviour was located in some aspect of the perpetrator's defective anatomy. By the 1890s, however, a new style of psychiatric reasoning had emerged which took as its starting point a belief in the existence of the so-called 'sexual instinct', the natural function of which, it was often assumed uncritically by many doctors, was reproduction. All aberrations were now mapped against this so-called natural function and constituted as 'sexual perversions', or psychic diseases of the sexual instinct, involuntary symptoms of a deeper personality structure, now intelligible through psychiatry.[12] Even though newly emerging conceptions of romantic love began to stress the importance of the enjoyment of sex independently of its reproductive function, deviations from a narrow range of acceptable heterosexual behaviours were increasingly viewed in terms of the defective psychology of those who practised them.

In this new intellectual climate, sexology was less interested in the classification of the vices than in the psychology of the perversions. Take, for example, the shift in thinking about sex between men. Forensic experts had often been called upon to measure physical evidence of sodomy; increasingly, however, such evidence was supplemented by an interest in the biological, and eventually the psychological, make-up of the offender who committed sodomy. In short, sexologists became interested in the broad personality structures of those who suffered from the so-called diseases of the sexual instinct. In 1877, Richard von Krafft-Ebing (1840–1902) identified a number of those diseases in his important article, 'Certain Anomalies of the Sexual Instinct', a precursor of the classificatory works that proliferated in the 1880s and 1890s, including his own major study, *Psychopathia Sexualis*. This was the period in which sexologists codified the perversions and devised criteria to demarcate the normal from the pathological; it was the era in which the terminology of sexual life we have inherited was formulated: 'exhibitionism' was coined in 1877, the master concept of 'sexual perversion' in 1885, 'masochism' and 'sadism', along with 'paedophilia', in 1890. As Robert Nye has argued, by around 1890 the perversions 'had crystallized into distinct types, each with its own symptomatology, archive of clinical cases, and small army of medical and legal specialists devoted to studying, curing or punishing them'.[13] Curing, rather than punishing, those who suffered from the perversions of the sexual instinct, became particularly important for many of those psychiatrists eager to enhance their own professional standing in society, leading to an array of new therapies, from hypnotism in the 1890s to psychoanalysis in the new century. Other sexologists, less enamoured of the increasingly prevalent psychiatric understanding of sexuality, however, still preferred to see the so-called sexual perversions as biological anomalies and remained dubious about the effectiveness of the cures being put forward by some of their more enthusiastic colleagues. Both groups, however, contributed to the mapping of sexual behaviour, to the new taxonomies of sexual pleasure that were being assembled and widely disseminated in the early years of the twentieth century.

Despite the existence of a number of shared assumptions that united sexologists across national borders, there were significant differences in national sexological traditions prior to 1914, indicative of the extent to which national political concerns shaped scientific research agendas. In France, anxieties about a declining birth-rate led sexologists to cast the perversions, especially homosexuality, as deviations from, and threats to, heterosexual norms that needed to be bolstered as a matter of national urgency.[14] Sexology in Germany and Austria was increasingly associated with movements of sexual reform, especially aimed at abolishing or revising the laws against homosexuality. In some of the earliest writing on the subject, Karl Heinrich Ulrichs (1825–1895) viewed homosexuality as a non-pathological variation of the sexual drive, advancing a biologistic theory of the phenomenon which was subsequently endorsed while being given a psychopathological inflection by Krafft-Ebing and Magnus Hirschfeld. On a lecture tour in the United States in 1930, Hirschfeld was heralded as the 'Einstein of Sex', espousing a theory of sexual relativity and refusing to characterize deviations from the norm as pathological.[15] Hirschfeld certainly saw himself in the forefront of a movement to bring social attitudes towards sexuality more in line with the findings of what he believed to be progressive science, as did Havelock Ellis in Britain (1859–1939), whose seven-volume work, *Studies in the Psychology of Sex*, was a milestone in the history of sexology. In Britain, however, the initial influence of sexology should not be exaggerated; it enjoyed only marginal status in medical circles while *Sexual Inversion*, the first volume of Ellis's *Studies*, was prosecuted as an obscene book.[16] Nevertheless, by 1914 sexological ideas circulated more widely than ever before in Western societies and were increasingly becoming a global phenomenon. Japanese experts had, as we have seen, engaged for many years in an ongoing, creative dialogue with Western sexology, while in India doctors also extolled the benefits of the new 'sexual science' – even if J.L. Chundra supplemented his own enthusiasm for Western science with traditional aphorisms culled from Sanskrit texts, leaving his readers to decide whether or not 'to accord them a hearty or cold reception'.[17]

Chundra cited the importance of sexological work emanating from the United States as well as from Europe. But there, more than elsewhere, concerns about public health, in addition to the strength of social purity movements, led to greater emphasis being placed on concrete, empirical studies of urban vice and prostitution, along with developing programmes of sex education that would teach the importance of purity. Nevertheless, despite the rise of an applied sexology, a number of American doctors engaged critically with current European thought, the ideas of Havelock Ellis and Sigmund Freud finding a receptive audience there. Freud's visit to the US, to lecture at Clark University in 1909, helped consolidate a significant following earlier there than elsewhere. His *Three Essays on the Theory of Sexuality* (1905) drew on contemporary sexological investigations even while extending them; ultimately his work would eclipse that of the earlier generation of sexologists altogether. While they often focused on deviant sexualities, he made normal sexuality an object of scientific investigation; while they explored the sexual problems of the individual, he showed how, more generally, sex was central to the functioning of civilization; while they examined what they took to be the innate sexual characteristics of certain types of people, he put forward a grand theory of psycho-sexual development that could account for the diversity of human sexual behaviour, both in terms of sexual aim (what one does) and sexual object (who one does it with).[18]

Between the wars, Freudian ideas were regularly contested, characteristic of the turf wars between various branches of sexology that became increasingly shrill. For example, his belief that homosexuality was a developmental anomaly conflicted with the findings of the new science of endocrinology, which argued that it was the result of hormonal imbalances. As research into human sexuality expanded, such debates became increasingly common. Nevertheless, most characteristic of the interwar years was an emphasis on the need for sex reform (bringing laws and customs into harmony with the latest scientific findings) and sex education (disseminating those findings on behalf of a healthier and more sexually-fulfilled populace). With respect to reform, new organizations were established in which individuals could exchange ideas and discuss ways of using scientific findings to influence legislation. This, however, remained a contested issue; while Hirschfeld had established his Institute of Sexual Science with the express intention of shaping policy, other sexologists eschewed activism and argued that science must not become a political tool. Hirschfeld convened the First International Conference for Sexual Reform on the Basis of Sexual Science in 1921, which led to the establishment of the World League for Sexual Reform in 1928. Amongst other goals, the League promoted sex education, access to birth control, racial betterment through eugenics, equality between the sexes, and liberalization of the divorce laws and the laws against homosexuality. A mutual reinforcement society for reformers, the League had many critics, the major German sexologist Albert Moll (1862–1939) establishing a rival body that stressed the need for the scientific study of sexuality to be above the political fray.[19]

If the interwar period witnessed disputes about the legitimate role of sexology in the public arena, it also witnessed the growing dissemination of sexological ideas to a broader audience. Before 1914, sexology remained an esoteric science; by the 1930s its ideas were being widely discussed and shaped the sexual advice literature increasingly encountered at most levels of society. The British champion of birth control, Marie Stopes (1880–1958), was hugely successful in creating a market for the rational discussion of sex and its problems, especially through her best-selling manual, *Married Love*, leading historian Lesley Hall to deem her 'the sexologist as agony aunt'.[20] Hardly the weighty tomes penned by the likes of Krafft-Ebing and Ellis for an educated readership, such works, which sought to restructure sexual practice along more rational lines, were indebted to the latest thinking about human sexuality, increasingly to that of the Freudians. By 1939, in the wake of these developments, the French sex radical René Guyon could look back at the progress that had been made on the road to 'sexual freedom', could wax lyrical about sexual acts being 'legitimate if they are performed under the aegis of science, reason, and logic', and could call for further progress in eradicating the neuroses that resulted from the repression of the sex instinct.[21] By 1939, however, the forward march of sexual emancipation, as Guyon viewed it, had come to an end. In May 1933 the Nazis suppressed Hirschfeld's Institute in Berlin, publicly burning its books. Two years later Hirschfeld died in exile in France. Sexological journals soon folded, institutes collapsed and researchers fled. Moreover, in 1939, Freud, Ellis and Moll all died, bringing to a close a vital period in the history of sexology.[22]

Some of the exiles fled to the United States, where Herbert Marcuse and Wilhelm Reich developed the radical potential of Freudian theory, inadvertently providing some of the philosophical underpinnings of the sexual revolution of the 1960s.[23] But in the US sexology as a theoretical enterprise was largely eclipsed by sexology as an investigative science. The belief that the problems of sex behaviour in the community – from illegitimacy to prostitution, from vice to divorce, from homosexuality to abortion – were amenable to objective empirical analysis, from which practical policy could be derived, flourished in the US as nowhere else between the wars. In 1921, the Committee for Research in Problems of Sex was founded, funded generously by the Rockefeller Foundation. While much of the research it sponsored was undertaken in the context of the 'social problem' paradigm, it also supported studies of the sexual practices and beliefs of 'ordinary' people, leading Havelock Ellis in 1931 to praise such work for advancing our knowledge of sexuality in society.[24] Crucial in this respect were the two monumental studies, based on some 12,000 interviews, conducted by Alfred Kinsey (1894–1956) and his colleagues – *Sexual Behavior in the Human Male* (1948) and *Sexual Behavior in the Human Female* (1953) – studies that 'propelled sex into the public eye in a way unlike any previous book or event had done'.[25] Despite his insistence on his scientific neutrality, empirical methods and resistance to theorizing (Freudian in particular), Kinsey's work was laden with special pleading and thinly-disguised opinions, aimed at challenging conventional morality; it was, claimed a recent biographer, an ode to Eros and a prayer to further liberation.[26] Ultimately, he believed that what occurred naturally was right and by documenting the prevalence of a variety of sexual practices – many of which had been seen as perversions of the sexual instinct by earlier sexologists – his work was implicitly an attack on their efforts to censure such practices.

Kinsey's work consolidated the status of the empirical survey of sexuality, the kind of survey that became ubiquitous throughout the postwar world. Lack of funding meant that an attempt to mount a study of sexual attitudes in Britain after the war was limited and Britain's 'Little Kinsey' remained very little indeed.[27] Nevertheless, major, national studies of sexuality were common by the 1960s, one of the more important being *Human Sexual Response*, by William Masters and Virginia Johnson. Their work marked a huge leap in the dissemination of knowledge about the physiological facts of sexual functioning. As Janice Irvine argues, it also furthered sexologists' consolidation of the market for their services by making it possible for people to seek help for their sexual problems.[28] In short, the role of the sex researcher was being augmented by that of the sex therapist, another category of sexological expertise that proliferated after 1945. In a postwar world infatuated by the potential of modern science, the expert in sexual matters had already become extremely influential, advising governments and spearheading state-sponsored projects of sexual normalization. In the United States, in the wake of the 'sex-crime panic' that flourished in the 1950s, when various constituencies all demanded action against the 'sexual psychopath' who could not control his behaviour, experts were called upon to establish new psychiatric and legal mechanisms for policing that behaviour. In Germany, in the context of a conservative, postwar pronatalism, experts urged the state to uphold the existing arrangements when called upon to testify with respect to the legality of existing laws against homosexuality. In Britain, more progressive experts testified before the Wolfenden Committee, established to examine the laws pertaining to prostitution and homosexuality – experts who relied on their authority to advance what they believed to be a superior, scientific understanding of sexuality.[29]

If sexological expertise enjoyed a heyday in the two decades after 1945, it was being eroded by the later 1960s. The anti-psychiatry movement of that decade, coupled with the rapid rise of second-wave feminism and the gay liberation movement, challenged what was 'normal' and 'natural', exposing the cultural bias of systems of expert knowledge production which upheld traditional gender roles and standards of sexual behaviour. This was certainly the case in the United States, where an assault by progressive psychiatrists and lesbian and gay activists influenced the American Psychiatric Association to remove homosexuality from its list of clinical disorders in 1973.[30] At least since then sexologists have not been able to monopolize the right to speak authoritatively about sexuality and its meanings. In the late nineteenth century, they articulated the 'truth' of sex, claiming the mantle of science. During the next century, they played a role in enabling sex to be debated more widely and seriously than ever before. In so doing, however, they helped empower individuals and communities to contest their authority and the cultural assumptions embedded in their work. Recently this can be seen in the politics of AIDS research which, as Steven Epstein argues, has entailed major 'credibility struggles' – battles to determine who can speak the truth of sex.[31]

Despite the vehemence of such disputes, sexology still remains a remarkably vibrant science, even if contested, even if its once bold claims have often been replaced by narrow research agendas. At a 2003 meeting of the World Congress of Sexology, papers explored a vast array of topics – from what Monica Lewinsky's affair with former president Bill Clinton tells us about women's strides in seeking sexual empowerment in the United States to how sex has been 'brought into the realm of discourse' in post-apartheid South Africa. Kinsey-like surveys were also ubiquitous, measuring, amongst other things, condom use in Poland, the typology of visitors to sex shops in Italy, the sexual knowledge and risk behaviour of African-American college students in the US, and sexual dysfunction amongst pathological gamblers in Spain.[32] The grand theorizing of a Krafft-Ebing or a Freud was conspicuous by its absence at this conference, but it is noticeable that historical interests – often influenced by the more recent theories of Michel Foucault – was not. It is to the relationship between historians and sexology that we must therefore now turn.

sexology and the historians

The history of sexology has often been written as a narrow form of intellectual history in which the ideas of sexologists have been dissected in some detail while their origins in the broad problems of social life, along with their political and social consequences, have not received the attention they deserve. Joseph Bristow has argued that we still need to know much more than we do about what gave rise to sexological research in the first place and what its impact in society has been; these 'urgent questions', he suggests, 'have been the subject of far less debate than one might expect'.[33] Although the historical narrative in this chapter is necessarily brief and overly schematic, it touches upon some of Bristow's concerns and identifies some of the ways in which sexology is as much a social and political practice as a disembodied commentary on the meaning of sexuality. In so doing it raises a number of questions with which historians are currently wrestling. How and why did sexology emerge when and where it did? What were the various problems faced by modernizing societies that sexology addressed? How in the process of addressing them did sexologists legitimate their work and enhance their professional status? How can we understand the turf wars between different sexological endeavours in the context of the politics of professional legitimation? What were the causes and consequences of sexology's conception of itself as an objective, value-free science? What role have cultural norms played in shaping sexological research agendas – and what role has sexology played in upholding those norms? Through what mechanisms has sexological research influenced public policy? How have sexological ideas taken root in other societies, transcending their place of origin? Through what channels have sexological ideas been disseminated in society, informing popular beliefs? How, when, why and by whom have the knowledge claims made by sexologists been contested? Questions such as these have generated much recent interest, but this has not always been the case. Indeed, historical assessments of sexology as a broad enterprise have shifted enormously over the years, as have the roles historians have granted to sexology in their histories of sexuality more generally.

In attempting to make sense of these shifts, it is crucial to emphasize that many early sexologists and their allies were themselves historians – or at least drew on a knowledge of the past in order to bolster their claims about the actual and ideal organization of sexuality in the present. Indeed, the history of sexuality as a field of academic enquiry can be said in part to have originated with the work of sexology and sexual reform. One of their endeavours, for example, was to map distinctive sexual types and to argue that those types were both part of the natural order and part of history – a project that led them to manufacture a useable past. Notable in this respect was John Addington Symonds, the English classicist and Ellis's initial collaborator in the writing of *Sexual Inversion*. Symonds called for homosexual emancipation and pillaged the past in order to bolster his claims about the legitimacy of homosexuality. An immersion in the past, he believed, would demonstrate that homosexuality was a natural part of ancient Greek society and not a modern pathology, a disease of the sexual instinct. As he wrote at the outset of his 1874 essay, *A Problem in Greek Ethics*: 'For the student of sexual inversion, ancient Greece offers a wide field for observation and reflection.' Here, he argued, was a society where homosexual passions were not only tolerated but considered spiritually valuable. Moreover, knowledge of this would 'be of service to the scientific psychologist', enabling him to approach the subject from 'another point of view than that usually adopted by modern jurists, psychiatrists, writers on forensic medicine'.[34]

While Symonds attacked the 'scientific psychologist' who discovered the causes of sexual inversion in hereditary degeneration for failing his history lessons, like-minded sexual reformers also immersed themselves in the past. Following Symonds, for example, many other advocates of homosexual rights sought to justify their own existence by pointing to the existence of men and women who shared their desires in the past – and not just in ancient Greece. Moreover, a number of sexual scientists also turned to the past to help them explain more recent sexual behaviour. Underneath the stockpiling of historical anecdotes in the work of Iwan Bloch, for example, was the belief that historical knowledge offered an important key to understanding contemporary problems of human sexuality. His comprehensive history of English sexual life transcended the mere 'manners and morals' school of historical writing – a simple accumulation of anecdotes about past beliefs and practices – and advanced a more sophisticated argument about the role played by the unique culture of a nation in shaping its sexual practices and attitudes to sexuality. In the case of England, he argued, its legacy of Puritanism influenced not only its prudery and hypocrisy with respect to sexual matters, but also the existence of sexual practices that were more prevalent in England than elsewhere – flagellation, for example.[35] If, for Bloch, ideas shaped sexual ideology and practice, then for Hirschfeld the dramatic changes in the sexual life of his own society could be explained by recourse to equally dramatic changes in the economic structure of society. Among other things, he argued, economic change underpinned the emerging equality of the sexes and, as a consequence, the growth of sexual freedom. Moreover, when he suggested that what 'the twentieth century accomplished in changes in the erotic realm is nothing more than a new stage of capitalist development initiated in economic life and accelerated by the war', he anticipated the kinds of arguments made by recent historians Estelle Freedman and John D'Emilio with respect to how economic changes in the United States created the social conditions that facilitated the emergence of new sexual identities.[36]

The role played by sexologists in the development of the history of sexuality has not yet been studied in detail; nor have the ways in which early sexologists and sexual reformers wrote themselves into the historical narratives they offered. Hirschfeld, for example, not only discussed the economic changes behind the 'erotic revolution' of his own age but attributed that revolution to the efforts of those who struggled against conventional morality, especially Bloch, Ellis, Forel, Freud, Krafft-Ebing – and, of course, himself.[37] Increasingly, the histories written by sexologists like Hirschfeld were self-congratulatory tales, narratives of progress – stories in which sexologists cast themselves as the heroes of reform and assumed that the cause of sexual emancipation and sexual science were one. By the interwar years, when the Freudians came to dominate the production of such narratives, the tale of repression and liberation was set, its form varying little over the next third of a century. In 1949, for example, the British analyst Edward Glover argued that in every age there were conflicts between the forces of sexual inhibition and the struggle against the restriction of sexuality and that it was the rise of 'an objective science of sexuality' (psychoanalysis) that facilitated understanding of that conflict and contributed to the widespread liberalizing of sexual attitudes.[38] This logic was central to the histories of sexuality written between the 1940s and the 1970s. It informed that of Gordon Rattray Taylor, who in 1953 characterized history as a struggle 'between the dangerous and powerful forces of the id, and the various systems of taboos and inhibitions which man has erected to control them'. It can be seen in the work of Wayland Young who, a decade later, envisaged the history of sexuality in terms of a pendulum swinging between repression and liberation – currently towards 'perfect sexual freedom'. It was central to the story told by Ronald Pearsall, who praised the work of Ellis, a 'monument to progressive thought' that helped liberate us from Victorian attitudes to sex. It structured the first major history of sexology, in which Edward Brecher argued in 1969 that society was convalescing 'from a sexually debilitating disease: Victorianism' and that we owed our current well-being to the work of sexologists, 'who ministered to us as we recovered step by step'.[39]

This narrative, a story in which sexologists were partly responsible for the progress from sexual repression to freedom – an explanatory edifice constructed bit by bit in the first two thirds of the twentieth century – suddenly came unstuck in the 1970s. No single work in that decade did more to undermine its purchase than Michel Foucault's *History of Sexuality*. This volume's editors discuss Foucault's impact on the writing of the history of sexuality in general; here what should be stressed is the extent to which his work effectively demolished the logic behind both the self-congratulatory posturing of various sexologists and the work of historians who celebrated their achievements. Foucault argued that it was not clear that the regulation of sexuality occurred simply through the forces of prohibition and denial. Instead, it was through the production and deployment of systems of knowledge – that mapped what was legitimate, that articulated norms, that specified perversions – that individual bodies and desires were controlled. According to Foucault, sexuality was not a force within the individual to be liberated or repressed, but an apparatus for constituting and regulating human subjects in particular ways – an apparatus to which sexologists contributed their expertise. Moreover, because Foucault argued that sexual repression was not an established historical fact, then the claims of sexologists to be liberating society from repression were dubious at best.[40]

To be sure, Foucault was not the first thinker to reorient our conceptions of the role of sexology in culture. As we have seen in the foregoing narrative, critiques of sexual science were voiced by the anti-psychiatry movement of the 1960s and 1970s and were central both to second-wave feminism and to the radical sexual politics of those decades. Moreover, as Jeffrey Weeks reminds us, he and other sociologists had already suggested that sexologists were not so much objective scientists of desire as 'diagnostic agents in the process of social labelling'.[41] Nevertheless, Foucault's work was ultimately decisive. In its wake, sexologists were dethroned as the arbiters of the historical importance of their own findings, while the triumphalist narratives that had defined the history of sexology were rendered problematic. Even Paul Robinson, who had written one such narrative in the early 1970s, argued in the late 1980s that it was now more difficult to write a cheerful story of the modernizing impulse of progressive sexology – in part because the sexual freedoms of the 1960s were now being eroded, in part because the traditional story of progress from repression to freedom had been challenged by the work of Foucault, among others.[42]

Foucault has not been without his critics. He has been lambasted for his empirical shoddiness, for writing a history without identifiable historical agents, for reducing the history of sexuality to a history of the classifications or representations of sexuality, for viewing the individual as little more than the passive victim of sexological discourse. And yet in the wake of his conceptual revolution – and in the context of the broader cultural changes of which it was part – it was no longer possible to cast sexologists as the emancipatory heroes they had appeared to be. Hence, from the mid-1970s to the early 1990s there was a tendency to veer towards the other extreme, to view sexologists as insidious agents of social control whose work functioned to discipline subjects by stigmatizing non-normative desires as deviant and by reinforcing patriarchal, heterosexual norms.[43] But if some historians in these years now viewed the sexological project less charitably than had once been the case, others became fascinated with what Foucault termed 'reverse discourse' – with those points of resistance when individuals whose proclivities had been mapped and rendered deviant embraced the categories through which they had been medically disqualified in order to assert with some pride the naturalness of their condition.[44] The problem with this work is that it repeated the old story of repression and liberation, albeit with a new twist: instead of sexologists liberating society from restrictive sexual norms, here was a narrative of grass-roots activists liberating themselves from sexological oppression. Moreover, there are two other problems with such approaches to the history of sexology. First was the tendency of those who viewed sexology as a means of control, and of those who celebrated the possibilities of 'reverse discourse', to assume the prior existence of sexological discourse and to focus on its presumed effects, paying little attention to its origins as a complex product of social interaction. Second, the boldness of a number of the claims made by both schools was seldom supported by the empirical evidence that would allow us effectively to judge them.

Literary critic Rita Felski has recently argued that it is 'as unwise to reduce sexology to a repressive disciplinary apparatus for the administration of psyches as it is to underwrite the self-description of sexologists as heroic pioneers aiding the cause of human progress'.[45] In the last decade writing on the history of sexology has tended more often than not to avoid these extremes, addressing the more vexing questions raised at the outset of this section. In the process the old, more confident narratives of progress and liberation have largely been abandoned – which is not a bad thing – although as a consequence any unitary story of the work of sexology is no longer possible. Foucault's impact on this shift in emphasis has been profound. Nevertheless, it has also exercised a limiting effect as well. For Foucault, the task of historians was to understand those discursive practices which make phenomena like sex socially significant and through which the social body is constituted and regulated. But the work of historians requires not only being attentive to the logic of discursive practices but to their *origins* and *effects*, to their operations in society. Hence the need to find ways to relate discourse to experience, to chart the manner by which discourses are shaped, circulate and come to demarcate the boundaries within which sexual subjects are constituted, understood and governed – and via which those subjects come to comprehend and experience their own selfhood. That this often remains a task to be fully undertaken is partly due to the legacy of Foucault. As Jeffrey Weeks has noted, he remained reluctant 'to discuss the actual relations between discourses, and between the discursive and the extra-discursive' – a reluctance that many enthusiasts for his work have shared.[46] Consequently, Joseph Bristow is not alone in his lament, cited above, that we know less than we might about the role of sexology in society. On a basic level, as Laura Doan has recently suggested, we still 'need to know far more about sexology's cultural status and significance', starting with the simple question, 'who knew what when?'[47]

sexology, the self and everyday life

The 1980s witnessed not only a rewriting of the history of sexology in the wake of Foucault's reconceptualization of its significance, but the expansion of sexuality as a field of historical enquiry more generally. In particular, the decade marked the rise of a new social history of sexuality that emphasized the reconstruction of the past sexual beliefs, behaviours and identities of ordinary people. Moreover, the new social historians often ignored sexology, or viewed it as peripheral to the experience of everyday life with which they were primarily concerned. In so doing, they often challenged the claims made by Foucault on its behalf. In 1985, finding sexological categories to have been virtually non-existent in shaping the self-understanding of those involved in a 1919 sex-scandal in Rhode Island, George Chauncey insisted that 'the role played by medical discourse has been exaggerated'.[48] Chauncey had made a similar claim at the beginning of the decade; at its close he insisted he would 'now argue more strongly' that sexologists did not create the categories around which individuals developed lesbian or homosexual identities in the early twentieth century and that therefore 'extensive and original research' was required to measure the influence of sexology.[49] In recent years much research has been undertaken addressing that influence, research that is beginning to yield important insights. In particular, scholars of the gay and lesbian past have pioneered three avenues of enquiry. First, they have explored the ways in which sexological knowledge has been *produced*, often the result of complex interactions between experts and their middle- and upper-class subjects. Second, they have mapped a number of the ways in which that knowledge has been radically *rewritten* and *used* by those who encountered it – often for different purposes than sexologists originally intended. Finally, they have focused on the various processes by which sexological ideas have become *institutionalized*, adopted and implemented by policy-makers concerned with the maintenance of social order.

In his recent study of Krafft-Ebing, Harry Oosterhuis has stressed the importance of doctor–patient interaction in shaping the sexological project. Suspicious of Foucault's claims about sexology as an apparatus of control, he has demonstrated that individuals who found their conditions mapped in *Psychopathia Sexualis* were not simply passive victims of forces beyond their control, without free will. Krafft-Ebing's work, he argues, gained its momentum from the intimate confessions of those who often willingly shared their life histories with him; it was a product of the 'confrontation and intertwining of professional medical thinking and patients' self-definition'.[50] Moreover, not only were his diagnostic categories and studies of the so-called perversions shaped by his encounters with late nineteenth-century Austrians, but his work also fuelled their self-awareness; it encouraged them to speak for themselves, to reflect on what was increasingly seen to be their authentic, inner being. In short, as Matt Reed has recently argued, the autobiographical case history, pioneered by sexologists such as Krafft-Ebing, became a privileged site for the manufacture of a new language of the self, for telling a particular kind of developmental life story.[51] In the next century, autobiographical narratives of sexual selfhood would proliferate, a form of writing that had once been elicited by sexologists, eager to expand their repertoire of case histories, but soon came to take on a life of its own as more and more individuals articulated a multi-dimensional sense of sexual selfhood through the stories they told about their own lives – through what would eventually come to be known as the 'coming out' narrative. In the 1930s, armed with their own 'life story narratives' that they believed would reveal the 'truth' of homosexual life and thereby serve as a vehicle for effecting social change, homosexual activists insisted on collaborating in a major scientific study of homosexuality in New York undertaken by the Committee for the Study of Sex Variants. Like many of Krafft-Ebing's correspondents, they believed they could advance the homosexual cause by aligning themselves with a scientific enterprise; like them, they shaped that enterprise as much as they were shaped by it.[52]

Work like this has charted some of the ways in which sexological ideas have been formed, suggesting that those individuals addressed by sexology often played a major role in its production. We also know more than we did about the effects of sexological discourse, about how, in specific situations, it has been contested, rewritten and used. We have that knowledge partly because of the work of historians who have begun to address the question posed by Laura Doan – who knew what when? – and have then gone one step further, asking questions about what they did with what they knew. Valuable in this respect are studies of the ways in which sexological and related cultural knowledge has been used by individuals in practices of self-fashioning, in articulating sexual subjectivity. Twenty years ago, Michael Lynch explored how the idea of 'adhesiveness' – a mental bond between men – originated in the Victorian pseudo-science of phrenology, was disseminated in the work of the poet Walt Whitman, and subsequently became an important conceptual framework through which men understood, and expressed, their sexual desire for other men.[53] Making similar arguments, Joanne Meyerowitz has shown how postwar transsexuals have also used medical discourse, becoming adept at structuring their life stories and sense of self to mesh with the institutional meanings and interpretations of their 'condition' in order to maximize chances of surgery.[54] Laura Doan has also contributed to such work, insisting that sexology has served multiple functions and conflicting historical agendas and cannot be viewed merely as a means of control in the hands of a patriarchal hegemony. In her examination of the work of interwar lesbian writers, she has argued that while sexologists 'shaped our discourse on sexuality through coining neologisms and inventing categories', the lesbian writer engaged in a 'strategic negotiation' of that work, imaginatively reconceptualizing the lesbian subject.[55]

Finally, historians have begun to detail the ways in which various sexological ideas influenced the work of policy-makers and became institutionalized, particularly through the criminal justice systems of various nations. In Britain, for example, we know that when Oscar Wilde was prosecuted and imprisoned for 'gross indecency', in 1895, no experts suggested at his trial that he should receive any kind of treatment for his condition. Moreover, when he wrote from prison to the Home Secretary seeking to be released into the hands of medical men, his understanding of contemporary medical thinking about homosexuality was wobbly at best – perhaps to be expected given the flux of ideas at the time. And yet by the 1950s, the behaviour that had led to Wilde's imprisonment was now being explained by many, both inside and outside of the courts, as a treatable aberration. This was primarily because of the ways in which the new, psychological understanding of the so-called sexual aberrations had, largely between the wars, influenced a number of criminologists and progressive magistrates and had slowly come to shape official policy. As early as 1924, in an article entitled 'Psycho-Analysis for Criminals', one British newspaper waxed lyrical about the benefits to be derived from the application of the new ideas, arguing that the legal system should take those ideas seriously because they offered hope for the treatment of the homosexual offender: 'If you can get at the man's mind you may find out where he has gone wrong, and if he is amenable to treatment it is possible to restore him to normal habits.'[56] Many in the 1920s and 1930s did take the claims of the psychologists of sexuality seriously and it is in these decades that we can therefore begin to map the ways in which they influenced state policy with respect to the regulation of homosexuality. Over twenty-five years ago, Foucault delineated the 'four great strategic unities' which, according to him, 'formed specific mechanisms of knowledge and power centring on sex', one of which he termed the 'psychiatrization of perverse pleasure'; nevertheless, it is only in more recent years that historians have actually begun to study the precise timing of the articulation and influence of these 'strategic unities', exploring in some detail the effects of sexological discourse in the arena of public policy.[57]

Work like this has now begun to address Chauncey's call for 'extensive and original research' into the operations of sexology. While it is no longer possible to see sexology as a monolithic repressive force, nor as a benign project of liberation, it is possible to view it as the complex social practice it is, a contested form of knowledge with effects that reach deep into the structures of everyday life. It is a practice through which power is both exercised and resisted, a practice that constitutes desires and identities – that shapes the self – and within which a number of selves can, on many levels, refashion their own self-understanding. In conclusion, the study of sexology should not merely be a study of disembodied ideas about sexuality; such a study should refuse any separation of the cultural and the social and think creatively about the interplay between social history and the history of discourse. As we all know, social history is about real people, real lives, not about mere texts. But it is also about how individuals understand themselves and hence go about their business in particular ways and not others; it is about selfhood and subjectivity – not only what people do, but the logic that underpins their actions and their understanding of those actions. Recent work on the history of sexology suggests just how important it has become in the shaping and regulation of sexual life in modern societies – and how important it must continue to be in the history of sexuality more generally.

notes

1. Gregory Pflugfelder, *Cartographies of Desire: Male–Male Sexuality in Japanese Discourse, 1600–1950* (Berkeley: University of California Press, 1999), pp. 232–3, 268–9.
2. *Oxford English Dictionary*, 2nd edition (Oxford: Clarendon Press, 1989), vol. 15, p. 112.
3. Quoted in Richard Cleminson and Efigenio Amezúa, 'Spain: The Political and Social Context of Sex Reform in the Late Nineteenth and Early Twentieth

Centuries', in Franz Eder et al. (eds.), *Sexual Cultures in Europe: National Histories* (Manchester: Manchester University Press, 1999), p. 184.

4. Elizabeth Willard, *Sexology as the Philosophy of Life: Implying Social Organization and Government* (Chicago: J.R. Walsh, 1867), pp. 11–16.
5. William Walling, *Sexology* (London: H. Sales, 1902), pp. 3, 18.
6. Paul Robinson, *The Modernization of Sex: Havelock Ellis, Alfred Kinsey, William Masters and Virginia Johnson* (New York: Harper & Row, 1976), p. vii.
7. Iwan Bloch, *The Sexual Life of Our Time in its Relations to Modern Civilization*, trans. M. Eden Paul (London: Rebman, 1908), p. xi.
8. Norman Haire (ed.), *Encyclopædia of Sexual Knowledge*, 2nd edition (London: Encyclopædic Press, 1952), pp. 7–8.
9. Jeffrey Weeks, *Sexuality and Its Discontents: Meanings, Myths & Modern Sexualities* (London: Routledge & Kegan Paul, 1985), p. 72.
10. Roy Porter and Mikuláš Teich, 'Introduction', in Porter and Teich (eds.), *Sexual Knowledge, Sexual Science: The History of Attitudes to Sexuality* (Cambridge: Cambridge University Press, 1994), p. 3.
11. For the importance of moral regulation in the practice of governance, see Frank Mort, *Dangerous Sexualities: Medico-Moral Panics in England since 1830*, 2nd edition (London: Routledge, 2000). This brief narrative has relied on a number of works which collectively offer the reader a comprehensive history of sexology: Lucy Bland and Laura Doan (eds.), *Sexology in Culture: Labelling Bodies and Desires* (Cambridge: Polity Press, 1998); Edward Brecher, *The Sex Researchers* (Boston: Little, Brown & Co., 1969); Joseph Bristow, *Sexuality* (London: Routledge, 1997); Vern Bullough, *Science in the Bedroom: A History of Sex Research* (New York: Basic Books, 1994); the two volumes edited by Franz Eder et al., *Sexual Cultures in Europe: National Histories* and *Sexual Cultures in Europe: Themes in Sexuality* (Manchester: Manchester University Press, 1999); Janice Irvine, *Disorders of Desire: Sex and Gender in Modern American Sexology* (Philadelphia: Temple University Press, 1990); Angus McLaren, *Twentieth-Century Sexuality: A History* (Oxford: Blackwell, 1999); Robert Nye (ed.), *Sexuality* (Oxford: Oxford University Press, 1999); Porter and Teich, *Sexual Knowledge*; Weeks, *Sexuality and Its Discontents*, esp. ch. 4.
12. Arnold Davidson, *The Emergence of Sexuality: Historical Epistemology and the Formation of Concepts* (Cambridge, MA: Harvard University Press, 2001).
13. Nye, *Sexuality*, p. 143. For Krafft-Ebing, see Harry Oosterhuis, *Stepchildren of Nature: Krafft-Ebing, Psychiatry, and the Making of Sexual Identity* (Chicago: University of Chicago Press, 2000).
14. Robert Nye, 'The History of Sexuality in Context: National Sexological Traditions', *Science in Context*, 4, 2 (1991), 387–406; Antony Copley, *Sexual Moralities in France 1780–1980: New Ideas on the Family, Divorce and Homosexuality* (London: Routledge, 1989).
15. James Steakley, '*Per Scientiam ad justitiam*: Magnus Hirschfeld and the Sexual Politics of Innate Homosexuality', in Vernon Rosario (ed.), *Science and Homosexualities* (New York: Routledge, 1997), p. 133.
16. See the work of Lesley Hall, especially 'Heroes or Villains? Reconsidering British *fin de siècle* Sexology and its Impact', in Lynne Segal (ed.), *New Sexual Agendas* (Basingstoke: Macmillan, 1997), pp. 3–16.
17. J.L. Chundra, *Laws of Sexual Philosophy: An Exposition of Eastern and Western Sexual Science from Medical, Moral and Social Point of View* (Calcutta: Mohes

Press, 1913), p. v. For Japan, see Pflugfelder, *Cartographies of Desire*, ch. 5. For China, see Frank Dikötter, *Sex, Culture, and Modernity in China: Medical Science and the Construction of Sexual Identities in the Early Republican Period* (Honolulu: University of Hawaii Press, 1995).

18. On Freud and earlier sexologists, see Frank Sulloway, *Freud, Biologist of the Mind: Beyond the Psychoanalytic Legend* (New York: Basic Books, 1983). On Freud in the US, see Nathan Hale, *Freud and the Americans: The Beginnings of Psychoanalysis in the United States, 1876–1917* (New York: Oxford University Press, 1971).
19. See Ivan Crozier, 'Becoming a Sexologist: Norman Haire, the 1929 London World League for Sexual Reform Congress, and Organizing Medical Knowledge about Sex in Interwar England', *History of Science*, 39, 3 (2001), 299–329; Atina Grossman, *Reforming Sex: The German Movement for Birth Control and Abortion Reform, 1920–1950* (Oxford: Oxford University Press, 1995).
20. Lesley Hall, '"The English Have Hot-Water Bottles": The Morganatic Marriage Between Sexology and Medicine in Britain Since William Acton', in Porter and Teich, *Sexual Knowledge*, p. 358.
21. René Guyon, *Sexual Freedom*, trans. Eden and Cedar Paul (London: John Lane, 1939), pp. 1–2.
22. See Erwin Haeberle, 'Swastika, Pink Triangle and Yellow Star: The Destruction of Sexology and the Persecution of Homosexuals in Nazi Germany', in Martin Duberman et al. (eds.), *Hidden from History: Reclaiming the Gay and Lesbian Past* (New York: New American Library, 1989).
23. See Irvine, *Disorders of Desire*, ch. 3; Paul Robinson, *The Sexual Radicals* (London: Temple Smith, 1969).
24. Bullough, *Science in the Bedroom*, p. 119.
25. John D'Emilo and Estelle Freedman, *Intimate Matters: A History of Sexuality in America*, 2nd edition (Chicago: University of Chicago Press, 1997), p. 285.
26. James Jones, *Alfred C. Kinsey: A Public/Private Life* (New York: Norton, 1997). See also Jonathan Gathorne-Hardy, *Alfred C. Kinsey: Sex, the Measure of All Things* (London: Chatto & Windus, 1998); Irvine, *Disorders of Desire*, esp. pp. 31–3, 37–8, 56; Robinson, *Modernization of Sex*, esp. pp. 49–54.
27. See Liz Stanley, *Sex Surveyed 1949–1994: From Mass-Observation's 'Little Kinsey' to the National Survey and the Hite Reports* (London: Taylor & Francis, 1995).
28. Irvine, *Disorders of Desire*, p. 75.
29. Estelle Freedman, '"Uncontrolled Desires": The Response to the Sexual Psychopath', in Kathy Peiss and Christina Simmons (eds.), *Passion and Power: Sexuality in History* (Philadelphia: Temple University Press, 1989), pp. 199–225; Robert Moeller, 'The Homosexual Man Is a "Man", the Homosexual Woman Is a "Woman": Sex, Society, and the Law in Postwar West Germany', *Journal of the History of Sexuality*, 4, 3 (1994), 395–429; Chris Waters, 'Disorders of the Mind, Disorders of the Body Social: Peter Wildeblood and the Making of the Modern Homosexual', in Becky Conekin et al. (eds.), *Moments of Modernity: Reconstructing Britain 1945–1964* (London: Rivers Oram Press, 1999), pp. 134–51.
30. See Ronald Bayer, *Homosexuality and American Psychiatry: The Politics of Diagnosis* (New York: Basic Books, 1981); Henry Minton, *Departing from Deviance: A History of Homosexual Rights and Emancipatory Science in America* (Chicago: University of Chicago Press, 2002), ch. 8.

31. Steven Epstein, *Impure Science: AIDS, Activism and the Politics of Knowledge* (Berkeley: University of California Press, 1996). On the current status of sexology, see Jeffrey Weeks, 'New Sexual Agendas', in Segal, *New Sexual Agendas*, pp. 43–59; Weeks, *Making Sexual History* (Cambridge: Polity Press, 2000), esp. pp. 1–14.
32. 'Abstracts of papers presented at the March 2003 Congress of Sexology, held in Havana', *Sexuality and Disability*, 22, 1 (2004).
33. Bristow, *Sexuality*, p. 56.
34. John Addington Symonds, *Male Love: A Problem in Greek Ethics and Other Writings*, ed. John Lauritsen (New York: Pagan Press, 1983); Joseph Bristow, 'Symonds's History, Ellis's Heredity: *Sexual Inversion*', in Bland and Doan, *Sexology in Culture*, pp. 79–99.
35. Ivan Bloch, *Sexual Life in England Past and Present* (Royston: Oracle, 1996 [1938]), p. 320.
36. Magnus Hirschfeld, *The Sexual History of the World War* (New York: Panurge, 1934), p. 17; John D'Emilio, 'Capitalism and Gay Identity', in his *Making Trouble: Essays on Gay History, Politics and the University* (New York: Routledge, 1992), pp. 3–16; D'Emilo and Freedman, *Intimate Matters*.
37. Hirschfeld, *Sexual History*, p. 18.
38. Edward Glover, 'Victorian Ideas of Sex', in *Ideas and Beliefs of the Victorians: An Historic Revaluation of the Victorian Age* (London: Sylvan Press, 1949), pp. 362–4.
39. G. Rattray Taylor, *Sex in History* (London: Thames & Hudson, 1959 [1953]), p. 13; Wayland Young, *Eros Denied* (London: Weidenfeld & Nicolson, 1964), p. 250; Ronald Pearsall, *The Worm in the Bud: The World of Victorian Sexuality* (Harmondsworth: Penguin, 1983 [1969]), pp. 301, 514; Brecher, *Sex Researchers*, pp. 315, 319.
40. Michel Foucault, *The History of Sexuality. Volume I: An Introduction* (New York: Pantheon, 1978), esp. pp. 10–11. The best, recent defence of Foucault is David Halperin, *How to Do the History of Homosexuality* (Chicago: University of Chicago Press, 2002), esp. ch. 1.
41. Weeks, *Making Sexual History*, pp. 53, 60–1.
42. Robinson, *Modernization of Sex*, preface to the 1989 Cornell University Press edition.
43. A classic example is Sheila Jeffreys, *The Spinster and Her Enemies: Feminism and Sexuality, 1880–1930* (London: Pandora, 1985).
44. See Foucault, *History of Sexuality*, p. 101; Weeks, *Sexuality and Its Discontents*, pp. 93–5; Bristow, *Sexuality*, pp. 178–9.
45. Rita Felski, 'Introduction', in Bland and Doan, *Sexology in Culture*, p. 3.
46. Weeks, *Making Sexual History*, p. 107; see also pp. 113, 120. For the fragmentation of the field, see Lucy Bland and Frank Mort, 'Thinking Sex Historically', in Segal, *New Sexual Agendas*, esp. pp. 18–21.
47. Laura Doan, *Fashioning Sapphism: The Origins of a Modern English Lesbian Culture* (New York: Columbia University Press, 2001), pp. 127, 130.
48. George Chauncey, 'Christian Brotherhood or Sexual Perversion? Homosexual Identities and the Construction of Sexual Boundaries in the World War One Era', *Journal of Social History*, 19, 2 (1985), 203.
49. George Chauncey, 'From Sexual Inversion to Homosexuality: The Changing Medical Conceptualization of Female "Deviance"', in Peiss and Simmons, *Passion and Power*, pp. 87–8, 108–9.

50. Oosterhuis, *Stepchildren of Nature*, p. 212; see also pp. 195–8, 211–16.
51. Matt Reed, '"La Manie D'Écrire": Psychology, Auto-Observation, and Case History', *Journal of the History of the Behavioral Sciences*, 40, 3 (2004), 265–84.
52. Minton, *Departing from Deviance*, p. 4. See also Jennifer Terry, *An American Obsession: Science, Medicine, and Homosexuality in Modern Society* (Chicago: University of Chicago Press, 1999), chs. 6–7.
53. Michael Lynch, '"Here is Adhesiveness": From Friendship to Homosexuality', *Victorian Studies*, 29, 1 (1985), 67–96. For recent work on how individuals shape a self out of the fragmentary cultural materials available to them, see Anna Clark, 'Anne Lister's Construction of Lesbian Identity', *Journal of the History of Sexuality*, 7, 1 (1996), 23–50.
54. Joanne Meyerowitz, *How Sex Changed: A History of Transsexuality in the United States* (Cambridge, MA: Harvard University Press, 2002), esp. ch. 4.
55. Doan, *Fashioning Sapphism*, pp. 162–3.
56. *Evening Standard*, 27 October 1924.
57. Foucault, *History of Sexuality*, pp. 103, 105. For an overview of the growing importance of the new psychology of sex in shaping criminological policy in interwar Britain, see Chris Waters, 'Havelock Ellis, Sigmund Freud and the State: Discourses of Homosexual Identity in Interwar Britain', in Bland and Doan, *Sexology in Culture*, pp. 165–79. For similar developments in the US, see Terry, *An American Obsession*; for the Soviet Union, see Dan Healey, *Homosexual Desire in Revolutionary Russia: The Regulation of Sexual and Gender Dissent* (Chicago: University of Chicago Press, 2001).

3
law

matt cook

introduction

This chapter explores the ways in which the law and the courts have helped us to understand sexual behaviour and ideologies in the past. In the historical analysis of homosexuality, prostitution, sexual violence, marriage and divorce, birth control, abortion and the circulation of sexual knowledge the legal framework has been difficult to ignore. It was one of the ways in which people came to know about the 'rights' and 'wrongs' of sex, and to understand their own desires and behaviour. It was also the primary means through which the state attempted to regulate 'morality' and people's supposedly private lives. The law was thus instrumental in shaping the relationship between state and citizen and creating conceptual distinctions between the public and private. The legal archive consequently allows us to address some key historical questions: how important was the law in delineating deviancy? How did the law demarcate privacy, and how did this square with the particular understandings of individuals and communities? How were different sexual spaces – parks, public toilets, hotels, homes – affected by the law? What impact did this have on individuals' sexual conduct?

The answers to such questions have a wide relevance not least because they relate to changing understandings of subjectivity and the kind of behaviour appropriate to the 'modern' citizen in the 'modern' nation state. Legal records thus not only give us unique access to voices, subcultures and behaviours which would otherwise be lost, but also reveal a link between concepts of modernity on the one hand, and ideas about family, relationships and sexual identity on the other. The scope of the archive is clearly tantalizing, but the material nevertheless needs to be handled with care: as the following pages suggest, an examination of legal and court records exposes some of the complexities involved in making sexual history.

cautionary notes

Michel Foucault's famous intervention in the history of sexuality in the 1970s was based in part on an examination of the law and relates closely to his work on crime and punishment.[1] Foucault argued that the law was not simply a series of institutions dispensing 'justice' but a powerful discourse which shaped understandings and experiences of sex and desire. It helped to propagate a series of apparently incontestable 'norms' and encouraged people to internalize them. Foucault used the law to uncover a particular system of power but perhaps more importantly he deployed it as a symbol of the historicity of sexuality.[2] Ideas about sex and sexual identity, he argued, were not stable, and shifts in experiences and understandings over time resulted partly from the machinations of the legislature and the courtroom, especially following the post-Enlightenment shift in moral policing from church to state. The 'homosexual', for example, was not simply regulated by the legal system but was also produced by it. While early work envisaged legal changes and particular court cases as important *events* in a narrative history of homosexuality,[3] historians following Foucault have focused more intently on the ways that parliament and the courts functioned in the circulation of ideas about – and experiences of – sexual identity and community.[4] In Britain, analyses of Oscar Wilde's trials have thus moved from accounts of the complexities of the case and Wilde's personal tragedy, to examinations of how the trials shaped and reflected ideas of masculinity, nationality, class, and art, combining to create a concept of a new deviant archetype. Similarly, section 11 of the Criminal Law Amendment Act of 1885, which criminalized all acts of gross indecency between men, has been seen not merely as a legislative event, but as a piece of legislation which shaped the conduct and understanding of male–male relationships for both external observers and the men involved.[5] The law's public authority, writes Nancy Cott, 'frames what people can envision for themselves and can conceivably demand'; state decree becomes important to the way we envisage and experience intimacy and the putatively private world of the senses.[6]

This take on sexual history – focused on the emergence of the 'modern' homosexual – is compelling, but critics have pointed to the tendency of these analyses to privilege the law and the courts as sites of cultural production and to ignore the subcultures and sexual identities that preexisted the legislation and sensational trials of the *fin de siècle*. They argue that the 'homosexual' has always existed as a being – if not a label – and that whilst court cases are invaluable in observing changing subcultures and responses to homosexual behaviour they do not shape identity itself.[7] These critical reflections have been helpful in one key respect: they suggest that we should not be seduced by the idea of a sudden rupture in ideas and cultures of sexuality. Rather we should acknowledge the complex intersection of different understandings, legal procedures, and philosophies of punishment from different periods.[8] Angus McLaren, for example, notes the anachronistic reintroduction of flogging for pimps in Britain in 1912. While the measure flew in the face of the nineteenth-century movement towards 'humane' punishment, McLaren uses this recourse to earlier penalties to highlight the sense of crisis surrounding normative masculinity and purported sexual abuse at this time.[9]

McLaren's analysis is especially sensitive to the relationship between courtroom events and decisions on the one hand, and broader concepts of cultural crises and sexual behaviour. It is a delicate balancing act which alerts us to some of the potential problems of using the law in making the history of sexuality. The law, first of all, is multifaceted, internally contradictory, and – most crucially – not the simple, neutral arbiter of justice it purports to be. In its formulation and application in England and Wales, for example, it extends from the executive and parliament through the various levels of courts to a complex police bureaucracy. Decisions are made at each level, and whilst these institutions often appear faceless, they are staffed (primarily) by men with different perspectives and preoccupations on the law's tenor and reach. Whilst Foucault describes a legal monolith, more recent historians have been careful to assess the significance of particular politicians, judges or police officers in exploring how the operations of the law might differ between times and places – the changing patterns of enforcement of the laws regulating sexual encounters between men in nineteenth- and twentieth-century Britain is only one example of this.[10]

This attention to specific detail is also needed in terms of national context. Foucault magisterially generalizes his arguments to Western Europe, but law was symbolically and functionally distinct between nations. As Joëlle Guillais observes, different societies 'perceive crime differently [...] and the attention and attitude to it are always peculiar to the social and historical context'.[11] Countries also have different legal systems, cultures and protocols – as well as differing in the kinds of behaviour deemed criminal – which can significantly shape the histories we write. The oral and adversarial tradition of the English courts, for example, is not the same as in France, where there is a greater reliance on written deposition. Legal arguments are consequently not presented in the same way and so ideas circulate rather differently. Thus although Katherine Fischer Taylor suggests that the architecture of the Parisian *Palais de Justice* was *more* theatrical than London's Old Bailey, the trials themselves were likely to be *less* disputational and performative.[12] In addition the English system of common law (which also operates with some differences in Scotland and most of the Commonwealth countries) means that courts have a greater power than in most continental European countries to create precedent and interpret the law. This can give individual courts in England a greater practical significance for the evolution of law. Much English legal history is consequently concerned with the implications of individual courtroom decisions and there is a particularly close relationship between the law and its own history.[13] The French legal system is based on the Napoleonic code rather than precedent, investing greater investigative power in the judge and their officials.[14] The United States meanwhile has complex and overlapping systems of state, federal and military law, each with their own protocols.[15]

To further complicate the issue, the multiple areas which make up the history of sexuality have different relations to the law, and historians tend to analyse its impact differently. Historians of homosexuality's focus on ideas of identity in legal discourse, for example, is not shared by those looking at abortion and birth control or rape and sexual violence. Although there are certainly shared concerns – the gendering of identity, for example – historians working in the latter fields have tended to use the law to examine issues of women's sexual autonomy, concepts of victimhood, and shifting understandings of male violence. It is important then to be clear about why and how we are using the legal archive and which legal jurisdiction and system we are referring to. These contexts are crucial to the ways in which we interpret the contemporary affects and reactions to legal change and particular court cases.

legislation

Frank Mort has argued that the British social purity movement in the second half of the nineteenth century began to see legislation 'as an instrument for improving public morals – as positively educative rather than just repressive'.[16] Viewed in this way, a country's legislation becomes a 'moral thermometer', giving an insight into public morals and the state's investment in improving or regulating them. Historians have consequently analysed sexual legislation to discern shifting social mores and cultural anxieties. The law has, they suggest, been pivotal in marginalizing particular groups and thereby in creating a sexual and moral 'norm'.[17] Consider, for example, recent work on Britain's Contagious Diseases Acts of 1864, 1866 and 1869. Historians have argued that the acts' provisions for the detention of female prostitutes for forced venereal examination and treatment in key port and military towns reflect a series of assumptions about female culpability in sexual 'sin' and 'contagion'. The prostitutes' clients – those servicemen whose health was seen as imperative to the nation's defence – went unexamined for fear it might damage their morale. Successive Tory and Liberal administrations were being legislatively proactive, giving us an insight into prevailing ideas about sex and desire. They also indicate a cultural departure: in seeking to regulate prostitution the government tacitly accepted the sex 'trade'. This shift has been taken by historians to show, variously, the level of concern about national prowess and security, the power of the market and of capitalist ideology, and the perceived difference in the libido of men and women. The legislation can further be seen as a form of class control over working-class women. The acts have thus served as a lodestone for the analysis not only of prostitution, but of gender and sexual difference and their relation to national culture, politics and economics in the 1860s.[18]

Historical analysis of these various acts has been enriched by feminist and gendered perspectives, exposing the law's broader character as what Joan Sangster characterizes as a vivid reflection of the patriarchy of Western cultures which symbolically and practically disempowers women whilst normalizing and naturalizing male power.[19] The law and the courts have thus not been a neutral instrument in the dispensation of 'justice', but rather operate from – and reproduce – a particular gendered and class-bound perspective. Carol Smart argues, for example, that whilst male sexuality is 'concretized' in violence and aggression under the law, female sexuality is conceived in terms 'of vulnerability and trauma'. In this sense, 'we should recognise the law as more a part of the problem (in the ways it genders, sexes and sexualizes the female and male body) than part of the solution'.[20]

This is important in our analysis of the past: although we need to recognize that individuals and groups have and experience power in diverse ways, it is also crucial to acknowledge that the state has what Jeffrey Weeks calls 'a monopoly of legal violence and power' and that because of the inherent inequities in the system 'some suffer and benefit from its provisions more than others'.[21] Leslie Moran, for example, has suggested that when gay men and women faced the law they were immediately in a skewed arena and found themselves undermined by being forced to dispute within a framework that did not accommodate their perspectives, needs and injustices.[22] In Britain, section 28 of the Local Government Act of 1988, which prohibited local authorities from 'intentionally promot[ing] homosexuality' or 'promot[ing] [...] the acceptability of homosexuality as a pretended family relationship', was fundamentally based on presumptions about 'pretence' and 'promotion' which were alien and made no sense to the targeted groups. The clause nevertheless demonstrates to historians an entrenched prejudice within the legislature. Simon Shepherd and Mick Wallis also suggest that the introduction of section 28 signalled burgeoning concern about the growing self-confidence of lesbians and gays, and about their position 'firmly on the agenda' of left-leaning local councils.[23] Such legislation is thus one means available to historians of identifying social norms *and* perceived challenges to them.

The government in these cases – the Contagious Diseases Acts and the Local Government Act – appears to be proactive, but legislation passed in reaction to particular pressures can also reveal pressing cultural anxieties and more localized moments of moral panic. Britain's 1885 Criminal Law Amendment Act, which raised the age of consent for girls to sixteen and regulated brothels, was rushed through parliament after a high-profile press campaign supposedly revealing an extensive network of child prostitution in London. The measure indicates the power of journalistic voices and also echoed a new and urgent cultural emphasis on the distinctiveness of childhood and the need to preserve it as a time of innocence.[24] Teenage and child prostitution was not new, but the eruption of concern, the ensuing parliamentary action, and the subsequent trials marked out their prominence in the cultural consciousness. The law can thus be used to tell us about social and cultural discontents at particular historical moments.

It is not to dispute such analyses to observe the need for caution in attempting to read a society's ideologies, norms and crises from its laws. One of the problems with Foucault's argument in this respect is that whilst he highlighted an institution with considerable power, he also chose one which was not especially responsive to – nor directly representative of – contemporary culture. Reactions to campaigns for age of consent legislation in 1885 were unusual, and whilst the act was indicative of a series of cultural concerns, it did not necessarily represent a consensus about how to deal with them. The statute book can make flat reading and is frequently constrained by an archaic and limited lexicon which suggests a simple problem and an easy answer. Whilst abortion in Britain was punishable with a life sentence under the 1861 Offences Against the Persons Act, for example, it was still the chief means available to women of controlling their reproductive health – not only relatively common but also tacitly accepted in some communities.[25] Despite this tacit acceptance – even amongst members of the legal profession – the law remained in place until 1967, thirty years after the Abortion Law Reform Association began campaigning. In the US the constitutional right to choose an abortion was not established until the famous *Roe* v. *Wade* Supreme Court decision of 1973. N.E.H. Hull and Peter Charles Hoffer argue that this decision was years too late: 'it had yet to catch up to the gains that women had made in the marketplace, academy and the media'.[26]

Despite in some ways falling into line with burgeoning 'women's rights', however, these measures did not represent a sudden groundswell of support for women's 'right to choose'. Indeed, where there is clear government strategy in respect of sexual regulation it often contravenes majority opinion. The 1967 Sexual Offences Act, which partially decriminalized male homosexuality in Britain, reflected a strategic retreat from the idea that the law had 'a right and a duty' to articulate and enforce a code of sexual rights and wrongs rather than a more tolerant and liberal culture.[27] While the act marked an official reconceptualization of the relationship between the state and the individual, it cannot be said to reflect public opinion as such. There is no straightforward correlation between the morality and norms of the law and the morality and norms of society.[28]

The issue here is not least the seemingly univocal nature of the law being pitched against the polyphony beyond. The latter cannot be represented by a singular piece of legislation, and neither can the power of the law to shape understandings of sexuality be easily gauged within a complex and pluralistic culture. Since the law is not the only mode of moral and social regulation, it can be difficult to observe a direct correspondence in our analysis of the past. The development of social history has shown the value of observing the multiple sites of power and resistance operating in society and also the contradictory forces shaping individual and group behaviour. To develop a full and sensitive understanding of the law's impact of the law it is important to examine these other factors.

Such an analysis might begin to explain why attempts at legal regulation so often misfired. Most obviously the existence or non-existence of particular laws has had a profound galvanizing impact on marginalized individuals and groups. Far from suppressing particular forms of behaviour, governments can bring it more fully into public view.[29] A central component of Foucault's theory of sexuality was the concept of 'reverse discourse', the idea that the implicit or explicit recognition of a particular form of deviance by governments offered individuals a language through which they might articulate and express pride in their 'deviance' and demand 'rights'. Section 11 of the 1885 Criminal Law Amendment Act, for example, thus became a focal point for George Ives' campaigning, prompting him to found the first support and pressure group for 'gay' men in the early 1890s and dedicate his life to legal reform and rebutting the criminality and putative pathology of homosexuality. Such activities were structurally crucial to the way Ives lived his life: to the friendships he forged, the work he undertook, the records he kept, and the profound, barely suppressed anger he felt – an anger evident in his extensive diaries.[30] For Ives, as for many other homosexual men in the past century, the law is observably important in creating a sense of personal and group identity.[31]

These responses cannot be generalized, however, and we cannot presume a uniform experience of, or reaction to, legal change. Truly collective action is rare and a pertinent historical question in fact relates to the apparent equanimity of many whose lives are braced by discriminatory legislation: what pressures or fears prevented them from either seeing the relevance of such laws to their lives or from actively campaigning against them? The impact of the law is clearly complex, and if it makes one man angry, it will also reinforce another's guilt or shame. The law clearly affects the extent to which an individual can feel legitimate in their sexual desires and activities, and this is why it is important for the historian of sexuality to look beyond *Hansard* and court records to other sources, personal testimonies amongst them. These often provide telling accounts of how the law affected individuals who may never have appeared in court themselves. They also allow us to write histories which are not only constructed from admonitory and pejorative legal records – records which often decry or ignore the friendships, relationships, and pleasures experienced by the likes of Ives.

In terms of the formulation of discriminatory measures, the state is often perceived to have a strategic and concerted agenda for moral and social control. We might look at nineteenth-century legislation on prostitution and observe a series of measures designed to control the working class through laws on sex and intimacy. That this was the case has been argued convincingly, but implicit in such arguments is an intentionality, the assumption of a joined up state policy to achieve these ends. This usually needs demonstrating more fully and there are often more signs of contingency and pragmatism. The state, it has more recently been argued, was less than enthusiastic in the late nineteenth century to take on the mantle of sexual regulation and when it did act it was often in piecemeal, incoherent, or reactive ways as a result of pressure from outside groups and individuals. If a coherent policy existed at all, it was to resist intervening further in sexual regulation and reform. Indeed, Lucia Zedner observes that during this period the family became increasingly central to the regulation of sexual and social behaviour, and that the law was beginning its long (though equivocal) retreat from the home.[32]

The Criminal Law Amendment Act was passed, as we have seen, on the back of mass protest, section 11 of the act – which criminalized acts of gross indecency between men – was a last minute addition, made by the maverick Member of Parliament Henry Labouchere and introduced and passed in a chamber that was virtually empty. It was not the subject of government comment and was barely mentioned in the press coverage of the act's passing.[33] Neither did it significantly add to the available statutes that could be deployed against men having sex with other men, all of which remained in force. The amendment was symptomatic of confusion rather than intentionality in the making of laws on sex in England, and raises the key question of whose will this law – but also other laws – enshrined. There can be no general answer to the question of intent, but keeping that question in mind as we explore the passage of sexual legislation allows us to identify the different forces which shape an 'official' moral line. This is useful in complicating our understanding of 'state action', a term which has become something of a bland catch-all and which suggests, often inappropriately, a coherent and driven government programme.

Addressing this question of intent and context also allows us to identify the particular problems in view when legislation was drafted. The nationwide reach of the law can obscure the quite specific reasons why and places where action was deemed necessary. In Britain, for example, the Obscene Publications Act of 1857 was passed as a result of concern about a London-based book trade, and, specifically, argues Lynda Nead, about bookselling in Holywell Street in central London.[34] This context is key to understanding the motivations of pressure groups and individuals demanding change, and of the government in responding to those demands. It also allows us to consider how the law may have been perceived more broadly once it had been passed; with an urban problem in view in this example, people living outside London may have felt little need to take heed.

Of course these questions should not detract from the impact of legislation. Whether a fully thought through aspect of the government's programme or not, section 11 blighted the lives of thousands of British men before it was finally repealed in 1967. If there was a general reluctance to legislate on sexual conduct and a legal retreat from the private sphere in the late nineteenth century, then section 11 was a cruel and anachronistic measure. It explicitly stated that gross indecency was illegal 'in public and private' and thus an offence to state and morality *wherever* it occurred. Such offences, in Labouchere's own words, 'put those who commit them beyond the pale of privacy'.[35]

The 'public and private' coda in Labouchere's Amendment marks the fundamental difference between English and French law on gross indecency between men at this time. Whilst in England it was the acts themselves that were at issue, in France it was whether they might be overlooked and cause specific offence. Later, in 1967, when sex between men in private was finally legalized in Britain, the statute was particular about the number of men involved: two was permissible; three or more rendered the activity illegal. The extra body/ies, it seemed, turned the private realm into a pseudo-public space. It was in this way that the state retained some control over homosexual sex even in private, laying down the boundaries of acceptability and implicitly reinforcing the ideal of monogamy. The extent to which legislators felt able to override a general trend against intervention in the private realm can be seen to indicate the level of cultural concern about – and interest in – sex between men. It also again brings into sharp focus the fraught relationship between public and private spaces and public and private lives. As Philip Hubbard observes in relation to the laws on prostitution, there is a tension between, on the one hand, 'notions derived from the liberal humanist philosophers about the sexual rights of individuals' and, on the other, the perceived need to assert 'that certain expressions of sexuality are morally unacceptable'.[36]

Finally, whilst this section has focused on the existence of particular laws and the ways in which they can help us to discern trends in state regulation and ideologies of sex and gender, it is important to remember that the absence of legislation can obscure behaviours. The lack of legal sanction against sex between women in England meant that the issue rarely entered the courts.[37] There was debate about criminalizing female–female sex in 1921, 1937 and 1956, but the proposed measures got nowhere, leaving male–male encounters centre stage in terms of the law. Women's lives – and their lives with each other – were certainly circumscribed by the law in multiple ways, but lesbianism itself entered the courts only obliquely, through divorce cases,[38] libel actions,[39] or literary sensations (like the 1928 prosecution of Radclyffe Hall's *The Well of Loneliness*).[40]

Cases like these came relatively infrequently, however; Lillian Faderman has found only twelve pre-1900 cases involving accusations of lesbianism.[41] In *Scotch Verdict* (1985) she takes one of these – the case of two female teachers accused of indecency in 1810 – and reconstructs events and testimony alongside her own first person commentary and diary.[42] The approach is similar in some ways to Neil Bartlett's inspirational analysis of Oscar Wilde in *Who Was That Man?* (1988),[43] and brilliantly combines early nineteenth-century voices with late twentieth-century analysis and personal reflection. But whereas Bartlett is able to refer to a number of cases involving male–male sex and relationships in the late nineteenth century, Faderman is necessarily dealing with an isolated trial. What her work highlights is the difficulty of building up a picture of shifting concepts of lesbianism through the law. The history of lesbianism in England has consequently been made somewhat differently from that of gay men,[44] reminding us that the law need not be primary in developing an account of sexual transgression in the past. We should instead see the law functioning within a broad framework of competing ideologies and contexts if we are properly to assess its contemporary impact and historiographical usefulness.

the courtroom

The law can have a significant impact without ever being directly applied. Section 28, for example, almost certainly had a censoring affect on British schools and libraries and prompted a powerful campaign for repeal even though no prosecutions were actually brought. But it was when the criminal law was evoked, when an individual took out a libel suit or sued for divorce that the law became personal and individuals felt its force first hand. Trials gave the law immediacy and a broader public the opportunity to put specific details, geographies, names and faces to abstract injunctions and vices. For the historian, courtroom testimony provides access to voices rarely heard in the public record, and gives us what Nancy Erber and George Robb call a 'vantage point' onto private codes and experiences, onto subcultures and communities.[45]

Trials helped to define the boundaries of normality and to rearticulate ideologies of gender, class, and nation. Convictions served to symbolically purge the pervert and – implicitly – the perversion from the social realm. Reports of Oscar Wilde's conviction seemed to suggest that London had seen the back not only of Wilde himself but also of men 'like him'.[46]

At the same time, though, the trials and their reporting broadcast the existence of male–male sex and relations, suggested a particular type of deviant, and indicated a lively West End 'scene'. These revelations may have been greeted by some with shock and outrage, by others with keen interest and understanding. Abstracted vices gained substance through such cases, and the affects were enduring. Wilde's shadow fell across the entire twentieth century, leading Neil Bartlett to write two moving letters to the dead playwright in 1988 – one embracing Wilde and his legacy, the other cursing him for stifling Bartlett's own voice ('you old queen', he writes, 'you've got your hand on my face, I can't talk now') and implicitly also a century of varied expressions and understandings of male–male love, sex and relationships.[47] As a result of the trial and the accompanying publicity 'Wilde' came to signify much more than a particular individual and personal tragedy.

Historians have justifiably complained that Wilde has dominated the analysis of late nineteenth-century (and also twentieth-century) homosexuality at the expense of other lives. It is also true, though, that such major sensations did have a disproportionate effect on the development of images of sexual deviance, even though they might be distant from the day-to-day realities of most people's lives. Some historians' accounts have uncritically replayed the sensationalism of such lives,[48] but it is this drama which itself needs particular critical attention. The sensations indicate the ways in which sexual transgression was understood and connected to popular prejudices and anxieties. They also suggest the terms on which society was able to cope with such transgression. Press coverage of cases of homosexual sex in London just before the First World War, for example, frequently emphasized the German roots of defendants, propagating an image of the foreign pervert during a period of concern about German militarism.[49] These representations reaffirmed the idea that such heinous activity could not be home grown. The British case of the rapist and murderer Peter Sutcliffe ('the Yorkshire Ripper'), to take a later example, reinforced a particular story of the unknown predatory rapist. Sutcliffe's trial in 1981 and the accompanying newspaper furore detracted from the disturbing fact that most rape and sexual violence occurred in the home and was perpetrated by an assailant known to the woman under attack.[50]

Recent analysis has linked the formation of such simplified sexual and criminal narratives to the intersection of trials, the press and popular culture. Judith Walkowitz, for example, has shown how the characterization of witnesses and defendants in court and in the press in the late nineteenth century was informed by Victorian melodrama. A cast of heroes and villains, cads and cowards provided a means through which chaotic experience and complex motivations could be condensed into simple stories and 'meaningful moral drama'.[51] The courtroom audience, Erber and Robb observe, frequently responded to courtroom events 'as they would to the action in the play',[52] and there is a sense in which such responses served to further demarcate the 'normal' (in the public gallery) from the 'abnormal' (in the dock). The modes of description and the priority given to particular pieces of information in court and by journalists are thus highly significant in developing an understanding of the formation and deployment of sexual and moral codes.

Equally important are the performances undertaken by those appearing in court. Lesley Hall has shown, for example, how the birth control campaigner Marie Stopes feigned sexual naivety for her divorce case, an act of 'good womanhood' many women in court have felt compelled to undertake.[53] Matt Houlbrook points to guardsmen deploying a similar language of innocent victimhood in cases involving sex with men in the first half of the twentieth century.[54] Earlier in 1871, in a strategic use of contemporary ideas of masculinity, the cross-dresser Frederick Park 'had grown stout' and sported a moustache for his courtroom appearance.[55] This latter transformation is familiar from earlier records of the courtroom appearances of Mollies in the 1720s: they frequently shunned the effeminate roles they took on in the Molly Houses in favour of more conventionally masculine deportment and bravado in court.[56]

Historians of sexuality have become increasingly attentive to such performances and to language in their analysis of courtroom events, drawing on literary and poststucturalist theory in their approaches. They insist that we must not see trial transcripts and reports as self-evident and transparent: in examining them we need to consider how individuals functioned, spoke, and behaved differently within the extraordinary setting of the courtroom, and so not fudge the distinction between this and other spaces – the home, the workplace, or the pub, for example. In court particular modes of behaviour are expected and particular performances undertaken relating in part to the kind of simplified narratives of crime I have been discussing. In addition the necessarily restricted range of available charges, the limited legal lexicon for describing human sexual relations, and the formulaic nature of courtroom procedure can serve to standardize experience, crimes and subjectivity. Defendants on felony charges were generally prevented from speaking in English courts at all in the nineteenth century. Instead we hear their voices refracted through witness statements and in letters of appeal and for clemency, documents similarly bounded by generic expectations and with a very particular aim in view. Oscar Wilde's case, H.G. Cocks observes, was a legal departure in this regard: 'it showed the willingness of the state to provide a platform for accomplices, and to admit their evidence as trustworthy, but also allowed Wilde to give evidence under oath, a privilege not granted to defendants in all criminal cases until 1898'.[57]

Cocks makes a specific point here about the ways in which defendants' voices were mediated by the legal process, and in so doing indicates the power dynamics of the courtroom and the ways in which they affected individual testimony. Similarly, in her work on child abuse Louise Jackson shows how sworn statements and reports of cross-examinations within the courts were woven from careful questioning. This questioning was often absent from the transcript, however, and so we lose a sense of the specific ways in which children were guided through their version of events. It is nevertheless obvious, Jackson suggests, that the questioning was designed to elicit 'information appropriate to the courtroom setting rather than an account of the child's views, thoughts, or feelings on the matter'.[58] We get, in other words, a reified narrative which is specific to the requirements of the law. This is not to say that this narrative does not give us an insight into the child's life, but rather that a story told in this context is not the same as that which may have emerged under different circumstances. Responses to that story might also differ from context to context. Joëlle Guillais, for example, shows how the local 'indulgent attitude' towards an incestuous couple in Paris in the 1870s was not reflected in court or indeed in the attitudes of those locals after the prosecution.[59]

The careful analysis of courtroom rhetoric and language has given us a fuller sense of the ways in which crime, the sexual criminal and the victims of crime are constituted. However, the ways in which these ideas relate to lived experiences and the complexities of sexual selfhood often remains obscure. The challenge is to explore how the two mesh and relate to each other.[60] Karen Dubinsky's work on rape and sexual violence in Canada has shown the analytical sensitivity needed to navigate the assumptions of juries, judges, and prosecuting and defence counsels when trying to reconstruct stories of sexual abuse and violence, or when trying to reclaim the voices of working-class men and women thrust into an arena controlled and directed by an educated elite.[61] Shani D'Cruze has undertaken related research in the British context and has also worked against the grain of the standardizing and simplifying tendency of the courts to treat women 'as actors and speakers as well as silenced victims'.[62] These historians have been careful to avoid seeing the court archive as a way of gaining unmediated access to sexual subjectivities. The telling insights into a particular mid-Victorian home provided by a little girl's deposition need to be balanced by our knowledge of where and how that deposition was taken down. It may well be that what was not said, what was not asked of the child, is as telling as what was communicated. Why, we might ask, were the child's feelings about the alleged abuse not seen to be significant? What might this lack of interest tell us about juridical and wider attitudes to childhood, sexual abuse, and emotional life at that particular historical moment?

The findings discussed above often emerge through the analysis of relatively low profile cases. However significant major sensations were in terms of the constitution of particular mythologies around sex and sexuality, they can also detract from other cases, which might yet help historians to formulate complex accounts of sexual conduct and the extent of its regulation through the law. Michael Rocke and Guido Ruggiero have used careful analysis of the law to reconstruct the dynamics of sexual cultures and identities in, respectively, Renaissance Florence and Venice, and they subtly detect particular patterns of, and participants in, sexual liaisons.[63] In his study of gay Toronto, Steven Maynard found that court records allowed him 'to begin to outline [...] the contours of [the city's] emerging subculture'.[64] Sangster has found that beyond the major trials and in 'the local, specific, mundane, lived encounters of women with the law' we can discover how 'power, domination, and resistance operated through and against the law', developing a convincing account of how such localized analysis might relate to broader patterns and definitions of sexual and family life for women. Crucially, though, she does not assume that the courtroom appearances of the few are necessarily representative or typical. Indeed she observes the ways in which the legal system might target criminality in certain social groups and be blind to that in others.[65]

The law was and is applied pragmatically and contingently. One of the implications of this is the need to be careful about the conclusions we draw from legal statistics. An increase in arrests and cases before the courts does not necessarily reflect an actual increase in sexual 'crime'; a new police commissioner, a moral panic, or a specific instruction from a civil servant or politician might result in the police being more or less active in respect of a particular law. Politicians or officials crusading against a certain crime can also manipulate and misrepresent figures in their reports. Statistics thus often tell us more about the regulation of, and attitudes towards, particular sexual crimes than they do about the prevalence or otherwise of the crime itself. We also need to be aware of the standardizing effects of statistics: columns of numbers relating to sodomy or gross indecency transform, as Maynard suggests, 'the diverse sexual experiences of men into a limited number of legal categories'.[66]

Whilst historians have been right to highlight the ways in which voices and experiences were marginalized in courts, it is also useful to observe how the courtroom sometimes provided the opportunity for overt dissent from domineering codes and values. Wilde's impassioned courtroom speech about the 'love that dare not speak its name' indicated alternative ways of conceptualizing sex and relationships between men, for example. His recourse to Hellenism and a long cultural and literary heritage helped Wilde and others to legitimize their otherwise criminal behaviour. H.G. Cocks details earlier cases in which defiant statements ascribed to defendants were rehearsed by witnesses in court. When he was accused of soliciting another man in 1726, for example, William Brown was said to have objected that 'there's no crime in making what use I please of my own body'.[67] Either directly, as in the Wilde case, or indirectly, as with Brown, the courtroom became a forum for rehearsing alternative values, systems of knowledge, and modes of conduct.

As well as these specific and localized challenges, the courts were also the site of larger epistemological conflicts. Ruth Harris has shown how medicine increasingly entered the courtroom in the later nineteenth century in the form of specialist testimony, presenting a 'competing system of values' and different 'perspectives on human nature'.[68] Whilst in many cases the legal, medical and scientific fields of knowledge complemented each other, they also frequently jostled for position. The emergent 'science' of sexology in the late nineteenth century, for example, presented theories of homosexuality as a pathology or intrinsic condition which were incompatible with the juridical conception of criminal sexual 'acts' rather than identities. The uneasy relationship between the two was compounded by the sexologists' intent to speak candidly about sex and sex problems in ways which could be seen to contravene English obscenity legislation. The embryonic sexology movement in England was partly stifled by the prosecution of George Bedborough for selling Havelock Ellis' *Sexual Inversion* in 1897 and by the restrictions placed on the English translation of Iwan Bloch's *Sexual Life of Our Times* in 1908. Such cases were a deterrent to other writers and publishers, and sexology remained chiefly a continental 'science' until at least the First World War.[69] In the Bedborough and Bloch cases no full defence was mounted, and as a result the superiority of the courts in identifying the best way of knowing – or not knowing – about sex seemed to be reaffirmed.

The courts were relatively successful in curtailing sexology, but their actions could as easily (and unintentionally) broadcast sexual knowledge.

Annie Besant and Charles Bradlaugh's feisty defence of their decision to re-publish the birth control tract *The Fruits of Philosophy* by Charles Knowlton in 1877 brought the issue – and more importantly specific methods of birth control – to a wide audience. The case indicates again the cultural conflict in terms of the appropriateness of sexual knowledge and practices, shows the threat particular non-conformist and radical individuals were seen to pose, and dramatically demonstrates how the courts could not fully control the consequences of their actions. Although Bradlaugh and Besant were prosecuted, the trial advertised rather than restricted information on birth control. The case came at a time when the birth rate in Britain was falling and although multiple factors were at play in the renewed desire to limit family size, the case, Sripati Chandrasekhar suggests, may have helped many to specific methods.[70]

These various cases indicate one of the key ways in which sex entered the courtroom: not because of what people had done but because of what they had said or written. We see this also in libel actions and the catalogue of trials involving literary texts. Such cases reveal the centrality of sex in the making or unmaking of an individual or a text's reputation, and through them historians have been able to assess shifting concepts of decency and the role of the law in sharpening public sensitivity to the *indecent*.[71] Literature trials, from Henry Vizitelly's prosecution in 1889 for publishing English translations of Emile Zola to the trial of the publishers Penguin over Lawrence's *Lady Chatterley's Lover* in 1960, articulated concern about the scope of fiction to explore sex and sensuality in new ways and to provide a forum for alternative ways of thinking. This was part of the challenge presented by Radclyffe Hall's 'poisonous' novel, *The Well of Loneliness* in 1928. Aside from Hall's scandalous willingness to write about lesbian desire, the furore and prosecution may also have related to wider concerns about female social and – in the year when women gained the vote on equal terms with men – political independence. In a similar way historians and literary critics have found courtroom contests involving literature in the late nineteenth century to be symptomatic of – and an attempt to resolve – crises in ideologies of sex and gender. The 'French' and 'foreign' literary 'plagues' were particularly at issue in the Vizitelly prosecution, in which sensual writing and sexual acts were seen to be closely related. The idea of cultural infection from abroad was a prominent aspect of both trials: they indicated concern about a nation vulnerable to attack from French naturalism and aestheticism, and marked attempts to guard against decadence, degeneration and supposed imperial decline.[72] These cases allow historians to attend to the complex ways in which societies regulate moral values and national and class cultures.

They also allow us to ponder the broader effects of such censorship in terms of art and creativity: literary critics, for example, have suggested the productive tension that exists between artist and censor.[73]

Sexual stories and issues of respectability and appropriateness again feature in libel cases. What is interesting with libel is that it is not about the state intervening uninvited, but rather about citizens using state apparatus to settle scores, and specifically to arbitrate in matters of public standing. Sexual lives and sexual attitudes were laid bare in such cases and we can see vividly the kinds of behaviour that were deemed beyond the pale and also the particular ways in which they were understood, observed and reported. On the one hand, Rosemary Coombe observes, libel suits were a particular means through which individuals strove 'to represent their experience of self as something other than that decreed by dominant discourses'.[74] Of course on the other hand those suing for libel were often trying to reclaim their respectability and so align themselves with prevailing norms and assumptions about sexual conduct and identity. The Australian actor and singer Jason Donovan sued *The Face* magazine in 1992 after they had referred to his 'bleached-blond hair' in an article about the campaign to 'out' him. His lawyer argued that in this context the reference to his supposed use of bleach was tantamount to an accusation of homosexuality. Donovan insisted he lightened his hair using lemon juice. We see here the urgency to deny accusations of homosexuality at this time, especially for celebrities and public figures, and also witness a series of assumptions about gay lives, preoccupations and fashions.

conclusion

Specific cases, I have argued in the second half of this chapter, are a valuable source in the reconstruction of past sexual behaviours and cultures. They bring us voices not generally found in the public record; reveal patterns of private behaviour, conscience and opinion; can both reaffirm and destabilize apparent ideological certainties; and often significantly trouble the distinction between public and private modes of behaviour, not least by bringing the supposedly private into the public sphere of the courtroom. Whilst Philip Hubbard is right to observe the ways in which the law articulates boundaries between 'good' and 'bad' subjects, partly through notions of normative sexuality,[75] it is also manifestly true that these boundaries are porous and often destabilized in the very process of law enforcement. Attending closely to the language of the courtroom, to its performativity, and the specificities of its protocols and procedures, can be a productive means of examining these challenges, and assessing critically the ways in which the law and the courts constituted particular versions of truth, morality, and justice, and interrogated alternative – sexological, literary, libellous – sexual stories.

Part of the rhetoric of the justice system is that it stands outside and in objective relation to society; 'its potency derives', Rosemary Coombe observes, 'from its ability to efface its character as representation and become socially accepted as [the social world] itself'.[76] This is one of the key claims which historians of sexuality have sought to discredit, showing instead that the law has much more than simply a regulatory function and is itself a site of cultural production which shapes our sense of who we are and our place within society. I have suggested, though, that one of the problems of this move towards discursive analysis has been that the individual gets neglected or has their experience absurdly generalized. We can easily lose a productive sense of how the justice system and its ideological imperatives play themselves out in a person's behaviour and self-conception, and of how the 'public' world of the law and the courts impact on the intimate and the 'private'. We need, as Steven Maynard argues, to 'come to terms with the ever-elusive realm of feeling and personal life', a realm which an exclusive focus on domineering discourses like the law and medicine can efface.[77] The most impressive accounts of past sexualities and sexual cultures have successfully held the courtroom and legal discourse and records in tension with other forces, spaces and sources which might also help us to understand past sexual subjectivities and behaviours. In this work, a sensitivity to the intersection of different forms of history (and in particular cultural, social, and legal history) has begun to illuminate the differential impact of the law and the courts, showing how individuals responded in various and often unpredictable ways to their injunctions.

notes

1. Michel Foucault, *History of Sexuality. Volume 1: An Introduction*, trans. Robert Hurley, 1976 (London: Penguin, 1990); Foucault, *Discipline and Punish: The Birth of the Prison*, trans. Alan Sheridan (London: Penguin, 1977).
2. See David Halperin, 'Forgetting Foucault: Acts, Identities, and the History of Sexuality', *Representations*, 63 (1998), 93–120.
3. H. Montgomery Hyde, *The Other Love: An Historical and Contemporary Survey of Homosexuality in Britain* (London: Heinemann, 1970).
4. This reflects broader shifts in the relationship between law and history over the past twenty years. See David Sugarman (ed.), *Law in History: Histories of Law and Society* (Aldershot: Dartmouth, 1996), vol. 1, pt. iv; and Louis Knafla

and Susan Binnie, *Law, Society and the State: Essays in Modern Legal History* (Toronto: University of Toronto Press, 1995), intro and pt. iii.

5. See, for example: Ed Cohen, *Talk on the Wilde Side: Towards a Genealogy of a Discourse on Male Sexualities* (London: Routledge, 1993); Alan Sinfield, *The Wilde Century: Effeminacy, Oscar Wilde and the Queer Moment* (New York: Columbia University Press, 1992).
6. Nancy Cott, *Public Vows: A History of Marriage and the Nation* (Cambridge, MA: Harvard University Press, 2000), p. 8.
7. Rictor Norton, *The Myth of the Modern Homosexual: Queer History and the Search for Cultural Unity* (London: Cassell, 1997); Netta Murray Goldsmith, *Homosexuality and the Law in Eighteenth Century London* (Aldershot: Ashgate, 1998).
8. See Mary Poovey, *Making a Social Body: British Cultural Formation 1830–1864* (Chicago: University of Chicago Press, 1995).
9. Angus McLaren, *The Trials of Masculinity: Policing Sexual Boundaries, 1870–1930* (Chicago, Chicago University Press, 1997), p. 18.
10. See Matt Houlbrook, *Queer London: Perils and Pleasures in the Sexual Metropolis, 1918–57* (Chicago: University of Chicago Press, 2005); Harry Cocks, *Nameless Offences: Homosexual Desire in the 19th Century* (London: I.B. Tauris, 2003); Matt Cook, *London and the Culture of Homosexuality, 1885–1914* (Cambridge: Cambridge University Press, 2003); Philip Hubbard develops a similar argument in relation to the policing of prostitution. See Philip Hubbard, *Sex and the City: Geographies of Prostitution in the Urban West* (Ashgate: Aldershot, 1999), p. 122.
11. Joëlle Guillais, *Crimes of Passion: Dramas of Private Life in Nineteenth Century France*, trans. Jane Dunnet (Cambridge: Polity Press, 1986), p. 12.
12. Katherine Fischer Taylor, *In the Theater of Criminal Justice: The Palais de Justice in Second Empire Paris* (Princeton: Princeton University Press, 1993), p. 13.
13. See Sugarman, *Law*, vol. 1, p. xiv.
14. See John Langbein, *The Origins of Adversary Criminal Trial* (Oxford: Oxford University Press, 2003).
15. Donal MacNamara and Edward Sagarin, *Sex, Crime and the Law* (New York: Free Press, 1977), p. 3.
16. Frank Mort, *Dangerous Sexualities: Medico-Moral Politics in England Since 1830* (London: Routledge, 1987), p. 104.
17. See, for example, Jeffrey Weeks, *Sex, Politics and Society: The Regulation of Sexuality Since 1800* (London: Longman, 1981).
18. See, for example, Lucy Bland, *Banishing the Beast: English Feminism and Sexual Morality 1885–1914* (London: Penguin, 1995); Miles Ogborn, 'Law and Disciplines in Nineteenth Century State Formation: The Contagious Diseases Acts of 1864, 1866 and 1869', *Journal of Historical Sociology*, 6, 1 (1993); M. Spongberg, *Feminizing Venereal Disease: Representations of Women in Victorian Britain* (Basingstoke: Macmillan, 1997). There have been similar analyses of legislation on divorce. See M.L. Shanley, 'One Must Ride Behind: Married Women's Rights and the Divorce Act of 1857', *Victorian Studies* (Spring 1982); M.L. Shanley, *Feminism, Marriage and the Law in Victorian England, 1850–1895* (Princeton: Princeton University Press, 1989).
19. Joan Sangster, *Regulating Girls and Women: Sexuality, Family and the Law in Ontario 1920–1960* (Oxford: Oxford University Press, 2001), pp. 2–3.

20. Carol Smart, *Law, Crime and Sexuality: Essays in Feminism* (London: Sage, 1995), p. 50. See also Shani D'Cruze, 'Approaching the History of Rape and Sexual Violence: Notes Towards Research', *Women's History Review*, 1, 3 (1993); Shani D'Cruze, *Crimes of Outrage: Sex, Violence and Victorian Working Women* (London: UCL Press, 1998).
21. Jeffrey Weeks, *Making Sexual History* (Cambridge: Polity Press, 2000), p. 117.
22. Leslie Moran, *The Homosexual(ity) of Law* (London: Routledge, 1996).
23. Simon Shepherd and Mick Wallis, *Coming on Strong: Gay Politics and Culture* (London: Unwin and Hyman, 1989), p. 18.
24. See Louise Jackson, *Child Sexual Abuse in Victorian England* (London: Routledge, 2000); Judith Walkowitz, *City of Dreadful Delight: Narratives of Sexual Danger in Late-Victorian London* (London: Virago, 1992).
25. Barbara Brookes, *Abortion in England, 1900–1967* (London: Croom Helm, 1988).
26. N.E.H. Hull and Peter Charles Hoffer, *Roe v. Wade: The Abortion Rights Controversy in American History* (Lawrence, KS: University of Kansas Press, 2001), p. 24.
27. Weeks, *Making*, p. 147.
28. David Cohen, *Law Sexuality and Society: The Enforcement of Morals in Ancient Athens* (Cambridge: Cambridge University Press, 1991), p. 12.
29. See Matt Houlbrook, '"Lady Austin's Camp Boys": Constituting the Queer Subject in 1930s London', *Gender and History*, 14, 1 (2002), 31–61. Steven Maynard, 'Through a Hole in the Lavatory Wall: Homosexual Subcultures, Police Surveillance, and the Dialectics of Discovery, Toronto, 1890–1930', *Journal of the History of Sexuality*, 5, 2 (1994), 207–42.
30. See Jeffrey Weeks, *Coming Out: Homosexual Politics from the Nineteenth Century to the Present* (London: Quartet Books, 1979), pp. 118–24 & pp. 130–6; Matt Cook, 'Sex Lives and Diary Writing', in David Amigoni (ed.), *Life Writing and Victorian Culture* (Aldershot: Ashgate, 2005); and Cook, *London*.
31. See, for example, Hall Carpenter Archives, *Walking After Midnight: Gay Men's Life Stories* (London: Routledge, 1989); Lesbian History Group, *Inventing Ourselves: Lesbian Life Stories* (London: Routledge, 1989). Eric Marcus, *Making History: The Struggle for Gay and Lesbian Rights, 1945–1990* (New York: HarperCollins, 1992).
32. Lucia Zedner, 'Regulating Sexual Offences Within the Home', in Ian Loveland (ed.), *Frontiers of Criminality* (London: Sweet & Maxwell, 1995).
33. F.B. Smith, 'Labouchere's Amendment to the Criminal Law Amendment Bill', *Historical Studies*, 17 (1976), 165–73.
34. Lynda Nead, *Victorian Babylon: People, Streets and Images in Nineteenth Century London* (New Haven: Yale University Press, 2000), pt. III.
35. Henry Labouchere, *Truth*, 28 November 1889, 983.
36. Hubbard, *Sex and the City*, p. 145.
37. See Alison Oram and Annmarie Turnbull, *Lesbian History Sourcebook* (London: Routledge, 2001), p. 155.
38. Martha Vicinus, 'Lesbian Perversity and Victorian Marriage: The 1864 Codrington Divorce Trial', *Journal of British Studies*, 36 (1997), 70–98.
39. See Philip Hoare, *Wilde's Last Stand: Decadence, Conspiracy and the First World War* (London: Duckworth, 1997); Lucy Bland, 'Trial by Sexology? Maud Allen, Salome and the Cult of the Clitoris Case', in Lucy Bland and Laura Doan (eds.), *Sexology in Culture* (Cambridge: Polity Press, 1998).

40. Laura Doan, *Fashioning Saphism: The Origins of a Modern English Lesbian Culture* (New York: Columbia University Press, 2001).
41. Oram and Turnbull, *Lesbian*, p. 156.
42. Lillian Faderman, *Scotch Verdict: Miss Pirie and Miss Woods v. Dame Cumming Gordon* (London: Quartet, 1985).
43. Neil Bartlett, *Who Was That Man? A Present for Mr Oscar Wilde* (London: Serpent's Tail, 1988).
44. There are some parallels here with the history of homosexuality (male and female) in France. The 'relative freedom' accorded by the Napoleonic code meant there were less criminal cases than in England. See Jeffrey Merrick and Bryant Ragan (eds.), *Homosexuality in Modern France* (Oxford: Oxford University Press, 1996).
45. Nancy Erber and George Robb (eds.), *Disorder in the Court: Trials and Sexual Conflict at the Turn of the Century* (Basingstoke: Macmillan, 1999), p. 5.
46. Cook, *London*, pp. 69–70.
47. Bartlett, *Who Was That Man?*, pp. 211–13.
48. See for example: G.H. Flemming, *Victorian 'Sex Goddess': Lady Colin Campbell and the Sensational Divorce Case of 1888* (Oxford: Oxford University Press, 1990).
49. Cook, *London*, p. 62.
50. Walkowitz, *City*, epilogue; Liz Stanley, *Accounting for the Fall of Peter Sutcliffe and the Rise of the So-Called Yorkshire Ripper* (Manchester: Manchester University Sociology Occasional Papers, 1985); Nicole Ward Jouve, *'The Streetcleaner': The Yorkshire Ripper Case on Trial* (London: Boyars, 1985).
51. See Walkowitz, *City*, pp. 83–4.
52. Erber and Robb, *Disorder*, p. 7.
53. Lesley Hall, '"The Subject is Obscene: No Lady Would Dream of Alluding to It." Marie Stopes and her use of the courtroom', paper delivered at the 'Outrageous Stories: Women, Scandal and Subversion in Britain' conference at the University of Warwick on 24 April 2004.
54. See Matt Houlbrook, 'Soldier Heroes and Rent Boys: Homosex, Masculinities and Britishness in the Brigade of Guards: c.1900–1960', *Journal of British Studies*, 42, 3 (2003), 351–88.
55. 'The Trial of Boulton and Park', *Reynolds*, 14 May 1871, 6.
56. See Randolph Trumbach, 'Sodomitical Subcultures, Sodomitical Roles, and the Gender Revolution of the Eighteenth Century: The Recent Historiography', in Robert MacCubbin (ed.), *'Tis Nature's Fault: Unauthorised Sexuality During the Enlightenment* (Cambridge: Cambridge University Press, 1987).
57. H.G. Cocks, 'Making the Sodomite Speak: Voices of the Accused in English Sodomy Trials, c.1800–1898' (unpublished paper), p. 33.
58. Jackson, *Child Sexual Abuse*, p. 92.
59. Guillais, *Crimes of Passion*, p. 1.
60. David Halperin, *How to do the History of Homosexuality* (Chicago: University of Chicago Press, 2002), p. 12; Rosemary Coombe, 'Contesting the Self: Negotiating Subjectivities in Nineteenth-Century Ontario Defamation Trials', in Austin Sarat and Susan Silbey (eds.), *Studies in Law, Politics, and Society* (New York: JAI Press, 1993), vol. 2, p. 5.
61. Karen Dubinsky, *Improper Advances: Rape and Heterosexual Conflict in Ontario, 1880–1929* (Chicago: University of Chicago Press, 1993), p. 7.

62. D'Cruze, 'Approaching', p. 378.
63. Michael Rocke, *Forbidden Friendship: Homosexuality and Male Culture in Renaissance Florence* (Oxford: Oxford University Press, 1996); Guido Ruggiero, *The Boundaries of Eros: Sex, Crime and Sexuality in Renaissance Venice* (Oxford: Oxford University Press, 1985).
64. Maynard, 'Through a Hole', p. 220.
65. Sangster, *Regulating Girls*, pp. 3 and 12.
66. Maynard, 'Through a Hole', p. 229.
67. Cited in Cocks, 'Making the Sodomite Speak', p. 8.
68. Ruth Harris, *Murders and Madness: Medicine, Law and Society in the Fin de Siecle* (Oxford: Clarendon, 1989), p. 18. Ivan Crozier, 'The Medical Construction of Homosexuality and its Relation to the Law in Nineteenth-Century England', *Medical History*, 45 (2001), 61–82.
69. See Cook, *London*, pp. 75–6.
70. Sripati Chandrasekhar, *'A Dirty, Filthy Book': The Writings of Charles Knowlton and Annie Besant* (Berkeley: University of California Press, 1981).
71. See, for example: Paul Hyland and Neil Sammells (eds.), *Writing and Censorship in Britain* (London: Routledge, 1992); John Sutherland, *Offensive Literature: Decensorship in Britain, 1960–1982* (London: Junction Books, 1982); Kathryn Temple, *Scandal Nation: Law and Authorship in Britain, 1750–1832* (Ithaca: Cornell University Press, 2003).
72. Cook, *London*, ch. 4. See also: Katherine Mullin, *James Joyce, Sexuality and Social Purity* (Cambridge: Cambridge University Press, 2003), p. 6.
73. Hyland and Sammells, *Writing and Censorship*, p. 10.
74. Coombe, 'Contesting', p. 23.
75. Hubbard, *Sex and the City*.
76. Coombe, 'Contesting', p. 4.
77. Maynard, '"Respect Your Elders, Know Your Past": History and the Queer Theorists', *Radical History Review*, 75 (1999), 65.

4
marriage and reproduction

george robb

For most of the history of the Christian West, the Church held that sex was exclusively the province of marriage and was exclusively for the purpose of reproduction. The Anglican *Book of Common Prayer*, for example, declared that God had instituted marriage firstly for 'the procreation of children' and secondly 'for a remedy against sin and to avoid fornication'.[1] This ideology has been considerably eroded since the nineteenth century, yet remains the subject of debate to this day. While religious influence has waned in modern society, new governmental and medical authorities as well as counter-cultural voices have continued to view marriage and reproduction as key areas connected to society's well-being and national strength. Critics have frequently damned marriage as sexual slavery, while others have defended the institution as the only defence against sexual anarchy. Likewise the bearing and rearing of children has been the subject of much contestation in modern society.

Of course marriage and the family are historical constructs, and, as such, have evolved over time, subject to legal developments, economic forces and cultural attitudes. Historians of the family, such as Lawrence Stone and Randolph Trumbach, have argued that from the eighteenth century marriage has been increasingly shaped by sentiment and notions of romantic love. The conjugal family was now emphasized over wider kinship networks, and a new fondness for domesticity meant that marriage was expected to bring one personal happiness, unlike earlier centuries when it was more often viewed as a practical arrangement. Marriage was also more likely to be a matter of personal choice, even sexual attraction, than in earlier periods, when one's family, friends and neighbours arranged marriages to strengthen property holdings and communal bonds.[2]

What constituted a legal marriage also changed dramatically over the course of the eighteenth century. Since the middle ages, people had 'married' in a number of ways – sometimes in church, sometimes through private betrothals, and at times through a variety of folk customs which still conferred social acceptance and were often recognized at common law. In addition to such 'irregular' unions, illegitimate births and pre-marital conceptions were also quite common, especially in the countryside.

This laissez-faire attitude toward marriage was undermined from the late eighteenth century by religious revivalism, the greater discipline of industrial society, and more rigorous legislation. In particular, in Britain, the 1753 Hardwicke Marriage Act defined a legal marriage in specific and unambiguous terms. Henceforth, the only legal marriages were those performed on specific days of the week and at certain registered churches. The wedding, to be valid, had to be held after a public reading of the banns three weeks in a row, or the purchase of an expensive licence. Both parties had to be over twenty-one or have the permission of their guardians. The Act also included heavy penalties for anyone officiating at an irregular wedding or falsifying a marriage licence.[3] Bastardy was also increasingly penalized. The New Poor Law of 1834 placed complete financial responsibility for illegitimate children on their unwed mothers, who could no longer sue the alleged father for maintenance. Over the course of the nineteenth century, illegitimacy, as well as irregular unions, decreased. The Victorian marital regime had become more severe, though by no means universal.[4]

Indeed, by the late nineteenth century, between 10 and 20 per cent of the population never married at all. Large numbers of 'redundant women' especially were seen as a serious social problem. Feminists urged that such women needed to earn their own living and therefore should have access to higher education and the professions. More conservative voices advocated emigration to colonies like Canada or Australia, which had excess populations of white men.[5]

The fall in birth rates was also cause for concern, with the average British household size declining from six in 1860 to four in 1900 to three by 1910. The eugenics movement, which sought to improve and increase the 'racial stock', was one response to depopulation and a perceived national degeneracy. Greater state intervention into family life and marriage also became apparent from the 1880s, in yet another attempt to shore up the Empire. The origins of modern European welfare states can be seen in legislation concerning child welfare, education and family allowances, as well as in debates over the state endowment of motherhood.[6]

The family has become an important locus of governance and marital stability is increasingly viewed as a measure of national well-being. Soaring divorce rates in the 1960s were often cited as evidence of social decay, just as today gay marriage is seen by conservatives as the death knell of the family, and hence civilization itself. Though, as John Gillis has argued, the contemporary social climate, with widespread cohabitation, unwed motherhood and domestic partnerships, is not so much a departure from traditional marriage as a return to an earlier historical pattern where what constituted a marriage was legally and socially imprecise and where 'so many people made their own private "little weddings"'.[7]

Not surprisingly, source materials for writing the history of marital sexual behaviour are both scarce and problematic. Most literary sources necessarily reflect elite and middle-class attitudes, though working-class sexual behaviour sometimes can be inferred roughly through demographic data on fertility, bastardy and so on. Much work on sexual attitudes utilizes prescriptive literature, which certainly tells us how certain people (religious authorities, medical experts, free love socialists) wanted their readers to behave, though not necessarily how readers actually responded. For example, it is doubtful whether the voluminous anti-masturbation literature of the nineteenth century had much effect in curbing the practice, though it may well have increased guilt and anxiety. On the other hand, twentieth-century sex manuals were avidly consumed by people eager for better sex lives. Yet, whether they had this desired effect, is more difficult to determine.[8]

The nineteenth century witnessed intense debates about the nature of marriage as well as the role of sex in human evolution. Early in the century, certain socialists had included companionate marriage and shared sexual pleasure as part of their utopian agenda. The Englishman William Thompson, for instance, called for 'mutual enjoyment' in sex to replace men's 'mere individual sexual gratification'.[9] Prominent socialists like Robert Owen in Britain and Charles Fourier in France condemned traditional marriage as legalized prostitution and the enslavement of women. They envisioned a future world where women and men would be free to change partners if they ceased loving one another and where children would be supported by society as a whole. In some cases, socialist communities practised forms of 'free love'. In the United States, the Oneida Community in upstate New York instituted 'complex marriage' whereby every man was married to every woman, and where the giving and receiving of sexual pleasure was celebrated as vital to the spirit of the community.[10] Such utopian experiments necessarily remained exceptional, isolated and the subject of intense hostility on the part of religious and political conservatives. Furthermore, given women's increasing economic marginalization during the nineteenth century, most women sought to maintain whatever security marriage afforded them despite the institution's obvious patriarchal bias.

For many women and men, sexual pleasure in marriage was always overshadowed by fears of pregnancy. Without some sort of birth control, there was a limit to how far couples could go in achieving mutual satisfaction. Robert Owen and other radicals had attempted to spread birth control knowledge, especially the work of the American physician Charles Knowlton, *Fruits of Philosophy* (1832). Socialist espousal of birth control, however, only discredited it in the eyes of many conservatives, as did the association with sexual licence. Opponents tended to damn birth control as libertine practices which concealed fornication and threatened to 'reduce' marriage to a purely carnal relationship. Defenders usually avoided discussions of pleasure, arguing instead that they merely wanted to shield women from the debilitating effects of frequent pregnancy and childbirth. As in so much nineteenth-century discourse on sexuality, reproduction was treated primarily as a problem and a shameful topic. For much of the period in Britain and the United States, birth control publications were actively repressed as obscene literature.[11]

By mid-century the Victorian sexual and marital regime seemed firmly in place. To the general public, 'Victorianism' is still a byword for prudery and sexual repression. The Victorians themselves certainly contributed to this popular understanding through a great deal of medical discourse and literary representation which celebrated female innocence and idealized motherhood as pure and untainted by sexual motives. According to the oft-cited nineteenth-century English physician, William Acton, 'normal' women had little sexual desire. The Victorian family was bursting at the seams, and yet, paradoxically, sex was taboo. In recent years, however, historians, following the lead of Michel Foucault, have vigorously refuted this image of Victorian sexual repression. Scholars such as Peter Gay, Michael Mason, Karen Lystra and Janet Farrell Brodie have unearthed a wealth of data suggesting that Victorian marriages were sexually active and that women as well as men enjoyed sex. Lystra and Brodie, in particular, have made effective use of letters and diaries, where women and men often wrote frankly of their sexual desire for their partners. One Victorian wife carefully marked an X in her diary each time she had sex with her husband. From 1849 to 1871 the couple had sex on average five times a month, a rate very similar to that of middle-class couples reported in 1970s family planning studies.[12]

Husbands and wives, however, did not enjoy sexual *equality* within marriage. That the male was naturally sexually active and the female sexually passive found expression in most Victorian scientific literature, such as Geddes and Thomson's influential *The Evolution of Sex* (1889). Women's sexual subordination to their husbands was further underscored by European marriage laws, from the English common law to the Napoleonic Code, which enshrined the double standard. Under British law, after 1857, men could divorce their wives for adultery, but women could not divorce husbands for extra-marital affairs unless compounded with another offence such as desertion or physical abuse.[13] Nor had wives the right to refuse sexual intercourse, as marital rape had no legal standing. According to John Stuart Mill, husbands could 'enforce the lowest degradation of a human being – that of being made the instrument of an animal function contrary to her inclinations'. Indeed, in the 1888 case *Regina* v. *Clarence*, the court ruled that a husband could not be found guilty of raping his wife even if she had refused sex because he was venereally infected.[14]

Victorian feminists hoped to reform the law, but they also sought to reconfigure marriage as a more spiritual union, downplaying the role of sexuality and asserting a woman's right to control her own body. A number of women's historians, most notably Susan Kingsley Kent and Lucy Bland, have documented the Victorian feminist critique of marriage and male sexuality, which feminists represented as 'a selfish, destructive, uncontrolled, brutalizing force'. Social purity feminism emerged in the 1870s as a challenge to the sexual basis of male power and an assault on the sexual double-standard. Women like Josephine Butler, Millicent Fawcett and Frances Power Cobbe embraced their society's assumption that women were morally superior to men, but they rejected the notion that this moral authority was to be exercised primarily in the home where it would be sheltered from the contaminating influences of the marketplace and politics. In fact, social purity feminists believed that a corrupt society could only be saved when women were liberated from male domination and free to bring their moral influence to bear upon the great social problems of the day. They especially sought to regenerate society by combating the corrosive effects of male viciousness such as pornography, prostitution, and venereal disease. They campaigned for temperance, to raise the age of consent and, most famously, against the Contagious Diseases Acts which enshrined the double-standard by subjecting prostitutes to forced medical inspections while leaving their male clients unmolested.[15]

At the most basic level, women needed greater control over the incidence of sexual intercourse within marriage, which some social purity activists argued was only permissible for the purpose of procreation. A number of British feminists thus turned to eugenics, the supposed science of selective breeding, in the hopes of arresting national decline through a more rigorous control of human reproduction. Eugenics exerted great influence at the turn of the century, and its popularity among women enhanced the dignity and importance of motherhood. Eugenics underscored and justified for many women the need to examine the health of prospective husbands, in particular possible exposure to venereal disease.[16]

Social purity feminists utilized eugenic language to argue that women actually represented a higher stage of evolutionary development than men. The influential American biologist Lester Ward put forth his 'gynaecocentric theory' in 1903 which held that femaleness existed before maleness and was more important to the development of life. The British suffragist and social purity activist Frances Swiney was much taken by Ward's theory. In her 1905 work, *The Awakening of Women*, she too argued for the biological superiority of women – a theme she was to develop over the next fifteen years in a series of books and articles that combined science with Theosophical mysticism. According to Swiney, 'science has abundantly proved that in the mysterious evolution of sex, the male element was first non-existent; and on its first initial appearance was primarily an excrescence, a superfluity, a waste product of Nature, discarded or expelled by the female or mother organism, and, unless reunited to the parent, perished'.[17]

Since women represented the upward path of evolution, male domination of society was viewed as a historical anomaly that would lead to racial degeneration if left unchecked. One frequently cited sign of women's greater evolutionary consciousness was the supposed fact that they would not mate freely with an 'inferior' race, but men would. Swiney declared: 'In spite of our Indo-European pride of race, the Aryan male has never failed to have relations with the lowest and most disgusting females of the most degraded races among whom his lot may be cast for the time being. Men have never had that instinctive pride of race, of intuitive self-respect, that, through the exercise of self-restraint, should keep their offspring free from tainted blood.'[18] Thus, woman was the guardian of racial purity and the true guide to the betterment of the race while male sexual excess posed the greatest threat to racial health and was the cause not only of race mixing, but also of prostitution and venereal disease.

At the turn of the century, a number of feminists, including Swiney, focused attention on venereal disease as the ultimate example of male sexual exploitation of women and as a leading factor in the supposed degeneration of the English race. According to Swiney, 'from the time that woman lost her power of selection, and man exercised upon her the abuse of sexual excesses, the race began to degenerate'. Women's independence was therefore a eugenic issue. In her controversial novel of 1893, *The Heavenly Twins*, Sarah Grand argued that the cycle of venereal disease could only be broken when women were free from dependence on marriage and thus free to reject diseased and degenerate suitors. Eugenicist Dr Alice Drysdale believed that women must have economic independence if they were to exercise 'that natural selective power in the choice of a mate, which was probably a main factor in the... evolution of the race'.[19]

The further evolution of the race depended on the emancipation of women. As Swiney argued in the feminist newspaper *The Awakener*, 'upon her selection of a mate depends the future of the race – physically, mentally and spiritually, as she is potentially, the creatrix of forms, the transmitter of hereditary traits, the primal impressionist on the embryonic brain, and the imparter of psychic gifts'. Indeed, if women were not freed from their sexual subjugation to men, the Anglo-Saxon race would degenerate and the British Empire would go the way of Rome. In *Woman and Labour*, the South African writer Olive Schreiner maintained that nations decay when their women are deprived of freedom and turned into sexual objects. By way of example, she condemned the 'Turkish harems, where one of the noblest dominant Aryan races the world has yet produced is being slowly suffocated in the arms of a parasitic womanhood'.[20]

Frances Swiney and other social purity feminists were instrumental in devising a feminist eugenic discourse that sought to empower women by making them the arbiters of sexual reproduction. In their view, men's uncontrolled sensual natures led to venereal disease, eugenically unsound marriages and excessive, debilitating pregnancies. To arrest this pattern of degeneration, men must submit to women's more finely developed sense of racial fitness. Swiney held that women must 'redeem men, in spite of themselves, from the bondage of their vices'. Chasteness before marriage was to be the rule for men as well as women, and men with 'pasts' would become social pariahs along with 'fallen' women. Within marriage, women would exercise restraint over their husband's sexuality, which would return to the natural function of species reproduction – 'an episode, not a habit'. 'Fewer, but better children' was a popular eugenic slogan. Swiney argued that no woman should have more than three or four children and that 'by natural law a woman, as the most highly evolved organism, should not produce a child under intervals of four to six years between each birth'. Significantly, Swiney herself had six children, born in rather swift succession. Since artificial means of birth control would only encourage men's carnality, most feminists, including Swiney, favoured marital restraint.[21]

In a startling transvaluation of values, Swiney contested her society's definition of 'natural'. Sexual desire, even for men, was not natural. In particular, the male dominance of society was unnatural. After all, the male was 'an afterthought of Nature', or in Swiney's words, 'the male, the immature organism, is produced by the female, of the female, from the female, for the female alone'. The natural superiority of women had been recognized by the earliest, matriarchal societies. According to Swiney, primitive man regarded the male with the greatest suspicion. Here, she argued, is a being unlike the Mother – smaller, weaker, unformed, unfinished, incapable of reproduction, less intelligent, more brutal and animal than the woman; essentially 'the hairy one'. Unfortunately the worship of the Divine Mother was overthrown by men, who replaced the natural law of sexual self-control with the cult of the phallus and sexual excess.[22] Swiney's use of terms like 'divine motherhood' reflects the influence of spiritualism and the occult in feminist circles.

The growing popularity of spiritualism and what today would be called 'new age' philosophies among middle- and upper-class English women at the turn of the century was in part a response to the 'biology is destiny' arguments of science. Recent scholarship by Alex Owen and Joy Dixon demonstrates that occultism attracted many feminists because it emphasized that women were more spiritual than men and that women were destined to lead men upwards, away from the physical and the sexual. In both Britain and America, many women found power and authority through mediumship. Scientists and educated people generally ridiculed the fascination with séances and ouija boards as superstitious nonsense, and some spiritualists sought to distinguish themselves from mere table rappers and achieve greater legitimation through a synthesis of occultism and science. Theosophy, which combined contacts with the spirit world, eastern religions and the language of evolutionary biology, was probably the most famous such synthesis.[23]

Theosophists envisioned motherhood as an essentially spiritual process and tended to downplay the physical side of sexual reproduction. Theosophy especially appealed to women through its emphasis on the equality of the sexes, the motherhood of God, and an evolutionary pattern that promised to transcend sex. Theosophists saw human evolution as a grand cosmic procession in which the Darwinian ascent of man from ape was but a tiny segment. Helena Blavatsky, one of the founders of the movement, explained that humanity would pass through seven 'races', or stages of development, on the road to perfection. The first two races had 'astral bodies' and were asexual. The third race began the descent to the physical, though it was originally androgynous or hermaphroditic. This race later developed differentiated sex and perished with the lost continent of Lemuria. The fourth race, of Atlantis, was the last to possess significant psychic powers before the fifth and present race which is purely physical. Theosophists believed that they were rediscovering the occult mysteries lost after the submersion of Atlantis and that humanity was on the brink of spiritual rebirth 'out of the bonds of matter, and even of flesh'. The coming six and seventh races would once again be astral and asexual.[24]

Just as Marx could only imagine an end to class conflict in a future 'classless' society, many nineteenth-century utopians believed that the sexual subordination of women would only disappear if society were somehow rendered 'sexless'. In 1884, for example, the spiritualist Laurence Oliphant published *Sympneumata* in which he foresaw a future androgynous society where children would be created non-sexually. The book was widely read, including by Queen Victoria, though the reaction of that mother of nine is not recorded. Theosophists, in particular, anticipated the creation of a higher being that would free humanity from sex altogether. Under the influence of Theosophy, the feminist Elizabeth Wolstenholme and her husband Ben Elmy predicted that in the future marriage would have no sexual expression but would be 'essentially a psychic alliance'.[25]

Other radical Edwardian feminists, such as Cicely Hamilton and Christabel Pankhurst, continued to warn women of men's sexual exploitation through marriage. In *Marriage as a Trade* (1909) Hamilton equated marriage with prostitution, since man provided economic support in return for woman to 'enkindle and satisfy the desire of the male'. Hamilton warned women that within marriage they had little control over sex or motherhood and were in real danger of venereal infection. According to Pankhurst, men believed that women were created primarily for men's sexual gratification. In her infamous pamphlet, *The Great Scourge* (1913), she asserted that 75 to 80 per cent of men were infected with gonorrhoea and a great number with syphilis as well. The pioneering woman doctor Mary Scharlieb also cautioned prospective wives about venereal disease in her book *What It Means to Marry* (1914).[26]

While most Victorian and Edwardian feminists sought to shield women from sex, new 'free love' feminists and other radicals advocated women's rights to sexual pleasure and to sexual freedom comparable to men. The writer Edward Carpenter saw sex as a vital force that would create new, more healthy and equal bonds between men and women. The pioneering sexologist Havelock Ellis was among the first to advocate sexual happiness as essential to marriage. A new generation of feminists, like Stella Browne and Catherine Hartley, sought to liberate the body and the spirit from the stifling confines of Victorian prudery. These 'New Women', along with progressive young men like H.G. Wells and George Bernard Shaw, were part of a generation that had come of age in the 1890s and were consciously lashing out at their Victorian elders. Self-styled iconoclasts who rejected the rhetoric of social purity feminists, they saw all talk of women's moral superiority as window dressing for sexual repression. The sex radicals, however, did not reject eugenics, although they favoured a variety far more sexually vigorous than had been endorsed by Swiney and her ilk. For example, in a 1909 article in the *Eugenics Review*, Maximilian Mugge emphasized 'how urgent is the need to stem the tide of Spritualisation and Intellectualisation' that he felt had been contaminating eugenic thought. The superman, he insisted, would be made through the *body*.[27]

The emphasis that sex radicals and 'progressive' eugenicists placed on physicality meant that sex and reproduction were often discussed in terms of animal husbandry. Consider the book *How to Beget and Rear Beautiful Children*, in which the American physician James Jackson argued the necessity of breeding better humans like livestock. Mothers, Jackson assured his readers, were like thoroughbred horses. And if a woman is 'a poor, spiritless thing herself, without a good strain of blood in her, with no constitution, no power of endurance, no tenaciousness of life; vapid in her moods, purposeless in aims, lacking in ambition, what is to be expected of her in the way of offspring?'[28] The delicate, wan Victorian lady was clearly not the ideal material for motherhood, but in this case, she was to be replaced by the buxom, uncorseted nymph, not the intellectual and moral paragon envisioned by Edwardian feminists.

Indeed, many eugenicists believed that the 'educated type' of woman was not sufficiently sexual to attract a mate. The fact that the birth rate of the professional classes had dropped more sharply than that of other social groups was particularly alarming. Feminists had celebrated women's power to regenerate the race by passing on their moral virtues to their children, but if the nation's noblest women had the fewest children, the power of motherhood was clearly being wasted. Francis Galton, the founder of the British Eugenic Society, had noted in his important work *Hereditary Genius* (1869) that the 'aunts, sisters and daughters of eminent men' had lower marriage rates and fewer children than their less accomplished sisters. Indeed, he wondered whether education and cultivated intellect actually robbed women of their appeal to prospective mates: 'One portion of them [educated women] would certainly be of a dogmatic and self-asserting type, and therefore unattractive to men, and others would fail to attract, owing to their having shy, odd manners, often met with in young persons of genius, which are disadvantageous to the matrimonial chances of young women.'[29] Galton feared that women of genius had the least opportunity to pass on their talents, due to their apparent lack of sex appeal.

Galton's intellectual heirs also argued that traditional 'womanly' attributes such as beauty, grace, and tenderness were not socially constructed, but in fact the modern expression of sexual selection. In a 1911 article in the *Eugenics Review*, the physician R. Murray Leslie affirmed that a girl should be intelligent, but not intellectual. 'The majority of men', he claimed, 'including even learned university professors themselves, exhibit a preference for the less highly educated type.' The New Woman's 'knowledge of mathematics, or even her efficiency in athletics', did not 'make her intrinsically a better potential mother than the natural, bright, intelligent girl interested in frocks and frills, dances and mild flirtations'.[30] Morality and high mindedness were all well and good, but not if they retarded eugenics.

In fact some advocates of eugenics and sexual liberation feared that too much concern with traditional sexual morality would be the ruin of the race because it stifled women's sexual desire and thus endangered the procreative urge. Havelock Ellis believed that the traditional 'marriage order' banished sexual pleasure for the woman. The whole cult of female purity 'rendered difficult for her the satisfaction of the instinct for that courtship [read foreplay] which is the natural preliminary of reproductive activity, an instinct even more highly developed in the female than in the male, and the more insistent because in the order of Nature the burden of maternity is preceded by the reward of pleasure'. The falling birth rate was thus attributable to sexual frustration. To the radical feminist Stella Browne, 'absolute freedom of choice on the woman's part, and intense desire both for her mate and her child, are the magical forces that will vitalize and transfigure the race'. A new and superior race of beings could be created through the experience of intense sexual pleasure. Or as Catherine Hartley prophesied, 'not in the enforced chastity of woman, but in her love, will man gain his new redemption'.[31]

Among the most passionate advocates of women's sexual liberation, Hartley, like Shaw, was greatly influenced by Nietzsche. In works such as *The Truth About Women* (1913), she argued that women would regenerate the race because they were closer to nature, more instinctual than men and thus better able to escape the stifling confines of a false civilization. Hartley completely rejected the Victorian idea that women were more spiritual, men more carnal: 'There is another error that I would wish to clear up now. It is tenet of common belief that in all matters of sex-feeling and sex-morality the woman is different from, and superior to, the man. I find in the writings of almost all women on sex-subjects, not to speak of popular novels, an insistence on men's grossness, with a great deal in contrast about the soulful character of woman's love.' All such sentiments, Hartley believed, were directed at repressing women's sexuality. But in fact 'There can be no such thing as the goodness of the other half. Love between woman and man is mutual, is continual giving. Not by storing up for the good of one sex or in waste for the pleasure of the other, but by free bestowing is salvation.'[32]

To those who proclaimed the gospel of free love, nature was not something to be resisted, as Evangelical Christianity had taught, but a source of endless instruction in the art of living. Progressive eugenicists saw the Victorian obsession with delicacy and good taste – 'that swathing up of all the splendours of the flesh', as H.G. Wells termed it – as sapping the vitality of civilization. According to Wells, 'a people that will not valiantly face and understand and admit love and passion can understand nothing whatever'. Sex should not be viewed as a dark contagion that must be controlled, but as a vital, redemptive force. Similarly, Havelock Ellis argued that 'sexual pleasure wisely used and not abused, may prove the stimulus and liberator of our finest and most exalted activities'.[33]

The eugenic emphasis on sexuality caused its adherents to see motherhood displacing marriage as the defining status of women. Some eugenicists even wondered whether marriage might put impediments in the way of better breeding. The choice of marriage partner was often influenced by considerations of money, class, and religion, all of which were extraneous to the primary goal of eugenics – better breeding. Ellis condemned 'the fatal influence of wealth and position and worldly convenience, which give a factitious value to persons who would never appear attractive partners in life were love and eugenic ideals left to go hand in hand'. In an article entitled 'Eugenics and St. Valentine', Ellis argued that 'the new St. Valentine will be a saint of science' and that sexual attraction was eugenic in its basis. Desire was sufficient, and if traditional morality imposed impediments to a eugenic union, traditional morality would have to go. Or, as the physician Caleb Saleeby put it, 'we might make a eugenist of Mrs. Grundy'.[34]

Creative works of the era frequently dramatized these issues. Grant Allen's notorious novel of free love, *The Woman Who Did* (1895), depicted a woman's decision to have a child outside of wedlock. In his play *Getting Married* (1913), George Bernard Shaw argued that many women rejected motherhood because it was inseparable from the legal subjection of marriage. His character Lesbia announces: 'I want children; and I want to devote myself entirely to my children, and not to their father. The law will not allow me to do that; so I have made up my mind to have neither husband nor children.' Legitimacy, according to Shaw, should be secondary to racial vitality, and any sensible statesman should 'prefer one healthy illegitimate child to ten rickety legitimate ones'. In a wartime play significantly titled *The Race*, the biologist Marie Stopes praised the decision of a young woman to have a child by her soldier lover. In response to her mother's assertion 'that for an unmarried woman to have a child is wrong', the heroine asks, 'Is it not *more* wrong that not only Ernest, but all the fine, clean, strong young men like him who go out to be killed, should have no sons to carry on the race; but that all the cowardly and unhealthy ones who remain behind can have all the wives and children?'[35] Motherhood was the supreme act of female patriotism, transcending the niceties of bourgeois morality.

In the conservative aftermath of the First World War, free love lost much of its appeal, but there were renewed calls to revitalize marriage through sex. After the war, there was an explosion of new marriage manuals which emphasized the need for sexual pleasure and provided necessary advice on technique. Marie Stopes' *Married Love* (1918) was the first and most successful of this new genre, outselling popular novels and going through numerous editions over the next forty years. The book's subtitle, 'A New Contribution to the Solution of Sex Difficulties', suggested that marriage was in fact in trouble and that good sex was the solution. Stopes included explicit advice about the sexual act, including the necessity of a husband arousing his wife before intercourse and the need for her to achieve orgasm. Part of Stopes' broad appeal and acceptability was her 'poetic' style and her insistence on the transcendent and spiritual nature of sex. In a typical passage, she celebrated the bodily union of husband and wife as 'the solid nucleus of an immense fabric of interwoven strands reaching to the uttermost ends of the earth; some lighter than the filmiest cobweb, or than the softest wave of music, iridescent with the colours, not only of the visible rainbow, but of all the invisible glories of the wave-lengths of the soul'. Stopes also advocated birth control, acknowledging that sexual pleasure brought couples closer together and that this was as worthy an end as procreation.[36]

Stopes' major competitor was Theo van de Velde, a Dutch gynaecologist, whose book *Ideal Marriage* (1926) also remained in print for decades. Translated into English by Stella Browne, it was the most widely known sex manual in the United States until the 1960s. According to van de Velde, 'sex is the foundation of marriage. Yet most married people do not know the ABC of sex. My task here is to dispel this ignorance, and show ways and means of attaining both vigour and harmony in monogamous sexual relations.'[37] Much of the book was occupied with dispelling myths and misunderstandings about sexual activity and with providing husbands and wives with more accurate information about their own and each other's bodies. As E.M. Brecher and Lesley Hall have both suggested, the popularity and success of marriage manuals had less to do with specific advice or sexual technique than with creating more openness and communication between husbands and wives.[38] These works also gained legitimacy by invoking eugenic arguments that good sex would improve the quality of the race.

Some historians, most notably Sheila Jeffreys, have argued that the new genre of sex manuals was actually oppressive to wives, who were now seen explicitly as sex objects by their husbands. Certainly advice books envisioned men as the initiators of sex. Lack of compliance on the woman's part was also viewed as problematic. What earlier generations had seen as woman's ideal purity was now labelled 'repression' or 'frigidity'.[39] Other historians, however, believe that the eroticization of marriage cannot be seen only as oppressing women. Marcus Collins, for one, emphasizes how sexologists stressed men's duty to subordinate their own sexual desires to what was 'pleasing' to their wives. Lesley Hall also points out that, far from initiating male licence, these new books often led to considerable anxiety among husbands, who wondered if they were capable of providing adequate sexual pleasure to their wives. Among the thousands of letters Stopes received from her readers, were many from confused and troubled husbands. As one correspondent shamefully confessed, 'I have not realized till now that I haven't given my wife the satisfaction to which she has a right.'[40]

If not a purely masculine concern, a better sex life did appear to be primarily a middle-class preoccupation. While Stopes' middle-class correspondents wanted advice on improved sexual technique, her working-class correspondents preferred practical information on birth control. There is little evidence that working-class marriages were much affected by the new advice books. Indeed, surveys of British working-class families during the 1940s and 1950s found that many wives identified a good husband as one who made few sexual overtures and 'never complained' when refused. A pioneering study of 200 couples in the mid-1940s by Eliot Slater and Maya Woodside found widespread 'puritanical attitudes' and a 'barely veiled sex antagonism' on the part of women to their husband's 'demands'.[41]

The new emphasis on conjugal bliss was also bourgeois in its heightened condemnation and policing of extra-marital and non-normative sexuality. Stopes, van de Velde and other sexologists were outspoken critics of homosexuality, prostitution and even masturbation. Van de Velde concluded his manual with a warning that 'Voluptuous pleasure *alone*, however refined and varied, cannot bring real happiness, without that solace to the soul which humanity desires, and *must* forever seek.' Stopes was also careful to disassociate her promotion of birth control with sexual libertinism. Her work was clearly within a familial, eugenic tradition that advocated fewer, but better, children and that favoured early marriage over pre-marital sex with prostitutes.[42]

British and American sex 'experts' certainly wanted to differentiate themselves from 1920s sex radicals like the Soviet writer Alexandra Kollontai. An ardent Bolshevik and feminist, Kollontai harkened back to Owenite views on marriage, believing the patriarchal family an individualistic institution that must be smashed. In a series of agitprop pamphlets, realist novels and a provocative memoir, *The Autobiography of a Sexually Emancipated Communist Woman* (1926), Kollontai argued for free, but comradely, sexual relations. She envisioned a kind of serial monogamy, where women and men would live together only so long as it suited them both. Communal living and childcare would free women from the tyranny of housework and free both partners from economic bondage to the family unit. State-funded birth control and abortion would also ensure that motherhood was voluntary. Kollontai represented the West's worst nightmares about 'Godless' communism undermining the foundations of Christian morality and the nuclear family. Her belief that sex was a natural function, not much different than 'drinking a glass of water', was especially cited as an example of Soviet depravity.[43]

Kollontai's eventual downfall and the suppression of her books under Stalin dramatize the conservative backlash against sexual radicalism during the 1930s. Throughout the West, efforts at promoting birth control and more liberal sexual attitudes came up against the hard realities of the Great Depression, falling birth rates and rising nationalism. Alarmist screeds like Dr Enid Charles' *The Twilight of Parenthood* (1934) predicted a bleak future of depopulation and national decline. For many Western nations, the mid-1930s marked the lowest point to date in their birth rates. A number of governments responded with pro-natalist rhetoric and policies. Totalitarian regimes, not surprisingly, furnish the most extreme examples. The Soviet Union re-criminalized abortion and reversed progressive employment policies that had encouraged women to work outside the home. Stalin, like Mussolini, created special medals for the parents of large families. The Nazis pushed eugenics to its furthest limits – both in horrific policies of exterminating 'inferior races' and in rather pathetic attempts to breed a master race at baby farms where German soldiers impregnated young women.[44]

Even in the United States and Great Britain there was a heightened emphasis on motherhood and domesticity in women's magazines, popular fiction and films. The fetishization of child stars like Shirley Temple or oddities like Canada's Dionne quintuplets underscores the premium placed on reproduction. Indeed, the Catholic Church in Quebec proclaimed the birth of the five identical girls in May 1934 'a public and decisive answer of God to those who are preaching and practicing birth control'. Complete freedom from childbirth had become unthinkable, and not only to Catholics. Even so sanguine an advocate of birth control as Marie Stopes emphasized that the avoidance of motherhood was unnatural. 'Every lover desires a child', she asserted. 'Those who imagine the contrary, and maintain that love is purely selfish, know only the lesser types of love.' Stopes even predicted that in the future all women would have children and that 'exceptional' women would have six or more. The massive loss of life during the Second World War only underscored the importance of each new child, and the postwar 'baby boom' seemed to confirm the regenerative power of the family.[45]

Meanwhile, the promotion of good sexual relations within marriage had ceased to be controversial and was even endorsed by former foes like clergymen. The new attitudes were exemplified in 1942, when the British doctor Eustace Chesser was prosecuted for obscenity for his book *Love Without Fear: A Plain Guide to Sex Technique for Every Married Adult*. The jury found for Chesser and the judge concluded 'in the year 1942, it is ridiculous and absurd to suggest that the discussion of sex and sex relationships in a book is obscene'. So far had the pendulum swung, that in the American obscenity trial of *Lady Chatterley's Lover* in 1959, the defence argued that Lawrence's novel was beneficial to society since it helped promote sexual compatibility in marriage. In his summation before the court, the defence attorney said that he did not find anything in *Lady Chatterley* that could not be found in the marriage advice columns of *Ladies Home Journal* and that it was now a truism among marriage counsellors that sexual fulfilment was essential to happiness.[46]

Soaring divorce rates in the postwar world cast doubt on sex's ability to save modern marriage. After all, heightened expectations were just as likely to create resentment when unfulfilled, or performance anxiety among the inexperienced. The new ideal of eroticized marriage put forth by advice manuals maintained that good sex was not innate, but needed to be learned and cultivated. Some young couples may have seen this as an exciting opportunity, though others were clearly intimidated by the prospect. Men sometimes felt insecure about their ability to give their wives pleasure, and women were afraid that if they responded too enthusiastically, their husbands would think badly of them.

As critics later pointed out, the great bulk of sexual advice literature well into the 1960s still posited a sexually active role for the husband and a passive one for the wife. David Mace, one of the founders in 1946 of Britain's influential Marriage Guidance Council, maintained that the husband should be 'the initiator' in sexual matters. The Council's most popular advice booklet, *How to Treat a Young Wife*, had sold over half a million copies by the 1960s, but as its title implies, it assumed more experienced husbands would initiate young virgin brides into the mysteries of sex. Sexual pleasure was deemed important for both partners, but men were still seen as the dominant one. Sex experts' longstanding preference for vaginal rather than clitoral orgasms further underscored their essential conservatism with regard to sex roles.[47] Despite the obvious limitations and biases of much marital advice literature, the fact that during the twentieth century sex in marriage was increasingly eroticized and separated from reproduction represented a seismic shift in the history of sexuality.

From the late 1960s, an even more radical position was adopted by young people and social critics who claimed the right to sexual pleasure *outside* of marriage. In particular, second-wave feminists like Germaine Greer and Ann Oakley condemned the nuclear family and women's sexual subordination to men. Women's need to pursue sexual satisfaction on their own terms and initiative without regard to male approval or within traditionally sanctioned relationships was promoted by a wide variety of sources, from Greer's feminist manifesto *The Female Eunuch* (1970) to Erica Jong's best-selling novel *Fear of Flying* (1973). But as always, the real difficulties came from envisioning parenthood outside of marriage. Given most women's limited earning power and the lack of affordable childcare facilities (even in nations with welfare provisions), households headed by a single mother often fall below the poverty line. This is especially true among African-American women in the United States.[48]

The early twenty-first century thus appears a critical and highly contentious moment in the history of marriage and sexuality. On the one hand, the institution seems to be losing its grip in many parts of the West where cohabitation and unwed motherhood are more common than ever before. In much of Scandinavia, for example, the majority of young people choose cohabitation over marriage and most children are now born out of wedlock. On the other hand, the desire for marriage has achieved a heightened urgency, reflected in a whole series of 'reality' television shows and popular advice books aimed at finding one's ideal mate. Some best-sellers like *The Rules* (1995) have even evinced nostalgia for 1950s-style courtship, where dating is a kind of game in which women are advised to ration sexual favours to control men and ultimately steer them into marriage.[49]

Nowhere is the uncertainty over conjugality more pronounced than in the current debates over 'gay marriage'. Since the 1980s conservative ideologues have increasingly invoked a homophobic rhetoric of 'family values' as an antidote to the supposed growth of sexual permissiveness. For example, in Thatcher's Britain schools were forbidden to discuss homosexuality as a 'pretended family relationship' and sex education was to teach students 'the benefits of stable married life and the responsibilities of parenthood'. Although some Western nations have enacted same-sex marriage (Netherlands, Canada) and others domestic partnership rights which approximate the legal status of marriage (France, Germany, Denmark), this has not occurred in either Britain or the United States, where conservative and religious opposition has proved especially tenacious. In the US the debate over gay marriage is approaching a political crisis, with certain liberal municipalities issuing marriage licences to same-sex couples while conservative politicians counter with a 'Defense of Marriage Act' and a proposed constitutional amendment banning gay unions. The 'essentially procreative' purpose of marriage is frequently cited against gay couples, even as parenthood and matrimony are increasingly separated in contemporary society.[50]

Same-sex marriage has also led to debates within the gay community, pitting conservatives like Andrew Sullivan against sex radicals like Michael Warner. As early as 1989, Sullivan, a British journalist working in the US, made the case for gay marriage as 'an anchor... in the chaos of sex and relationships to which we are all prone'. 'Like straight marriage', he argued, 'it would foster social cohesion, emotional security, and economic prudence.' Much of his argument was aimed at potential opponents, assuring them that same-sex marriage was not an attack on 'family values', but an 'extension of them'. Unlike Sullivan, whose position is based on a rather idealized view of marriage, Michael Warner, an American academic and activist, is far more critical of the institution, which he sees as hopelessly enmeshed in patriarchal values. In *The Trouble with Normal: Sex, Politics, and the Ethics of Queer Life* (1999), Warner offers a defence of 'sexual autonomy' and a warning that the drive to marriage is founded on a false morality that will sanctify 'some couples at the expense of others'. Gay marriage, he argues, will privilege those couples who enter it while leaving 'unmarried queers looking more deviant'.[51]

Over the past two centuries, marriage and parenthood frequently have been portrayed as being 'in crisis'. Although some few voices have conspired to overturn or radically reconfigure these institutions, most people have positioned themselves as trying to 'save' marriage and the family. These rescue operations have been directed variously against perceived external threats (feminists, socialists, homosexuals) as well as possible internal weaknesses (patriarchy, sexual repression). That certain types of sexual desire or sexual expression have been thought to be either essential to or incompatible with marriage and parenthood, testifies to long-held assumptions that 'the family' is primarily a moral entity and is absolutely necessary to social stability. That so many gay men and women are clamouring for marriage also suggests that the institution, far from being on its last legs, is remarkably vital.

notes

1. *Book of Common Prayer, 1559* (Washington, DC: Folger Shakespeare Library, 1976), p. 290.
2. Lawrence Stone, *The Family, Sex and Marriage in England, 1500–1800* (London: Weidenfeld and Nicolson, 1977) and Randolph Trumbach, *The Rise of the Egalitarian Family: Aristocratic Kinship and Domestic Relations in Eighteenth Century England* (New York: Academic Press, 1978).
3. John Gillis, *For Better, For Worse: British Marriages, 1600 to the Present* (New York: Oxford University Press, 1985), pp. 11–54, 135–60.
4. Peter Laslett et al., *Bastardy and Its Comparative History* (London: Arnold, 1980).
5. Martha Vicinus, *Independent Women: Work and Community for Single Women, 1850–1920* (Chicago: University of Chicago Press, 1985), pp. 10–45.
6. Richard Soloway, *Demography and Degeneration: Eugenics and the Declining Birthrate in Twentieth-Century Britain* (Chapel Hill: University of North Carolina Press, 1995), Anna Davin, 'Imperialism and Motherhood', *History Workshop Journal*, 6 (1978), 9–65, and Susan Pedersen, 'Gender, Welfare and Citizenship in Britain during the Great War', *American Historical Review*, 95 (1990), 983–1006.

7. Gillis, *For Better, For Worse*, p. 310.
8. For a good discussion of source materials, see Michael Anderson, *Approaches to the History of the Western Family, 1500–1914* (Cambridge: Cambridge University Press, 1980), pp. 4–5, 14–15, 26–7, 31–2.
9. Quoted in Marcus Collins, *Modern Love: An Intimate History of Men and Women in Twentieth-Century Britain* (London: Atlantic Books, 2003), p. 4.
10. Spencer Klaw, *Without Sin: The Life and Death of the Oneida Community* (New York: Penguin Books, 1993), pp. 167–89. See also Raymond Lee Muncy, *Sex and Marriage in Utopian Communities* (Bloomington: Indiana University Press, 1973), and Barbara Taylor, *Eve and the New Jerusalem: Socialism and Feminism in the Nineteenth Century* (New York: Pantheon Books, 1983).
11. Janet Farrell Brodie, *Contraception and Abortion in Nineteenth-Century America* (Ithaca, New York: Cornell University Press, 1994), and Roy Porter and Lesley Hall, *The Facts of Life: The Creation of Sexual Knowledge in Britain, 1650–1950* (New Haven: Yale University Press, 1995).
12. Michel Foucault, *The History of Sexuality: An Introduction* (New York: Vintage Books, 1978); Peter Gay, *The Bourgeois Experience: Victoria to Freud, Volume 1: Education of the Senses* (New York: Oxford University Press, 1984); Karen Lystra, *Searching the Heart: Women, Men, and Romantic Love in Nineteenth-Century America* (New York: Oxford University Press, 1989); Brodie, *Contraception and Abortion*, pp. 9–12; Michael Mason, *The Making of Victorian Sexuality* (New York: Oxford University Press, 1995).
13. Susan Kingsley Kent, *Sex and Suffrage in Britain, 1860–1914* (Princeton: Princeton University Press, 1987), pp. 80–113.
14. Lucy Bland, *Banishing the Beast: English Feminism and Sexual Morality, 1885–1914* (London: Penguin Books, 1995), pp. 127–35.
15. For histories of the Victorian social purity movement, see Kent, *Sex and Suffrage*; Bland, *Banishing the Beast*; Frank Mort, *Dangerous Sexualities: Medico-Moral Politics in England Since 1830* (London: Routledge and Kegan Paul, 1987); Judith Walkowitz, *Prostitution and Victorian Society* (Cambridge: Cambridge University Press, 1980).
16. Among the considerable literature on eugenics, see especially Daniel J. Kevles, *In the Name of Eugenics* (Berkeley: University of California Press, 1985); and Lyndsay Farrell, *The Origin and Growth of the English Eugenics Movement, 1865–1925* (New York: Garland, 1985).
17. Frances Swiney, *The Awakening of Women, or Woman's Part in Evolution* (London: William Reeves, 1905), p. 20. For an evaluation of Swiney's work, see George Robb, 'Eugenics, Spirituality, and Sex Differentiation in Edwardian England: The Case of Frances Swiney', *Journal of Women's History*, 10 (1998), 97–117. Women's participation in the eugenics movement is also examined in Rosaleen Love, 'Alice in Eugenics-Land: Feminism and Eugenics in the Scientific Careers of Alice Lee and Ethel Elderton', *Annals of Science*, 36 (1979), 145–58.
18. Swiney, *Awakening of Women*, p. 133.
19. Frances Swiney, *The Mystery of the Circle and the Cross, or the Interpretation of Sex* (London: Open Road Publishing Co., 1908), p. 45, and Alice Drysdale, 'Women and Eugenics', *Sociological Papers*, 2 (1905), 21–2. The feminist response to prostitution and venereal disease is an important chapter in the history of the Victorian women's movement. See, for example, Walkowitz,

Prostitution and Victorian Society and Greta Jones, *Social Hygiene in Twentieth-Century Britain* (London: Croom Helm, 1986).

20. Frances Swiney, 'Education in the Law of Sex', *The Awakener*, 1 February 1913, 5 and Olive Schreiner, *Woman and Labour* (New York: Frederick A. Stoker, 1911), p. 97.
21. Frances Swiney, *The Bar of Isis* (London: Open Road Publishing Co., 1907), pp. 15, 17, *The Awakening of Women*, p. 101, and *Mystery of the Circle and the Cross*, p. 44.
22. Swiney, *Mystery of the Circle and the Cross*, p. 28.
23. Alex Owen, *The Darkened Room: Women, Power and Spiritualism in Late Victorian England* (Philadelphia: University of Pennsylvania Press, 1990), and Joy Dixon, *Divine Feminine: Theosophy and Feminism in England* (Baltimore: Johns Hopkins University Press, 2001).
24. H.P. Blavatsky, *The Secret Doctrine: The Synthesis of Science, Religion, and Philosophy* (London: Theosophical Society, 1888), vol. 2, p. 446.
25. Laurence Oliphant, *Sympneumata, or the Evolutionary Forces Now Active in Man* (London: William Blackwood, 1884), and Ellis Ethelmer, *Life to Woman* (Congleton: Women's Emancipation Union, 1896), p. 66.
26. Kent, *Sex and Suffrage*, p. 86, and Bland, *Banishing the Beast*, p. 245.
27. Maximilian Mugge, 'Eugenics and the Superman', *Eugenics Review*, 1 (1909), 189. See also George Robb, 'The Way of All Flesh: Degeneration, Eugenics, and the Gospel of Free Love', *Journal of the History of Sexuality*, 6 (1996), 589–603.
28. James Jackson, *How to Beget and Rear Beautiful Children* (Dansville, New York: Sanatorium Publishing Co., 1884), pp. 3–4.
29. Francis Galton, *Hereditary Genius* (London: Macmillan, 1869), p. 318.
30. R. Murray Leslie, 'Woman's Progress in Relation to Eugenics', *Eugenics Review*, 2 (1911), 284–5.
31. Havelock Ellis, *Objects of Marriage* (London: British Society for the Study of Sex Psychology, 1918), p. 7, Stella Browne, *Sexual Variety and Variability Among Women* (London: British Society for the Study of Sex Psychology, 1915), p. 13, and Catherine Gasquoine Hartley, *The Truth About Women* (London: Everleigh Nash, 1913), p. 328.
32. Hartley, *Truth About Women*, pp. 258, 328.
33. H.G. Wells, *The New Machiavelli* (London: John Lane, 1911), pp. 96, 133, and Ellis, *Objects of Marriage*, p. 20.
34. Havelock Ellis, 'Eugenics and St. Valentine', *Nineteenth Century and After*, 49 (1906), 785–6, and Caleb Saleeby, *Woman and Womanhood* (London: Heinemann, 1912), p. 139.
35. George Bernard Shaw, *Getting Married* (London: Constable, 1913), pp. 337, 404, and Marie Stopes, *The Race* (London: A.C. Fifield, 1918), p. 70.
36. Marie Stopes, *Married Love* (New York: Eugenics Publishing Company, 1918), p. 2. See also Porter and Hall, *Facts of Life*, pp. 208–12.
37. Theo van de Velde, *Ideal Marriage: Its Philosophy and Technique* (New York: Random House, 1926), p. 6.
38. Edward Brecher, *The Sex Researchers* (London: Andre Deutsch, 1970), p. 102, and Lesley Hall, 'Impotent Ghosts from No Man's Land, Flappers' Boyfriends, or Crypto-Patriarchs?: Men and Social Change in 1920s Britain', *Social History*, 21 (1996), 66–7.

39. Sheila Jeffreys, *The Spinster and Her Enemies: Feminism and Sexuality, 1880–1930* (London: Pandora Press, 1985) and Margaret Jackson, *The Real Facts of Life: Feminism and the Politics of Sexuality, 1850–1940* (London: Taylor and Francis, 1994).
40. Collins, *Modern Love*, pp. 31–2, and Hall, 'Impotent Ghosts from No Man's Land', 63.
41. Jeffrey Weeks, *Sex, Politics, and Society: The Regulation of Sexuality since 1800* (London: Longman, 1981), pp. 210–11, and Lesley Hall, *Sex, Gender and Social Change in Britain since 1880* (London: Macmillan, 2000), pp. 139–40.
42. Van de Velde, *Ideal Marriage*, p. 321.
43. Cathy Porter, *Alexandra Kollontai* (New York: The Dial Press, 1980).
44. Enid Charles, *The Twilight of Parenthood* (New York: W.W. Norton and Co., 1934), p. 89; Sir Leo Chiozza Money, 'Renew or Die!', *Nineteenth Century and After*, 120 (1936), 668–83; Sheila Fitzpatrick, *The Russian Revolution, 1917–1932* (New York: Oxford University Press, 1982), pp. 150–1, and Claudia Koonz, *Mothers in the Fatherland: Women, the Family, and Nazi Politics* (New York: St Martin's Press, 1987), pp. 185–7, 398–400.
45. For the sexual conservatism of the interwar years, see Deirdre Beddoe, *Back to Home and Duty* (London: Pandora, 1989). Pierre Berton, *The Dionne Years: A Thirties Melodrama* (New York: W.W. Norton and Co., 1977), p. 61; Marie Stopes, *Radiant Motherhood* (London: G.P. Putnam's Sons, 1920), p. 11; and Stopes, 'Married Women: In the Future – Free', *The English Review*, 34 (1922), 431.
46. Hall, *Sex, Gender and Social Change*, pp. 121–2, 136–7, and United States Post Office Department, *Excerpts from transcript from the hearing held May 14, 1959 to determine whether Grove Press, Inc. may use the facilities of the U.S. Post Office for its complete and authorized edition of Lady Chatterley's Lover* (New York: Post Office, 1959), p. 24.
47. Collins, *Modern Love*, pp. 90–8, 125; Weeks, *Sex, Politics, and Society*, p. 237.
48. Alice Echols, *Daring to be Bad: Radical Feminism in America, 1967–75* (Minneapolis: University of Minnesota Press, 1989), Anna Coote and Beatrix Campbell, *Sweet Freedom: The Struggle for Women's Liberation* (Oxford: Blackwell, 1982), and Sara Maitland, *Very Heaven: Looking Back at the 1960s* (London: Virago, 1988).
49. Jane Lewis and Kathleen Kiernan, 'The Boundaries between Marriage, Non-marriage, and Parenthood: Changes in Behaviour and Policy in Postwar Britain', *Journal of Family History*, 21 (1996), 372–87.
50. Weeks, *Sex, Politics, and Society*, pp. 294–5; Sarah Lyall, 'Legal Alternatives to Wedding Vows', *New York Times*, 15 February 2004, 3.
51. Andrew Sullivan, 'Here Comes the Groom: A (Conservative) Case for Gay Marriage', *New Republic*, 28 August 1989, 20, 22. See also Sullivan's *Same-Sex Marriage: Pro and Con* (New York: Vintage, 1997). Michael Warner, *The Trouble with Normal: Sex, Politics and the Ethics of Queer Life* (New York: The Free Press, 1999), pp. 82, 109–16.

5
race and empire

ross forman

introduction

In his essay 'The Present Phasis of Ethnology', which forms the concluding chapter to the second edition of *The Races of Men: A Philosophical Enquiry into the Influence of Race over the Destinies of Nations* (1892), Robert Knox tells his readers, 'I had but to look at the map of the world at any time in the stream of history to perceive that in all great questions of civilization, religion, national power, or greatness, the element which chiefly influenced these was in reality the element of race.'[1] Race, Knox avers, is everything, and its integrity can only be safeguarded by practices of endogamy (i.e. marriage within the group) and by the avoidance of hybridity (i.e. intermarriage with members of other groups). History, according to this theory, unfolds as a race war – a war based not primarily on real battles, but on the politics of sex. For it is through sex, through procreation, that the continuity of races is or is not maintained, and it is through sex that empires rise or fall, survive or disappear.

Knox may or may not epitomize the views of his contemporaries with his particular theory of the race war and his contention that – by analogy with the mule – human hybridity brings on sterility.[2] (Indeed, scientists during the early nineteenth century hotly debated whether human races constituted separate species, or whether they were all subspecies of a single, common race.) Nonetheless, the doctor and anatomist is undeniably representative of his age in seeing race and sex as indelibly intertwined. From at least as early as the eighteenth century – when modern Western ideas about the individual began to consolidate themselves – conceptions of race and of sexuality not only started to coalesce, but to coalesce around each other. And because this was an age of great expansion overseas, imperialism lay at the heart of this process.

Philosophical, scientific, legal, and social developments all colluded to link sexuality to race and empire. Evolutionary theory – Jean Baptiste Pierre Antoine de Monet de Lamarck as much as Charles Darwin – connected the characteristics of the individual to the fate of the 'race'; the notion that ontogeny recapitulates phylogeny – i.e. that the lifecycle of an individual mirrored that of the species to which it belonged – became the cornerstone of this new perception of subjectivity, or personhood.[3] And its corollary was that the 'perversions' – i.e. non-normative sexual acts – that were increasingly being concocted and classified at this time were themselves intimately tied to the success or failure of racial groupings. Human evolution, in short, was the sexual history of race through time.

Bearing this view of history in mind, the fundamental goal of this chapter is to sketch out some of the interconnections between race, ethnicity, empire, and sexuality. More importantly, however, the chapter underscores the centrality of this nexus to understanding the history of sexuality – not to mention 'History' itself – in the West and in the Western academy more generally. I suggest that the history of sexuality – since long before Michel Foucault published his seminal work on the topic – bases itself in notions of difference, and that race and ethnicity constitute one of the key areas of difference around which sexual subjectivities historically have been organized. Theories of sexually based difference, as Foucault emphasized, are invested with political and social authority. They form part of a complex of relations that Foucault referred to as 'biopower', meaning a form of power exercised through the body, from the inside, in such a way that an individual's sexuality becomes linked to larger issues of national, cultural, or imperial policy. Biopower therefore structures the relationship between the individual and the social whole, and life itself becomes implicated in power relations.

Foucault's assumption – but more especially that endorsed by many of his followers – that the 'discursive' explosion around sexuality in the late eighteenth and nineteenth centuries was an affair primarily internal to Europe has engendered significant criticism in recent years. Foucault was, in the words of Tony Ballantyne and Antoinette Burton, 'notoriously myopic about the domain of the colonial in his analyses of both the history of sexuality and of state-sponsored surveillance'.[4] Since the 1980s, scholars studying a wide range of colonial contexts – among them Ann Laura Stoler – have argued that, in fact, interaction with non-Western societies was crucial to the development of normative notions of sexuality in the West, as well as to the ever expanding list of perversions enumerated by Foucault in his *History of Sexuality*.[5] And scholarship showing the pervasiveness of imperialism on everyday life 'at home' in the 'mother' countries – noteworthy among them the work of Catherine Hall and Linda Colley – has demonstrated that disconnecting the metropole (or colonial centre) from the colony paints an inaccurate picture of internal, intra-European isolation.[6]

Instead, the last ten years has seen a marked shift towards understanding metropoles and colonies as part of a single analytical field.[7] As Mrinalini Sinha points out, the study of sexuality in colonial arenas therefore makes a contribution to two seminal areas of historical thinking: 'one, how to go beyond the reductive choices offered in political critiques concerned only with one or another isolated aspect of social relations; and, two, how to recast the historiographical unit of both metropolitan and colonial histories to recognise their interaction in the age of imperialism'.[8]

the rules of the race

To fully appreciate the impact that scholarship in this field has had more widely, a working definition of what we mean by 'race' and 'ethnicity' is necessary, not the least because these words have powerful political and social connotations today. We should also consider how they interact with concepts of class. Traditionally, the West has conceived of race in terms of innate characteristics, such as skin colour and body shape. Racial identity is a matter of fixity, of genetics, and races are mutually distinct. Race is lineage, and it is marked by levels of conformity to a specific standard of purity. And race is secured through bloodlines, through procreation and heritage. Because of some of the obvious problems with this concept, however, many scholars today prefer the word 'ethnicity'. In contrast to race, ethnicity acknowledges the cultural component of difference. It is mutable and contingent. It allows dangerous notions of purity – notions which carry a hint of racism and anti-Semitism and which conjure up an unsavoury legacy of Nazism, racial 'cleansing', eugenics, and discrimination – to be swept away. Above all, because ethnicity is perceived as constructed, rather than innate, it is a flexible concept that not only encompasses the definitional characteristics of the term 'race' but also goes beyond them to incorporate a number of other factors crucial to a group's sense of identity, including language, religion, and nationality. Ethnicity, for instance, allows us to account for how the Jews historically functioned as the internal 'other' in Western societies and how the Jewish man came to be defined as a sort of 'woman' within

Europe.[9] In this chapter, therefore, 'race' is used in its historical sense. It is not taken to indicate a true and measurable dividing line between different ethnic or cultural groups.

The slipperiness of the terms 'race' and 'ethnicity' encapsulates one of the most significant problems that historians of sexuality face in analysing the past in terms of imperialism and cultural difference: namely, how to avoid using terms and methodologies that contain residues of their imperialist or racist origins.[10] The problem is encapsulated by Ifi Amadiume's summation of the parallel shortcomings of social anthropology, in particular, its 'racist division of the world [into "their own the 'civilized' and others the 'primitive'"] and the indifference to those being studied'.[11] As this critique indicates, historians also have to beware of importing concepts of gender and sexuality from their own cultures which might have little local importance.[12]

Class is also an important factor in the way that race and sexuality interact. Colonial elites certainly developed for themselves, and were held to, different standards of propriety than the rest of the populace. At the same time, working-class Europeans were often likened to 'primitives' in their sexual proclivities.[13] The slums of 'darkest London' were analogues to the wilds of 'darkest Africa', places where middle-class codes of morality were suspended, if not entirely absent. This – mainly bourgeois – bias against working-class citizens and colonized peoples alike hints at the complexity of the negotiations within races and cultures that were brought to bear in the larger structures of imperial relations. Meanwhile, the notion that imperialism was itself a middle-class endeavour – that those who went out to the empire effectively became middle-class whatever their social origins – offers a conception of homogenization that relations 'on the ground' did not necessarily manifest.

The association of 'lower classes', 'lower races' and excessive sexuality of all kinds, which was a characteristic feature of Victorian thinking about race, has produced its own distortions. On the one hand, early histories of imperialism reflected a general tendency to excise sexuality, and especially sexual deviance, from their accounts. On the other, the imperial project and its proximity to the 'uncivilized' also meant that it was taken as a place of sexual licence. This once popular thesis – which posits that homosexual men and other sexual non-conformists were drawn into the empire because, through it, they could escape the strictures of their own societies – tended to redress the balance of omission too far in the other direction. This theory draws on nineteenth-century ideas such as the Sotadic Zone, Richard Burton's geography of permissive homosexuality, but inverts its perspective. Burton believed that in many parts of the non-Western world, 'the Vice [of sodomy] is popular and endemic, held at the worst to be a mere peccadillo, whilst the races to the North and South of the limits here defined practise it only sporadically among the opprobrium of their fellows who, as a rule, are physically incapable of performing the operation and look upon it with the liveliest disgust'.[14]

The sexual licence theory asserts that Western men avoided repressing their unconventional desires or becoming sexual outlaws by going out to empire, where they could take advantage of greater permissiveness in their host culture, as well as their greater distance from their own culture's moral codes. The paucity of Western women; the men's potential isolation from other Westerners in remote outposts; and the prevalence of all-male environments, such as the barracks, the boarding house, and the prison, all contributed to the invisibility of homosexuality in this context – an invisibility that allowed same-sex practices to flourish. In the 'white' colonies, like Australia, the 'great open' blank spaces of forest, deserts, and prairies allowed for similar evasions of moral strictures. Without disputing the relevance of these ideas, it is nonetheless essential to identify the liberationist thrust which underlies them and which may have led scholars in the past to overemphasize their importance – as well as to overlook the more variegated pattern of indigenous condemnation of homosexuality and of colonial enforcement of metropolitan moral standards.

By the early twentieth century, women, too, might take advantage of this apparent permissiveness. Lesbians or women-identified women, those pursuing relationships outside of wedlock, stigmatized divorcees, and others all might look to the colonies for a better life. We have only to remember that the protagonist of Radclyffe Hall's *The Well of Loneliness* (1928) escapes to the Canadian forests to be a lesbian for an example of this thesis at work.

Ronald Hyam's groundbreaking *Empire and Sexuality* (1990) was the prime example of the 'empire as space of sexual liberation' theory. Whatever its excesses, Hyam's work rightly insisted that 'sexual dynamics crucially underpinned the whole operation of British empire and Victorian expansion'.[15] Yet he also falls into this trap of uncritically asserting that there was greater scope for homosexuality in the colonies than at home. In a similar vein, Robert Aldrich's *Colonialism and Homosexuality* (2003) directs his exploration of the sexual possibilities that empire afforded to male colonists towards the celebratory and recuperative. Imperialism was, at best, merely uneven in its application of moral and legal discrimination against non-normative sexuality. At worst, it could be even more draconian than the metropole. Philippa Levine's recent study of the application of contagious diseases legislation to regulate prostitution in

British colonies has, for instance, unearthed significant variation in the severity of enforcement and also shown that in some contexts, repressive measures far outlasted those in Britain. As all this work indicates, we need to be careful with methodology and terminology in histories of race and sexuality. In particular, we should perhaps beware of describing the supposedly 'liberated' space of the empire, since concepts like this reflect embedded notions about the intersection of class, race and geography that were inherent to the imperialist project and have their origins in Victorian imperialism.

adventures in the imperial archive

The issue of terminology raised above, in turn, points to another challenge: the nature of the evidence that historians in this field have at their disposal. Here, too, the field is diverse. Patterns for the regulation of sex, the rhetoric about it, and even sexual tastes themselves naturally have varied according to region and climate, according to the ethnicities of the different parties involved, and according to the specific temporal moment. In addition, there is usually much more to say about the colonizer's perspective than about the colonized's. The reason for this imbalance is in part because of issues of illiteracy (on the part of colonial subjects) and translation and because the colonizers were the main record-keepers; in addition, the imbalance persists in part because scholarship on sexuality is itself concentrated in the Western academy. Thus while anthropology tells us much about the sexual behaviour of different societies around the world over the last few hundred years, it is not without historical biases; sometimes it tells us more about the ethnographers than about the ethnographic subject. And especially with oral cultures, there can be no 'means testing' of the realities that these colonial or anthropological documents represent: we may have little access to what cultures without writing thought about sexuality before the moment of 'first contact' with Western outsiders.

For the same reason, studies of the relationship between race and empire and the history of sexuality have tended to concentrate on the post-Enlightenment period; records for earlier periods or about earlier empires are necessarily sparser.[16] And consistent with the way in which sexuality as a whole has been studied, much more attention has been paid to urban sites in both colonies and metropoles than to rural ones, where source material is harder to access, in part because of the lack of organized communities of sexual subcultures.

Issues of documentation have also affected our picture of same-sex behaviours among women in the empire. Because legal restrictions on homosexuality nearly always centred on sex between men and because empire was often (if unfairly) conceptualized as a male endeavour, lesbianism and other forms of female desire have received less attention than they merit. This is not to say that there are no sources, just that they are fewer in number than those on male homosexuality, and those that do cover these areas (such as the 1904 *Crossways of Sex: A Study in Eroto-Pathology* by one Dr 'Jacobus X') were often written by men.[17]

Partly for this reason of documentation, prostitution has proved to be a major area of study. The history of the Contagious Diseases Act in Britain and the extensive archive surrounding the regulation of the sex trade in the colonies has proved a fruitful way to examine tensions between colony and metropole.[18] Materials about prostitution provide important information about women's position in various colonial settings, about their physical attributes, and about the interface between local social customs and imperial sexual policies. Nevertheless, although prostitution brings non-European women's perspectives into the fold, the women themselves remain relatively voiceless.

Sex scandals have also proved a popular subject of study because they, too, engender a wealth of information about sexual norms; in addition, they generally offer a diverse documentary base, running the gamut from court proceedings to newspaper articles to cartoons and dramatic sketches. Indeed, the Oscar Wilde trial in the 1890s reverberated across the British Empire and beyond, inaugurating wide-ranging discussions of homosexuality in a variety of arenas.

Another way in which the availability of source material has affected the field comes in the use of literature. Literary sources have played a fundamental role in informing studies of race, empire, and sexuality. There are two reasons for this cross-fertilization. On the one hand the interdisciplinary nature of much writing on the connection between literature and imperialism encourages such meetings. On the other, fiction has been an important site for examining questions of hybridity thrown up by interracial relationships and colonial encounters. Two classic examples might suffice here: first, Edward Said's account of the imperial connections behind the English wealth portrayed in Jane Austen's *Mansfield Park*. In drawing these links out, Said shows that a seemingly neutral literary canon, apparently distant from the fact of empire was in fact minutely implicated in Caribbean colonial wealth. In contrast, Jonathan Dollimore's account of how Andre Gide and Oscar Wilde met briefly in a Morroccan brothel in 1895 demonstrated how the quest for sexual fulfilment might also be shrouded by racial ideologies and imperial contexts.[19] Literary scholars have also generated interest in imperial histories of affect or sentiment. Taking its cue from Foucault's contention that 'all sentiments have a history', the study of affect in different colonial contexts aims to recover what the anxieties (on both sides) about sentimental relationships between Europeans and non-Europeans were, and what the benefits were, too. This study identifies the family as a crucial site for the production of and intervention into colonial discourses; it brings aspects of childrearing, education, and camaraderie into larger debates about sexuality and biopower.[20]

What the history of sexuality's healthy interaction with the fields of literary and cultural studies points out is the inherent necessity of an interdisciplinary background for analyses of race and empire. Some political and economic historians have expressed scepticism about history's 'cultural turn' (of which the use of literary theory to think about sexuality and race is a symptom), largely because of its lack of interest in empiricism. Yet most have embraced the change enthusiastically. In imperial studies, dialogue with other related fields – notably art history, museum studies, film theory, and anthropology – have proved similarly fruitful.[21]

Much of this work typifies a wider trend towards identifying new archival sources. Seemingly neutral sources like census reports or apparently non-colonial popular cultural artefacts like folk art and pornography have been made to speak important details about sexual and racial histories. Vicente L. Rafael's book *White Love and Other Events in Filipino History* (2000) takes the census as its main archive, and refers in its title to the policy of 'benevolent assimilation' pursued by the Americans after taking control of the Philippines following the 1898 war with Spain. Rafael reads the US government's 1903 census of the Philippine Islands as a crucial tool in this policy because it ordered native races into '*a* people'. A census, he reminds us, confirms 'the state's ability to represent, and so govern itself. In enumerating and classifying the resources and population of the state, censuses render visible the entire field of colonial intervention.'[22] In Latin American Studies, the eighteenth-century tradition of *casta* painting has come under similar scrutiny: these allegorical paintings show the union of a man and woman of different races and their offspring (e.g. 'Spanish with black makes mulatto'); in so doing, they elucidate how racial categorization provided an important mechanism for controlling Spain's colonial subjects.

As Sarah Leonard shows in this volume, pornography has also been recently added to the colonial archive and has been made to yield detailed information about sexual fantasies and their interpolation within cultures. At the same time, pornography provides a map of how and what sex was practised – and by whom. Malek Alloula's *Colonial Harem* (1986) was a notable example in this area. His analysis of pornographic postcards of Algerian women uncovered widespread and largely unknown patterns for the circulation of erotica, charted the process by which individuated images of women became amalgamated into (and erased by) a conception of the 'femme Arabe', and highlighted an extremely invasive aspect of imperialism: its penetration into the private sphere – in this case the harem, one of the most hidden corners of 'native' life – for the purposes of sexual gratification.[23] The increasing variety of sources and methodologies in imperial histories of sexuality can only be glimpsed here, but this diversity is fundamental in reinserting both race and the colonial subject into the history of 'Western' sexuality. In fact, these histories show that the idea of a European and American 'West' isolated and sealed off from the influences of its empires is both false and, more perniciously, invested with all kinds of ideological assumptions, some of which will be dealt with below.

miscegenation: a topic for our times

One of the central axes around which thinking about race and sexuality has revolved is the issue of miscegenation. This term and its many variants – *mestizaje, mestizo, métisse,* and so on – refer to the union of two people of different 'racial' stock and to their children, normally called hybrids, or, in racist discourse, half-breeds or half-castes. Discussions of miscegenation often invoke the notion of the 'colour line', an imaginary boundary between 'races' that is crossed when members of different groups have sex with each other and reproduce. This line, sometimes also called the 'colour bar', has been an important metaphor of ethnically 'transgressive' sex for at least the last century.

The reasons for miscegenation's prominence in this field are perhaps obvious, but a brief outline of them clarifies why the topic has proved so enduring: First, scholarly investment in miscegenation reflects the interest in (and anxiety about) immigration that has become a staple part of the political and social landscape of Western Europe and North America since the end of the Second World War. Second, scholarship on miscegenation responds to changing sexual values in the West that have seen interethnic/'interracial' marriages go from being taboo and stigmatized to being widely visible in the media and on the street. Third, miscegenation as an act reduces the encounter between cultures to its most basic and controversial components, so it is only natural that historians should want to engage with it. Miscegenation illuminates the boundaries between cultures, races, ethnicities, and nations; it provides the perfect illustration of the popular civil rights maxim that the personal is political. Fourth, the explosion of research on sexual violence has had its impact on the field of race and the history of sexuality by drawing attention to the way in which rape (in places such as Rwanda and Kosovo) forms a part of programmes of 'ethnic cleansing'. What could be worse than having to bear and to raise an enemy's children? Finally, literary scholars such as Homi K. Bhabha have argued persuasively that hybridity is inherently subversive, providing a location from which power can be challenged. This thesis has encouraged scholars on the left to pursue miscegenation and hybridity in order to recover a genealogy of anti-imperialist sentiment, although work since the late 1990s has acknowledged, as Stoler puts it, that 'mixing could provide access to some privileges while it sharply blocked access to others'. 'Recurrent debates about who was "mixed",' she continues, 'could as easily confirm as contest truth-claims about other bold-faced social categories.'[24]

To better understand how historians have conceptualized the links between miscegenation and imperial cultures, it may be helpful to delineate who was mixing with whom. Scholars normally divide colonies into two types: settler colonies, where people from Europe tended to immigrate on a permanent basis, and occupation colonies, where a small colonial elite presided over a much larger indigenous population. The so-called 'white' colonies – such as Canada, Australia, and South Africa in the British case – are examples of the former group. The bulk of the West's colonies – such as Indochina in the French case or Indonesia in the Netherlands's – were of the latter type.

The way sexuality was treated and, consequently, the way it has been studied differ between the two groups of colonies. To generalize, places with large white populations and small indigenous communities pursued assimilationist policies, whereby white models of masculinity and femininity were imposed on the rest of the populace. In Australia, for instance, the state removed Aboriginal children from their parents until as late as the 1970s, placing them with white foster parents in order to separate them from their 'primitive' origins. Meanwhile, places with small white populations focused on strategies for endogamy. In late Victorian India, for example, women unable to find partners in Britain took advantage of free passage on steamships to marry colonists in the subcontinent. These 'odd women' – there were statistically more men than women in Britain at the end of the nineteenth century – thus helped to safeguard the racial 'integrity' of the British population overseas.

However, both settler colonies and occupation colonies – not to mention the multiracial societies that they left behind – placed great emphasis on policing racial boundaries, severely restricting and penalizing sex across colour lines. Because race and power were so intimately intertwined, transethnic sex could serve as a weapon of empowerment or disempowerment. In the Caribbean, families often encouraged women to 'marry up' – to find a partner of lighter skin than their own – so that their children, over progressive generations, would become increasingly whiter. Some light-skinned people adhered to the practice of 'passing': that is, they passed themselves off as white in order to access the privileges attached to that racial designation.

In the post-Civil War American South, the Jim Crow laws were used to prevent sex between black and white people. It was not until the case of *Love* v. *Virginia* in 1967 that the US Supreme Court struck down legislation prohibiting interracial marriage. As part of the legacy of slavery, US states regularly applied the 'one drop' theory in classifying people racially. In some states, anyone who was 1/32 or more black could be legally considered black. This theory prompted a famous response by the Haitian dictator 'Papa Doc' Duvalier. When asked in an interview with an American publication what percentage of Haiti's population was white, Duvalier replied that over 98 per cent were – since one of the consequences of slavery was that nearly everyone had some drops of white blood in them.[25] Policies as repressive as those in the American South also applied in South Africa during the apartheid era, where the Prohibition of Mixed Marriages Act of 1949 and the Immorality Act of 1950 made interracial sex a serious crime.

As Kevin Mumford points out in his study of Chicago and New York, 'In our culture, when a black person has sexual relations with a white person, the act is often controversial and always extraordinary. Because of history – slavery, racism, gender relations, sexual repression, power politics – sex across the color line always represents more than just sex.'[26] In other words, transethnic sex constitutes a particularly dense 'transfer point' for cultural negotiation of all kinds, and it is not surprising that since the 1970s and 1980s scholars have turned to the history of sexuality in large numbers to study such phenomena as imperialism, slavery, and domesticity. These studies have been intimately tied to larger political movements, such as the growth of civil rights activism, the rise of feminism, and the development of organized gay, lesbian, and transgender groups not just in Europe and the United States, but across the globe. As notions of normative masculine and feminine roles are increasingly contested, so too are ideas of racial essentialism and of the automatic mapping of race onto culture. The emergence of the category of the 'bi-racial' has been a particularly salient intervention into this debate in the last fifteen years. Although society may pressure them to adopt a particular position, children who have parents of different races no longer feel that they must choose to belong exclusively to either one group or the other.

Of course, miscegenation has not always been seen in a negative light, either by people living in multiethnic societies or by scholars. In the 1930s, Brazilian anthropologist Gilberto Freyre developed a highly influential theory in favour of miscegenation in his book *Casa-grande e senzala* (*The Masters and the Slaves*), as well as his subsequent work.[27] Known as lusotropicalism, this theory claims that there was a major difference in the way that the Portuguese carried out their overseas expansion in comparison with the French and the British. Whereas the latter powers restricted contact between Europeans and those they ruled, the former welcomed miscegenation. For Freyre, Portugal's encouragement of miscegenation was its greatest success. It had, he argued, turned Brazil into a land of racial harmony, a racial paradise, based on fraternity and love. Slavery, he insisted, had therefore been a more benign institution in Brazil (which, in 1888, was the world's last country to abolish it) than elsewhere, and was characterized by a beneficent paternalism that contrasted sharply with the brutality of the Caribbean or the American South. Freyre compared Brazil to Texas where, in the 1920s, he had witnessed horrific levels of racism and racial segregation.

Freyre's concept of lusotropicalism was hotly debated in the American academy. It was also adopted (with some variations) by the Portuguese dictator Antonio de Oliveira Salazar, who used it to shore up repressive policies in colonial Africa in the postwar period.[28] Today, lusotropicalism has been widely discredited – not least because other scholars have exposed the highly racist organization of Brazilian society. But it has remained an important intervention into the history of imperialism because of the way in which it places race and sex at the heart of colonization and the way it makes them central to the legacy of imperialism in the contemporary world. Freyre's emphasis on distinguishing between European powers and their differing methods of colonization also turned scholars' attention to what is now one of the most dynamic areas of empire studies: research with a comparative focus, rather than one defined by specifically national or area studies boundaries.

Ironically, though, this turn to conceiving of colonialism in a comparative frame has elicited further proof that Freyre's claims for the uniqueness of Portugal's promotion of miscegenation were misguided. For however much sex across the 'colour line' came to be stigmatized, especially in British and French colonies, most historians of sexuality agree that this interdiction was a product of modernity, industrialization, and the rise of scientific racism, rather than a pattern of longstanding tradition. In fact, it seems clear that until some time in the nineteenth century, formal or informal relationships between male colonists and women of the local community were the norm. Most men involved in empire-building – especially before the nineteenth century's improvements in transport and communication, such as the telegraph, steamship, and railways – were young, and they stayed abroad for considerable periods, if not for the rest of their lives. So it was only natural that they sought to satisfy their desires for sex and affection within local communities. In many places, these men's relationships with native women often were consecrated as marriages. At the same time, a system of concubinage applied, where a man had an indigenous mistress who lived with him but did not attend official functions as the man's spouse. These relationships were especially common among men of the colonial civil service or merchant communities, who might or might not be settling permanently in the colony. They might persist for life, or they might be suspended when the colonizer either returned to his 'mother' country during a period of leave or obtained a rank that obliged him to acquire a Western wife.

During the nineteenth century, changes in the structures of imperialism, combined with changes in the intellectual climate, meant that relations between Western men and indigenous women became increasingly restrictive – or at least, more clandestine. (Recent scholarship on the British Empire has demonstrated that rates of concubinage did not decline as rapidly as had been thought during this period.) The growth of scientific racism made sex across colour lines more dangerous and taboo, converting what had been personal choice into an issue of national and racial integrity. The increased immigration of women and families from the West to the colonies made it socially unacceptable to prefer a member of the colonized race to one's own. And political insurrections in places such as India led to new modes of regulating contact between colonizers and colonial subjects. The 1857 Mutiny or Sepoy Rebellion in India, for instance, was a watershed, marking the point at which corporate colonialism carried out under the auspices of the British East India Company transmuted into direct, formal imperialism under the aegis of the British Crown. Concomitant with this change, as Jenny Sharpe has shown, was a change in sexual politics. Reporting of the Mutiny stressed the sexual violation of white women by Indians, and after 1857, Sharpe argues, rape became a governing metaphor of imperial relations.[29] Confrontation replaced concubinage as a model for cultural interaction.

Racism frequently depends on mutual dislike, even if one side of the equation enjoys greater power over the other. So it is therefore not surprising that on the other side of the colour bar, many colonized societies were equally resistant to relations with white men (and occasionally women). In areas where Europeans and the Chinese rubbed shoulders, for instance (such as Hong Kong, Shanghai, and the Malay peninsula), women might be considered dead by their families if they took up with a 'white ghost'. (Jewish groups traditionally have treated marriage 'outside the tribe' similarly, sitting *Shiva* – i.e. mourning – members who marry non-Jews.) Conversely, East Asian men entertained a fascination with white women – no doubt according to the principle that forbidden fruits taste the sweetest. As Joseph Crad was told by his guide to brothels in Shanghai in *Traders in Women: A Comprehensive Survey of 'White Slavery'* (1940), 'A Chinaman, or for that matter any man of the Mongolian races, will pay ten times as much to have an Englishwoman or American for his bed-mate as he will pay for one of his own race and colour.'[30] During the interwar period, when large numbers of Russian Jews emigrated to Shanghai following the upheavals of the Russian Revolution, brothels catering to this taste for white 'flesh' burgeoned – often causing moral outrage among white observers.

Paradoxically, as legitimate relationships across colour lines became more and more circumscribed during the nineteenth century, they also became rhetorically more important. This turn was especially prominent in the newly independent countries of North and South America, where a process of nation-building encouraged the search for the mythic origins of discrete communities. This search led to the establishment of what Doris Sommer has called 'foundational fictions' – narratives of national identity that generally grounded themselves in 'originary' acts of miscegenation.[31] Sommer points to crucial texts, such as the writer José Alencar's *Iraçema* (1865), in which the title character (whose name is an anagram for 'America') is an Indian woman who gives birth to the first Brazilian child through her union with a Portuguese colonist. More controversial is the figure of La Malinche, the Aztec noblewoman who helped her lover Hernán Cortés to conquer Moctezuma's empire. Depending on one's perspective, La Malinche either gave birth to the first Mexican or was a traitor who helped to destroy and enslave millions of indigenous people. In North America, the invention of traditions such as Thanksgiving relied on a similar story of miscegenation – that of John Smith and Pocahontas – to allegorize the US as a benign, modern nation, founded on peace and goodwill. Such a narrative of positive miscegenation thus sutures over the history of violent contacts between colonists and First Peoples and the genocidal practices in which some colonists engaged in order to 'clear' the land for their own uses, including giving blankets infected with smallpox to Native Americans.

scientific racism and the study of sexuality

As noted above, restrictions on the practice of miscegenation have varied significantly according to the groups being examined and the time period being studied, and there is often an inconsistency between the theory governing such interaction and the sex people actually had with each other. However, one of the central arguments which Foucault and the 'social construction' school which came after him have made is that the regulation of sexuality changed radically in the eighteenth and nineteenth centuries. Foucault famously argued that this was the period in which acts transformed into identities, in which people's sexual behaviours became constitutive of their subjectivity. As a result, a plethora of sexual categories were formulated, and an ever-expanding list of 'perversions' was produced. What scholars of race and empire have widely noted is that during the same period, race also became a category that was similarly constitutive of identity. The fact that these developments in the understanding of race and sexuality occurred at the same time is no accident, and many scholars have contended that contact with the world outside of Europe was to a fair degree responsible for the general trend according to which taxonomies of individual behaviour began to be applied to groups (thus creating categories like the 'homosexual').

One of the ways in which these changes manifested themselves is in the development of scientific racism, a social theory which argues that race conforms to scientific principles and manifests itself in specific, measurable ways. Scientific racism treats the body as a text and claims that it can be read for signs of normality or abnormality, degeneracy, criminality, and so on. Until the wide-scale spread of Darwin's theory of evolution in the mid-nineteenth century, such scientific studies of race tended to fall into two general camps: monogeny and polygeny. As Siobhan Somerville explains, 'Monogeny, which had been the prevailing theory in eighteenth century studies of racial difference, held that all of the so-called races were members of the same species and that they descended from common ancestry.' Monogenists believed that environmental conditions, such as climate and civilization, were responsible for differences in race. Polygeny, by contrast, 'held that different races were actually different species with distinct biological origins'.[32]

After the publication of *The Origin of Species* in 1859, concepts of polygeny began to die out. They were replaced, however, with evolutionary models of race that expounded a theory of the hierarchy (or ladder) of races. This was the 'great chain of being', according to which some races were more evolved or civilized than others, and all races could be ranked according to their levels of 'primitivity'. The most 'primitive' races, such as the Aboriginals of Australia, were said to be without culture. Those of African stock were low on the scale, whereas white northern Europeans were usually at the top. 'By the middle of the nineteenth century', Nancy Stepan points out in *The Idea of Race in Science* (1982), 'everyone was agreed, it seemed, that in essential ways the white race was superior to non-white races.'[33] The power dynamics implicit in this hierarchy are clear, and scientific racism was widely used to justify a range of oppressive policies in colonial and ex-slave contexts.

Crucially for our purposes here, sexual conduct became an important way that races came to be categorized. How different racial groups reproduced, the level to which they indulged in any of the new list of perversions, and their adherence to taboos against incest were all linked to their place in the ladder of races. In the eighteenth century, theorists and philosophers had invested in a notion of the 'noble savage', according to which non-Western peoples were in a state of blissful ignorance about the evils of civilization, living pure and simple lives. However, with the expansion of colonization and the concurrent development of scientific racism, non-Western societies – particularly those in Africa, Australia, and the Americas – were taken to represent an earlier stage in the historical evolution towards the civilized – i.e. towards Western modes of social organization. Consequently, primitive peoples were inherently libidinous; they lacked the ability to control their desires. They might therefore indulge in a variety of unacceptable sexual behaviours, including incest, homosexuality, and bestiality. Marriage was often by 'bride capture' or purchase, polygamy and polyandry were rife, and child marriages common. (Polygamy usually is defined as the state of having two or more wives at the same time, while polyandry refers to the state of having two or more husbands simultaneously.)

At the perverse end of the spectrum were a variety of practices of genital mutilation: female and male circumcision, castration, and the like were all the province of the primitive. (Traces of these attitudes persist today in some of the debates about female genital mutilation in Africa, where notions of 'civilization' are invoked to brand 'traditional' African societies as intrinsically 'barbaric'.) Another perverse custom was footbinding, where Chinese women's feet were crippled in girlhood to make them more sexually appealing to men. This custom was a source of endless fascination to nineteenth-century observers; more recently, it has become a subject of interest among feminist critics. Also at this end of the spectrum were practices such as widow sacrifice, where a Hindu widow known as a *sati* (or *suttee*) immolated herself on her husband's funeral pyre, and *purdah* and other forms of secluding women, such as the harem.[34]

The more 'primitive' the race, the more aberrant its sexual practice and even its physiognomy were thought to be. Black men became mythically well-endowed, the large size of their genitals symbolizing their low levels of morality. They were as much like apes as like men, a convention lent legitimacy by Darwinian ideas about sexual evolution. The most famous of black women was the deformed 'Hottentot Venus', a South African woman named Saarjite or Sara Baartman, who was put 'on display' as an example of savage primitivism in London in 1810. Her steatopygia, or enlarged buttocks, announced a racially marked perversity that she ostensibly shared with all other black women, regardless of their appearance or background.[35] As Frantz Fanon somewhat crudely concluded in *Black Skins, White Masks* (1952), 'For the majority of white men the Negro represents the sexual instinct (in its raw state). The Negro is the incarnation of a genital potency beyond all moralities and prohibitions. The women among the whites, by a genuine process of induction, invariably view the Negro as the keeper of the impalpable gate that opens into the realm of orgies, of bacchanals, of delirious sexual sensations…'[36] Other groups were similarly subject to stereotyping around presumed sexual issues. The Trobriand Islanders, in the South Pacific, were believed to be so primitive that they could not even make the connection between sex and pregnancy.[37]

Male–male sexual contact was also an indication of levels of savagery versus civilization; what Rudi Bleys has termed a 'geography of perversion' unfolded during the course of the eighteenth and nineteenth centuries to embrace the non-Western world. (Earlier writers had also linked homosex to the state of civilization. Edward Gibbon, for instance, claimed in *The History of the Decline and Fall of the Roman Empire* (1776–78) that homosexual acts contributed to the degeneration of Roman power under the emperor Hadrian. However, these writers relied on a notion of decadence, rather than assuming a trajectory of civilization leading from the primitive to the modern.) The emerging field of psychoanalysis linked homosexuality to stunted intellectual growth – homosexuals were those who failed to progress along the Freudian schema of development from the oral stage to the anal stage through to the genital stage – thereby creating a parallel with the idea that 'natives' were like children. The presence of homosex among 'primitive' peoples 'eventually consolidated the analogical structure of human anthropology in an evolutionary context. More specifically, it sanctified the newly conceptualised medical stigmatization of same-sex praxis at once as a sign of inferior evolutionary status ("endemic sodomy/pederasty") and of "degenerate", pathological heritage ("homosexuality").'[38]

If sexual excess and aberration characterized less evolved groups, temperance and control, by contrast, was the hallmark of 'modern' man. In Europe and North America, unnatural desires were curbed, subject to legal and social checks, and systems were put into place to prevent inappropriate sexual behaviour from occurring. These norms were simultaneously exported to the colonies. Scientific racism thus worked hand in hand with religious missionaries (who constituted an informal colonial force across the world) to promote the 'civilizing mission' that would instil similar methods of control onto the benighted heathens. The 'white man's burden' was therefore intimately tied to the control of sexuality. Eugenics – the attempt to engineer a society towards specific, racially defined goals through the regulation of heredity – also blossomed as a result of the identification of these norms and the ways in which racial others ostensibly failed to achieve them.

Projecting these models back in time also gave rise to some of the fundamental theories of civilization. From the nineteenth century until at least as late as the mid-twentieth, social theorists widely assumed that 'primitive' societies represented earlier moments in a trajectory of cultural evolution, as well as physical evolution. In these societies' customs and beliefs, therefore, a self-affirming history of civilization could be grounded. And that history was usually, in one form or another, a history of sexuality. In contrast to earlier ideas of the social contract as the foundation of civilization, these histories averred that it was prohibitions and regulations around sexual conduct that gave rise to civilization.

For example, in *Totem and Taboo*, subtitled 'Some Points of Agreement between the Mental Lives of Savages and Neurotics' (1913), Sigmund Freud attributes the birth of civilization to two factors: the development of the taboo against cannibalism and the repression of homosexual desire.[39] Catherine Mayo's exoneration of British imperialism in South

Asia in *Mother India* (1927) blamed the 'whole pyramid of India's woes' on the Indian man's 'manner of getting into the world and his sex-life thenceforward'.[40] As late as the 1930s, American anthropologist Margaret Mead relied on a similar timeline between primitivity and civilization in her study *Sex and Temperament in Three Primitive Societies* (1935): 'I studied this problem in simple societies because here we have the drama of civilization writ small, a social microcosm alike in kind, but different in size and magnitude, from the complex social structures of people who, like our own, depend upon a written tradition and upon the integration of a great number of conflicting historical traditions.'[41] Claude Levi-Strauss's anthropological works in the postwar period also viewed restrictions on incest in 'primitive' societies as the source of social organization.

Needless to say, all of these theories have come under attack in the last twenty to thirty years, mainly by scholars from or located in the West. Yet they have also engendered other, more socially conservative reactions from Africa and Asia. Foucault's powerful assertion that sexual acts transmuted into identities has prompted the response from within the former sites of imperialism that 'non-normative' sexualities like homosexuality have no basis in indigenous practice. Instead, they are simply another one of the 'negative' consequences of colonialism itself. In Africa in particular, cultural critics, politicians, and religious authorities alike often have united in their insistence that homosexuality is 'un-African' and did not exist before the arrival of Europeans.[42] In effect, the Western colonist's assertion that sexual depravity emanates from beyond Europe's pale has been turned back on itself: here, a pre-colonial paradise has been tainted by Western sexual perversity, just as self-sufficient agrarian economies in Africa were ruthlessly impoverished by the process of colonialism and its aftermath.

Whatever moral high ground this position lays claim to, however, it does not tally with history. Anthropological research indicates that homosocial behavioural patterns and homosexual acts are longstanding practices in sub-Saharan Africa. Nonetheless, such a belief in homosexuality as 'un-African' has been used to legitimate legal and social repression against gay men in many African nations. In places such as Zimbabwe, this belief has had wide political ramifications; the dictatorial leader Robert Mugabe has enlisted homophobia as part of his campaign to blame Britain for the country's failing economy and to justify the political repression of opposition groups, as well as devastating land reform policies, all under the banner of freeing his people by returning to 'authentic' African values. Homophobia also played a part in the persistent denial by Thabo Mbeki's government in South Africa that HIV causes AIDS, which has had a disastrous effect on millions of people's access to anti-viral medication. As AIDS activist Zackie Achmat pointed out as early as 1993, 'In Southern Africa, the attempts to fix ethnic and political identities through "culture and tradition" necessarily enforce prejudices against lesbians, gay men, women and youth.'[43] Achmat goes on to say that against the backdrop of the AIDS/HIV pandemic, recovering the historical genealogies of queer identity in prisons and labour compounds is central to transforming power relations in the region.

In the Caribbean, particularly in Jamaica and Trinidad, legal structures according to which the final court of appeal resides in Britain's Privy Council have come under threat in good part because of claims that homosexuality is antithetical to traditional moral beliefs. As a result, in 2002, West Indian leaders agreed to create a Caribbean Court of Justice to replace the Privy Council. Questions of sexual morality have therefore led independent states to conclude that the former colonial power, which designed their legal system, should no longer have the right to be its ultimate arbiter. Thus it could be argued that the final acts of decolonization are taking placing around the contest between Europe's liberalization of sexual polices and its former colonies' refusal to participate in this project. In Britain's five remaining territories in the Caribbean, the Privy Council was forced in 2001 to impose the decriminalization of consensual homosexuality after local legislatures refused to repeal anti-gay laws. The move sparked widespread protest, particularly by religious leaders, who claimed that Britain was interfering with legitimate cultural expression in the Caribbean. Elsewhere in the former colonial world, high rates of divorce, sexual violence, and promiscuity have similarly been ascribed to the erosion of indigenous moral systems by the forces of empire.

Within the West, social conservatives and politicians have also manipulated the relationship between race and sexuality to promote their agendas, often with an anti-immigrant bias. Islamophobia has, in part, led to the conceptualization of Muslims, particularly those from the Arab world, in racial terms, which, in turn, has brought their sexuality into the public domain. For instance, recent debates in France and Italy about Muslim women's right to wear veils or headscarves in schools and in passport and identity card photographs have sought to construct Arabs in particular as unwelcome aliens; their 'refusal' to assimilate is thereby constituted as a threat to the secular, humanist state. The difficulties faced by European governments in recognizing polygamy has also had a tragic effect on some people from north and sub-Saharan Africa (many of whom are refugees). Upholding legal structures of monogamy has destroyed families by denying 'lesser' wives and their children permission to immigrate, rights of residence, and welfare benefits. The wide debate in many European states (not to mention Japan) about whether citizenship should be based on place of birth (*jus solis*) or on 'blood' ties measured through notions of common 'racial' or ethnic heritage (*jus sanguinis*) is another instance in which racial and sexual politics have come together in the contemporary world.

The point of these examples is not to give a polemical overview of contemporary politics, but to illuminate why studying the history of sexuality is so vitally stimulating. Not only has the history of sexuality offered tools to all sides of these debates by identifying the longstanding links between sex, race, and empire and by tracing the patterns of the West's engagement with the 'rest' through the imbrication of sexuality and race. It has also played a dynamic role in shaping the very terms of these debates themselves, one that it should continue to play in the future. By studying what Judith Butler has called 'bodies that matter', the history of sexuality goes beyond the hallowed halls of the academy. In short, it has the critical potential to make a difference in the world today.

notes

1. Robert Knox, *The Races of Men: A Philosophical Enquiry into the Influence of Race over the Destinies of Nations*, 2nd edn (London: Henry Renshaw, 1862), p. 563.
2. Peter Mandler has recently suggested that critical interest in Knox exceeds his own influence during his lifetime and argues that biological discourses of race have been overstated. See 'The Problem with Cultural History', *Cultural and Social History*, 1, 1 (2004), 97–103.
3. Lamarck's belief that acquired characteristics could be inherited was extremely promiment and remained relevant to debates about acquired or innate homosexuality throughout the period.
4. See Tony Ballantyne and Antoinette Burton, 'Postscript: Bodies, Genders, Empires: Reimagining World Histories', in Tony Ballantyne and Antoinette Burton (eds.), *Bodies in Contact: Rethinking Colonial Encounters in World History* (Durham: Duke University Press, 2005), p. 406.
5. See Ann Laura Stoler, *Race and the Education of Desire: Foucault's History of Sexuality and the Colonial Order of Things* (Durham: Duke University Press, 1995).
6. See, for instance, Catherine Hall, *Civilising Subjects: Metropole and Colony in the English Imagination 1830–1867* (London: Polity, 2002); Catherine Hall (ed.), *Cultures of Empire: Colonizers in Britain and the Empire in the Nineteenth and Twentieth Centuries* (Manchester: Manchester University Press, 2000).
7. For an excellent analysis of this shift, see Frederick Cooper and Ann Laura Stoler, 'Between Metropole and Colony: Rethinking a Research Agenda', in Frederick Cooper and Ann Laura Stoler (eds.), *Tensions of Empire: Colonial*

Cultures in a Bourgeois World (Berkeley: University of California Press, 1997), pp. 1–56.

8. Mrinalini Sinha, *Colonial Masculinity: The 'Manly Englishman' and the 'Effeminate Bengali' in the Late Nineteenth Century* (Manchester: Manchester University Press, 1995), p. 181.
9. See Daniel Boyarin, *Unheroic Conduct: The Rise of Heterosexuality and the Invention of the Jewish Man* (Berkeley: University of California Press, 1997), p. 5.
10. See, for instance, bell hooks, *Black Looks: Race and Representation* (New York: Between the Lines, 1992), p. 89.
11. Ifi Amadiume, *Male Daughters, Female Husbands: Gender and Sex in an African Society* (London: Zed Books, 1987), p. 2.
12. On the usefulness of Western notions of effeminacy in studying South Asia see Peter Jackson and Gerald Sullivan who discuss some of the issues around Western scholarship on Asia in 'A Panoply of Roles: Sexual and Gender Diversity in Contemporary Thailand', *Lady Boys, Tom Boys, Rent Boys: Male and Female Homosexualities in Contemporary Thailand* (New York: Harrington Press, 1999), pp. 1–27.
13. Seth Koven, *Slumming: Sexual and Social Politics in Victorian London* (Princeton: Princeton University Press, 2004), p. 61.
14. See Sir Richard Burton, 'Terminal Essay', *A Plain and Literal Translation of the Arabian Nights' Entertainments, Now Entituled The Book of the Thousand Nights and a Night with Introduction[,] Explanatory Notes on the Manners and Customs of Moslem Men and a Terminal Essay Upon the History of The Nights*, vol. 10 (Benares: Kamashastra Society, 1886), p. 207. Burton considered the Sotadic Zone to be more climatologically and geographically determined than racially.
15. Ronald Hyam, *Empire and Sexuality* (Manchester: Manchester University Press, 1990), p. 1.
16. Notable exceptions include Richard Trexler, *Sex and Conquest: Gendered Violence, Political Order, and the European Conquest of the Americas* (Ithaca: Cornell University Press, 1995).
17. Jacobus, X... [pseud.], *Crossways of Sex: A Study in Eroto-Pathology*, 2 vols (Paris: British Bibliophiles Society, 1904).
18. Philippa Levine, *Prostitution, Race, and Politics: Policing Venereal Disease in the British Empire* (New York: Routledge, 2003), p. 34.
19. Edward Said, *Culture and Imperialism* (London: Chatto and Windus, 1993), pp. 95–116; Jonathan Dollimore, *Sexual Dissidence: Augustine to Wilde, Freud to Foucault* (Oxford: Clarendon, 1991), pp. 3–6.
20. See Ann Laura Stoler, *Carnal Knowledge and Imperial Power: Race and the Intimate in Colonial Rule* (Berkeley: University of California Press, 2002), pp. 112–39.
21. See, for instance, Richard Dyer, *White* (London: Routledge, 1997); Kaja Silverman, *Male Subjectivities at the Margins* (New York: Routledge, 1992); Jennifer Robertson (ed.), *Same-Sex Cultures and Sexualities: An Anthropological Reader* (Oxford: Blackwell, 2005); Alison Griffiths, *Wondrous Difference: Cinema, Anthropology and Turn of the Century Visual Culture* (New York: Columbia University Press, 2002).
22. Vicente Rafael, *White Love and Other Events in Filipino History* (Durham: Duke University Press, 2000), pp. 34, 25.

23. Malek Alloula, *The Colonial Harem*, trans. Myrna Godzich and Wlad Godzich (Minneapolis: University of Minnesota Press, 1986); see also Lisa Sigel, *Governing Pleasures: Pornography and Social Change in England, 1815–1914* (New Brunswick, NJ: Rutgers University Press, 2002), p. 1.
24. Stoler, *Carnal Knowledge and Imperial Power*, p. 208.
25. Cited in Ania Loomba, *Colonialism/Postcolonialism* (London: Routledge, 1998), p. 119.
26. Kevin Mumford, *Interzones: Black/White Sex Districts in Chicago and New York in the Early Twentieth Century* (New York: Columbia University Press, 1997), p. xi.
27. See Gilberto Freyre, *The Masters and the Slaves: A Study in the Development of Brazilian Civilization*, trans. Samuel Putnam (New York: Knopf, 1946).
28. On Salazar's adoption of lusotropicalism, see Cristiana Bastos, 'Race, Medicine and the Late Portuguese Empire: The Role of Goan Colonial Physicians', *Journal of Romance Studies*, 5, 1 (2005), 24–5.
29. See Jenny Sharpe, *Allegories of Empire: The Figure of Woman in the Colonial Text* (Minneapolis: University of Minnesota Press, 1993), p. 3.
30. Joseph Crad, *Traders in Women: A Comprehensive Survey of 'White Slavery'* (London: John Long, 1940), p. 135.
31. Doris Sommer, *Foundational Fictions: The National Romances of Latin America* (Berkeley: University of California Press, 1991).
32. Siobhan Somerville, *Queering the Color Line: Race and the Invention of Homosexuality in American Culture* (Durham: Duke University Press, 2000), p. 22.
33. Nancy Leys Stepan, *The Idea of Race in Science: Great Britain 1800–1960* (London: Macmillan, 1982), p. 4. See also Stepan, *'The Hour of Eugenics': Race, Gender, and Nation in Latin America* (Ithaca: Cornell University Press, 1991).
34. See Gayatri Chakravorty Spivask, 'Can the Subaltern Speak?' in Cary Nelson and Lawrence Grossberg (eds.), *Marxism and the Interpretation of Culture* (Urbana: University of Illinois Press, 1988), p. 297.
35. See Sander Gilman, 'Black Bodies, White Bodies: Toward an Iconography of Female Sexuality in Late Nineteenth-Century Art, Medicine, and Literature', in Henry Louis Gates (ed.), *'Race', Writing, and Difference* (Chicago: University of Chicago Press, 1985), pp. 228–38.
36. Frantz Fanon, *Black Skin, White Masks*, 1952, trans. Charles Lam Markmann (New York: Grove Press, 1967), p. 177.
37. See Bronislaw Malinowski, *Baloma: The Spirits of the Dead in the Trobriand Islands* (London: Royal Anthropological Institute, 1916), p. 219. See also his *The Sexual Life of Savages in North-Western Melanesia: An Ethnographic Account of Courtship, Marriage and Family Life among the Natives of Trobriand Islands, British New Guinea* (London: Routledge & Kegan Paul, 1929).
38. Rudi Bleys, *The Geography of Perversion: Male-to-male Sexual Behaviour outside the West and the Ethnographic Imagination, 1750–1918* (London: Cassell, 1996), p. 192. For a comprehensive survey of representations of homosexuality in non-Western sites, see David Greenberg, *The Construction of Homosexuality* (Chicago: University of Chicago Press, 1988).
39. See Diana Fuss, *Indentification Papers* (New York: Routledge, 1995), p. 36. Fuss describes the mechanism through which, for Freud, desexualized sublimated love for other men becomes a basis for social group ties in toto.

40. Catherine Mayo, *Mother India* (London: Jonathan Cape, 1927), p. 29.
41. Margaret Mead, *Sex and Temperament in Three Primitive Societies* (London: Routledge & Kegan Paul, 1935), p. xvi.
42. For a discussion and debunking of this view, see Gaurav Desai, 'Out in Africa', *Genders*, 25 (1997), 120–43.
43. Zackie Achmat, '"Apostles of Civilised Vice": Immoral Practices and Unnatural Vice in South African Prisons and Compounds, 1890–1920', *Social Dynamics*, 19, 2 (1993), 108.

6
cities

matt houlbrook

introduction

It's rare that historians find themselves writing about a hot cultural issue, but for those exploring the relationship between sex and the city that's been the case over the past ten years. At present, indeed, it's difficult to escape popular representations of the ways in which sexual practices and identities are shaped by contemporary urban life. On our television screens, for example, *Sex and the City* suggests how experiences of place – Manhattan – are inexorably connected to distinct sexual practices, problems, and personalities – embodied in the ubiquitous figure of Carrie Bradshaw. Whether in its Pittsburgh or Manchester settings, *Queer as Folk* locates a specific queer lifestyle in a particular urban locale. The visual and print media generates a constant stream of reports about urban red-light districts, urban prostitution, 'gay ghettos' or the sexual dangers of Amsterdam or London after dark. Little surprise that, as Pat Califia suggests, 'the city has become a sign of desire: promiscuity, perversity, prostitution, sex'.[1]

The city's status as a 'sign of desire' has also become an increasingly hot academic issue. As historians and sociologists have turned their attention to sexual practices and identities in the two decades since Foucault's *History of Sexuality* was first published, they have, more often than not, focused overwhelmingly upon the European and North American city. In modern times the association between sex and the city has become almost axiomatic. From the correlation between urbanization and the 'making of the modern homosexual', to narratives of sexual possibility and peril – 'cities of dreadful delight' – the city and the sexual appear culturally and conceptually inseparable.[2]

This chapter offers a critical reflection on what might be called urban histories of sexuality. It explores three discrete questions. First, why have a generation of historians been so obsessed with the city? Second, in what ways has urban culture shaped the experience, organization and understanding of sexual behaviour since the early nineteenth century? How, in turn, has sexuality shaped a distinctive urban culture? Third, what problems are there in the ways in which historians have handled these themes? The chapter works thematically, rather than chronologically, introducing material from a range of European and North American cities. In developing a series of arguments about the relationship between sex and the city, however, it returns repeatedly to a particular case study: the sexual culture of London's parks.

foundations

In many ways, the urban focus of historians of sexuality is understandable. The modern city is, after all, the site of many of our most familiar images of sexual practices and identities. To explore the formation of red-light districts or public queer cultures in the past thus represents an attempt to understand contemporary urban culture within its historical context. It is, moreover, for the nineteenth- and twentieth-century city that institutions, newspapers, and public commentators have generated the most extensive evidence of such practices. In his chapter above, Matt Cook rightly emphasizes the centrality of legal records to research in this field. This material, however, contains an inherent urban bias. Official regulation – from the watches of late eighteenth-century London to the bureaucratic police forces of mid-nineteenth-century European cities – has always been most pervasive in urban areas. Urban police and courts enforced legislation against brothel keeping, prostitution, or public sex more vigorously than their rural equivalents. Urban culture in general – and urban sexual practices in particular – were more heavily policed. They were, as a result, more heavily documented.

The city's centrality in the historical record, however, needs further explanation. *Why* have urban sexual practices been subject to such pervasive surveillance? Police forces, modes of municipal governance and sexual offences laws are, in themselves, cultural artefacts, reflecting hegemonic understandings of urbanization's impact on personal morality and sexual behaviour. From the early nineteenth century onwards, anxieties about urban culture generated ongoing official attempts to control individuals' sexual practices. Louise Jackson, for example, convincingly attributes the 1885 Criminal Law Amendment Act to fears over the visibility of 'vice' on London's streets.[3] The enforcement of such legislation by police and magistrates, in turn, shaped the material available to historians. Such anxieties generated other rich sources: published social investigations and exposes of urban 'vice' like Michael Ryan's *Prostitution in London* (1855) or Erwin Seligman's *The Social Evil* in New York (1902).

The influence of such anxieties in orienting historians towards the city is clear in recent work on nineteenth- and twentieth-century America. Timothy Gilfoyle, George Chauncey and Kathy Peiss, for example, draw heavily on the papers of social purity societies like the Society for the Suppression of Vice in their work on New York prostitution, homosexuality, and heterosociability.[4] The work of such societies regulating working-class and immigrant street life reflected a pervasive sense that, as Chauncey suggests, 'the city posed a threat not just to the morality of individuals but to the survival of American society as a whole'.[5] Like the London Council for the Promotion of Public Morality – founded in 1901 – they considered themselves right-minded citizens 'banded together to try as far as possible to check the torrent of vice which floods our streets'.[6]

Why was urbanization equated with immorality, viciousness and danger? For many commentators, the apparent anonymous and atomized qualities of urban life, the sheer size of the metropolis, and the concomitant distance between work, neighbourhood, leisure and family life, threatened to erode established social boundaries. In New York, the Committee of Fifteen suggested,

> the main external check upon a man's conduct, the opinion of his neighbors, which has such a powerful influence in the country or small town, tends to disappear. In a great city one has no neighbors. No man knows the doings of even his close friends; few men care what the secret life of their friends may be... [T]he young man is left free to follow his own inclinations.[7]

In the early twentieth century, urban sociologists, particularly those associated with the Chicago School, developed such analyses further. Walter Reckless, writing on the 'Distribution of Commercial Vice in the City' (1926), thus characterized urban culture by its sense of 'personal disorganization'. The result was the release of 'impulses and desires... from the socially approved channels' which could result 'not merely in prostitution, but also in perversion'.[8]

The inherent archival bias towards urban sexualities has been reinforced by broader trends in critical academic thought over the past two decades, particularly the 'spatial turn' within history, cultural studies and human geography. As the work of David Harvey, Henri Lefebvre or Edward Soja suggests, space – the city – is not simply a passive backdrop against which social and cultural processes are enacted, but a 'constitutive part of the cultural and social formation of metropolitan modernity'.[9] Like Walter Reckless, recent research has started from the premise that sexual practices do not just take place *in* the city, but are shaped *by* the physical and cultural forms of urban life, just as they in turn shape that life. 'The city', suggests Mark Turner, 'is an active force, an agent that *creates* certain kinds of behaviour, true to the modern urban sensibility.'[10] Taken together, contemporary images of sex, the archive's nature and historiographical trends mean that the historian's gaze is inexorably re-directed to the city.

themes

Historical anxieties over urbanization's moral impact and contemporary historiographical debates both coalesce upon one central assumption: the city actuates particular desires, practices, ways of being and forms of encounter. To put it another way: modern urban culture has shaped the experience, organization and understanding of sexual behaviour in such a way as to constitute a unique sexual space. Working on Lord Hardwicke's 1753 Marriage Act, the British historian Miles Ogborn suggests two approaches to an urban history of sexuality. First, by relating sites of sexual encounter and identity to geographies of leisure, sociability, work, and state regulation, thereby 'weav[ing] sexuality into the complex social relations of the cityscape'. Second, by analysing how regulation enables and constrains different sexual practices, thereby articulating particular understandings of the boundaries between 'good' and 'bad' sexualities. The social, cultural and physical geography of urban life, Ogborn suggests, shapes *both* where and how individuals interact sexually *and* the meanings participants and observers invest in those interactions. Following Ogborn, this section identifies five key motifs in historical analyses of the interrelationship between sex and urban culture. The central question is very simple: what 'kinds of behaviour' have been considered 'true to the modern urban sensibility'?[11]

the erotics of the street

As commentators sought to evoke a 'modern urban sensibility' from the mid-nineteenth century they usually focused on the bustling streets of metropolises like Paris and New York. Walter Benjamin, Charles Baudelaire and Georg Simmel, for example, saw in the rapidly circulating crowds the fluidity, fragmentation and anonymity that seemed to characterize modern life. This transient public realm meant two things. First, it was impossible to fully know a passing individual's identity. Second, visuality – the act of *seeing* – was the intrinsic sensory quality of modern urban culture. In imaginative literature this sensibility was embodied in the flaneur – the man passing through the crowds, compulsively watching, categorizing and consuming the urban spectacle.[12]

Modern street culture, moreover, generated particular forms of sexual behaviour and interaction. Indeed, the opportunities to gaze upon passersby were often imaged as a near-erotic source of pleasure. During the First World War, for example, the student Robert Hutton regularly wandered the bustling streets of London's West End.

> Men in uniform, hucksters, hawkers, prostitutes and people like myself, killing time and enjoying the crowds, jostled and strolled from the Pavilion to Leicester Square and back again... When dusk fell a feeling of restlessness and excitement crept over me.[13]

Like those he glimpsed in the crowds, Hutton was drawn by the district's imaginary status as a public realm of pleasure, leisure and consumption. Here men and women of all classes found opportunities for public sociability, spectatorship and pleasure. As the journalist H.V. Morton noted in 1932, 'the bright lights call them night after night, if only to saunter for an innocent hour in the slow, exciting crowds'.[14]

Hutton's immersion in these 'slow, exciting crowds' generated the heightened sensations of arousal evident in the 'excitement and restlessness' recalled years later. Amidst the bustling flow of humanity his gaze was fleetingly yet repeatedly drawn to the men who passed by, anonymous and distant, yet tantalizingly close. His experiences of London's streets actuated disconcerting desires; gripped by an unexplainable longing, Hutton never wanted to return home.

> Some day I promised myself I would stay as long as I liked and mingle with the crowds instead of being... an onlooker... I would have liked to get into conversation with one or other of the young men in uniform and once or twice, I tried it, but did not get much response. They were looking for something and in a vague way so was I. I hoped that some day I might meet someone who felt the same way.[15]

As Hutton's longings suggest, moreover, the sexual pleasures of the urban crowd went far beyond spectatorship. Amidst the bustling crowds, men and women could forge connections with passing strangers, exchanging glances with potential partners, enjoying what Mark Turner calls 'the excitement of the passing moment'.[16] In 1916 Hutton was browsing at the bookstall in Victoria Station, when he glanced at a 'well-dressed man of 35'. The man returned his gaze, they began talking, before walking to a nearby park, where they had sex.[17]

Such encounters suggest how public *urban* culture shaped a complex and vibrant public *sexual* culture, predicated upon moving through the city, gazing and searching for contact. In European and North American cities alike, queer men cruised certain streets and parks. Streetwalking prostitutes sought partners in the passing crowds. And young men and women transformed the streets of crowded working-class neighbourhoods into bustling centres of heterosocial interaction and encounter. They gathered on corners, or walked the parks or local streets, talking, gazing at shop windows and each other. Finding partners amidst the ebb and flow of the crowd, they then sought moments of privacy elsewhere – in darkened alleyways or parks. Both 'homosexual' cruising and its 'heterosexual' equivalent – known as the 'monkey parade' in Britain – were sexual practices appropriate to the modern urban sensibility.

urbanization and the 'making of the modern homosexual'

The sexual interactions associated with the urban crowd were shared by diverse social groups. By contrast, a second strand in historical analyses of the relationship between sex and the city has focused upon urbanization's narrower impact on the organization and experience of sexual difference, particularly male 'homosexuality'. Consider, for example, the story of Cyril L. Cyril moved to London in 1932, aged 20. He quickly began to frequent certain commercial venues, making a kind of home for himself in nightclubs like the Caravan. Here he made friends and socialized, found sex and, eventually, love. In 1934, he reflected on these experiences in a letter to his friend Billy. Seventy years on, Cyril's excitement at the world in which he had only just begun to move remains tangible. He talked about his relationships, his feelings, and the life he was forging in the city. He wrote 'I have only been queer since I came to London about two years ago, before then I knew nothing about it.'[18]

In mapping his own changing sense of self and sexual practices onto his encounter with London, Cyril established a productive relationship between space, the social, and subjectivity. Geographical, temporal, and subjective movements blend together. 'Being queer' is equated with the cultural experience of urban life – 'coming to London about two years ago'. Retrospectively, self-knowledge – self-realization – is correlated with that moment of migration. Here the city is both a symbolic and experiential rupture, a productive space that generates and stabilizes a new form of selfhood and way of life. Cyril's story pivots upon an implicit opposition between silence and speaking out, repression and fulfilment, non-being and being. This can easily be a recognizable tale of the big city as a space of affirmation, liberation and citizenship – the city as a queer space.

In linking sexual selfhood and place Cyril thus began to talk about familiar themes – the association between 'homosexuality' and the city. It is, after all, in cities like San Francisco or Berlin that queer cultures have assumed their most visible and characteristic forms – where networks of commercial and public spaces and residential enclaves have taken hold. As Matt Cook recently observed, 'think of "gay" men and "gay" culture and we think of cities'.[19] As I suggest above, moreover, such patterns of thought have permeated popular culture, through books like Armistead Maupin's *Tales of the City*.[20] And in a growing number of historical studies of sexual difference there has been an overwhelming focus on the organization of queer sexualities in their urban setting. Together, the work of George Chauncey, Marc Stein, and others comprises a dynamic queer urban history.[21]

Within this field, *the* dominant paradigm in historical analyses of male sexualities has been the correlation of the emergence of visible queer cultures with the experiential dimensions of urban modernity. Just as Cyril mapped 'being queer' onto 'coming to London', so historians taking their cue from Foucault have mapped the 'great paradigm shift' of the 'making of the modern homosexual' onto the process of urbanization. In the early work of John D'Emilio or Jeffrey Weeks, urbanization – by disrupting structures of authority, weakening the family, challenging established forms of community surveillance and offering the anonymity of the modern metropolis, is a precondition of the emergence of the 'homosexual' as an identity, state of being, and social world from the mid-nineteenth century onwards. In recent essays Michael Sibalis and Gert Hekma, for example, analyse the historical emergence of queer social networks organized around public (urinals, parks, and streets) and semi-private commercial (bars and clubs) spaces, in Paris and Amsterdam respectively. Both emphasize how men seeking men have exploited the cultural and physical forms generated by metropolitan life to construct meeting places and spheres of relative cultural autonomy.[22]

Such analyses of the temporal conjunction of space and sexuality reach their apogee in Henning Bech's *When Men Meet* (1997). Drawing upon his work on Scandinavian cities, Bech's starting point is the notion that 'being homosexual... is not primarily a matter of discourse and identity but a way of being'. He locates this particular 'homosexual form of existence' within modern experiences of urbanity, in particular the flux, anonymity, and visuality of the crowd. Here the city is a productive space, generating specific forms of desire and conventions of social interaction. Bech concludes with an axiom: the city is 'the social world proper of the homosexual... to be homosexual he must get into the city'. Simultaneously, this is a suggestive historical analysis and a profound cultural imperative – an imperative which has led countless queer men and women to migrate to cities in Europe and North America over the past century.[23]

the sexual dangers of the city

Historical analyses of the erotic pleasures of the urban crowd and the 'making of the modern homosexual' both treat the city as a site of sexual possibilities. A third strand of analysis, however, has emphasized how the city became associated with sexual danger and disorder from the late eighteenth century onwards. Prostitution, the sale of pornography or public forms of heterosociability associated with working-class or immigrant neighbourhoods were, in this context, a disturbing sign of the city's deleterious effect on the established social and moral order. Urban culture, for many observers, held the constant threat of social disorganization and the collapse of the boundaries and constraints on which national stability depended.

Alongside these generalized anxieties, the city has also been constructed as a site of sexual danger for particular groups. Judith Walkowitz and Karen Dubinsky, for example, suggest how women have been excluded from the public city through narratives of rape, sexual assault, harassment or indecent exposure.[24] Notions of the city's perils have, moreover, often crystallized in fears over the safety of children. After the First World War, for example, a number of children's charities and moral purity organizations began to demand that the British state take action to protect the nation's youth. Their lobbying efforts utilized a stereotypical narrative of sexual danger – a paradigmatic 'assault' that took place in the public leisure spaces where children and men met, and where the 'natural' boundaries between generations collapsed. Groups like the Hammersmith Juvenile Organisation Committee regularly forwarded 'particulars of known cases of molestation of children' to the London

County Council and Home Office, demanding Women Police patrols to 'protect' children. This coding of public space as dangerous reshaped public understandings of good parenting and childhood freedom, and the policy decisions made by municipal authorities. In 1923, for example, the secretary of the Hampstead Heath Protection Society noted how 'the things that go on the Heath... are such that... most careful parents would not allow their youngsters to sit on the Heath alone, I certainly never allow mine to go off the... paths'.[25] By 1925 the Parks and Open Spaces Department were asking that the Education Department 'arrange for children in the schools maintained by the Council be warned periodically against conversing with or accepting gifts from strangers in parks or open spaces'. Through official warnings and regular newspaper reports, the public city was constructed as a threatening place, populated by dangerous men who preyed on vulnerable children.[26]

As this suggests, in the modern city sexual possibilities and dangers exist in a constant tension – the balance between the two shaped by differences of age, gender, class, race, place and time. The urban park, for example, is simultaneously a site of anonymous sexual encounters, a source of privacy or somewhere for a romantic stroll, just as it is a threatening no-go area. As Pat Califia observes:

> The warning 'don't go into the park after dark'... is more than just a simple notice of potential physical danger. It is also an acknowledgement of the shift in the park's function – which takes place when the sun goes down – from a place where nature lovers eat lunch and children feed squirrels, to a place where one can buy drugs or get one's cock sucked.[27]

the sexual politics of the city

If modern urban culture has been associated with particular sexual possibilities and perils, it has also underpinned attempts by municipal authorities to control their citizens' sexual practices. Anxieties over disorderly sexualities have thus exercised a profound influence on municipal politics, official and quasi-official policing, and urban planning. Since the mid-nineteenth century, from its political organization to the built environment, the modern city has taken shape within an ongoing relationship with the sexual practices of its inhabitants. 'The politics of space', suggests Beatriz Colomina, 'is always sexual.'[28]

Although the introduction of legislation regulating sexual behaviour was often ad hoc and haphazard, in practice the law came to constitute a pervasive system of moral governance, defining sexual 'normality' through the symbolic ordering of urban space. Acceptable sexual conduct was defined around the bourgeois nuclear family – it took place in private, and between consenting adult 'heterosexual' married couples. Legislation against homosex, prostitution or public sex thus, in Philip Hubbard's terms, made 'dominant moral codes clear, tangible and entrenched, providing a fixed point in the attempt to construct boundaries between good and bad subjects'.[29] In so doing, the law collapsed the notional distinctions between public and private space. As Leslie Moran suggests, public space was understood as the realm of law's full presence – 'a space of order and decency through the law'. The private, by contrast, was 'an alternative place where the law is absent'.[30] The law's 'absence', however, depended upon conforming to notions of normative sexual and social behaviour. The 'bad subject' – the sexual deviant – remained subject to state intervention, deemed sufficiently dangerous as to warrant intrusion into the sanctified private sphere.[31]

Whilst official regulation often collapsed the public–private distinction, however, *public* urban culture was considered particularly dangerous. Left alone, the unfettered sociability of the city's streets and open spaces threatened to corrupt working-class men, women and youths, seducing them away from 'respectability'. Such anxieties coalesced around the intrusion of sex into public life. Set against the growing ideological correlation between sexual intimacy and domesticity from the early nineteenth century onwards, public sex was defined as dangerous, immoral, and promiscuous. Such fears were further shaped by the assumption that public spaces were a sensitive indicator of a nation's moral well-being. Nominally an idealized realm of order, purity, and respectability, they were subject to a perpetually anxious surveillance.

In 1920s Britain such anxieties were articulated most powerfully around London's parks, where the 'immoral' spectacle of working-class couples, prostitution and queer men seemed to threaten the nation's youth. Purity organizations repeatedly demanded official action. In 1922, for example, Reverend Peel complained of the 'scourge of immorality' in Hyde Park to the Office of Works:

> One only has to walk through Hyde Park... to see couples... lying on top of each other... the sights to be seen near Marble Arch are disgusting. The harm being done to young people... is serious beyond words. That Park is little less than a brothel... a disgrace to a civilised country.[32]

Within this context, municipal authorities sought to delineate the proper boundaries between public and private conduct, articulating a singular notion of the appropriate location of sexual intimacy which precluded men and women's use of public space to meet and then have sex. From the late nineteenth century onwards, the Metropolitan Police and London County Council arrested countless men and women found engaging in 'public indecencies'. After the 1900s, moreover, they began to close or demolish public urinals in which men engaged in homosex, and discussed fencing and locking parks overnight. On occasion authorities were prepared to physically dismantle the public sites of sexual interaction.[33]

These actions, however, sat uneasily against the citizen's right to move through the city and local government's concomitant responsibilities – they could never demolish every urinal or close ever park. Unable to *remove* such sites, the authorities thus policed their *use*. Law enforcement was informed by dominant understandings of acceptable public practices, articulating a moral politics of space that associated public sex with danger and immorality.

Alongside regular police patrols, municipal authorities policed the boundaries between public and private by reconstructing London's built environment, reconfiguring physical space to extend surveillance into those urban niches where men and women regularly had sex. In 1926, for example, police asked the LCC for 'material assistance' in controlling 'indecency on Clapham Common' by 'improving the lighting of the Parish Path [and] Bishop's Walk'.[34] Two years later, an Office of Works official identified 'certain areas [in Hyde Park] which are notoriously the haunts of loose characters... increased lighting in these areas will be a discouragement to these people'.[35] The movement from darkness to light was also the symbolic movement from disorder, depravity and dangerous privacy to order, morality and the purity of full publicity.

The interplay between public sexual practices and a bourgeois moral politics of space thus had a productive impact on *both* modern police systems *and* urban planning. In 1933–34, for example, a House of Commons committee discussed redeveloping the Adelphi Estate. Built on sloping ground between the Strand and the Thames, the Adelphi stood upon a series of vaulted arches. Above and below ground it was a rabbit warren of narrow alleys and passageways. By the 1920s it was, noted Inspector Woods, a well-established 'resort of persons of the sodomite class', heterosexual couples and prostitutes because of its 'position and surroundings' – in central London – and since 'the locality is badly lighted' and housed several urinals.[36] In debating 'the desirability of closing the lower roads under the Adelphi... on the grounds of good order, decency and public morality', the committee proceedings were thus driven by their engagement with one particular urban space.[37] The modern city's redevelopment deliberately sought to exclude those sexual practices deemed 'disorderly' and 'indecent'.

regulation and the individual

The modern city has thus been shaped through an ongoing relationship with the sexual practices of its inhabitants. In turn, the operations of municipal governance have shaped individual sexual practices and identities. The most convincing analysis of this interrelationship is Philip Hubbard's recent work on geographies of prostitution in the urban West. Hubbard's starting point is the historical representation of female prostitution as deviant, which has underpinned ongoing attempts at its regulation. For Hubbard, regulation seeks to exclude a disorderly sexual presence from the city, defining the limits of acceptable sexuality through the symbolic ordering of space.[38]

Hubbard moves to explore the relationship between the discursive and legal exclusion of prostitution from 'normal' urban life and the practices and identities of individual sex workers. Analysing geographies of social control through eighteenth-century London to contemporary Hull, Hubbard argues that the regulation of prostitution focuses on those urban zones where it is perceived to be 'out of place'. Drawing on the notion of sex work as a threat to the nuclear family, police officers target soliciting only when it is situated in residential and 'respectable' neighbourhoods. Thus 'the historical evolution of red light districts... needs to be viewed as part of an ongoing process involving the exclusion of disorderly prostitution from imagined sites of orderly sexuality' (180). Prostitution is tacitly removed to – and tolerated in – industrial or inner-city zones where it is 'in place'.

In focusing on the everyday encounters between street policemen and prostitutes, Hubbard thus connects pejorative sexual discourses and official regulation to prostitutes' lives. Potential legal hostility means these working lives are characterized by attempts – not to oppose law and order – but to 're-work and divert [urban] spaces to create an alternative meaning of space – a space that often has its own alternative morality, rhythms and rituals – often invisible to outsiders' (183). The spatial marginalization of prostitutes – the obstacles to work from (traditionally safer) domestic locations in some cities, or their reliance on the cover of night – creates very real, everyday problems. On one hand, the adoption of specific beats and working practices such as 'pairing' are tactics to 'establish social spaces and socio spatial networks that are, at least in part, insulated from control and surveillance' and to protect women from dangerous clients (183). On the other, this moral re-mapping of the city sustains an identity apart from pejorative constructions of their immorality. Thus prostitutes may maintain a rigid division between domestic and working life and experience that life as a profession, imbued with concomitant pride and skills.

Hubbard, finally, closes the circle between discourse and experience. The discursive and pragmatic removal of solicitation to the city's margins means that when the police or media 'discover' prostitution, dominant constructions of their status as marginal sexual subjects are sustained through their association with a particular location. In the public imagination, sex workers assume the characteristics of the place in which they are found, at the same time as their presence defines that location. For Hubbard 'the moral contours of society are mapped on to (and out of) specific urban spaces' in a process that ensures the place of the prostitute – and other transgressive sexual practices – at the symbolic heart of definitions of legitimate heterosexuality (16).

problems

This chapter has traced several key themes in urban histories of sexuality. Whilst the field is increasingly vibrant, generating a productive debate about the spatial constitution of sexual practices and identities, this section focuses upon the historiographical, conceptual and methodological problems inherent to much recent work. As such, I raise a series of questions about historians' approach to the relationship between sex and the city.

The first problem follows from Foucault's enduring influence, particularly his focus on the emergence of modern sexual categories and identities. Whilst historians have engaged productively with broader aspects of Foucault's work – particularly on surveillance, power and knowledge – attempts to frame their discussions within the chronological parameters delineated in the *History of Sexuality* have hindered the development of an urban history of sexuality, effacing the complexities of sexuality's relationship with the city. Urban history's characteristic strength lies in its attentiveness to the minutiae and diversities of city life. If Foucault came to recognize space as a profound category of analysis, the singular linearity of the *History of Sexuality* sits uneasily with such approaches. Attempting to map changes *across time* within a Foucauldian framework, obscures the persistent differences in the organization of sexual practices *across space*.[39]

What do I mean? Individuals' engagement with urban life was shaped by their age, gender, race, status or economic status. Kevin Mumford's work on Chicago and New York, for example, suggests their relative poverty together with formal and informal racial exclusions meant black men and women forged a sexual culture very different from that of their white counterparts.[40] Such differences, moreover, determined whether the city was experienced as opportunity or danger. Whilst many men were able to move through the public city by day or night, for example, women's access to public space has been historically more problematic. The association between femininity and domesticity, familial and neighbourhood surveillance, anxieties surrounding the moral status of public women, and circulating narratives of sexual danger constrained women's movements. Their marginal position in the labour market lessened their ability to access commercial venues or private residential space. For women, the city held very different problems and possibilities to men.[41]

The tensions between chronology and difference are particularly marked in the equation between urbanization and the 'making of the modern homosexual'. Too often, in this schema, the city is treated as a universal agent of social change, producing a hegemonic singular 'homosexuality'. As Scott Bravmann suggests, 'the modernist narrative logic of social constructionist accounts of gay identity formation… elides the multiple differences among gay men' – differences of class, race, age, gender, and place. Thinking of urbanization as a 'grand, universalizing historical process' thus 'obscures recognition of effective and meaningful difference within that overarching process of change'.[42] The key point is very simple: men are different from one another, and those differences shape their experiences of the city, the lives they lead, and their sense of selfhood.

George Chauncey's work on New York, for example, is underpinned by a persistent tension between two different modes of analysis. *Gay New York* can be read, in part, as a sophisticated ethnography of diverse sexual practices and identities and their inflection by differences of class, place and race. At the same time, Chauncey positions that exploration within a chronological framework that effectively marginalizes those differences. His narrative of the making of modern sexual categories – borrowed directly from Foucault – maps a transition from multiple modes of queerness to the singular identity of 'gay'. This inexorable movement from difference to sameness was, in Chauncey's schema, completed around the middle of the twentieth century. As a chronological narrative of origins, *Gay New York* reifies certain contemporary cultural conceptions of homosexuality that preclude the recognition of the differences between queer men.[43]

Much recent work has successfully addressed this issue, moving beyond the simple correlation between urbanization and a singular 'homosexual' identity, to explore the complexities of the interrelationships between sexual practices and the city. Such work remains attentive to the differences between queer historical subjects. As such, it emphasizes the city's role in constituting diverse discourses, forms of desire, and ways of being. Influenced by conceptual insights derived from queer theory, and drawing upon an ever-widening body of empirical research, the result has been increasingly sophisticated analyses of the relationship between sex and the city.

As an example, take Matt Cook's recent *London and the Culture of Homosexuality, 1885–1914*. Cook begins with a provocative reading of sexual interactions in London's railway stations. Drawing upon newspaper reports, court records and diaries, Cook uses these encounters to underscore the 'axiomatic connection between urban material and cultural change and the proliferating discourses of homosexuality'. Yet rather than following Bech in conceptualizing these characteristically modern urban sites as constitutive of a singular 'homosexual' way of being, Cook carefully scrutinizes the competing understandings of homosexual and homosocial relationships that structured men's participation in such encounters – and relates these competing understandings to differences of class, education, background and place. For Cook, ideas of comradeship, platonic love, socialist rhetoric, notions of the city as a sexual playground, and the desire for masculine intimacy and material reward converged upon this one urban space. This is a compelling analysis that 'demonstrates the impossibility of conjuring a unitary gay metropolis or a singular gay urban type, and indicates instead the controlled plurality which characterized the relationship between London and homosexuality'.[44]

Yet in taking this idea of 'controlled plurality' as an organizing theme this kind of approach can be just as problematic as the linear chronologies discussed above. The relationship between sexual difference and urban culture, for example, is so ubiquitous that it can obscure the process of meaningful change over time. Too often the 'modern city' is taken as a static category of analysis, creating the impression that the modern 'homosexual' and the modern city came into being at the same time – at some point in the mid-nineteenth century – and have remained unchanged ever since. Paradoxically, queer urban history has tended to become ahistorical. It remains alive to the complexities of men's relationship to the city and how sexual identities are shaped by differences of class, race or age, but has been unable to fully incorporate change over time. Working within the overall framework of urbanization and the 'making of the modern homosexual' it is difficult to account for the changing sexual landscape since the mid-nineteenth century.

This, I would suggest, is the second problem facing historians. In part, it is an issue of historical practice – the need for a form of analysis that can simultaneously account for differences over time and space. But it is also an issue of how we think about the city. This thing called the modern city is an organic and fluid entity that changes over time. Paris is not the same in the late nineteenth century as in the 1940s, let alone in the twenty-first century. And, if the experience of being modern and urban is constantly shifting, then so too is the geographical and cultural organization of sexual practices and identities. Sexual practices, identities and – indeed – cities themselves, have their own unique chronologies.

Beyond these particular changes, however, it is possible to suggest one long-term trajectory in the spatial organization of sexualities since the late eighteenth century – what we might call a process of 'privatization'. In European and North American cities alike, rising real wages and consumerism, an increasingly compelling connection between respectability and privacy, and official regulation have underpinned a broad movement away from *public* forms of sexual interaction. From the 1920s, for young working-class men and women, for example, the 'monkey parade' on the local main street gave way to the coffee house, dance hall or saloon as places to meet partners. The 'knee trembler' in park or alley gave way to sex in private. Street prostitution gave way to the call girl's flat. Sex in the city has been privatized in the sense of becoming centred on the home or particular semi-private sites of commercial sociability, and in the sense of becoming increasingly invisible. Since the early nineteenth century, public sexual practices have been displaced to an increasingly marginal urban position.[45]

The third pervasive problem within urban histories of sexuality is underpinned by the vagaries of academic fashion. To a remarkable extent, historians have devoted their attentions to 'marginal' and 'dangerous' sexualities – prostitution, cross-dressing, promiscuity, public sex and homosexuality. 'Perversion is chic' in academic circles, Rita Felski observes. Focusing on marginality and difference, however, has obscured the relationship between the city and 'normal' or 'conventional' sexualities. As Felski rightly argues, historians need to 'separate the study of sex from the obsession with transgression'.[46] This might, for example, involve analysing the suburban familial bedroom as part of a broader geography of urban sexualities, alongside the park, urinal or brothel. It might include an analysis of how spaces coded as 'marginal' or 'transgressive' can be sexed in ways that are understood as unproblematic. The park may have been the site of diverse illicit sexual encounters, but it also afforded opportunities for respectable forms of sexual interaction – the romantic stroll.

Finally, I would caution historians to engage critically with the very ubiquity of the association between sex and the city. Our obsession with the city as *the* sexual space of modern times has rendered non-urban and non-Western historical subjects invisible. The recent play *The Laramie Project*, for example, explores events surrounding the 1998 murder of Matt Shepherd, a gay student at the University of Wyoming. Whilst the play's setting is ostensibly rural, the city is all-pervasive in its representation of Shepherd's death. It is the utopian space to which he aspires, yet from which his exclusion is ultimately fatal. Laramie is subjected to a judgemental urban gaze that contrasts the city's assumed tolerance and freedoms to a 'backward' rural milieu: only there could this happen. *The Laramie Project* serves as a salutary confirmation of urban privilege and the impossibility of being queer anywhere else. And yet, as John Howard's groundbreaking work on rural Mississippi suggests, men and women *did* engage in homosex elsewhere, forging social networks and identities different from, but often equally vibrant and affirmative as, those of San Francisco. Above all, Howard's work is a powerful reminder of the need to remain alive to sex *outside* the city.[47]

futures?

The social and cultural forms associated with urban life have, I've suggested, exercised a defining influence on the understanding, organization and experience of sexuality in modern Western cultures. In turn, sexual practices and anxieties have profoundly shaped our cities. Increasingly, however, the axiomatic nature of this relationship is being questioned by new information technologies. If the city became a defile for the problematic and alluring nature of sexuality from the nineteenth century onwards, those problems and possibilities are being displaced onto the realm of the virtual – onto cyberspace.

The circulation of information through the Internet challenges the city's integrity as *the* paradigmatic site of sexual encounters. Each month around 1.5 million men visit the website <www.cruisingforsex.com> – 'devoted to helping horny cruisers find one another'. They find searchable 'sex listings', which identify places for men to meet in European and North American cities. A message board allows them to make virtual contact and arrange real-time meetings. If such features allow men to negotiate the city safely, however, they simultaneously disrupt the link between cruising and the urban crowd. Men no longer *have* to cruise parks to find sex. The 'sex listings', moreover, include rural areas like North Dakota, alerting men to local sexual opportunities. The British media's recent obsession with 'dogging' – watching/being watched while engaging in public sexual encounters – suggests a similar shift in the geography of public sex. Websites like <www.dogging-central.com> list established – often rural – meeting places, and allow couples to arrange rendezvous. Whilst cruising is predicated upon a recognizable and bounded urban place, the Internet affords opportunities for sexual encounters that transcend those boundaries.[48]

In allowing access to global sources of information and the formation of social connections between individuals across national boundaries, cyberspace has similarly reconfigured geographies of sexual community. This process has been most pronounced in the emergence of what Nina Wakeford calls the 'cyberqueer'. For Wakeford, the Internet's anonymity creates a private safe space in which individuals can explore their desires and forge affirmative queer identities. 'There are', an advertisement in *The Advocate* claimed recently, 'no closets in Cyberspace.'[49] As well as becoming central to the formation of individual *identities*, the Internet has also reshaped queer *communities*. The Australian website <www.mogenic.com> calls itself

> A special place on the net where gay and lesbian youth have the freedom to exchange ideas, share experiences, discuss coming out, make friends, read interesting content and most importantly: make contact... Mogenic [is] help[ing] gay, lesbian bisexual and transgender youth know that they are not alone, that there is a community of acceptance, vibrancy support, beauty and pride.[50]

Envisaging the Internet as a primary source of information about and contact with other queers, the 'community' imagined by Mogenic is dis-embedded and boundless. It is, still, tangible and affirmative, countering the isolation often experienced by those living in rural areas. Challenging Bech's assumption that 'to be homosexual he [sic] must get into the city', cyberspaces like Mogenic undermine the city's centrality to the formation of queer communities.

The sheer number of websites like <www.gay.com> suggests how the Internet has changed the organization of queer sexual encounter, sociability and community. The transformative potential of cyberspace has been further manifest in more utopian claims that it is redefining the very meanings of sex, intimacy and selfhood. For Aaron Ben-Ze'ev 'computers have changed not just the way we work but the way we love', generating a 'new kind of romantic relationship' between individuals whose most intense intimacies are conducted with people they may never see.[51] Similar claims have been made about cybersex – the shared enactment of sexual fantasies to the point of orgasm. In part, as Shannon McRae suggests, cybersex mirrors the 'fleeting, anonymous erotic experiences' normally associated with the city: chatrooms are imagined as a physical public space in which individuals 'cruise' for partners. Like public sex, such encounters are often stigmatized as alienating, disembodied and meaningless – 'one handed typing'.[52] Others, however, find an alluring freedom of sexual expression and experimentation in the anonymity and safety of cybersex, together with opportunities to assume alternative public identities that 'drastically unsettle the division between mind, body and self'.[53]

The sexual possibilities invested in cyberspace cohere in the notion that it constitutes an unfettered site of social interaction – equivalent to urban public spaces. For many commentators, however, this simultaneously figures cyberspace as disorderly and disruptive. As the site of a growing number of narratives of sexual danger, the Internet has provoked profound anxieties amongst governments and the media. Such narratives include the phenomenon of 'cyberstalking' – men exploiting the privileges of anonymity to send women sexually aggressive messages. Their classic form, however, coalesces upon the ubiquitous figure of what the British newspaper the *Daily Mirror* calls the 'cyber pervert' – the predatory older man using chatrooms to 'groom' minors for 'sexual abuse'. In Britain, twenty-six such cases have been directly linked to the Internet.[54] The contrast between the innocent young victim and the predatory and threatening 'paedophile' inhabiting the shadowy unregulated world of cyberspace has become a staple of tabloid newspapers, children's charities and moralizing politicians.[55]

What is most striking about such narratives, are the parallels with nineteenth- and twentieth-century fears over urbanization's cultural impact – particularly the emphasis on the Internet as a site of unfettered social interaction and the impossibility of knowing an individual's 'true' identity. 'The internet fosters anonymity', one journalist remarked, 'and enables some to take advantage of the innocent and unwary.'[56] Moreover, in evoking the dangers to children, commentators utilize narrative tropes established through persistent exposes of the dangers of public urban space. Explicitly, the Internet is understood within broader cultural knowledge of the city's sexual dangers. It is, suggested the manager of UK Chat,

> A big wide world which to many is a foreign place... This presents a serious challenge to parents' ability to supervise their children's activities... Parents who would not dream of letting their children roam the streets unsupervised seem to have no problem with allowing them unrestricted access to the net... We drum into our children the need to follow road safety precautions and be cautious of strangers. It is time that we did the same for Internet use....[57]

The correlation between the Internet and public urban space is further evident in attempts to regulate cyberspace, particularly to 'protect' children. Chat rooms routinely police their users' behaviour through online moderators. In 2003, moreover, Microsoft UK closed the MSN Chat rooms 'to provide consumers with a safer, more secure and positive overall online experience [and] to better protect children from inappropriate communication online'.[58] If the nocturnal park can be locked, so virtual sites of public sexual interaction can be dismantled.

Such modes of commercial self-regulation have been reinforced by a series of government initiatives in Britain, under the aegis of the Internet Watch Foundation and Taskforce on Child Protection on the Internet in order to 'make [the] UK the best and safest place in the world for children to use the Internet'. The state's powers of surveillance have expanded massively – including a new offence of 'Sexual Grooming' online explicitly aimed at intergenerational interactions short of sexual contact. An extensive advertising campaign – focused upon the websites <www.haltabuse.org> and <www.thinkuknow.co.uk> – has tried to raise parental awareness of the Internet's dangers and provide advice on dealing with online abuse.[59] Just as anxieties surrounding the disorderly nature of the city's streets sustained increasingly elaborate regulatory bureaucracies from the nineteenth century, so the Internet has become subject to official surveillance and intervention.

This is not to suggest that the city is no longer an important site in the production of sexual knowledge, or that the interrelationship between urban space and sexual practices is irrelevant today. Indeed, in many ways the association between 'sex and the city' is more compelling than ever. The urban crowd still generates eroticized opportunities for seeing and being seen. The city's commercial and public geography still shapes distinct sites of illicit or semi-licit sexual encounter and consumption. Whether hetero or homosocial, urban nightlife is still an idealized space for sexualized interactions. And the city continues to generate shifting narratives of sexual danger.

Whilst cyberspace is challenging urban space's hegemonic position within cultural understandings of sexuality, moreover, the association between sex and the city retains sufficient power to shape the ways in which new forms of virtual sociability are understood, represented and policed. Like nineteenth-century Paris or New York, the Internet is a disorderly space, threatening established social structures just as it opens new opportunities for sexual encounters, practices and identities. Yet perhaps at precisely the moment at which the relationship between sex and the city has become most visible, sexual geographies are changing fundamentally.

notes

1. Pat Califia, *Public Sex: The Culture of Radical Sex* (San Francisco: Cleiss Press, 2000), p. 216.
2. See Michel Foucault, *The History of Sexuality: Volume 1: An Introduction*, trans. Robert Hurley (London: Allen Lane, 1979).
3. Louise Jackson, *Child Sexual Abuse in Victorian England* (London and New York: Routledge, 2000), p. 105.
4. See, for example, George Chauncey, *Gay New York: The Making of the Gay Male World, 1890–1940* (London: Flamingo, 1995). Timothy Gilfoyle, *City of Eros: New York City, Prostitution and the Commercialization of Sex, 1790–1820* (New York: Norton, 1992). Kathy Peiss, *Cheap Amusements: Working Women and Leisure in Turn of the Century New York* (Philadelphia: Temple University Press, 1986).
5. Chauncey, *Gay New York*, p. 137.
6. London Metropolitan Archive [hereafter LMA]: A PMC 97: Annual Report of the London Council for the Promotion of Public Morality, 28 February 1901.
7. Chauncey, *Gay New York*, p. 131.
8. Walter Reckless, 'The Distribution of Commercial Vice in the City: A Sociological Analysis', in Ernest Burgess (ed.), *The Urban Community* (Chicago: University of Chicago Press, 1926), pp. 192, 202.
9. Frank Mort and Lynda Nead, 'Introduction: Sexual Geographies', *New Formations*, 37 (1999), 6.
10. Mark Turner, *Backward Glances: Cruising the Queer Streets of London and New York* (London: Reaktion Books, 2003), p. 127. See also Henri Lefebvre, *The Production of Space*, trans. David Nicholson-Smith (Oxford: Blackwell, 1991). David Harvey, *The Condition of Postmodernity: An Enquiry into the Origins of Cultural Change* (Oxford: Blackwell, 1989). Edward Soja, *Postmodern Geographies:*

The Reassertion of Space in Critical Social Theory (London and New York: Verso, 1989). Michel de Certeau, *The Practice of Everyday Life*, trans. Steven Randall (Berkeley: University of California Press, 1984).

11. Miles Ogborn, 'This Most Lawless Space: The Geography of the Fleet and the Making of Lord Hardwicke's Marriage Act of 1753', *New Formations*, 37 (1999), 12. See also Edward Laumann, *The Sexual Organization of the City* (Chicago: University of Chicago Press, 2004).
12. This account draws upon Turner, *Backward Glances*, passim. Richard Sennett, *The Fall of Public Man* (London: Faber, 1993). Georg Simmel, 'The Metropolis and Mental Life', in K. Wolff (ed.), *The Sociology of Georg Simmel* (New York: Free Press, 1950), pp. 409–24. Marshall Berman, *All That Is Solid Melts Into Air: The Experience of Modernity* (London: Verso, 1983).
13. Robert Hutton, *Of Those Alone* (London: Sidgwick and Jackson, 1958), pp. 9–10.
14. H.V. Morton, *The Nights of London* (London: Methuen and Co., 1932), p. 5. See also Erika Rappaport, *Shopping for Pleasure: Women in the Making of London's West End* (Princeton, NJ: Princeton University Press, 2000).
15. Hutton, *Of Those Alone*, pp. 9–10.
16. Turner, *Backward Glances*, p. 118.
17. Hutton, *Of Those Alone*, pp. 9–10.
18. Public Record Office [hereafter PRO]: MEPO 3 758: Caravan Club 81 Endell Street WC1: Disorderly House / Male Prostitutes: Minute 8c: Cyril L. to Billy: 16 August 1934.
19. Matt Cook, *London and the Culture of Homosexuality: 1885–1914* (Cambridge: Cambridge University Press, 2003), p. 2.
20. Armistead Maupin, *Tales of the City* (New York: Harper and Row, 1978).
21. See, for example, Chauncey, *Gay New York*. Dan Healey, *Homosexual Desire in Revolutionary Russia: The Regulation of Sexual and Gender Dissent* (Chicago and London: University of Chicago Press, 2001). Steven Maynard, 'Through a Hole in the Lavatory Wall: Homosexual Subcultures, Police Surveillance and the Dialectics of Discovery: Toronto, 1890–1930', *Journal of the History of Sexuality*, 5, 2 (1994), 207–42. Steven Maynard, '"Without Working?" Capitalism, Urban Culture and Gay History', *Journal of Urban History*, 30, 3 (2004), 378–98. Arne Nilsson, 'Creating Their Own Private and Public: The Male Homosexual Life Space in a Nordic City during High Modernity', *Journal of Homosexuality*, 35, 3/4 (1998), 81–116. Marc Stein, *City of Brotherly and Sisterly Love: Lesbian and Gay Philadelphia: 1945–72* (Chicago and London: University of Chicago Press, 2000). Elizabeth Armstrong, *Forging Gay Identities: Organizing Sexuality in San Francisco, 1950–1994* (Chicago: University of Chicago Press, 2002).
22. Michael Sibalis, 'Paris', and Gert Hekma, 'Amsterdam', in David Higgs (ed.), *Queer Sites: Gay Urban Histories since 1600* (London and New York: Routledge, 1999). See also Jan Lofstrom, 'The Birth of the Queen/The Modern Homosexual: Historical Explanations Revisited', *Sociological Review*, 45, 1 (1997), 24. John D'Emilio, *Sexual Politics, Sexual Communities: The Making of a Homosexual Minority in the United States 1940–1970* (Chicago and London: University of Chicago Press, 1983). Jeffrey Weeks, *Coming Out: Homosexual Politics in Britain from the Nineteenth Century to the Present* (London: Quartet Books, 1977), passim.

23. Henning Bech, *When Men Meet: Homosexuality and Modernity*, trans. Teresa Mesquit and Tim Davies (Oxford: Polity Press, 1997), pp. 98–9, 104–16. For contemporary explorations of this relationship see Gordon Brent Ingram, Anne-Marie Bouthilette and Yolanda Retter (eds.), *Queers In Space: Communities/Public Places/Sites Of Resistance* (Seattle, WA: Bay Press, 1997).
24. Judith Walkowitz, *City of Dreadful Delight: Narratives of Sexual Danger in Late-Victorian London* (London: Virago, 1992). Karen Dubinsky, *Improper Advances: Rape and Heterosexual Conflict in Ontario, 1880–1929* (Chicago and London: Chicago University Press, 1993).
25. LMA: LCC MIN 8945: JG Pearce to Committee: 30 June 1923.
26. LMA: LCC MIN 8776: Minutes: 13 November 1925.
27. Califia, *Public Sex*, p. 217.
28. Beatriz Colomina, 'Introduction', in Colomina (ed.), *Sexuality and Space* (New York: Princeton Architectural Press, 1992), p. 1.
29. Philip Hubbard, *Sex and the City: Geographies of Prostitution in the Urban West* (Aldershot: Ashgate, 1999), p. 103.
30. Leslie Moran, *The Homosexual(ity) of Law* (London and New York: Routledge, 1996), p. 56.
31. See, for example, legislation against incest and male homosexuality. Anthony Wohl, 'Sex and the Single Room: Incest among the Victorian Working-Classes', in Wohl (ed.), *The Victorian Family: Structure and Stresses* (London: Croom Helm, 1978).
32. PRO: MEPO 2 5815: GR 26 PA 199: Hyde Park Policing: HG Peel to HM Office of Works: 1 July 1922.
33. PRO: MEPO 2 5815: GR 139605: Supt A Bean to Commissioner 28 April 1903.
34. LMA: LCC MIN 8715: 16 July 1926.
35. PRO: HO 45 16223: Powers under the Hyde Park Regulations: Section 509445/8: Office of Work Minutes: 21 May 1928.
36. PRO: MEPO 2 4309: Adelphi Estate Bill: Minute 3a: Abstract of evidence given by ASDI Woods: 17 July 1933.
37. Ibid.: Minute 1a: Mr L. Fladgate to HM Howgrave (Secretary NSY): 14 July 1933.
38. Hubbard, *Sex and the City*, passim.
39. For Foucault's later interest in space see Paul Rabinow (ed.), *Foucault Live: Interviews, 1966–84* (New York: Columbia University Press, 1989).
40. Kevin Mumford, *Interzones: Black/White Sex Districts in Chicago and New York in the Early Twentieth Century* (New York: Columbia University Press, 1997).
41. See Walkowitz, *City of Dreadful Delight*. Elizabeth Wilson, *The Sphinx in the City: Urban Life, the Control of Disorder and Women* (Berkeley: University of California Press, 1991). Elizabeth Kennedy and Madeline Davis, *Boots of Leather, Slippers of Gold: The History of a Lesbian Community* (London and New York: Routledge, 1993).
42. Scott Bravmann, *Queer Fictions of the Past: History, Culture and Difference* (Cambridge: Cambridge University Press, 1997), pp. x, 9.
43. See Chauncey, *Gay New York*, passim.
44. Cook, *London and the Culture of Homosexuality*, introduction.

45. See, for example, Hubbard, *Sex and the City*, passim. Matt Houlbrook, *Queer London: Perils and Pleasures in the Sexual Metropolis, 1918–57* (Chicago: University of Chicago Press, 2005).
46. Rita Felski, 'Domesticated Porn', *New Formations*, 37 (1999), 130.
47. See <www.tectonictheaterproject.org/Laramie/Laramie.htm>. Beth Loffreda, *Losing Matt Shepherd* (New York: Columbia University Press, 2000). John Howard, *Men Like That: A Southern Queer History* (Chicago: Chicago University Press, 1999).
48. Turner, *Backward Glances*, pp. 162–4. The British media's obsession with dogging was triggered by the high-profile revelations surrounding soccer player Stan Collymore. See 'Stan Collymore's "Dogging" Sex Shame', *Daily Mirror*, 2 March 2004.
49. Quoted in Nina Wakeford, 'Cyberqueer', in David Bell and Barbara Kennedy (eds.), *The Cybercultures Reader* (London and New York: Routledge, 2000), p. 404. David Bell, *An Introduction to Cybercultures* (London and New York: Routledge, 2001), pp. 128–9.
50. Quoted in Turner, *Backward Glances*, p. 175. See also Dave Ford, 'How Cyberspace Helps Gay Teens', *San Francisco Chronicle*, 22 June 1995.
51. Aaron Ben-Ze'ev, *Love Online: Emotions on the Internet* (Cambridge: Cambridge University Press, 2004). Andrea Orr, *Meeting, Mating and Cheating: Sex, Love and the New World of Online Dating* (Upper Saddle River, NJ: Reuters, 2004).
52. Shannon McRae, 'Flesh Made Word: Sex, Text and the Virtual Body', in David Porter (ed.), *Internet Culture* (London and New York: Routledge, 1997), p. 74.
53. Allucquere Rosanne Stone, 'Will the Real Body Please Stand Up? Boundary Stories about Virtual Cultures', in David Trend (ed.), *Reading Digital Culture* (Oxford: Blackwell, 2001).
54. 'Ex-Marine Jailed for Sex with Girl, 12', *Guardian*, 12 April 2004. Helen Carter, 'Microsoft Chatrooms to Close after Abuse Fear', *Guardian*, 24 September 2003.
55. Neil McIntosh, 'Cyberstalking on Coronation Street', *Guardian*, 10 July 2001.
56. Katie Jones, 'Room for Improvement', *Guardian*, 24 September 2003.
57. Ibid.
58. See <http://groups.msn.com/Editorial/en-gb/Content/chat.htm>.
59. See <www.protectingthepublic.homeoffice.gov.uk>. Perry Aftab, *The Parents' Guide to Protecting Children in Cyberspace* (New York: McGraw Hill, 2000).

7
religion and spirituality

h.g. cocks

Histories of sexuality have tended to recapitulate existing stories of modernity, one of which is the apparently increasing secularization of the world. Our ideas of sexuality appear to follow the same pattern as the decline of religion. Until the nineteenth century, so the story goes, sexuality was dominated by religious terms of understanding, but these have been gradually replaced by legal, medical and psychological models of normality and pathology. The history of sexuality appears to run from sin to crime to sickness: from the religious to therapeutic. Traditionally, historians posited a decisive break between these modes of knowledge, but in many ways they are more analogous than separate.[1]

Michel Foucault argued in the *History of Sexuality* that religious confession – the revelation of the sins and hidden truths of the self to a father confessor – has been at the centre of Western culture in various forms since the middle ages and that this process also informed modernity. Indeed, he suggested that the agencies which dominate modern life perform an analogous function to religion by forcing a similar kind of confession from secular subjects. Psychiatry, psychoanalysis, consumerism, law, medicine, the family, schools and welfare systems all demand the compulsory 'confession' of the details of selfhood, including sexuality. 'One confesses', Foucault observed, 'in public and private, to one's parents, one's educators, one's doctor, to those one loves.'[2] The 'truth' of the self, once the object of solely religious investigation, is thereby demanded at every turn. As Foucault suggests, the historical importance of a religious inheritance to this process of self-making, in which personal experience and sexual desire becomes the bedrock of selfhood and identity, cannot be overestimated.

Ironically though, Foucault's followers have tended to concentrate on the formation of identity via medical and legal sources such as sexology and psychiatry. In this context, a focus on the importance of religion and spirituality acts as an antidote to those histories that concentrate on medicine, the state and the law as chief determinants of sexual identity. Including religion in these histories allows us to do three related things. Firstly, we can show how religion was frequently the location for the expression of unconventional sexuality. Secondly, we can see how early scientific efforts to understand the psychology of sex were informed by spiritual matters. We can therefore see the rise of psychology and psychiatry as intimately linked to non-scientific discourses like spiritualism. Thirdly, we can see how vastly important spiritual and religious matters were in the making of modern science, literature, and culture. This focus therefore allows us to reshape the history of modernity not as a simple story of secularization which is shaped by the death of religion, but one that is informed by a dialogue between the secular and the spiritual.

Where studies of Western sexuality and spirituality intersect, there have been two principal approaches. The first of these deals with the making of individual or collective identity, and the second, derived more from intellectual history, places religion and sexuality at the heart of certain influential cultural trends. A large part of this historiography of personal identity has examined the extent to which religion and spirituality provided a congenial location for the expression of unconventional sexuality, both homosexual and heterosexual. More recently, however, normative heterosexuality has also come under sustained and specific investigation, with the result that spirituality has been located at the heart of the Victorian marriage, as a key ingredient of sexual intimacy. In fact, when speaking of the various intimacies, sexual or otherwise, of the Victorians, it is impossible to understand them without reference to a religious or spiritual context. As well as using the intersection of religion, spirituality and sexuality to understand personal identity and intimacy, historians have also placed this trinity at the heart of important social and cultural trends such as religious revivals, socialism, state formation, spiritualism, and the making of modern Christianity.

Aside from the influence of this investigative technique, religious thought and practice has had an enormous influence on secular institutions and morals, especially since the religious revivals which began in America and Britain in the late eighteenth century and lasted – at least in America – until the 1850s. Religion is therefore now taken much more seriously by historians than it used to be. Whereas in the

1980s religious belief tended to be dismissed as the ideological window dressing for genuine class interest, especially on the part of the middle class, historians now accept that religion informed a diverse collection of secular processes such as state formation, social policy, public health and the law which collectively have had an enormous influence on morality, the social organization of desire, perceptions and practices of sexuality, gender, and the family.

One of the key influences on this kind of social thought and on the perception of sexuality in the nineteenth century was a British clergyman and early sociologist, the Rev. Thomas Malthus. Malthus highlighted what, to him, was the central contradiction of the age: sexual desire was necessary, pleasant and central to human happiness and social being, yet excessive sex – and hence reproduction – could lead to social disaster. Human reproduction, Malthus argued, was likely to outstrip food supply in the long run. Early marriages – and hence more children – thus must be avoided. Catherine Gallagher has pointed out that Malthus' work therefore sets out the central dilemma of the age: sexual passion and the body were universally regarded as good when properly expressed in a prudent marriage, but the misuse of the body might lead to immorality, improvident early marriages, unchecked population increase and social collapse. This simultaneous valuation and problematization of the body was reproduced in a great variety of nineteenth-century discourses in Britain, America and Europe. Partly as a consequence of Malthusian thought, the 'appropriate' use of sexuality became one of the principal themes of nineteenth-century Western culture.

In a post-Malthusian world, in which moral and social certainties were rent asunder by social and political change, various solutions were offered to the problem of sex. One of these was to lay stress on the spiritual content of desire, which redeemed it from the animal, the lustful and the merely physical. Another solution was to try and regulate desire and reproduction according to strict rules based on rationality and the Malthusian dilemma. These features are evident across Anglo-American culture, but were developed most fully amongst those reformers and social leaders who were trying to remake the world. Such trends are most obvious among religious communitarians and the emerging middle classes of the early nineteenth century. In particular, the application of spirituality to sexuality was a feature of the religious revivals and consequent communitarian experiments which took place in the US before 1850, especially the northeastern states. It became easier to start society – and sex – anew in the small communities of like believers which were a feature of American revivalism on the western fringes of settlement in the early nineteenth century. These groups, as well as reforming property so that it was held in common, also faced the difficulty of how to perpetuate their communities. This led them to various experiments in restricting and organizing courtship, sex and reproduction.

One branch of communitarianism tried to banish sex altogether. These were the Shakers, a Quaker sect whose origins lay in northern Britain in the 1780s. They were led by Ann Lee, an English woman who was convinced that she was a prophet, the 'woman clothed with the sun' mentioned in Revelations, and a second, risen Christ. Taking inspiration from a New Testament passage in which Jesus praises the unique sanctity of the unmarried, the Shakers banned all sexual relations in their communities and sought to sublimate sexual energy through energetic rituals such as dancing. Similarly, the 'Perfectionists', who settled in Oneida, New York, took inspiration from the same biblical passage, although they interpreted it to mean that marriage and permanent sexual unions with one person – what they called 'special love' – should be prevented. In their place, the Perfectionists – so called because they claimed to have attained a kind of inner spiritual perfection – instituted a system of partner swapping, or 'complex marriage', which lasted from 1848, when Oneida was founded, until 1879, when the practice was partially abandoned.

In the view of the Perfectionist leader, John Humphrey Noyes, and of European communitarians like Robert Owen and Charles Fourier, marriage was the source of human selfishness, not to mention a system of gender subordination bordering on slavery. While Owen and his followers in Britain tried to abandon marriage and replace it with a relatively unregulated 'free love', Perfectionist complex marriage involved a complicated system of rules governing sexual relations and intimacy between the sexes. These regulations – partly inspired by Malthus' dire predictions about population – were bolstered by incessant debate on what emotional relationships were permissible within the community. Deep attachment to one individual, or 'special love', was discouraged in order to foster allegiance to the larger 'family' of the community itself. Regulation extended to questions of sexual practice. In particular, men were required to practise 'male continence'. This meant not ejaculating during sex, largely as a means of birth control, but also in order to free women from the onerous task of childbearing and allow them to participate more fully in the work of the community.

These practices were regarded by critics of communitarians as an encouragement to sexual licence, but, as Lawrence Foster has explained, part of the popularity of Shakerism, Perfectionism and of Mormonism – which introduced marriage reform in the shape of polygamy in the

1840s – was that these groups promised a solution to the difficulties of frontier life, one of which was the widespread breakdown of conventional marriage. Foster suggests that the problems associated with economic expansion, social mobility and competing value systems in areas of westward growth had made it impossible to maintain conventional bourgeois marital ideals and practices. The Shakers, Perfectionists and Mormons were, he argues, 'only the tip of an iceberg of dissatisfaction with prevailing marriage, family, and sex roles'. He notes that a widespread practice in disrupted communities on the fringes of westward expansion was 'spiritual wifery', a vague term which at best suggested 'rationalised infidelity'.[3] Polygamy, complex marriage, celibacy and free love were therefore concerted attempts to reinforce and rethink marriage and sexual intimacy in the face of social upheaval and the breakdown of conventional morals.

Sexuality was at the centre of religious revivals and communitarian experiments and was hedged about by complex rules and rituals. As such, the form taken by millennial religion on both sides of the Atlantic would seem to bear out Gallagher's point about the problematic centrality of the body and sexuality to early nineteenth-century thought. Another area in which sexuality was simultaneously valued and problematic was in the formation of the middle class. Middle-class identity, forming in Britain and urban America from the 1830s onwards, was initially predicated on superior morals and religious, usually evangelical, purity. Historians have identified the emergence of separate spheres (public for men, private for women) as a key component of this class identity, an idea which also placed great stress on the sanctity of home and on the purity and sexual passivity of middle-class women. The polar opposite of such purity and morality was an unrestrained sexuality. While Nancy Cott and others have argued that sexual and moral purity was embraced as a source of power for middle-class women in America, abundant evidence exists of the passionate sex lives of some women. Peter Gay, for instance, uncovered in the 1970s the intimate diary of one New England woman, Emily Dickinson's friend and editor Mabel Loomis Todd. Despite coming from the very stern Puritan tradition which produced evangelical revivals on both sides of the Atlantic, and living at the heart of haute bourgeois culture, Todd's sex life was passionate, frequent, guiltless and satisfying. Such women therefore faced what seems to us like a contradiction in their very self-image. They addressed the central problem in marriage of how to admit the centrality and pleasure of legitimate sexuality without allowing that sexuality to descend into an immoral sensuality.[4]

As Steven Seidman has pointed out, the way to redeem sexuality, solve the dilemma posed by Malthus, and to ensure that sex did not damage the soul by becoming a mere sensual indulgence, was by insisting on its spiritual nature. Marriage, therefore, became a species of spiritual love, primarily a communion of souls rather than bodies. According to one American writer of the mid-century, marriage was constituted by a 'perfect oneness of feeling and confluence of soul', by 'the complete solution of every feeling and faculty of each with every feeling and faculty of the other, and [by] longing for its attendant spiritual communion'.[5]

According to Seidman, sexuality was in this way 'de-eroticised', divorced from carnal impulses, and rendered safe through its confinement to heterosexual, spiritual marriage.[6] Spiritual love of this kind was a very common presence in the nineteenth century, in both Britain and America, and did not only sanction sexual desire within marriage. Intense, passionate friendships between men and between women were also characterized by a similar kind of pure, spiritual communion. However, although these romantic friendships were loving, they were not necessarily sexual in the twenty-first-century meaning of that term.

Jonathan Katz argues that a religious understanding of the separation between spiritual and physical was what allowed these friendships to be so intense. Physical and spiritual love were two very different things, and in most circumstances were not allowed to be confused. Donald Yacovone, in a study of the anti-slavery movement in America, argues that spiritual forms of love were inherently Christian. Abolitionism on both sides of the Atlantic was cemented as a movement by a Christian love, or agapé, which imitated God's love for his children and sought to repair the damage wrought by the Fall. Similarly, the Abolitionists looked to the early Christian church as their model of community, and thought of themselves as apostles in the same way. These religious associations allowed some Abolitionists to say openly that they 'sometimes felt really in love' with their intimate friends without feeling that this implied an 'unnatural' or 'morbid' physical attraction.[7] In a similar way, Lillian Faderman has suggested that romantic friendships between women were characteristic of Western societies in the nineteenth century, and were legitimate and encouraged. Faderman suggested, famously, that the homosocial nature of life at the time, and the pervasive idea that female sexuality was inherently passive, created a space in which intense, usually chaste relationships between women became the norm. The nineteenth century, then, was in some ways a golden age of same-sex love.

Were these friendships ever sexual? Earlier historians, writing at a time when any hint of same-sex desire might be discreditable, usually took a defensive line on this question. The biographers of some key nineteenth-century figures who experienced these friendships such as Walt Whitman, Abraham Lincoln or William Lloyd Garrison, were keen to exonerate their heroes of any taint of homosexuality.[8] Later writers, more from concern over accuracy than any disdain of homosexuality, also caution against 'mistaking the language of religious ecstasy... or agapé, for homoeroticism or outright "homosexuality"'.[9] Since no language of sexual identity based around the categories of homosexual/heterosexual existed for much of the nineteenth century, it is anachronistic to suggest that romantic friends be subsumed within these categories.

While this is a useful principle to observe, it would be wrong not to recognize that romantic friendship did have a physical component, but perhaps not in a way which connects these relationships to the modern idea of 'sexual identity'. Yacovone, for instance, admits that physical intimacy, such as kisses of greeting, was at the heart of Abolitionist culture. Similarly, Lillian Faderman's thesis that all spiritual friendships between women were chaste has been substantially revised in the light of Anne Lister's diaries. These journals, compiled in the 1820s and 1830s in the north of England, show a young, aristocratic woman enjoying a spirited sex life with a variety of female lovers, all of whom presumably appeared to the outside world as her (chaste) friends.[10] Similarly, Katz shows that as the nineteenth century progressed, many men tried to assemble a language of homoerotic love out of the tradition of spiritual friendship, thereby blurring the lines between them. Also, as Seidman shows, the spiritual could in some circumstances be the vehicle for physical love. In addition, other writers have argued that the tradition of chivalry, which was revived in the nineteenth century, always contained a sexually ambiguous element, especially in the hands of particular poets such as Gerard Manley Hopkins.[11]

The question of whether spiritual intimacy and religious dissidence was actually hiding physical homosexual relationships has been at the centre of one of the major controversies of nineteenth-century British religious history. This controversy, which revolves around the question of whether leading figures in the Anglican (Episcopalian) church were homosexual, is not merely of academic interest at a time when modern Anglicanism worldwide is seriously divided over its attitude to gay priests. This debate has centred on the Oxford Movement, a reform group within the early Victorian Anglican church which attained its strongest influence in the period c.1830–60. The Oxford Movement, also known as the Tractarians from their practice of publishing controversial religious tracts, had many different facets. Firstly, the Tractarians wanted to effect a rapprochement between the Protestant Anglican church and the Catholic church from which it separated at the Reformation. To this end they argued that, with some modifications, the Anglican church could maintain its identity, but also resume its place as a branch of the one, true church. Their proposed reforms centred on ritual, into which they incorporated particular high church practices normally associated with Catholic liturgy such as rich ornamentation, elaborate vestments, Latin mass, decorated altars, celibacy and monasticism. In addition, they continually stressed the common historical inheritance of both the Protestant and Catholic churches and revived the ostensibly Catholic practice of writing and celebrating lives of the saints, a genre associated with the early, Catholic, church.

To their low-church critics, the Tractarians seemed to be diluting Protestantism to the point where it ceased to exist and instead became a form of Catholicism. Although these arguments might now appear arcane, at the time they went right to the heart of national identity. The Protestant, Anglican church was the established church of Britain, and as such maintained strong links with the state. In the early nineteenth century, the link between church and state was frequently held to be a vital pillar of the constitution, especially by conservatives. It was feared that any weakening of the Protestant church might therefore have extensive political ramifications at a time when other major constitutional changes, such as the extension of the franchise, were being made. Moreover, Catholicism was simply un-English, being associated with foreign despotisms which as recently as 1745 had tried to overthrow the English crown by encouraging internal rebellion, and with Irish immigrants who were commonly portrayed as feckless, undisciplined and rebellious.

The most famous attack on the Tractarians came from within the Church of England. In 1851, Charles Kingsley, a mainstream Anglican clergyman, denounced the Oxford Movement, and especially its leader John Henry Newman, in terms which seemed to hint that the Tractarians' deviance was not only religious, but transgressed ideals of manliness and perhaps even sexuality. 'In all that school', Kingsley wrote, 'there is an element of foppery... a fastidious, maundering, die-away effeminacy, which is mistaken for purity and refinement.'[12] David Hilliard has read Kingsley's attack on Tractarian effeminacy as 'the usual nineteenth-century caricature of male homosexuality', and as such, a denunciation of the barely hidden sexual deviance of the entire Anglo-Catholic movement.[13] In addition, Hilliard suggests that the movement as a whole, with its emphasis on transcendent purity, spiritual friendship and lush ritual, provided a refuge for homosexual men in an otherwise hostile culture. Celibacy in particular appealed to young men unable to recognize or express their sexual feelings, and who instead devoted themselves to a life of purity and virginity 'in the company of like-minded friends, as a religiously-sanctioned alternative to marriage'.[14] Hilliard is not alone is noticing a correspondence between homosexuality and high-church practice. Ellis Hanson has noted a similar affinity between Catholicism, *fin de siècle* decadence and homoerotic aestheticism.[15]

It is certainly the case that some of the leading figures of the Oxford Movement developed intense and loving friendships. Newman, for instance, insisted on being buried in the same grave as his constant companion Ambrose St John, while the Oxford don Frederick Faber wrote many effusive poems to his male friends. In addition, the Oxford Movement led to the establishment of numerous brotherhoods and Tractarian theological colleges, such as Newman's at Cuddesdon near Oxford. Hilliard suggests that the atmosphere of male brotherhood, along with the exaltation of celibate purity may have been 'especially attractive to homosexually-inclined young men'.[16] Moreover, Christian brotherhoods were dogged by actual homosexual scandals. The establishment of the self-styled Father Ignatius (real name John Lyne) in Norfolk aroused particular suspicion when a Norwich newspaper published a love letter written by the choirmaster to a boy. In addition to this kind of scandal, the liturgy, dress and general atmosphere of the Oxford Movement was thought transgressive of particular gender ideals. In particular, the sensual rituals of Tractarian churches were thought at the time to attract 'sentimental ladies and womanish men-youths of a lachrymose turn of mind'.[17]

Although some of the late-Victorian historians of the Oxford Movement remarked on the womanly nature of its leaders, the possibility of their homosexuality was first raised by Geoffrey Faber's *Oxford Apostles*, published in 1933, a book which subjected Tractarian leaders to posthumous psychoanalysis. Faber argued that the celibacy of Newman and his Oxford associate Hurrell Froude, a spiritually intense young man whose early death turned him into a combination of saint and martyr for the movement, probably had a homosexual origin. Moreover, Froude's private journal, discovered by his friends after his death, is full of tortured self-reproach about painful emotions, dangerous friendships, and 'thoughts which... are too shocking even to name'. Faber concluded that Froude's self-torture was 'the unmistakable language of conflict with sexual temptation', a battle which was resolved through the idealization of pure, virginal, Christian love.[18]

In spite of this evidence there are many problems with trying to identify 'homosexuals', in the modern sense of the term, in the Oxford

Movement. As Katz and others have suggested, these terms of sexual identity are anachronistic in the extreme when applied to Victorian expressions of intimacy which kept the erotic and the spiritual entirely separate. In addition, attacks on the movement's 'effeminacy' were not directed against any visible homosexuality. In 1851, effeminacy did not necessarily denote homosexual desire. Attacks on the effeminacy and ritual of the Tractarians such as that by Kingsley were not specifically about gender, but instead included a cluster of fears about national identity, religious ethics, secrecy, manliness and the role of the church in the world.

Kingsley's attacks on celibacy were motivated by his particular view of marriage, nature and the role of the church. He belonged to a section of the church to which has been attached the somewhat pejorative label 'muscular Christianity'. This was a form of liberal Anglicanism which sought engagement with, and active intervention in, the problems of the world, and also rejected dogmatic distinctions between truth and error. As a result it set itself against the ethos of ascetic purity and withdrawal associated with Tractarianism. According to this view, it was celibacy rather than any more 'unnatural' passion that was the worst crime of Anglo-Catholicism because it alienated man from his natural self. As John Maynard has shown, Kingsley's enthusiastic embrace of marital sexuality, and the placing of sexual desire at the heart of his religious worldview, gave his assaults on the Tractarians a very personal edge. Kingsley, in common with the men and women written about by historians like Steven Seidman and Peter Gay, regarded marital sex as a religious and spiritual rite, a kind of 'communion' between husband and wife.[19] Although, as Seidman argues, the spiritual was introduced to mitigate sensuality, it nevertheless took its place at the centre of Christian sexuality. For Christians like Kingsley, the spiritual and the sexual were not necessarily separate, but, Maynard suggests, were aspects of each other, mutually reinforcing modes of expression. Kingsley saw in Tractarianism the belief that man was an essentially spiritual, non-sexual being, and this contradicted his own view of the nature of humanity, the role of religion and the place of sexuality within it. Therefore, the controversy between Tractarians and evangelicals, Kingsley and Newman, was in fact sexual, but it was not only about effeminacy and possible homosexuality in the way earlier historians have assumed.

More recent approaches guided by queer theory offer a way through the thicket of argument about both the Oxford Movement and the nature of spiritual friendship. Queer approaches suggest that instead of trying to read homosexuality into past friendships, we should understand those attachments on their own terms. On the one hand, queer interpretations simply compel us to be more careful with the sources, and not to foist modern categories of understanding on the past. On the other, queer theory recognizes that sexuality cannot necessarily be subsumed within categories like heterosexual/homosexual. As a result, queer approaches are profoundly historical in suggesting that we recognize the fundamental otherness of past sexual experience or desire. Frederick Roden, Ellis Hanson, and literary scholars such as David Alderson and Julia Savile therefore suggest that understanding the intimacies of men like Newman, Froude and Frederick Faber as profoundly indeterminate, as resistant to modern understandings of gender and desire, is a far more radical step to take than simply identifying them as homosexual using the interpretive terms of the present. As we have seen, when such identification is attempted, there is always some doubt, some extra multiplicity, something left over that the sources cannot recount. Roden, for instance, focuses not on sexual identity, but on 'an erotic energy that might be expressed as love, sublimated in friendship, used as the driving force for the creation of literary art, or embraced as religious ecstasy'.[20] The fundamental otherness of past sexuality must therefore be confronted.

As the Newman–Kingsley controversy shows, anti-Catholicism in British culture had a profoundly sexual element. Conflicts over the nature of Catholicism were also imported into the US because of the conflicting religious allegiances of immigrants from northern and southern Europe. One of the most pernicious aspects of Catholicism, according to its critics, was the fact that it made specific threats to morality and the family, especially through the practice of confession. Anti-Catholic agitators in Britain argued that the practice of confession was particularly threatening to women, since it involved a detailed interrogation about their secret sins which could extend to sexual matters. Fears about the apparent secrecy of Catholic practices extended not just to the confessional, but also to anxieties about what went on in Tractarian brotherhoods and Catholic convents. Walter Arnstein has described the career of one leading anti-Catholic Member of Parliament, Charles Newdegate, who continually demanded an inspectorate for nunneries and monasteries, while at the same time employing private detectives to try and discover salacious convent scandals.[21]

The sexual danger posed by Catholicism was the theme of much anti-Catholic writing on both sides of the Atlantic in the nineteenth century. As Hanson has pointed out, anti-Catholic writing frequently functions as the 'pornography of Puritanism', in the sense that it portrays Catholicism as inherently sexual: it is 'vampiric... seductive, perverse, decadent, often feminine, and certainly fatal'.[22] The sexual peril lurking in the confessional was the theme of the most famous anti-Catholic pamphlet in Victorian Britain. *The Confessional Unmasked: Showing the Depravity of the Romish Priesthood, the Iniquity of the Confessional and the Questions Put to Females in Confession*, was first published in Britain in 1836. It purported to expose the teaching of Catholic priests at the seminary in Maynooth, Ireland, which in the face of much controversy, was funded by the British government. The pamphlet consisted of extracts from eighteenth-century instruction manuals for priests, and focused particularly on questions about sexual sin. Some of these extracts governed 'the Carnal sins which man and wife commit with one another', and specified sinful sexual positions, while others dealt with 'Touches, Looks and Filthy Words' and the sin of Onan.[23] These instructions were said to pose a grievous threat to the virtue of women and the sanctity of the family. 'Are not these questions', the author asked,

> Questions pressed by celibate priests on maids and married women – on British subjects and British legislators – in private and under terror of damnation *admirably* adapted, by their PIOUS OBSCENITY and RELIGIOUS MALICE, to convert an Eden into a Sodom, a hospitable people into fanatical assassins?[24]

Whereas attacks on the Oxford Movement had been inexplicit in their assaults on effeminacy and 'sentimental' young men, anti-Catholic propaganda like *The Confessional Unmasked* used language specifically designed to inflame sexual terrors and associate sexual depravity with Catholics and Irish immigrants. 'Romish priests', it declared, were trapped in the contradiction of their faith. They were supposed to be moral but confession demanded that they traffic in intimate and indecent sexual knowledge. As a consequence, a priest was both 'pure as an angel, yet more corrupt than a Sodomite... the slave of the most debasing sensuality', guilty of 'exposing the nakedness and perverting the faculties of those who put themselves under his influence'.[25] Women were especially at risk from these 'mesmerists', who would usurp the authority of fathers if allowed. A lecture tour to publicize the book drew supporters and opponents in vast numbers to British cities, with as many as 100,000 people gathering in Birmingham in 1867 in support of or in opposition to the lecturer Patrick Murphy. Wherever he went across the north and midlands of England, 'Murphy riots' broke out. Sexual matters, in this case, were at the very centre of Victorian questions of religion, race and immigration.

The example of the *Confessional Unmasked*, as well as the Kingsley–Newman controversy, shows that there were moments in the nineteenth century when sexual matters did become linked explicitly with questions of religion and spirituality. In addition, towards the end of the century there was a noticeable turn among homosexual writers towards religion. Hilliard's work suggests that in the late nineteenth century the homoeroticism which was always present in the spiritual friendships established in Anglo-Catholic monasteries became far more explicit and open. Ellis Hanson also maintains that many decadent writers, including Walter Pater and Oscar Wilde, turned to Catholicism in the 1890s because of its similarity to aspects of aestheticism. Moreover, a number of writers turned to ideas of spiritual comradeship to argue for the legitimacy of homosexual desire, and to take a stand against late-Victorian discourses which identified that desire as low, brutal and wholly physical.

The moment when the language of spiritual love and attachment changed, and became openly available to describe sexual, and specifically, homoerotic desire, can be glimpsed in the 1890s. The language of comradeship was one of the key resources of English writers like Edward Carpenter and John Addington Symonds, two of the most famous homophile authors of the late nineteenth century. Both argued tentatively for the nobility of homosexual desire against the prevailing view that it was a species of moral wickedness. A key element in this reformulation of comradeship was the poetry of Walt Whitman. Whitman's work was a celebration of the working man, of 'comrade love', and the beauty of the physical body. Symonds in particular found in Whitman the perfect unity of spirit, body and love, a trinity which had the potential to ennoble all attachments between men. In addition, this 'democratic chivalry' promised to help bridge the distance between the classes. Whitman's writing was not only a vision of manly love, but also provided an account of how comradeship could cement a progressive social movement based on love that would build a new Jerusalem – a 'City of Friends'. Whitman promised to 'make the most splendid race the sun every yet shone upon', to 'Make divine magnetic lands/ With the love of comrades,/ With the life-long love of comrades'.[26]

Whitman's idea of comrade love always contained something ineffable and spiritual, 'something fierce and terrible in me, eligible to burst forth, I dare not tell it, even in these songs'. This ineffability lent itself to spiritual and homoerotic readings, especially of the 'Calamus' sections of *Leaves of Grass*. The spiritual or the transcendent was vital to Whitman, as it was to his followers in Britain, Europe and North America. As modern critics have noted, Whitman equates desire and death. For him, death is a means of transcending the spiritual and bodily agonies brought about by an intense passion:

> O I think it is not for life I am chanting here my chant of lovers, I think it must be for death,
> For how calm, how solemn it grows to ascend to the atmosphere of lovers,
> Death or life I am then indifferent, my soul declines to prefer
> (I am not sure but the high soul of lovers welcomes death most)[27]

Such visions of transcendent love provided a common theme in the writing of the 1890s, especially in attempts to legitimize homosexuality. In particular, the ineffable nature of Whitman's poetry, his equation of death, desire and spiritual love proved useful to those men who sought to escape the supposed 'morbidity' of homoerotic desire by insisting on its transcendent quality.[28] In the writing of the *fin de siècle* we can see the language of chivalry, and spiritual comradeship turning tentatively into an explicit vocabulary of sexual desire.

This is particularly visible among the followers of Whitman and Carpenter, although it is by no means confined to them. The remarkable diaries of a Scottish doctor give some clue as to how the ideas of spirituality, comradeship, homoerotic desire and transcendent spiritual love coalesced. John Johnston, who lived in Bolton in the northwest of England, belonged to a small group of friends who knew Edward Carpenter and informed his theories of the 'intermediate sex'. Johnston and his confreres also took a keen interest in many contemporary movements and intellectual trends, including socialism, Whitman, theories of homosexuality, theosophy and spiritualism. In spite of having little connection with literary circles, they met Walt Whitman and tried, with some success, to use his 'teachings' on the nature of comradeship to influence the early Labour party. The significance of these men lies in the way they used spirituality as a resource to understand their desire.

Johnston and his friend J.W. Wallace habitually expressed an effusive, romantic love for each other, and both borrowed ideas from Carpenter and Whitman to examine their own desires. They exalted comrade love, and found its pure expression in Whitman's poetry, but they also began to entertain the idea that a new type of person was evolving who would develop what they called 'cosmic consciousness'. This mystical new form of awareness was, they thought, evident in Whitman, and to an extent in Carpenter. It involved the sudden development of a higher awareness, an experience akin to both religious conversion and sexual awakening.

Undergoing such a revelation gave one a realization of the oneness of the universe, and heralded the development of acute powers of perception. One of the signs of cosmic consciousness was the ability to develop a transcendent love for one's comrades. Both Wallace and Johnston fell under the spell of a young American Whitmanite named Philip Dalmas, a man who seemed to have developed cosmic consciousness. In his case this was expressed in an extravagant, sometimes physical love which he assured Johnston would endure after death, in synaesthesia and various other manifestations of acute psychical development including the self-professed development of an 'astral body'.

The idea of cosmic consciousness, which was originally developed by Whitman's doctor R.M. Bucke, influenced Edward Carpenter in his attempt to describe homosexual or 'intermediate' types of people. Carpenter argued that men and women who experienced homosexual desire combined the characteristics of both sexes. As a result, they tended to have the beneficial features of both masculinity and femininity, and to represent a higher stage in evolution. Such 'higher' types, like Walt Whitman or Philip Dalmas could be seen infrequently in the world already. On a more mundane level, the invert who had not attained quite such a high state of consciousness would nevertheless typically have a talent for art, music and social reform.[29]

The experiences of men like Johnston and Dalmas therefore reinforced Carpenter's theories. As Joy Dixon and Andrew Elfenbein have pointed out, these ideas had partly emerged from continental anthropology, and had a strong influence on early sexual science.[30] Carpenter's travels in Ceylon and India, as well as his reading of anthropology, provided ample evidence that in 'primitive' societies priests and shamen frequently took on female roles, lived as wives to men, and were in fact 'intermediate types'. This realization, along with the astonishing personality of men like Philip Dalmas, seemed to confirm Carpenter's suggestions.

Far from being an isolated and unconsidered idea, the association between higher perception, advanced evolutionary stages and homosexuality informed a number of different discourses. Joy Dixon points out that Havelock Ellis' pioneering work of sexology, *Studies in the Psychology of Sex*, incorporated Carpenter's insights and included case studies of homosexual men who felt themselves to have developed the same advanced psychic and intellectual qualities that he and others had identified as characteristic of the invert. Whereas a previous generation of historians have stressed the medical and scientific aspects of sexology in making homosexual identity in this period, it is much more accurate to see sexual science as informed by a variety of progressive discourses, one of which was this spiritual-evolutionary understanding of the self. Andrew Elfenbein has argued that the association of special gifts with androgyny and even sexual transgression was also a much older idea, dating back to the Romanticism of the late eighteenth century. Lord Byron was the most significant figure in this idea of the sexually transgressive, queer romantic genius. His work, Elfenbein argues, cemented 'an association between genius and mysteriously unfathomable depths of erotic transgression'.[31] The idea of the specially gifted homosexual continued to have vitality well into the twentieth century.

In addition to these associations, other, less radical writers sought to use ideas of 'higher consciousness' to rethink the nature of same-sex desire. In Germany, the idea of the homosexual as a super-masculine type and a more highly evolved individual caught on much more widely than in Britain.[32] There, homosexual desire was claimed by homophile writers to be merely an extension of masculine association, or *mannerbund*. Other discourses used the idea of a higher self to present a more pacific and respectable face to the world. The French émigré and aesthete Marc Andre Raffalovich, for example, sought to make sexual inversion palatable to society by denuding it of its erotic content. The 'higher' invert was capable, according to him, of developing a spiritual being that could sublimate sexual desire through art, religion and friendship, unlike the lower pervert/sodomite who was defined solely by his passion for sex. Other aesthetic writers, such as the poet John Gray, embraced religion to escape their decadence and sexuality. Hanson points out that writers like Raffalovich and Gray were going against the trend of the times. Instead of using the spiritual as a resource for erotic desire, they were using religion and the idea of higher consciousness to put eroticism back in its place.[33]

The idea that the self might harbour another kind of consciousness, whether higher or lower, was a prevalent idea in the last two decades of the nineteenth century, especially among spiritualists. As I will explain, spiritualism also had strong links with gender transgression and unconventional sexuality. It originated in the northeastern United States, an area which was visited repeatedly by millenarian religious revivals before 1850, and which also produced the communitarian experiments discussed earlier. In this turbid atmosphere two young sisters in Rochester, New York claimed to have heard unearthly knockings and to have talked to the spirits. These 'Rochester rappings' became a national sensation and the craze for spiritualism soon spread to Britain where it became most popular in places where nonconformist Protestant sects and freethinking movements such as Owenite socialism had thrived. Alex Owen divides the spiritualist movement into three phases. The first evolved from the 1850s onwards, when spiritualism became immensely popular among the working classes, partly because of its strong association with radical politics. By the 1870s, a number of young, working-class women had become famous as mediums. However, by the late 1880s many of these women had been exposed as fraudulent or had confessed their imposture. After that, the focus of spiritualism turned away from mediumistic manifestations to scientific investigation of trance states, dreams, telepathy and automatic writing under the auspices of the educated intellectuals who led the Society for Psychical Research (SPR).

Alex Owen's classic work on spiritualism and gender, *The Darkened Room*, shows how spiritualism, like earlier religions of enthusiasm and millennial socialism, provided a space in which gender and sexuality could be transgressed safely. An indication of this status was that free love, women's rights, and other radical causes were often espoused by the same people who embraced spiritualism. Moreover, Owen points out that mediumship was a means for ordinarily powerless young women to assume status and celebrity, make a living, and gain social cachet by mixing with higher classes. In addition, the darkened room of the séance was a place where the normal rules of morality and decorum were suspended. Physical intimacy such as holding hands around the table was usual, while mediums and 'spirits' would often caress the sitters, kiss them or sit in their laps. The séance was, Owen argues, a kind of arena for the play of the unconscious, a place for the acting out of unconventional and uncanny desires. The séance was, to use a more recent theoretical idiom, queer. By focusing on physical manifestations of all kinds, Owen says, it disclosed 'the polymorphous, paradoxical, deviant, erratic, eccentric, even scandalous nature of desire and its enactment'.[34]

But was Psychical Research queer in a more obvious way? Did it provide a useful location for homosexual men and women to investigate alternative selves? Roger Luckhurst has certainly shown that what were earlier regarded as intimate, spiritual friendships were often rethought in the 1880s and 1890s as a kind of telepathic relation.[35] Some of the SPR leaders were homosexual, and this reinforces the impression that spirituality, 'higher' or 'alternate' states of mind and body, which were the dominating preoccupation of many late-Victorian homosexuals, and which later became central to self-making and to modern culture in general, have been largely overlooked by historians of sexuality. These ideas also have a much wider historical relevance. What we now consider supremely modern, secular ideas and discourses, were informed at crucial points by ideas like spiritualism and psychical research. The beginnings of modern psychiatry, psychoanalysis and psychology had their origins in research into the dynamic unconscious mind carried out by the SPR and its associates.[36]

The association between research into an alternate self and same-sex desire is by no means coincidental. Searching for a higher self which might be the source and location of homoerotic desire should not be seen as a form of repression. Instead, spiritualism, Whitmanite spirituality, Anglo-Catholic aestheticism and mediumship might all enable the expression of awkward passions which in other locations were regarded as at best immoral and at worst unnatural. Therefore it is relevant to a history of homosexual identity that some of the principal figures in the SPR were homosexual, including its leading researchers Frederick Myers, Frank Podmore and others. Myers had been at Cambridge with the homosexual and Whitmanite writer John Addington Symonds, and had also been interested in Whitman's poetry and Hellenism, although he later married.[37] The death of another SPR researcher, Edmund Gurney, in 1888 was also rumoured to have been suicide in anticipation of homosexual blackmail and consequent exposure. Gurney and Podmore had taken rooms in Brighton to conduct experiments in telepathy with a local stage hypnotist who claimed to be able to read minds. The subjects of these experiments at length confessed themselves fraudulent, and, according to one theory, Gurney's despair at the ruin of his life's work led him to suicide.[38]

Does Gurney's death or possible suicide show that there was a homosexual element to SPR researches? Gurney was working closely with Frank Podmore, who, in addition to his efforts for the SPR, worked for the Post Office in London. The office in which Podmore worked in St Martin's Lane became notorious in 1889 when the Cleveland Street scandal revealed that telegraph messengers from that office had been entertaining members of the aristocracy in a male brothel in the West End of London. Long before the scandal broke, telegraph boys had been notorious for their willingness to have sex with men for money, a fact of which Podmore must have been aware.[39] This fact makes it all the more surprising that Gurney and Podmore were prepared to lock themselves away in a Brighton hotel with a number of working-class youths, including several telegraph messengers, in order to conduct intimate experiments into their states of mind.

The association between 'higher' states or selves, psychical research and unconventional sexuality persisted in the twentieth century, and informed the emergence of another predominantly secular creed: literary and cultural modernism. Richard Dellamora has suggested that early modernism was marked strongly by its association with same-sex desire. Moreover, the decentring of consciousness, and the play with conventional gender roles which was so central to the work of Edward Carpenter, to the Whitmanites, and to many leading spiritualists, were later the stock in trade of modernist writers.[40] The British pacifist novel *Despised and Rejected* (1918), the hero of which is a classic type of the 'higher' invert in combining the best characteristics of either sex, was clearly inspired by the work of Edward Carpenter.[41]

More famous modernists also belonged to this tradition. Andrew Elfenbein has identified this trend in Radclyffe Hall's classic novel of lesbian self-discovery, *The Well of Loneliness* (1928). As well as being an enthusiastic Catholic, Hall herself was keenly interested in spiritualism, not only visiting a medium to contact her former lover Mabel Batten, but also publishing a paper with the SPR on the subject. The protagonist of the *Well*, the mannish lesbian 'Stephen' Gordon, is also a mixture of the higher invert, the classic sexological case study, and the 'intermediate type'. As Elfenbein points out, Stephen is a kind of genius who embodies masculine and feminine characteristics, and is also a classic type of invert who believes that her 'fine brain' and superior consciousness should be recognized as useful by society.[42]

However, in spite of its queer beginnings, twentieth-century modernism was more usually defined by its rejection of same-sex desire and its preference for hard facts over spiritual speculations. In this sense it reflected a general de-coupling of the link between religion-spirituality and sexuality which has gone on apace in the last hundred years. After sexology and psychoanalysis it became harder to argue that religious enthusiasm or spiritual comradeship did not have a primarily sexual origin, especially since Carpenter, Whitman and others had shown that this might be the case. By 1918, in wartime America, even the very idea of Christian brotherhood had to be defended against allegations that it was inherently homoerotic.[43] Whereas nineteenth-century religion had been allowed to be truly queer, in the sense that its cultural prestige and immense social authority meant that it might cover a variety of polymorphous and unspecific transgressions of gender and sexuality, by the early twentieth century religion had come under suspicion and fallen into decay as one of the principal locations for sexual expression of all kinds. Exceptions to this rule existed, not least in the form of Marie Stopes, whose best-selling writings on birth control and marital sex continued to characterize heterosexual sex as a mystical and ineffable communion.[44]

In spite of the persistence of this mystical idiom in the writings of Stopes, the place of religion in discussions of sexuality became increasingly insignificant. After the First World War, many modernist writers became increasingly impatient with the professed religious motivations of their eminent Victorian predecessors, and saw in their careers not the pure love of God but a self-serving hypocrisy. Progressive writers on sexuality also began to attack the entire structure of Western morals which had produced the catastrophe of war and what they saw as widespread ignorance about the facts of life. According to the advocates of wider sex education, religious morals were one of the key obstacles to sexual knowledge and were the mainstay of prudery and ignorance. This association was cemented by the religious origins of many social purity organizations in Britain, America and Western Europe.

Until the beginning of the twentieth century, spirituality reigned supreme as the desired ingredient of all passionate intimacy, including sexual desire. Since then, the spiritual element of sexual passion has lost its eminence along with the declining status of religion in Western societies as a whole. In much of Western Europe, the church, faith and the spirit no longer occupy a central role in the guidance of married couples, romantic friends, gay or straight men and women. Although the rise of the religious right in the US since the 1970s has provided a powerful challenge to liberal ideals and reforms from sex education to gay partnership laws, this evangelical zeal remains a localized American phenomenon. In spite of calls by evangelical Christians for new, more restrictive moral codes, it remains the case that in America religious discourses have not displaced medical or therapeutic versions of sexuality. Psychotherapy in all its forms, but most obviously in the shape of popular guides to relationships whose nostrums are reflected in TV, radio, novels, magazines and across the culture as a whole, remains largely unchallenged by fundamentalist Christianity. In fact, it is a measure of the dominance of the therapeutic model of selfhood that evangelical Christianity tries repeatedly to merge its own language with that of popular psychotherapy.

The fact that psychotherapeutic discourses are so dominant in European and American societies provides a good reason to study spiritual passion and religious sexuality. One of the main differences between past and existing structures of sexuality and intimacy is their spiritual content. This fact allows us to examine the fundamental otherness of sexual desire and the self even in the immediate past. Incidents such as the Newman–Kingsley controversy, the history of American communitarianism, or the nature of spiritual romantic friendship shows us that sexual desire cannot be reduced simply to the categories which are currently employed. Studies of this sort lend themselves very well to queer readings of the past. Insofar as queer refers to kinds of sexual expression which exceed available categories of gender and sexuality, the study of spirituality and sexuality is an eminently queer project.

notes

1. On this theme see Alex Owen, *The Place of Enchantment: British Occultism and the Culture of the Modern* (Chicago: University of Chicago Press, 2004); Molly McGarry, 'Ghosts of Futures Past: Spectral Sexualities in Nineteenth-Century Anglo-America', unpublished paper delivered at Queer Matters Conference (Kings College London), 29 May 2004.
2. Michel Foucault, *The History of Sexuality, An Introduction*, trans. Robert Hurley (London: Penguin, 1984), p. 59.
3. Lawrence Foster, *Religion and Sexuality: Three American Communal Experiments of the Nineteenth Century* (Oxford: Oxford University Press, 1981), p. 131; and *Women, Family and Utopia: Communal Experiments of the Shakers, The Oneida Community, The Mormons* (Syracuse: Syracuse University Press, 1991).
4. Nancy Cott, 'Passionlessness: An Interpretation of Victorian Sexual Ideology, 1790–1850', *Signs*, 4 (1978), 219–36; and *The Bonds of Womanhood* (New Haven: Yale University Press, 1977); Carroll Smith-Rosenberg, *Disorderly Conduct: Visions of Gender in Victorian America* (New York: Oxford University Press, 1985); Peter Gay, *The Bourgeois Experience, Vol. 1, The Education of the Senses* (New York: Oxford University Press, 1984).
5. Orson Fowler, *Love and Parentage* (New York, 1850), p. 88, quoted in Steven Seidman, 'The Power of Desire and the Danger of Pleasure: Victorian Sexuality Reconsidered', *Journal of Social History*, 24, 1 (1990), 47–67, 53.
6. Seidman, 'Power of Desire', 62.
7. Samuel Joseph May, of his Harvard classmate, quoted in Donald Yacovone, 'Abolitionists and the "Language of Fraternal Love"', in Mark C. Carnes and Clyde Griffen (eds.), *Meanings for Manhood: Constructions of Masculinity in Victorian America* (Chicago: University of Chicago Press, 1990), p. 90.
8. See on this Robert Martin, *The Homosexual Tradition in American Poetry* (Austin: University of Texas Press, 1979); Gary Schmidgall, *Walt Whitman: A Gay Life* (New York: Dutton, 1997). The controversy over Lincoln continues in C.A. Tripp, *The Intimate World of Abraham Lincoln* (New York: Free Press, 2004).
9. Yacovone, 'Abolitionists', p. 94.
10. See Jill Liddington, *Female Fortune: Land, Gender and Authority, The Anne Lister Diaries and Other Writings, 1833–36* (London: Rivers Oram, 1998); Helena Whitbread, *I Know My Own Heart: The Diaries of Anne Lister, 1791–1840* (London: Virago, 1988).
11. Julia F. Savile, *A Queer Chivalry: The Homoerotic Aestheticism of Gerard Manley Hopkins* (Charlottesville: University of Virginia Press, 2000); David Alderson, *Mansex Fine: Religion, Manliness and Imperialism in Nineteenth Century British Culture* (Manchester: Manchester University Press, 1998); Richard Dellamora, *Masculine Desire: The Sexual Politics of Victorian Aestheticism* (Chapel Hill: University of North Carolina Press, 1990).
12. Quoted in James Eli Adams, *Dandies and Desert Saints: Styles of Victorian Masculinity* (Ithaca: Cornell University Press, 1995), p. 98.

13. David Hilliard, 'Un-English and Unmanly: Anglo-Catholicism and Homosexuality', *Victorian Studies*, 25, 2 (1982), 181–210, 188.
14. Ibid., 185.
15. Ellis Hanson, *Decadence and Catholicism* (Cambridge, MA: Harvard University Press, 1997).
16. Hilliard, 'Un-English', 192.
17. Quoted in John Shelton Reed, *Glorious Battle: The Cultural Politics of Victorian Anglo-Catholicism* (Nashville: Vanderbilt University Press, 1996), p. 211.
18. Quoted in Geoffrey Faber, *Oxford Apostles: A Character Study of the Oxford Movement* (London: Faber and Faber, 1933), p. 218.
19. John Maynard, *Victorian Discourses on Sexuality and Religion* (Cambridge: Cambridge University Press, 1993), p. 96.
20. Frederick S. Roden, *Same Sex Desire in Victorian Religious Culture* (Basingstoke: Palgrave Macmillan, 2002), p. 4.
21. Walter L. Arnstein, *Protestant Versus Catholic in Mid-Victorian England: Mr Newdegate and the Nuns* (London: University of Missouri Press, 1982).
22. Hanson, *Decadence and Catholicism*, p. 264.
23. Anon., *The Confessional Unmasked: Showing the Depravity of the Romish Priesthood, the Iniquity of the Confessional and the Questions Put to Females in Confession* (London: Protestant Electoral Union, 1871), pp. 56–72.
24. Ibid., p. iii.
25. Ibid.
26. Walt Whitman, 'For You O Democracy', in Francis Murphy (ed.), *Walt Whitman: The Complete Poems* (Harmondsworth: Penguin, 1977), p. 150.
27. Whitman, 'Scented Herbage of My Breast', in Murphy, *Walt Whitman*, p. 147.
28. See H.G. Cocks, *Nameless Offences: Homosexual Desire in the Nineteenth Century* (London: I.B. Tauris, 2003), ch. 5.
29. Edward Carpenter, *The Intermediate Sex: A Study of Some Transitional Types of Men and Women* (London: George Allen and Unwin, 1908), ch. V.
30. Joy Dixon, 'Sexology and the Occult: Sexuality and Subjectivity in Theosophy's New Age', *Journal of the History of Sexuality*, 7 (1997), 409–33; and *Divine Feminine: Theosophy and Feminism in England* (Baltimore: Johns Hopkins University Press, 2001); Andrew Elfenbein, *Romantic Genius: The Prehistory of a Homosexual Role* (New York: Columbia University Press, 1999).
31. Elfenbein, *Romantic Genius*, p. 203.
32. On this see James D. Steakley, *The Homosexual Emancipation Movement in Germany* (New York: Arno Press, 1975).
33. Hanson, *Decadence and Catholicism*, p. 323.
34. Alex Owen, *The Darkened Room: Women, Power and Spiritualism in Late Nineteenth Century England* (London: Virago, 1989), p. 222.
35. Roger Luckhurst, *The Invention of Telepathy, 1870–1901* (Oxford: Oxford University Press, 2002), p. 226.
36. See Janet Oppenheim, *The Other World: Spiritualism and Psychical Research in England, 1850–1914* (Cambridge: Cambridge University Press, 1985); Adam Crabtree, *From Mesmer to Freud: Magnetic Sleep and the Roots of Psychological Healing* (New Haven: Yale University Press, 1993); Henri F. Ellenberger, *The Discovery of the Unconscious: The History and Evolution of Dynamic Psychiatry* (New York: Basic Books, 1970); Helen Sword, 'Modernist Mediumship', in Lisa

Rado (ed.), *Modernism, Gender and Culture: A Cultural Studies Approach* (New York: Garland, 1997).

37. Frederick Myers, *Fragments of Inner Life*, revised edition (1900), unpublished, Myers Collection, Trinity College Cambridge.
38. Trevor Hall, *The Strange Case of Edmund Gurney* (London: Duckworth, 1980).
39. See Cocks, *Nameless Offences*, chs 1 and 4.
40. On these links see Richard Dellamora (ed.), *Victorian Sexual Dissidence* (Chicago: University of Chicago Press, 1999); Sword, 'Modernist Mediumship', quoted in Luckhurst, *Invention of Telepathy*, p. 256.
41. A.T. Fitzroy, *Despised and Rejected* (London: C.W. Daniel, 1918).
42. Elfenbein, *Romantic Genius*, p. 205.
43. On this see Luckhurst, *Invention of Telepathy*, p. 229; George Chauncey, 'Christian Brotherhood or Sexual Perversion? Homosexual Identities and the Construction of Sexual Boundaries in the World War One Era', *Journal of Social History*, 19 (1985), 189–211.
44. Marie Stopes, *Married Love* (London: Putnam, 1919).

8
pornography and obscenity

sarah leonard

introduction

A peculiar thing began happening in the 1980s and 90s: pornography and obscenity, long relegated to the margins of serious scholarship, began showing up at the centre of influential historical work. As new generations of historians returned to vital questions – how power operates, why revolutions occur, how belief systems change – a small but important group of scholars began to consider 'scurrilous', 'obscene' and 'pornographic' texts. Sources that an earlier generation of historians would have dismissed as trivial or opaque were now expected to yield important information about the past. What was remarkable about this work was that it was not the history of pornography *per se* – the history of genres and borrowings, printers and collectors. Instead, historians were using 'pornographic' materials as a means of asking new kinds of questions about the past. They were also using these sources to demonstrate links between realms of experience long thought to have no relationship to one another – among them, sexuality and politics; family identity and economics. In short, these historians were in the process of breaking down boundaries that had long been kept distinct and redefining what it meant to talk about politics and the political.

Historians turned to pornographic and obscene sources in part because they hoped to shed light on an emerging field of research: the history of sexuality. In the 1960s, it still flew in the face of conventional wisdom to suggest that sex (understood in its double sense of the act of physical intercourse *and* as sex roles or gender) had a history. For most professional historians, History was thought to be synonymous with dynamic change in the *public* sphere. They looked for developments in the world of economics, political institutions, and the military. Sex, gender, and the world that adhered to them, were considered 'natural', 'static', and therefore ahistorical. It was also assumed that 'private matters' – the history of the family, gender, sexual identity – had little if no bearing on important 'public' concerns. In the 1960s and 70s, this began to change, as it became increasingly clear that sexuality and sex had histories, and that so-called 'private' concerns often intersected with 'public' transformations.

At the same time, scholars began to insist that the concept of 'pornography' was the product of the nineteenth century. Pornography was not simply out there to be found, but was instead a category created over time by police and judges, readers and librarians who relegated certain texts and artefacts to a separate category of representations labelled 'pornographic', or 'obscene'. In his important history of the modern concept of pornography, Walter Kendrick advanced the thesis that pornography was not a *thing*, but an *argument*.[1] He explained that the terms of that argument changed over time, yielding new concepts of what was meant by pornography and an ever-changing body of 'pornographic' texts. Thus, pornographic sources were not only historically relevant, but pornography was itself historical.

I will argue that the story of how pornography and obscenity came to be treated as topics worthy of serious historical scholarship is also the story of the transformation of the historical profession since the 1960s. This chapter will not only describe what historians have said about the history of obscenity; it will also try to account for the emergence of interest in pornography since the 1960s. How and why did such things begin to be of interest? Interest in the obscene, the scurrilous, and the modern term, pornographic, emerged from several impulses and converged into a history of pornography that integrated a seemingly marginal set of ideas and works into proximity with many of the fundamental questions that concern historians. The history of this interest can be traced to some of the major social and political, but also to important intellectual movements of the second half of the twentieth century. These included the growing influence of post-structuralism in the 1980s – and especially the work of Michel Foucault. Just as importantly, they included social and political transformations – particularly the sexual 'revolution' of the 1960s and 70s and the feminist movement of the 70s and 80s. These social and intellectual movements converge in important places, but they are not reducible to one another, and need to be examined separately.

Both movements were important to historiographical developments because of their insistence that sexuality and gender relations were political and historically contingent. Sex and gender roles were political because they were tied explicitly to an agenda of liberation and de-repression. Sexual repression, according to the parlance of the 1960s and 70s, was symptomatic of a broader culture of hypocrisy – one that ignored and repressed presumably 'natural' and 'healthy' instincts. Some of the early works of historical scholarship were generated during this period. This chapter will examine the social, intellectual and disciplinary developments affecting the study of pornography and attempt to suggest ways they are related. It will also consider how these initial impulses transformed as historians began to explore pornography both as a source and a subject matter in relation to the world in which they developed. Finally, we will consider how ideas have developed linking pornography to violence, and to the violation of the body's integrity, as well as to the post-colonial context.

early histories and historians

Scholars agree that the modern concept of 'pornography' emerged in nineteenth-century Europe. Obscenity, Walter Kendrick argues, has existed since the advent of language and collective value systems (that is, since there has been human society); the concept of pornography was generated by ongoing debates between publishers, authors, librarians, pedagogues, policemen, and legal courts over the effects of certain texts or images on the individual and on public society. 'From the start', Kendrick writes, '"pornography" named a battlefield, a place where no assertion could be made without at once summoning up its denial.'[2] The historical preconditions for these debates were urbanization, increasing literacy, innovations in publishing and the growth of public institutions like the library or museum that made texts and images available to an increasing number of readers and viewers.

Similarly, Lynda Nead's *Victorian Babylon* argues that 'obscenity' in its modern incarnation must be seen in the context of an emerging popular culture rooted in the industrial urban landscapes of the mid-nineteenth-century city. 'Obscenity', she argues, 'was… simply the most explicit and dangerous instance of the many new cultural forms that had emerged within the modern city.'[3] Street literature, or the 'Boulevard Press', played a dual role: on the one hand, it was an expression of the new dangers of the city, which opened up new spaces in which anonymous consumers were exposed to potentially obscene texts and images.[4] At the same time, Nead argues, the continuing presence of the boulevard press seemed to undermine modern claims that the city could be rationalized.

Thus modern notions of obscenity were linked with mass literacy, the anonymity of urban spaces, and a newly prolific popular press.

It is not surprising, therefore, that the first histories of pornography were produced in the nineteenth century. Yet these histories were not the work of professional historians; instead they were produced by bibliographers, librarians, and book collectors. In the late eighteenth and early nineteenth centuries, long before such sources were considered worthy of serious study by historians, collectors and bibliophiles were intrigued by the challenges of documenting obscene works. Interest in these works emerged in part because many publishers of illegal works actively hid their material origins. Publishers would print false imprints to throw the authorities off the track; authors would use pseudonyms and booksellers would often falsify their marks. The challenges of historical reconstruction intrigued those fascinated by the material history of book production and the detective work involved in historical reconstruction. This was especially the case with this kind of material because so much of it was illegal, and therefore the origins of such were hidden from view. The process through which certain forms of literature were designated 'dangerous' was by no means one-sided – authors, publishers and booksellers were also complicit in this process. Indeed, many profited from the free publicity that attended trials and prohibitions.

In one of the first serious attempts to write a history of obscenity, Steven Marcus devoted considerable time to the work of the famous nineteenth-century bibliophile, Henry Spencer Ashbee. Publishing his work under the pseudonym *Pisanus Fraxi*, Ashbee devoted himself to tracing the publication histories of illicit and 'curious' literature. Such collectors were important figures in part because their material efforts to document, catalogue, collect and preserve collections made it possible to consult such works, but also for the work they did in defining pornography as separate categories. Questions of value, rarity and condition preoccupy such collectors; but their work has been extremely important in terms of collecting the artefacts. Much of the initial work – on legal frameworks, legal cases and publication details – was done by these earlier historians, bibliographers and bibliophiles. We think, for instance, of the great nineteenth-century book collectors who wrote on erotic literature: among them collector-historians such as Gustave Brunet (1807–1896); P.L. Jacob (1806–1884) who wrote under the pseudonyms Paul Lacroix and Pierre Dufour; Frédéric Lachèvre (1855–1945); and Louis Perceau (1883–1942). While many bibliophiles and bibliographers, among them Hugo Hayn (1843–1923), were particularly concerned with the physical condition of the books and the market price they commanded, there were also collectors who expressed genuine interest in the content and ideas expressed in the texts.[5] Among the latter category was the Bavarian privy councillor Franz von Krenner, who collected widely on the theme of 'love' as discussed in dissertations, medical treatises, and legal texts, in addition to pornographic works.[6]

A similar process attends the early history of pornographic film – stag films, for example, which might have been collected out of pleasure for the material object, but which nonetheless formed the basis for collections such as that of the Kinsey institute, which were invaluable for later scholars.[7] Long before scholars saw value in pornographic works or even considered them historical sources at all, bibliographers, collectors, and librarians were treating these objects as important cultural artefacts. The key to most of this early work was its focus on the materiality of the text – on the physical qualities of the book, pamphlet, film, image. These scholars concerned themselves with where and by whom they were produced, where they were sold or shown, and to the technological change related to the creation of these artefacts.

One other expression of interest in pornography came during the first two decades of the twentieth century within the development of sexology, expressed in the work of Krafft-Ebing and Magnus Hirschfeld. German sexologists like Iwan Bloch and Paul Englisch began to study sexually explicit literature for clues about the evolution of human sexual behaviour. In the 1920s and 30s, Englisch himself published two major histories of erotic literature in which he revealed his encyclopaedic knowledge of the subject matter.[8] Englisch was still focused primarily on the history of pornography itself – treated as something unrelated to transformations taking place in the world around it. Instead, he was interested in the material history of books and other publications – with publishers, imprints, speculation about pseudonymous authorship and distribution routes. At the same time, Englisch hoped that the serious study of pornographic texts would provide insight into the history of human sexual behaviour. He approached the material hoping to find serious the untold histories of customs and morals (*Sittengeschichten*) that reigned in particular eras.

This impulse to mine obscene works for information about human sexuality was itself historical. Sexologists' laborious efforts to document and analyse the history of sexuality were undertaken in the 1920s and 30s, a period that saw the fundamental transformation of relationships between the sexes throughout Western Europe. Perhaps it is not surprising that sexology and the new preoccupation with the science of sex emerged in post-First World War Europe. With 10 million men dead, and millions more returning home as invalids, women took on new roles, divorce rates rose, and fewer people married; the extent to which sexuality was mutable and historical must have been readily apparent to these new 'experts' on sex.[9]

We might even consider the thesis that histories of sexuality are not only rooted in new ideas of expertise, but also in the collective experience of new social realities. This is a thesis we will have ample opportunity to explore in the discussion that follows. But it is nonetheless worthwhile to keep in mind not only the emerging historical research on pornography and obscenity, but also how contemporary concerns informed the questions historians asked about the past.

1960s scholarship

Given the nineteenth-century impulse to classify and catalogue, it should not be surprising that one of the first major pieces of scholarship on the history of pornography came from the world of collectors and librarians. In the early 1960s, David Foxon, by profession a librarian and bibliographer, published an important series of essays on the history of what he termed 'libertine literature'. These essays played an important role in opening the door to interest in the literature of this period.[10] Foxon describes what emerged out of his unexpected engagement with the history of seventeenth-century libertine texts.

> To my mind, the most important and unexpected discovery in this study is the way in which pornography seems to have grown to maturity in a brief period in the middle of the 17th century... it seems to me to show that however much men remain the same in their erotic preoccupations, the form in which these are expressed does vary, and that at this period sex becomes to some extent intellectualized.

Foxon insisted that pornography had a history – that is, that its form and subject matter changed over time. And perhaps even more importantly, he suggested that perhaps pornography might reveal the 'unacknowledged attitudes of different periods'.[11]

Foxon's tentative hypothesis, since pursued by other historians, was that the seventeenth century marked a turning point in the history of 'libertine' literature.[12] In this work, the history of pornography was for the first time framed in terms of the history of modernity – in the seventeenth century sex was 'intellectualized' as interest in the human body (but also in physical bodies like spheres and planets) grew. As historians have worked to write the history of pornography, the seventeenth century continues to be one of the central foci of research, as sexuality was linked in seventeenth-century science, philosophy, materialism and critiques of the church. That is, Foxon suggested that historical modernity and the evolution of obscenity had something to do with one another.

Finally, Foxon historicized obscenity in another key way: he suggested that a nascent interest in pornography among scholars was related to transformations – and in his view a new openness – in the contemporary world: 'our increased psychological self-knowledge should help us to view the subject more rationally and to trace the beginnings and inter-relations of sexual writings more dispassionately'.[13] Foxon, like many others in the 1960s, implicitly linked the study of such taboo topics as pornography to growing self-knowledge, and however subtly, to a politics of liberation.

In 1966 – only a few years after Foxon published his three essays on seventeenth-century libertine literature – Steven Marcus published *The Other Victorians*.[14] Marcus set out to study the neglected history of Victorian England – the 'sexual subculture' marked by the prostitution, pornography and sexual promiscuity that accompanied the age of science, domesticity and liberal economics. In this work, Marcus made extensive use of pornographic memoirs and novels to explore historically specific attitudes toward the body, sexuality and the nature of male and female desire. In addition, Marcus devoted energy to studying Ashbee, the work of whom Marcus describes as 'the first bibliography in the English language devoted to writings of a pornographic or sexual character'.[15]

For Marcus, the study of sexual subcultures required an anthropological method. That is, the metaphors, attitudes and perceptions of sexuality, the body and gender were fundamentally different from our own – and to approach this world was to approach a foreign country. Marcus's work was important in several respects. First, Marcus insisted that sexuality had a history. He took this one step further and argued that this history was linked to visions of the economy, of the human subject and to medical models of the body – the history of sexuality was linked to context and place. Second, Marcus took seriously a body of sources that were previously unexplored – that is, pornographic memoirs, novels, flagellation literature and the bibliographical labours of a nineteenth-century bibliophile – to generate new insights into the history and culture of Victorian England. By so doing, he argued convincingly that such literature could be effectively mined for information about the past.

Marcus's work on pornography and sexual culture was very important then, insofar as it suggested that sexuality had a history. He also linked this history to subjects long considered 'important', such as medicine, economic theory, visions of the self and society. Finally, he used sources that few 'serious' scholars had dreamed of touching, demonstrating the importance of the collecting and classification efforts that had begun in the eighteenth century.

the transformation in historical studies: 1950–80

It is perhaps not surprising that such questions and sources began to seem relevant to scholars in the 1960s and 70s. Marcus and Foxon wrote during a period of social and political transition. Movements in the United States and Western Europe towards increased sexual 'openness' were followed by the organized efforts of feminists who insisted that sexuality, gender and reproduction were serious political matters. Like the sexologists of the 1920s and 30s, historians writing in the 60s and 70s took up the study of sex and its history at a moment when the historical variability of sexuality was especially palpable.

We should be cautious, however, about drawing facile connections between scholarship and social context. While social change may suggest and inspire new historical questions and methods, it does not *determine* the intellectual agenda of scholars in any clear-cut way. During the 1960s and 70s, there were also important transformations at the level of epistemology and the historical method that also affected the growing interest in the topics of obscenity and in pornographic literature.

For the moment, then, we will be occupied with transformations in the social sciences and humanities and the approach taken by each to questions of knowledge and its relationship to power. Knowledge of these major shifts is important to understanding how and why professional historians found themselves by the 1980s and 90s using scurrilous, obscene and pornographic works as important documents for understanding major historical developments. Before turning to examples of this scholarship, let us first consider three major developments in the 1960s and 70s that paved the way for the treatment of pornography and obscenity as subjects worthy of historical study: first, the emergence of social and later cultural history associated with the influential French historical movement, the Annales School; second, the growing influence of post-structuralist thought in the social sciences; and finally, the achievements of scholars working in the new and related fields of women's history, gender history and the history of sexuality.

The first of these three influences emerged in the heart of the historical profession, which found itself at a crossroads following the Second

World War. 'A new world', Fernand Braudel wrote in 1950, 'requires a new history.'[16] Historians began to take cues from influential scholars associated with the Annales School – among them Lucien Febvre, Marc Bloc, Fernand Braudel and Emmanuel Le Roy Ladurie. In the wake of two world wars and the genocide that accompanied it, scholars insisted that a new world – post-holocaust, post-atomic, increasingly post-colonial – required a new history. The narratives of the triumph of progress and science and civilization that had once framed historical study in the West seemed bankrupt. One of the tenets of this new history, according to Annales historians, was to move away from the history of events – of presidents, kings, wars – and consider the longer-term and deeper structures that shaped human existence. Braudel famously embarked on his studies of 'unchanging history' – geography, environment and climate. But in the 1960s, a younger generation of Annales historians began to be interested in the history of mentalities – that is, the structures of thought that framed the lens through which people – often 'ordinary' people or non-elites – saw the world. To do this, they turned to new sources and began to borrow methods from sociologists who were used to thinking about the structures that frame social existence, and anthropologists, practised in the art of studying non-elite cultures and oral sources.

These historians began to identify topics as worthy of study that would have been inconceivable to historians working in previous generations. Thus in his influential study, *Montaillou*, Emmanuel Le Roy Ladurie examined such topics as body language, sexuality, love and marriage in medieval *langue d'oc*. These were topics that had not previously been part of mainstream professional historians' purview – in part because such questions seemed to have little bearing on the 'important' developments of history. Social history, itself an outgrowth of Annales School and Marxist historical frameworks and questions, meant that historians became increasingly concerned with popular politics, the terms of legitimacy. The transformation of political history – particularly the shift towards looking at political order and disorder through the lens of popular politics – would be one of the key places that historians would begin to consider the history of obscene, scurrilous literature. We will discuss this further below, but in the meantime, let us consider the other two transformations that affected historians' relationship with the topics of obscenity and pornography.

The second development in the historical profession that made pornography a subject worthy of historical study was the profound influence of Foucault's publications – particularly *Discipline and Punish* (1977) and *Madness and Civilization* (1965). In 1976, Foucault published the first volume of *The History of Sexuality*. The importance of Foucault's work is difficult to overestimate. Just as historians in the 1970s were turning to anthropology and sociology for hints on method, the fundamental assumptions on which these disciplines rested was being subjected to challenge. Foucault's work was important to the growing interest among historians in obscenity for a number of reasons. This influence is probably best understood by considering Foucault's critique of Liberalism and the Enlightenment – a critique that opened up questions relevant to the history of pornography and obscenity. But what were the elements of this new critique of the orthodoxies of Western Liberalism, and how did this critique suggest new methods for studying pornography and obscenity?

To begin, Foucault insisted that, contrary to popular belief, the approach taken to sexuality in the West was *not* marked by silence or repression. Nothing, he argued, was further from the truth. Western societies were instead marked by multiple imperatives to speak about sex – in the confessional, the physician's office, on the psychiatrist's couch. Slowly, over time, to reveal the truth about sex was to reveal the truth of the self. Furthermore, Western societies 'spoke' of sex through the arrangement of physical spaces – middle-class Victorian homes, for example, 'spoke' of the sex that took place between adults by placing children far from their parents' bedrooms and therefore implying that something took place that was secret and even shameful.

Foucault proposed that the history of sexuality since the early-modern period is one of putting sex into forms of speech – be they legal, medical, pedagogical or religious – in which sexuality was not merely documented, but also constituted. This second point is crucial to Foucault's argument – he argues that 'sexuality' describes not a natural and universal impulse that exists prior to culture; instead, it is the putting into discourse, or language of sex. Furthermore, Foucault argued that this putting of sex into discourse was one of they key ways power operated on the Western self. He proposed that power did not simply operate through repression; it also worked through the incitement to speak, and to take pleasure in the speaking. Foucault argued instead, that 'knowledge' about sex – that is, the production of sexuality through the putting of sex into language – was in fact fundamentally tied to a form of power internalized and replicated by the individual self.

These arguments were crucial to historians' growing attention to pornography and obscenity as a topic of serious study. For one thing, he suggested that speech about sex was crucially tied to power. By revising operating assumptions about power, Foucault undermined assumptions that power existed only in the public world – of the state, government, institutions. Instead, he described power as operating at the micro-level of the subject – that is, at the most intimate level of the self. Thus liberal assumptions about power and the idea that there was a 'public' world permeated by power and a 'private' or 'intimate' world were challenged. In their place, Foucault saw a world in which the most private and seemingly intimate realms of the self were increasingly penetrated by the 'microphysics' of power. This challenge was crucial to defining intimacy, sexuality and 'private life' as subjects worthy of serious scholarly consideration. Furthermore, this opened the way for historians to begin to imagine how public power – that is, political power – was informed by particular understandings of sexuality and private life. Simply put, the liberal division between public and private was eroding as more and more work suggested links between the performance of power and the constitution of the self.

As one of the central forms of 'discourse' about sexuality in Western culture, pornography and obscenity were tied to power, rather than existing outside of it. If 'sexuality' – the putting of sex into speech – was shot through with power, this suggested that pornographic writing could no longer be seen as 'transgressive' in any straightforward way. Furthermore, it implicated pornography in its discussion of 'intimate' matters in the workings of power, both at the level of the individual subject and at the level of other forms of power. Finally, Foucault's challenge to the strict separation of public (powerful and historical) and private (power-free and ahistorical) would be crucial to the historical profession's growing interest in new topics. After Foucault's work, obscenity and pornography could no longer be dismissed as 'trivial' – that is, private, unimportant, not bound up with power. By fundamentally challenging received notions of power – what it was, how it operated, where it was located, and which realms of existence it permeated – Foucault opened up new ideas about where to look to study power. Pornography and obscenity was one of these new places to look.

The third impulse to study pornography and obscenity came from the growing importance of feminist theory within the humanities and social sciences. Once again, the 1970s were a crucial decade. In history, the first theoretical framework for women's history emerged out of labour history. Women's historians were quick to point out that, after all, women had always been labourers. Furthermore, labour history's debt to Marxism meant that it provided a strong theoretical basis for the analysis of power. Historians of women, and later of gender, wanted not only to *describe* but also to *account for* women's structural inequality. For some feminist scholars, as we will see, pornography was an agent of women's inequality – promoting a vision of women as sexual objects subject to the actions and desires of an active (and often violent) male viewer.

Yet the analysis of the history of pornography did not stop there. Feminists were also interested in new ideas put forward by Foucault. In particular, historians of women and gender explored the proposal that social identities and selfhood were created within culture – that is, that law, medicine, pedagogy and psychology actively produced, rather than simply described, social identities. In the hands of women's historians this became a crucial tool towards historicizing gender and sex roles. The category of woman could be seen not as a biological – and therefore fundamentally ahistorical – category, but instead an identity that was produced in different ways at different times, and as a result, historically variable. In this sense, post-structuralism was crucial in opening up gender to historical analysis. This also meant that pornographic and obscene texts and images, which took relations between the sexes as their subject matter, became important historical sources for the study of gender.[17]

transformations in the world outside academia

Thus by the 1970s, things were brewing in academic circles: historians were reconsidering what were the appropriate objects of study; social scientists were reconsidering the politics of claims to 'objectivity' and the status of knowledge as leading to liberation was up for question. At the same time transformations were taking place in the world outside the academy that would play a crucial role in drawing people's attention to obscenity and pornography. Of particular importance was the growth of an active feminist movement. Women associated with the feminist movement of the 1970s struggled to gain access to public life: to political office, male-dominated professions, graduate programmes and so on. They also insisted that realms of experience long relegated to the status of the 'private' and therefore of the apolitical were in fact shot through with real power, real consequences and real inequalities.

The feminist movement also provoked open and heated public debates about pornography. On the one hand, the movement of pornographic film and literature closer to the mainstream, brought with it women readers, women viewers. Another important strand of feminist theorists – whose position was most rigorously articulated by the feminist legal scholar Catharine MacKinnon – posited that pornography 'acted' upon women, rendering them mute and passive objects of male domination. Women who watched pornography were not liberated; instead they were complicit in their own objectification. MacKinnon further argued that *words* (particularly hate speech) could in certain circumstances function as *acts*; seen in this light, the 'speech' of pornography was akin to a violent assault on women.[18]

MacKinnon's interpretations of pornography were convincing to many. But they also opened deep rifts among feminists, some of whom criticized MacKinnon for basing her argument against pornography on the vision of an inert, passive and asexual female subject 'acted' upon by violent and sexualized men. Where, her opponents asked, was there room for women's agency? For women's desire? Was it not antithetical to feminism's goals to strip women of sexual desire, or to encode into law a vision of women as child-like victims of a patriarchal society?

Historians are not legal scholars, however, and they begin with different questions and assumptions. Thus, in their approach to the topic, feminist historians insisted that the meaning, content and social impact of pornography changed dramatically over time. One of the best accounts of the transformation in the content and social context of pornography is Linda Williams's *Hard Core: Power, Pleasure, and the 'Frenzy of the Visible'*, originally published in 1989. Williams set herself the task of historicizing the evolution of hard-core pornographic film, a topic far outside the realm of acceptable scholarly topics. To historicize this genre meant, on the one hand, attention to the evolution of technical features – genre, sound, shots, venue and audience – that changed considerably over the course of the twentieth century. It also meant considering the evolution of hard-core pornographic film against the backdrop of the political and social transformations in the 1950s, 60s and especially the 70s. For Williams, the evolution of pornography as a genre was linked to the identification of sex and sexuality as topics of social and political concern.

Williams illustrated this connection by pointing to the 1957 Supreme Court case *United States* v. *Roth*. The defendant in the case, Roth, had been convicted of mailing sexually explicit magazines, and the Supreme Court upheld the conviction on the grounds that the hard-core centre of pornography had only one 'idea' – that is, sex – and was therefore of no social value.[19] Thus the First Amendment protection of free speech, intended to protect 'ideas', did not apply. Williams insists that this ruling had unintended consequences – throwing open the door to suppressing many sexually explicit works on grounds that they had social or intellectual value. Writing for the majority, Justice Brennan defined sex as a topic of vital social importance, rather than simply as a 'private' matter: 'Sex, a great and mysterious motive force in human life, has indisputably been a subject of absorbing interest to mankind through the ages; it is one of human interest and public concern.'[20] Williams argued that Brennan's decision identified sex as a 'problem' to be debated, discussed, viewed, and analysed; this, she argues, became important to the evolution of pornographic film as a genre in the 1970s and 80s.

Williams argues that something crucial was happening to pornography in the 1970s – it was emerging from its hiding place and becoming a cultural document with political resonance. In 1972, for example, *Deep Throat* was shown on college campuses in New York and Los Angeles. The film not only began to be shown in mainstream venues as well as college campuses, but it also became the subject of academic conferences and debates, including a well-publicized conference in 1972 at Barnard College in New York City. Against the backdrop of the feminist movement in the US, women's desire and sexual pleasure were being identified as important political questions.

What is important for our purposes is understanding the complex links between three developments: the emergence of feminism in the 1970s and 80s; the growing visibility of pornography as the genre began to reach new audiences; and the insistence within politics and the academy that sexuality was linked to politics and power (and not simply a matter of 'personal' choice, and therefore stripped of political importance). These things would converge, as we will see below, in a growing interest in the topic, and in the 1980s, fierce debates among feminist scholars in several disciplines about the meaning and politics of pornography.

Looking at this development in historical hindsight, it is impossible to ignore how transformations within the academy were linked to the political questions of the day. Speaking about the historical discipline, we can perhaps be even more concrete. As sex roles, gender, the sexual division of labour and women's position began to change in the 1970s, the *historical mutability* of divisions long termed 'natural' and therefore ahistorical was an obvious and apparent fact. Classical Liberalism – with its strict division of private and public interests, and insistence on the liberatory potential of knowledge – was subjected to serious scrutiny by thinkers like Foucault just as feminists were insisting on the political nature of the 'private sphere'.

It was against this backdrop that historians began to take a serious interest in the evolution of pornography and obscenity. Pornographic books and film began to be considered sources that could potentially shed light on broader political, social and cultural changes within a given society. It is to this second impulse – the impulse to link pornography, blasphemy, and obscenity to some of the major developments of modern history – that we will now turn. For it is here that we find most historians working. Historians are, after all, interested in context and meaning, therefore the history of pornography *per se* – that is, separate from other social, legal or political developments – interests them less that the often unexpected intersection between these realms of experience.

historians, political culture, and pornography

As we saw above, historians in the 1980s began to engage in a serious exchange with anthropologists and literary scholars. From anthropologists, they learned methods for studying communities, ritual practices, for analysing oral sources and collective rituals. From literary scholars, they also borrowed new strategies for reading sources, looking not only for what was said, but also for what was unsaid. Historians began to dip their toes into the world of popular literature – no longer were they confined to presidential papers, letters, memoranda, speeches. A whole new body of sources seemed to reveal a world of popular beliefs and practices that had previously been invisible to the historical record.

During the 1970s and 80s, historians of Europe, many influenced by Marxism, began to be particularly interested in the nature of political subversion. They began to consider how scandal, libel, and sexual exposure could be used to undermine the legitimacy of historical centres of authority – the Catholic Church, the clergy, aristocrats and monarchs. Shifting their view of politics to the terms of legitimacy – to people's understanding and acceptance of political authority – historians began to consider how scandal and libel could be used as tools to erode the authority and thereby the legitimacy of existing authorities.

One of the most influential works among historians was the Russian literary critic Mikhail Bakhtin's *Rabelais and His World*, not published in English until 1968.[21] Bakhtin's subject was the literary, linguistic, and social context of sixteenth-century France. He took the bawdy, ruckus, explicit language of Rabelais' *Gargantua and Pantagruel* as a jumping off point for a larger argument about subversion and reversal of existing power structures – in the case of Renaissance France, of the clergy, learned humanists and aristocrats. Rabelais' literature, Bakhtin wrote, captured the earthy, physical language of the marketplace – a language of physical necessity, bodily function, and open (not closed) orifices, open to the world and rejecting of all that was closed, finished, completed – that is, pre-existing orthodoxies.

A generation of historians studying early-modern Europe were influenced by Bakhtin's vision of bawdy subversion. Revolutions began to be seen as not simply events involving the transformation of institutions

– instead, what was explored was the process by which authority had been eroded in the minds of average people. The righteousness of the clergy, for example, could not be maintained in the face of pamphlets accusing priests of fornicating in the confessional, or seducing unsuspecting nuns ready for conversion. Similarly, following the invention of print and the rise of literacy, kings, queens and influential statesmen were regularly subjected to exposure and conjecture about their moral, sexual activities. For the most part, these historians did not concern themselves directly with pornography or sexuality. Nonetheless, the vision of political subversion they advanced – and their willingness to consider street ballads, broadsides, anonymous pamphlets – changed historians' understanding of the 'political' and what it meant to study 'politics'.[22]

Books such as Iain McCalman's *Radical Underworlds: Prophets, Revolutionaries and Pornographers in London, 1795–1840* (1988) took up the nature of British political radicalism and its connection to sexual politics and sexual scandal. As the idea that people's understanding of politics was inflected by their understanding of sexual morality began to circulate, historians began to consider the history of pornography as something that could actually shed new light on important questions. Awareness that our understanding of authority often entails sometimes implicit understandings about bodily practices and sexual morality helped turn historians towards such topics.

Furthermore, this new vision of politics – termed 'political culture' insofar as it proposed to study people's unexampled presuppositions about authority, legitimacy and power – opened new doors to questions about gender. How, historians began to ask, did gender influence people's understanding of the nature of authority? How did sexual narratives about political figures, for example, evoke visions of gender disorder in the minds of political subjects or citizens?

By 1991, a conference organized by American historian of France, Lynn Hunt, at the University of Pennsylvania, on 'The Invention of Pornography', gathered together scholars of different national contexts and disciplines, conducting research on topics related to pornography. The conference resulted in the publication of *The Invention of Pornography: Obscenity and the Origins of Modernity, 1500–1800*, edited by Hunt, a well-received volume of essays by major scholars which reflected current state of work on the subject.[23] Drawing on previous scholarship as well as new work, the volume made a convincing case for the historical importance of pornography.

What did this case look like in its details? Like Kendrick, Hunt insisted on the historicity of pornography and obscenity. Pornography, she wrote, 'developed out of the messy, two-way, push and pull between the intention of authors, artists and engravers to test the boundaries of the "decent" and the aim of the ecclesiastical and secular police to regulate it'.[24] Hunt's volume contained a series of nine essays organized around a working hypothesis: obscenity, she suggested, emerged in the West in conjunction with the development of modernity. That is, obscenity seemed to be intimately connected to the major transformations that historians identify as the origins of modernity: with Renaissance Humanism; scientific method; religious scepticism; democratic theory and (later) revolution; mercantile activity and the growth of the bourgeoisie. Hunt and the authors in her volume were also interested in exploring Foucault's thesis that speech about sex and sexuality were, in the modern world, increasingly bound up with power that operated through the production of certain kinds of selves; but the theory needed exploration within particular historical contexts.

In Hunt's volume, the modern history of obscenity begins with Humanism in the sixteenth century. The first essay, by Paula Findlen, considers the importance of the Italian Renaissance writer, Pietro Aretino (1492–1556). Aretino was the author of two infamous works of obscene literature: the first a set of *Dialogues* in which a prostitute discusses the proper profession for her daughter; the second, a series of verse poems describing the 'postures' of love making, which were widely printed in the Renaissance with detailed illustrations depicting Renaissance nudes in active postures.[25] What would justify the attention of a historian to such 'marginal' texts? Findlen argues that Aretino's works were published in an age in which access to knowledge – of classical authors, of the physical universe, and of the human body – was highly contentious. Scientific discoveries were officially disputed and closely guarded, and knowledge of the human body endangered the principles of religion; Aretino's writings offered information about sexuality, the human condition, and the nature of physical love. Furthermore, Aretino used obscenity as a means to critique existing political structures – poking fun at kings, dukes, princes and priests while elevating the monkey and the whore.

The sixteenth century also marked one of the first legal articulations of specific categories of knowledge. With the Council of Trent, and the Counter-Reformation efforts of the Catholic Church to designate which publications were permitted to be circulated and those proscribed, the Church attempted to continue the monopoly of the clergy on knowledge.[26] Thus, in addition to a whole host of other kinds of publications, the Catholic Church characterized a new category of publications: 'Books which professedly deal with, narrate, or teach things lascivious or obscene are absolutely prohibited, since not only the matter of faith but also that of morals, which are usually easily corrupted through the reading of such books, must be taken into consideration.'[27]

Findlen argues that Aretino's works, largely ignored by historians of the Renaissance, reveal information about printing and publishing (as well as manuscript culture); politics; and the status of knowledge. Margaret Jacob's contribution to Hunt's volume, 'The Materialist World of Pornography', also picks up on these themes of science, knowledge of the physical world and sexuality.[28] Jacob identifies unlikely points of intersection – such as the parallels she draws between the philosophy of Thomas Hobbes, and the notorious pornographic work of the period, *Therese Philosophe.* In an era in which scientists began to discover that the laws of the physical universe were characterized by the uniform motion of bodies in space, materialist philosophers began to apply these physical laws to the world of human bodies and thus to human nature. Hobbes described humans as atomized bodies in motion, acted upon by the laws of attraction and repulsion. Human thoughts were not a result of spirit or consciousness; they were strictly material, originating in the individual body being pressed upon by an object outside itself. Like other materialists, Hobbes seemed to call into question the existence of the human soul; he also described a world of atomized individuals mutually contracting to form a polis, but in a state of nature fundamentally separate from one another.

This vision of human society as composed of atomized (and therefore also equal) bodies in motion, Jacob argues, was taken up by some of the most notorious pornographic works of the time. *Therese Philosophe,* for example, revolves around a young woman, Therese, who desires to be educated in philosophy and love. Her initiation to physical love is simultaneously a series of lessons on Free Will, personal autonomy and the physical properties of the body. The radical implications of Materialist philosophy – that bodies were alike, and therefore theoretically equal, that intention originated in the material rather than the spiritual – opened up new possibilities to imagine the political and philosophical relevance of sexuality.[29] Here again, sex was bound up with knowledge – in this case, philosophical knowledge of a variety that undermined the teachings of the Catholic Church. Jacob argues, pornography like *Therese Philosophe* popularized materialist philosophy by making it compelling, concrete, and entertaining. Like Findlen, then, Jacob focuses on connections between politics, sexuality, and knowledge in early-modern Europe.

Nowhere is this connection made more apparent than in the large – and still growing – body of work linking pornography to the emergence of new democratic forms of government (and new theories of the self) during the European Enlightenment.[30] In her contribution to her volume, 'Pornography and the French Revolution', Hunt evokes one of the central questions of modern European history: namely, the origins of the French Revolution. She is not alone in linking this question to obscenity; other prominent historians of pre-Revolutionary France, most notably Robert Darnton, have found that the world of illicit literature reveals much about the political culture of this well-studied period.

To understand the significance of pornography to the political world of pre-Revolutionary France, we must begin with eighteenth-century ideas of political legitimacy and power. Historians have argued that under the Old Regime, the legitimacy of the King rested on the collective belief that his power was sacred – that is, linked to the authority of the Catholic Church and to God. The political symbolism of the period rested on a vision of the King's two bodies: an earthly, human body that lived and died; and a sacred and immortal body that connected him, and through him the French nation, to God.[31] During the eighteenth century Louis XVI and Marie Antoinette were the subject of a large pamphlet literature by anonymous writers that focused on their earthly physical bodies engaged in acts of incest, sodomy and even bestiality. Historians have referred to the effects of such literature as the process of 'desacralization' – that is, the process whereby the monarch and his queen were stripped of their sacred bodies and reduced to the level of common human beings with less than stellar moral constitutions.[32] In this work, obscene texts reveal important insight into the terms of legitimacy – located, in this case, increasingly in the attitudes of the French public.

Yet there remains one more point to be mentioned about Hunt's collection, for lurking behind much of the discussion of philosophy and politics is also the question of gender, and its relationship to power. And it is precisely because of this question that feminist scholars of many stripes – from those who condemn pornography as akin to hate speech against women, to those who embrace the radical implications of sexual women – have gravitated towards pornography. In her essay on pornography and the Revolution, Hunt is concerned with the position of the Queen, Marie Antoinette. She argues that pre-Revolutionary obscene texts consistently depicted the Queen as the active agent in the corruption of the royal family – she was repeatedly accused of lesbianism, emasculating the King and even incest with her son the Crown Prince. By contrast pre-Revolutionary obscene texts depicted the King as meek and emasculated, incapable of standing up to the voracious sexual appetite of the Queen and his mistresses.[33] At stake in Hunt's argument is an implicit question: why were women, who were active in the Revolution from the beginning, the only group to be excluded from political rights in the new Republic? How did a political system founded on principles of universal human rights justify the exclusion of half the human population? To answer this question, Hunt argues, requires attention to political culture, and to the terms by which the power of the Old Regime was undermined. It is not, therefore, unimportant that in the popular imagination, Marie Antoinette was perceived as the agent of the King's destruction. Such visions of femininity – and of women in power – were central to the ultimate decision to exclude women from power. Once again, we find ourselves considering how pornography sheds light on connections between 'intimacy' and politics.

recent developments

Though much of the historical work written on pornography and obscenity has focused on early-modern Europe, recent historians have used the history of pornography and obscenity to explore other questions: in particular, links between violence and pornography; cultural exchange (particularly in colonial contexts); and the 'obscenity' of foreign imports.

A small but important body of work has recently begun to examine the relationship between obscenity, pornography and the violation of the body. In a world in which images of death, mutilation, and violence are often described as 'obscene' and 'pornographic', historians have begun to ask questions about the meaning of such images. The consumption of violence – and our responses to images of violated bodies – has motivated excellent work on the subject. One of the best examples of this kind of work is Carolyn Dean's *The Frail Social Body: Pornography, Homosexuality and Other Fantasies in Interwar France.*[34] The book examines the meaning of bodily integrity and the violation of that integrity in the aftermath of the First World War. In the wake of the war, fantasies arose surrounding the vulnerability of individual bodies – seen as subject to violation. These fears about individual bodies, Dean argues, extended to broader concerns about the fragility of the larger social body – subject to assault by pornography and homosexuality, two things believed to violate the integrity and autonomy of the individual body. Like Hunt, Dean explores the relationship between particular bodies – in Hunt's case, the bodies of the King and Queen; in Dean's case, the bodies of men – and the social body. Both describe power and politics as being rooted in fantasies about the body politic. Another historian who has pursued the links between violence and pornography is Karen Halttunen, who has examined images of physical violence against slaves in the early nineteenth-century United States.[35] Her interest is in the relationship between humanitarianism, anti-slave campaigns, and graphic (and often titillating) images of violence against slaves.

Indeed, in our modern media-saturated world, in which images of violence and destruction are played over and over again on multiple media outlets, there have been subtle shifts in our use of the word 'obscene'. These shifts have been, and I believe will continue to be, reflected in historical work on the subject. It is now not uncommon to use the word 'obscene' to describe images of the mass destruction of bodies in German concentration camps during the Second World War – or, perhaps better put, the use of 'pornographic' to describe the combination of horror and pleasure with which we view such images. In an era in which the tape of Daniel Pearl's execution-style murder at the hands of Islamic militants is available on a frequently visited website on the Internet, questions of the violation of the body, privacy and public consumption of images become matters of great concern. One source of this concern surrounds the status of events *as images*. Pearl's execution was produced as an image, that is, the act was secondary to the publicity that attended the act. Thus those who view the videotape are complicit in the event – for the event itself was produced for the image.

The public consumption of Daniel Pearl's execution is 'obscenity' not because it has an obscene 'essence', but instead because of the *desire* it produces in the viewer to watch the event. That desire itself is disquieting, even obscene, because it plays into the hands of those producing the *event as image* and because it raises questions about why we feel compelled to watch. Fascination with images of tortured or mutilated bodies makes us uneasy about the integrity of our own culture as well as the 'progress' attending technological development. Even more fundamentally, this provokes debates about the contemporary subject, who is often suspected of passivity (vis-à-vis images) coupled with an insatiable appetite for shock and novelty.

Yet similar questions are at stake in the United States government's insistence that the bodies of dead soldiers returning from the Iraq war should not be photographed or publicized. Such tensions reveal essential questions about our own society and the role of images. Where does the privacy of the individual (to be shielded from having images of his or her violated body distributed) begin? What about the imperative of democracies to ensure transparency and publicity, especially if the bodies returning from war have been killed in the name of the public? When is it responsible to view injured bodies, and when does the viewing of such bodies constitute exploitation and voyeurism? Such are the pressing questions that might inform the contemporary relevance of obscenity (though often they do not).

The recent widely-publicized images of torture involving Iraqi prisoners at the Abu Ghraib prisoner camp are particularly relevant. Critics have pointed out that the photographs of the prisoners resemble nothing more that pornography. Visions of hooded men forced to fake fellatio or anal sex with other prisoners for the camera evoke the visual language of pornographic film. Images of men forced to stand in place with electrical wires connected to their genitals raises a second understanding of pornography as the pleasure attending the viewing of others' pain. At stake in all of it seems to be the desire to document – and by extension, to view – other people in extreme states (of excitement, fear, pain, even death). What disturbs us is perhaps what this reveals about us as subjects – have images rendered us insensitive to others' pain? Are we no longer capable of differentiating between artificial images (disaster movies, horror flicks), and real destruction, real wars, real mutilations?

A second set of historical questions has also arisen in the context of a post-colonial world in which 'westernization' is increasingly associated with materialism, moral laxity, and secular values. Thus questions of cultural exchange, often in the context of colonialism, have begun to interest historians studying pornography. Anne Hardgrove, for example, is at work on a book project concerning the translation of the Kama Sutra into English in the context of British colonization of India.

In her recent book, *Reading Lolita in Tehran*, Iranian scholar Azar Nafisi describes a group of Iranian women who met secretly at her house in Tehran. They gathered regularly to read and discuss banned American and European books. Nafisi argues that the reading practices of young Iranian women are highly political. They link gender and sexuality to Iranian Nationalism and to the perceived threat of Western Imperialism and culture.[36] Such chains of association between reading and political change are not peculiar to post-1979 Iran – and they are worth sustained study, because they help us understand how people symbolize change. In my own work on obscenity in nineteenth-century Germany, questions of cultural exchange were certainly at stake in people's perceptions of what was 'obscene'. French books, which flowed across German borders in unprecedented numbers after 1815, brought with them an image of a newly democratic nation that was also a hotbed of sexual laxity; thus the understanding of democracy in early nineteenth-century Germany was also bound up with visions of the destruction of the family and the corruption of young women.

conclusion

If historians have been drawn to the study of pornography and obscenity since the 1960s, it is because they have taken from this study new methods of examining historical events and developments. In particular, this study has allowed historians to link the bodies of individuals to broader metaphors and understandings of the 'body politic', and in so doing, it has allowed historians to shed new light on the relationship between gender and political power. In addition, it has redirected historians' attention to the meanings and effects of images, and enabled them to explain how images affect public opinion, and as a result, the legitimacy of governments.

It seems to me that questions of what constitutes the 'obscene' and the 'pornographic' are likely to continue to interest historians. In a world experiencing increasing tensions between the commercialism and image-saturated culture of the West and fundamentalist movements (all over the world, including in the West) attempting to return to domestic order, the nature of 'obscenity' continues to be a compelling question. And while historians are not in the business of writing the history of the present, critically engaged historians often ask questions of the past informed (though not dictated) by the struggles and questions of the world around them.

notes

1. Walter Kendrick, *The Secret Museum: Pornography in Modern Culture* (New York: Viking Press, 1987).
2. Ibid., p. 31. Kendrick argues that the modern definition of 'pornography' as a shifting body of representations that are potentially harmful is distinct from an older definition of pornography as, literally, writing about prostitution.
3. Lynda Nead, *Victorian Babylon: People, Streets and Images in Nineteenth-Century London* (New Haven: Yale University Press, 2000), p. 149.
4. For an example of the outcry over street literature in a different context, see Laura Engelstein, 'From Avant-Garde to Boulevard: Literary Sex', in her *The Keys to Happiness: Sex and the Search for Modernity in Fin-De-Siecle Russia* (Ithaca: Cornell University Press, 1992).
5. The bibliomaniacal tendencies of these figures are expressed in the number of publications they produced; in the case of some, like Gustave Brunet, a good research library will have hundreds of entries under their names. Thus I only name a few here as examples of the kinds of works they produced. Wherever possible, I mention the English translation. See, for example, Brunet, *Livres Perdus: Essai Bibliographique sur les livres devenus introuvables* (Bruxelles: Gay & Doucé, 1882), and *Bibliomania in Present Day France and England* (New York: J.W. Bouton, 1880). See also P.L. Jacob, *History of Prostitution Among*

All the Peoples of World by Paul Lacroix, translated from French (New York: Covici, Friede, 1931); Hugo Hayn, *Bibliotheca Germanorum erotica: Verzeichniss der gesammten deutschen erotischen Literatur mit Einschluss der Uebersetzungen* (Leipzig: H. Nay, 1875); Louis Perceau, *Enfer de la Bibliothèque nationale* (Paris: Bibliothèque des Curieux, 1919).

6. For further information on Franz von Krenner's collection, see Sarah Leonard, *The Cultural Politics of 'Immoral Writings': Readers, Peddlers and Police in German, 1820–1890* (PhD dissertation, Brown University, 2001), and Stephen Kellner, 'Bibliotheca erotica Krenneriana – eine Bürgerliche Privatsammlung um 1800', *Bibliotheksforum Bayern*, 22, 1/2 (1994), 64–86.
7. Al Di Lauro and Gerald Rabkin, *Dirty Movies: An Illustrated History of the Stag Film* (New York: Chelsea House, 1976).
8. Paul Englisch, *Geschichte der erotischen Literatur* (Stuttgart: J. Püttman, 1927), and *Irrgarten der Erotik: Eine Sittengeschichte über das gesamte Gebiet der Welt-Pornographie* (Leipzig: Lykeion, 1931). Also, see Iwan Block, who wrote under the pseudonym Eugen Dühren, *The Sexual Life of Our Time in its Relation to Modern Civilization*, trans. M. Eden Paul (New York: Rebman, 1908), and his *Sex Life in England* (New York: Panurge Press, 1934).
9. There is a growing body of historical literature on the transformation of gender roles in the decades leading up to and following the First World War. See, for example, Mary Louise Roberts, *Civilization without Sexes* (Chicago: University of Chicago Press). Allen Frantzen, *Bloody Good: Chivalry, Sacrifice and the Great War* (Chicago: Chicago University Press, 2004); Paul Friederick Lerner, *Hysterical Men: War, Psychiatry, and the Politics of Trauma in Germany, 1890–1930* (Ithaca: Cornell University Press, 2003); George Mosse, *The Image of Man: The Creation of Modern Masculinity* (Oxford: Oxford University Press, 1996).
10. The essays were entitled 'Libertine Literature in England, 1660–1745', and they were published initially in *The Book Collector*, XII, 1,2,3 (Spring, Summer, Winter 1963).
11. David Foxon, *Libertine Literature in England, 1660–1745* (New Hyde Park, New York: University Books, 1965), p. ix.
12. On the seventeenth-century context of 'obscene' publications, see for example: Ian Frederick Moulton, *Before Pornography: Erotic Writing in Early Modern England* (Oxford: Oxford University Press, 2000); and James Grantham Turner, *Schooling Sex: Libertine Literature and Erotic Education in Italy, France, and England, 1534–1685* (Oxford: Oxford University Press, 2003). For an excellent analysis of obscene texts in the context of seventeenth-century philosophical and scientific debates, see Margaret Jacob, 'The Materialist World of Pornography', in Lynn Hunt (ed.), *The Invention of Pornography: Obscenity and the Origins of Modernity, 1500–1800* (New York: Zone Books, 1993), pp. 157–202.
13. Foxon, *Libertine Literature*, p. x.
14. Steven Marcus, *The Other Victorians: A Study of Sexuality and Pornography in Mid-Nineteenth-Century England* (London: Weidenfeld and Nicolson, 1966).
15. Ibid., p. 35.
16. Fernand Braudel, 'The Situation of History in 1950', in his *On History* (Chicago: University of Chicago Press, 1980).
17. Excellent examples of this kind of scholarship include Thomas Laqueur, *Making Sex: Body and Gender from the Greeks to Freud* (Cambridge: Cambridge

University Press, 1990); and Londa Schiebinger, *Nature's Body: Gender and the Making of Modern Science* (Boston: Beacon Press, 1993).

18. This argument is argued systematically in Catharine MacKinnon, *Only Words* (Cambridge, MA: Harvard University Press, 1996); see also MacKinnon and Andrea Dworkin, *Pornography and Civil Rights: A New Day for Women's Equality* (Minneapolis, MN: Organizing Against Pornography, 1988) and Dworkin, *Pornography: Men Possessing Women* (New York: Perigee Books, 1981). For a different perspective see the feminist defence of pornography offered by another legal scholar, Nadine Strossen, *Defending Pornography: Free Speech, Sex, and the Fight for Women's Rights* (New York: New York University Press, 2000).
19. See Linda Williams, *Hard Core: Power, Pleasure, and the 'Frenzy of the Visible'* (Berkeley: University of California Press, 1989).
20. Justice Brennan, quoted in ibid., pp. 88.
21. Mikhail Bakhtin, *Rabelais and His World* (Bloomington: Indiana University Press, 1984).
22. See Christopher Hill, *The World Turned Upside Down: Radical Ideas During the English Revolution* (New York: Viking Press, 1972); Lynn Hunt, *Politics, Culture and Class in the French Revolution* (Berkeley: University of California Press, 1984); David Underdown, *Revel, Riot and Rebellion: Popular Politics and Culture in England, 1603–1660* (Oxford: Clarendon Press, 1985).
23. Hunt, *Invention of Pornography*.
24. Ibid., p. 10.
25. Paula Findlen, 'Humanism, Politics and Pornography in Renaissance Italy', in Hunt, *Invention of Pornography*, pp. 49–108.
26. *Canons and Decrees of the Council of Trent*, trans. Rev. H.J. Schroeder (St Louis: B. Herder Book Co., 1941).
27. Ibid., p. 275.
28. Margaret Jacob, 'The Materialist World of Pornography', in Hunt, *Invention of Pornography*, pp. 157–202.
29. Ibid., p. 178.
30. This literature includes Jean Marie Goulemot, *Forbidden Texts: Erotic Literature and its Readers in Eighteenth-Century France*, trans. James Simpson (Cambridge: Polity Press, 1994); Roy Porter and Lesley Hall, *The Facts of Life: The Creation of Sexual Knowledge in Britain, 1650–1950* (New Haven: Yale University Press, 1995); and G.S. Rousseau and Roy Porter (eds.), *Sexual Underworlds of the Enlightenment* (Chapel Hill: University of North Carolina Press, 1988).
31. Ernst Kantorowicz, *The King's Two Bodies: A Study of Mediaeval Political Theory* (Princeton: Princeton University Press, 1957).
32. Lynn Hunt, 'Pornography and the French Revolution', in Hunt, *Invention of Pornography*, pp. 301–39. For a detailed discussion of the production and circulation of illicit literature as well as a discussion of content and anti-Revolutionary sentiment, see Robert Darnton, *The Forbidden Best-Sellers of Pre-Revolutionary France* (New York: W.W. Norton & Co., 1996). A similar process, Darnton argues, was at work in stripping the Catholic clergy of its claim to moral righteousness. Literature – from the cheap pamphlet literature of the *bibliothèque bleu*, to the high literature of philosophes like Voltaire and Diderot – depicted the Catholic clergy as being greedy, lascivious, bawdy, perverse – everything but pious. If the religious authority of the French

monarch depended to a great extent on the moral authority of the Church, the Church too was systematically exposed to slander and exposure that often took the form of entertaining and pornographic literature. And while it is impossible to do justice to the complexity of these arguments and the wealth of empirical evidence brought to bear on the topic here, it is nonetheless important to suggest why the most important recent interpretations of Revolution have turned to pornography for insight.

33. For a longer version of this argument, see Lynn Hunt, *The Family Romance of the French Revolution* (Berkeley: University of California Press, 1992).
34. Carolyn Dean, *The Frail Social Body: Pornography, Homosexuality and Other Fantasies in Interwar France* (Berkeley: University of California Press, 2000).
35. Karen Halttunen, 'Humanitarianism and the Pornography of Pain in Anglo-American Culture', *American Historical Review*, 100, 2 (1995), 303–34.
36. Azar Nafisi, *Reading Lolita in Tehran: A Memoir in Books* (London: Fourth Estate, 2004).

9
prostitution

elizabeth clement

introduction

> Of the young women patrons of the premises, a large percentage are store employees, telephone girls, stenographers, etc. Their morals are loose and there is no question that they are on terms of sexual intimacy with their male companions. Another class of young women is plainly discernible about these premises. Though probably working girls, that are what may be characterized as 'near whores' or 'whores in the making'. They are more sporty in appearance than the girls mentioned.... Their favorite portion of the premises is the ladies toilet which is by far the busiest place in the room. There they smoke cigarettes and converse for long periods of time... A few 'kept women' and professional prostitutes patronize these premises, but the latter do not ply their trade in this rear room. It is their custom to 'pick up' a man on the street, then come into the rear room for a few drinks before going to their designated or chosen place for performing the act of sexual cohabitation. These 'kept women' and professional prostitutes also... patronize the ladies toilet and from their example and conversation the 'near whores'... gain further impetus in their downward spiral.[1]

Charles Briggs, an undercover investigator for one of New York's pre-eminent private vice societies, filed this written report in 1913. In his estimation, the women of this particular club fit into no fewer than four categories: 'working girls', 'near whores' (or 'whores in the making'), 'kept women' and 'professional prostitutes'. Although other contemporary observers might have called all of these women prostitutes, Briggs carefully acknowledged the moral, sexual, and economic differences between them. To the modern ear, Briggs uses an exotic vocabulary, but on closer inspection his categories are actually quite familiar. Working girls on terms of '*sexual intimacy with their male companions*' would seem the most normal to us; they were young women who had sex with their boyfriends and fiancés. By 'near whores' and 'whores in the making' Briggs probably meant 'charity girls', an emerging identity in early twentieth-century American cities. Charity girls had sex with men they met in exchange for an evening's entertainment, but stopped short of exchanging sex for cash.[2] Kept women are another familiar group, as are the 'professional prostitutes' whose very presence, in Briggs' opinion, threatened to draw all the other women into a 'downward spiral' of depravity.

This investigator's care in delineating the complex world of sex work highlights one of the fundamental problems in the historical study of prostitution: that of definitions. Just who was a prostitute, and who was not? Of course we face similar problems today. Even though the commonly accepted definition of prostitution – the exchange of sex for money – seems clear, most of us also acknowledge that this narrow legal definition does not encompass the range of activities in which people profit from sex. Furthermore, it does not begin to explore the reasons why people sell or barter sex, nor does it indicate the myriad of moral gradations that most of us use when we evaluate different kinds of work (stripping, lap dancing, work in pornography, prostitution) or different kinds of intimate relationships (marriage, domestic partners, dating, one-night stands, sex work). Prostitution may seem easy to define but, in reality, it is suspended in a complex web of economic, cultural, and moral systems.

I wrote this chapter as a way of exploring the place that prostitution has in Western society, but like a cat with a string, really thinking about prostitution as a category tends to tangle rather than untangle the stories that emerge. Instead of simplifying the questions inherent to the study of prostitution down to a linear narrative, I complicate the story, and at times pose more questions than I answer. Given the complex, contested and often violent history of prostitution in the West, this is entirely appropriate. We have often assumed with prostitution that we 'know it when we see it', but a broad historical approach makes it clear that few of us can agree on what we are seeing.

Beginning with a discussion of the difficult question of cultural and legal definitions of prostitution, this chapter briefly explores the history of prostitution in Europe and the United States in the context of the profound changes that occurred between 1600 and the present.

Urbanization, industrialization, the decline of agriculture, the emergence of class systems, and the rise of the nation state have all shaped both prostitution and societal reactions to it. The historians of prostitution writing about every period of the modern West address the way that these enormous economic, social, and governmental developments interacted with the sale of sex. Paradoxically, however, historians have also found that when compared with other kinds of work, prostitution has changed very little. Street walking and brothel prostitution, forms of sex work very familiar to us, can also be found in medieval England, early-modern Seville and nineteenth-century France.[3] What other work process has maintained the same organization and has been performed in basically the same way for nearly a thousand years? It is almost as if having evolved several very efficient forms of organization, prostitution merely alternates between these forms depending on the political, economic, or social situation. In this regard, prostitution can be seen as both uniquely sensitive to local conditions, and oddly timeless.

The same cannot be said of the academic study of prostitution, which changed dramatically with the advent of the feminist movement in the West in the 1970s, and then again when vitriolic arguments between feminists challenged basic societal assumptions about the degraded and degrading character of prostitution. Feminist sex workers – strippers, lap dancers and women in pornography as well prostitutes – argued that sex work did not have to involve coercion, violence and degradation and that some women chose prostitution as an alternative to other poorly paid 'women's work'. Prostitute Donna Marie Niles summarizes this position eloquently:

> when I was nineteen years old I made what seemed like a conscious decision to become a prostitute... Any woman who has ever been on a date, who knows what it is to exchange affection or sex for dinner, or kindness, or survival, is quite prepared to be a hooker. Learning to serve, please and appease men is something that binds all women together. It's why secretaries, nurses, waitresses, wives, sales clerks, etc. are on the low paying end of the stick. To separate our experiences too much, or to believe that the ways we get by in this woman-hating world are so different, is a mistake.[4]

In the wake of these passionate disagreements between feminists, historians have had to change our research questions and agendas. We now view prostitution as a form of work, as well as a social and moral category. Perhaps even more important, historians also now include the perspectives, life choices and motivations of prostitutes themselves. More than any other factor, these painful debates changed the way we think about prostitution in the modern West.

defining our terms

While definitions of prostitution may be cultural and social, the legal definition of prostitution is undoubtedly the easiest to trace. However, even in the cold, dry arena of law, prostitution's definitions have been ambiguous. In her work on medieval England, Ruth Karras argues that jurists did not see the taking of money for sex as essential to definitions of 'whoredom'. Ecclesiastical courts emphasized 'indiscriminate availability rather than exchange of sex for pay'.[5] The law thus embraced fuzzy descriptions that focused as much on women's 'promiscuity' as they did on the exchange of sex for cash, or involvement in a particular practice like street walking or brothel work.

Legal definitions of prostitution have continued to be vague. By the mid-nineteenth century, most people in France, England or Germany defined prostitution as the exchange of sex for money. The law, by contrast, continued to include 'promiscuous' women who did not receive cash for sex. As Judith Walkowitz has shown in her work on Victorian England, the Contagious Diseases Acts, passed to regulate prostitution near military concentrations, never defined prostitution and simply directed police to identify 'common prostitutes'.[6] In order to protect the health and safety of the Empire's troops, the CD Acts cast a wide net that could, under some circumstances, trap any working-class woman found near a military camp. Similarly, New York's 1886 Wayward Minor Law allowed police to arrest girls 'found in a reputed house of prostitution' and those 'in danger of becoming morally depraved'.[7] Since moral depravity in this period simply meant sexual activity before marriage, the Wayward Minor Law, if enforced now, would apply to most female high school students in America.[8] As both of these laws indicate, perceived promiscuity in sexual relations, rather than an actual monetary exchange, continued to function as an important legal definition of prostitution even as most people made accepting cash the important distinction between licit and illicit sex.

Furthermore, these distinctions mattered a great deal to the women accused, and varied in the racial and class-based effects. Working-class families vehemently protested what they saw as arbitrary incarcerations, overly vague legal language, and the high handedness of social workers and judges. As Mary Odem has shown in her discussion of the development of juvenile courts in Los Angeles, many working-class parents brought their daughters before the court as a way of asserting their own authority over girls and their economic and sexual behaviour. Families turned to the courts when girls stayed out late or had inappropriate boyfriends, but they also objected when girls refused to turn their earnings over to the family. Families thus used the courts as a way of enforcing economic and sexual morality. To their astonishment, however, families found that the courts blamed them, and their social class, for their daughter's sexual behaviour, and removed girls from the home.[9] In one case from Bedford Reformatory in 1919, an African-American father begged for the return of his daughter. As her social worker reported, 'Daisy's parents feel very badly because she was sent here. The father says that he did not intend to have her sent away but simply wanted to scare her so she would know she must obey him.'[10] When discussing whether to release her, one social worker commented that 'It really was not a legal commitment', to which another replied 'With that record I should not care to have the responsibility of letting her go out. I don't see how they can control her any better now than before.' Deciding not to release Daisy, they noted in her file that 'She does not seem to realize that she has committed any offence and is quite unwilling to admit that she has been bad.'[11] But of course by Daisy's definition, she had not committed an offence by having sex with friends in exchange for dinner and presents. Adding insult to injury, the state allowed middle-class parents to deal with the issue of sexual discipline within the privacy of their own home, even when police found girls in bars or noted a history of 'incorrigible behaviour'.[12] Thus, working-class girls bore the burden of the state's vague definitions of prostitution, and more broadly, its desire to regulate women's sexuality.

Young women also protested outdated or inappropriate legal definitions of prostitution. In conversations with their social workers they made clear moral distinctions between sex for fun and sex for profit. Rose Hansen lectured her social worker 'that having intercourse occasionally with a man was very different from being in "the racket" and not caring whom you took or with whom you went out'.[13] To Hansen the difference between moral sex and immoral sex lay both in a woman's engagement with the formal prostitution business, 'the racket', and in evaluations of her intentions and state of mind. Having sex with men you liked was normal: walking the streets, working in a brothel, or taking cash was prostitution.

The shift in popular definitions of prostitution also marked real changes in sexual behaviour and understandings of morality by the early twentieth century. For example, in the United States, many young girls began to engage in an activity they called 'charity'. First identified by historian Kathy Peiss, charity involved the exchange of sex for entertainment expenses like theatre tickets, dance hall admissions and meals. Lacking cash because of their family responsibilities, working-class girls relied on sexual barter to gain access to the glittery world of urban amusements. These young women made a clear distinction between sexual barter, which they practised, and sexual sale, which they saw as immoral.

The social worker of one African-American girl reported that 'she has had sexual intercourse with three different friends but has never taken money from them. They have sent her presents and have taken her out to dinner and the theatre often.' When asked about prostitution the girl commented that '"in a way prostitution is the worst crime anybody can commit because you have to do things that take away your self respect"'.[14]

As I argue elsewhere, charity and other pre-marital sexual activities opened up space between chastity and prostitution, which both changed understandings of sexual morality and affected sexual behaviour. These activities increased rates of pre-marital intercourse in the United States, and by the 1920s fundamentally changed the way Americans thought about pre-marital sex and prostitution. Pre-marital sex became more common and more accepted for women. As a result, men began to look to non-commercial relationships for sex. This changed the market for sex, further stigmatizing the exchange of sex for money, and marginalizing prostitution in American sexual culture.[15] By the 1940s, visits to prostitutes had become so rare that white soldiers with venereal disease named prostitutes as their source of infection in only 6 per cent of cases, and black soldiers blamed prostitutes 14 per cent of the time.[16] Visiting prostitutes, even for soldiers away from home during wartime, had become an uncommon occurrence.

As this suggests, legal and cultural definitions of prostitution overlapped, yet at times remained distinct. Legal definitions remained vague for far longer than popular ones did, and at times failed to respond to major shifts in average people's understanding of sexual and economic behaviours and values. As the twentieth century progressed, legal definitions did begin to adopt the popular 'sex for money' definition, but the exigencies of enforcing bans on prostitution have resulted in laws that give police as much leeway as possible. California's laws thus still allow police to entrap women (by soliciting them for sex) and have even allowed police to argue that making eye contact represented consent in the place of verbal agreement or a nod. These laws continue those nineteenth-century statutes that cast all working-class women as possible prostitutes. Arrests and prosecutions for prostitution continue to rely more on location, race and class, than on actual activity. Los Angeles police are far more likely to target an African-American woman standing on the corner of Hollywood and Vine than a white woman standing on the corner of the ritzy Rodeo Drive. But of course, this reflects a different sort of imprecision in the law. Unlike the medieval jurists who saw promiscuity as more important than a cash transaction, current laws remain vague to bolster the enforcement power of the state. Sexual behaviours and values have changed dramatically and 'promiscuity' no longer distinguishes prostitutes from 'respectable' women.

a brief history of the world's oldest profession

The pre-eminent French historian of prostitution, Alain Corbin, once wryly observed that 'the oldest profession in the world seems to be the only one to have escaped history'.[17] In itself, this rejection of prostitution as a valid topic for historical study reveals enormously contradictory assumptions. Such assumptions at once naturalize prostitution (it has always existed, and thus does not need to be explained) and marginalize it (it is too vile an activity to merit our attention). How, then, might we contextualize and historicize something often seen as timeless and unworthy of study? In the last fifteen years historians have increasingly challenged these assumptions. In this burgeoning historiography, prostitution is treated as a lens through which we see the development of the modern West, and a mirror that reflects the anxieties people going through those changes felt. Prostitution, historians have argued, has played a practical role in the economic and sexual lives of many individuals and has been an important symbol for interpreting and challenging the modern social, political and economic order. However, we must be careful not to link prostitution too tightly to the conditions of modern life. Whilst, as Timothy Gilfoyle noted recently, historians have a tendency to see prostitution as a metaphor for modernity, 'recent research increasingly reveals that issues of regulating female sexuality, licensing brothels, restraining male promiscuity, and maintaining the "social order" were significant components of pre-modern society'.[18] The 'world's oldest profession' does provide an excellent metaphor for human relations in the modern world, but it is also a real economic and social practice that has remained remarkably stable over the last millennia.

Prostitution has evolved alongside the staggering changes that have occurred in the organization of economic and social life since the seventeenth century. In England, for example, over-population and soil exhaustion combined with movements that eliminated common lands to disrupt the agricultural economies that supported poor and middling folk. Bereft of their traditional employment, some moved directly to cities looking for work while others undertook a seasonal economic migration between country and city. Soon industrialization began to offer work to some of these newly displaced people, but at very low wages and under appalling working conditions. By the mid-eighteenth century, English industrialists combined de-skilling with mechanization, replacing skilled tradesmen with machines and poorly paid workers. Elsewhere in Europe and North America, industrialization began later, but advanced more rapidly. By the mid-nineteenth century few in the West's poor or middling classes remained unaffected by these radical economic changes. All of these factors led to increased urbanization, some freedom from community and family supervision and a population of impoverished people concentrated in cities competing for what little low-wage work existed.

Although women and men both experienced these changes, they had a differential impact on the sexes. Economic changes made it difficult for poor men to earn enough to support a family, and thus to get married. Seasonal work drew young men to the cities creating large pools of unmarried men who might want to engage the services of a prostitute, particularly if their prospects for marriage seemed dim. Industrialization and urbanization inhibited stable family formation for some, and delayed it for others, creating larger markets for prostitution than had previously existed in either the rural areas or small cities of early-modern Europe and colonial America.[19]

While I am not arguing for a transhistorical understanding of heterosexual male sexual desire, most historians and the communities they study assume that single men will turn to prostitution for sex if they have no other options. The Contagious Disease Acts, for example, restricted prostitution only in cities with military concentrations, thereby implicitly acknowledging the assumption that servicemen wanted sex with women and would, given the opportunity, avail themselves of the services of prostitutes. George Chauncey, by contrast, posits a more general male desire for sex that could be resolved in either homosexual or heterosexual ways. Chauncey found that the rootless young men who flooded New York City in the 1890s often used female prostitutes and male 'fairies' interchangeably.[20] Furthermore, Chauncey's earlier work on the Newport Naval Base suggested that sailors turned to other men for sex after the War Department's massive propaganda campaigns blamed female prostitutes for venereal disease.[21] Historians and their subjects have tended to assume that men have innate sexual desires that they will go to great lengths to satisfy.

If industrialization and urbanization created a larger market for prostitution, these forces also had gendered effects that propelled many young women into the trade. Sexual discrimination in the labour market made it impossible for women to live on the wages their work paid and faced fierce competition for particular forms of work. Employers also argued that women only worked for 'pin money' – money to buy luxuries.[22] Since it was assumed that women did not support either themselves or families, they did not need to be paid as much as men. This gender segregation of the labour market kept women's wages desperately low. For example, a state investigation into wages in New York State in 1853 found that a working man needed to earn $600 dollars a year to support a family of four, but that seamstresses only made an average of $91.[23]

Not surprisingly, numerous historians of Europe and the United States have found that low wages led many women into prostitution. Despite periodic modern examples of middle-class women going into prostitution and ancient traditions of well-educated courtesans, the majority of prostitutes came (and continue to come) from the working class. While working-class women's economic needs proved dire, they were also often temporary or cyclical. As a result, many women prostituted casually, rather than professionally, combining it with other temporary work. Women arrested for prostitution often reported a number of other low-paying jobs in industry or domestic service. As one New York woman explained to in court in 1814, 'I sometimes go out to days work [domestic work] and also live by prostitution.'[24] The seasonal nature of industrial work added to women's need to supplement their wages from time to time. When laid off from jobs making paper flowers or sewing shirtwaists, some women turned to casual prostitution to make ends meet. Prostitution also provided a temporary solution for family emergencies, such as the death, maiming or unemployment of a husband, or the illness of a child.

Industrial labour and urbanization contributed to women's participation in prostitution in other non-economic ways. The mobility and the anonymity of city living allowed women more freedom from traditional family and community supervision, making sexual activities, either for pay or for fun, easier to undertake. In her study of prostitution in Victorian England, Judith Walkowitz found orphans and half orphans disproportionately over-represented among the prostitutes registered under the Contagious Diseases Acts. These women may have turned to prostitution because the death of parents forced them to shift for themselves. However, they may also have taken advantage of the lack of family supervision to engage in prostitution. In areas as diverse as New York and Cape Town, South Africa, historians have noted the strong connection between the death of a parent (particularly the father) and prostitution.[25] Undoubtedly both economic need and relative freedom drove these women's activities.

Finally, while prostitutes clearly and overwhelmingly come from the working class, not all of them cite economic need as their primary motivation for working in the trade. Christine Stansell's analysis of William Sanger's exhaustive study of New York's prostitutes in 1850 showed that over a quarter of them answered 'inclination' when asked why they prostituted.[26] Poor girls might go into prostitution to buy fancy clothes, because they liked dancing and drinking, or because prostitutes convinced them that 'they led an easy, merry life'. Sanger's 'exhaustive queries revealed a great deal about the roots of prostitution in economic desperation, but they also produced compelling evidence about more complex sources... Inclination, whatever its moral connotations, still indicated some element of choice within the context of other alternatives.'[27] And of course, as Stansell reminds us, many desperate women in disastrous economic situations chose *not* to go into prostitution. For me, as for many other historians of prostitution, the question is never why some women went into prostitution, but why so many others did not.

Studies of the European empires indicate that the process of colonization also produced urban areas with large numbers of single men, and large numbers of economically precarious women and families. In Kenya, Luise White found that prostitution resulted from the disruption of traditional agriculture. Although the British designed Nairobi to function as a way station for large groups of single male wage-earners, White argues that prostitution resulted more from women's attempt to preserve family land in the face of catastrophic changes to agriculture, than from the large 'market' of men who might buy sexual services. Prostitution in Europe's colonies, it seems, developed differently, but still responded to many of the same sorts of social forces.[28]

By the mid-nineteenth century in European and American cities, prostitution appeared to be a growing problem. However, historians have had trouble ascertaining whether or not prostitution actually increased as a result of widespread industrialization and urbanization. Certainly contemporaries believed it had. But as researchers in many fields have discovered, prostitutes are notoriously difficult to count, a problem that is compounded by historians' reliance on fragmentary records. Estimates often say more about the fears of those commenting than actual conditions. Timothy Gilfoyle provides an excellent discussion of this problem for nineteenth-century New York. He noted that in 1833 the *Journal of Public Morals* suggested that 10,000 prostitutes made their homes in New York. If true, he points out, this meant that 20 per cent of the city's female population between the ages of sixteen and thirty-six sold sex for money. While the *Journal of Public Morals* may have inflated their numbers to raise public concern, police reports, by contrast, usually under-reported the numbers because high numbers of prostitutes indicated their failure to maintain the public order.[29] Historian Christine Stansell also wrestled with these conflicting estimates for nineteenth-century New York and concluded that even the hysterically inflated estimates of prostitution indicated that prostitution increased at pace with the rapidly growing population. 'There were', she commented wryly, 'more prostitutes simply because there were more people.'[30]

Historians like Gilfoyle or Carroll Smith-Rosenberg believe that the inflated estimates of prostitution reflected middle-class anxieties about the changes brought by industrialization and urbanization. In this context, they argue, prostitution became a symbol for fears about the idle and dissolute poor who crowded into the cities in search of work. The middle class who saw prostitution as a growing threat to their authority and to the morality of their cities began to organize against it. One clear outcome of urbanization and industrialization was the creation of social and political movements to study, contain, and at times eradicate the 'social evil'. These movements debated the relative value of either abolishing prostitution or segregating prostitution into vice districts to keep it from contaminating the rest of society. However, these reformers shared many of the same fears about the effects of prostitution on society, and differed more in their strategy for how to deal with the problem, than in their analysis of what caused it.

Male reformers in the 1840s in France saw prostitution as a necessary evil, which led them to establish state-sponsored brothels and a complex system of registration and tracking. As one pre-eminent authority observed, 'prostitutes are as inevitable, where men live together in large concentrations, as drains and refuse dumps... they contribute to the maintenance of social order and harmony'. Men's lustful nature made prostitution necessary, as without it, 'the man who has desires will pervert your daughters and servant girls... he will sow discord in the home'. Such fears about moral contagion and men's sexual needs drove the movement to enclose and supervise prostitution. While the system developed in France in the mid-nineteenth century required the inspection of prostitutes for venereal disease, disease remained a secondary concern to fears about the moral problems that might erupt should prostitution be unavailable.[31]

Early nineteenth-century Americans shared the French analysis of the causes of prostitution ('unrestrained male lust'), but differed in their solutions. Influenced by the intense religious revivals that lashed the eastern seaboard of the United States in the 1820s and 1830s, a group of middle-class women in New York founded the Female Moral Reform Society in 1834 to 'convert New York's prostitutes to evangelical Protestantism' and to close the city's brothels.[32] They pursued these goals by, in Caroll Smith-Rosenberg's terms, 'systematically visiting – or, to be more accurate, descending upon – brothels, praying with and exhorting both the inmates and their patrons. The missionaries were especially fond of arriving early Sunday morning – catching women and customers as they awoke on the traditionally sacred day.'[33] While the Society did not manage to rid their city of prostitution, their experiences led them to a radical and implicitly feminist analysis of social problems. Unlike French male reformers who saw prostitution as a necessary outlet for male lust, they railed against the sexual double standard, arguing that men should learn to control their sexual desires, instead of dragging innocent women down to their level. By the 1840s, the Society had broadened their analysis, concluding that both licentious men and inadequate wages drove women to prostitution. To them, and to many feminists since, prostitution represented both the sexual double standard that punished women for the same sexual activities tolerated in men and women's economic exploitation under capitalism.

By the late nineteenth century concerns about the role prostitutes played in the spread of venereal disease introduced new urgency into these 'social purity' movements, but did not change the direction they took. Efforts in France to control casual prostitution increasingly relied on doctors and medical inspections. In the United States social purity movements used a perceived epidemic of venereal disease as a rallying cry for closing brothels and red light districts.[34] Unfortunately for both prostitutes and their clients, the ability of doctors to diagnose and treat venereal disease lagged far behind society's desire to curb it.[35] Instead, the new focus on disease did little more than complicate the lives of women engaged in prostitution, increasing the level of harassment and exploitation in the trade. By the early twentieth century, venereal disease had changed the rationale for attacking prostitution, shifting attention from moral contagion to physical contagion. However, the solutions offered for these problems remained the same, as did their damaging effects on the lives of prostitutes.

My own research has shown how laws introduced to curb venereal disease during the First World War led to the incarceration of nearly 20,000 women for the duration of the war. Increasing numbers of indefinite incarcerations led women who had previously worked as independents to turn to pimps and madams for protection which in turn resulted in higher levels of violence and exploitation in the trade. By the early 1920s, investigators reported older women engaging in 'charity' rather than prostitution to avoid these new dangers. As one woman told an investigator who propositioned her, 'as far as going out and picking men up on the street for the mere sake of money, I would not consider it, the dangers are too great'.[36] Wartime repression had a devastating impact on prostitutes' families. Prostituting with soldiers became grounds for the removal of children from their mother's custody. In one case, reformers wrote to the Superintendent of the Society for the Prevention of Cruelty to Children, stating that a twelve-year-old girl should be removed from her mother's care because 'it [was] being alleged, with a good deal of positiveness, that Mrs. Eid has immoral relations with the soldiers'.[37] Women who had gone into prostitution to preserve and support families now found that the state viewed them as unfit mothers. These wartime policies remained in force after the war and cast a pall of violence, coercion, and corruption over prostitution in New York that never lifted.

England's experience with prostitution and venereal disease combined all of the responses to prostitution seen in the US and France. In 1864 the English parliament passed the Contagious Diseases Acts in an attempt to curb venereal disease in the military. Under the CD Acts police could arrest women they perceived to be prostitutes in English (and Imperial) military towns, force them to have medical exams, register them as prostitutes, and if found infected, commit them to 'lock hospitals' until doctors declared them cured or non-contagious. By the 1870s an alliance of middle-class feminist and radical working men challenged this regulationist approach and demanded the repeal of the Acts. Raising similar criticisms and concerns to those developed by the Female Moral Reform Society, they argued that the CD Acts discriminated against poor women and perpetuated the sexual double standard.[38] More broadly, Judith Walkowitz argues, the repealers saw 'prostitution as a paradigm for the female condition, a symbol of women's powerlessness and sexual victimization'.[39] This grass-roots campaign had a profound impact on the logic and organization of nineteenth-century feminism, and on the push by women for suffrage in the late nineteenth and early twentieth century. Prostitution raised larger issues than just the treatment of the women involved, indicting patriarchy, the class structure, conditions caused by capitalism, and new understandings of the role of the state in people's lives and health.

Tied both to local and national politics, prostitution remained sensitive to local legal, political and economic conditions. For example, the CD Acts only applied to military and garrison towns. As a result, the state heavily regulated prostitution in Southampton and Plymouth, but not in nearby London. Furthermore, political campaigns and judicial and police scandals all have had profound impact on prostitution in local areas, and can change the form of prostitution most prevalent from one town to the next. Brothel prostitution may have thrived alongside casual street prostitution in some areas, but be temporarily driven out of others. The prevalence of particular forms of prostitution over others mostly depends on local and national economies and anxieties.

By the mid-twentieth century the West had also experienced a rise in what modern theorists refer to as 'sex work'. Coined by women working in the sex industry in the early 1980s, the very term 'sex work' broadens our understanding of what constitutes sexualized labour to encompass a variety of legal and illegal activities including stripping, lap dancing, peep shows, pornography, and prostitution. In cities like London, Berlin, and San Francisco in the 1920s, women began to work in legal jobs such as stripping, or selling sexual or sexualized performance as a form of entertainment. A New York tabloid, the *Broadway Brevities*, described one aspect of the trade when it published an article on what it called 'nude modeling'. Hired as 'entertainment' at private parties, models would strip for men, dance, and share drinks and conversation. 'But the parties are the least annoying part of the model's job', the author explained, 'it's the pawing punks who burn 'em up. A large majority of the girls in the game are dead on the level, and while they don't mind a supper and a show, they do object to a strange sap trying to play the Lost Chord on their vertebrae.'[40] The *Brevities* article exposes the tension created when women sold sexualized entertainment, but stopped short of selling sex. The benefits of sex work, though, far outweighed these liabilities for the women involved. Sex work eliminated many of the dangers inherent to prostitution, while preserving the high wages women could earn. Because sex work did not involve intercourse, it could remain legal, which kept women out of jail, and reduced the spread of venereal disease, which preserved their health. Today legal sex work accounts for far more of the jobs in the industry than prostitution. Although still heavily stigmatized, sex work's legality has created a popular and profitable multi-million dollar industry, and provides high-paying and legal work for women.[41]

research and writing after the 'sex wars'

The rise of modern feminism had a profound impact on academic analysis of prostitution. These debates, in turn, have shaped historians' understandings of prostitution in the past. In the early 1980s, radical feminists began to call for the abolition of prostitution as the ultimate expression of men's sexual exploitation of women. As the legal theorist Catharine MacKinnon argued, 'Because the stigma of prostitution is the stigma of sexuality is the stigma of the female gender, prostitution may be legal or illegal, but so long as women are unequal to men and that inequality is sexualized, women will be bought and sold as prostitutes.'[42] In this vision, prostitution emerged more as a symbol of all women's victimization than an actual practice, an analysis that irritated those working in the sex industry. Stung by the way other women classified them as passive victims of the patriarchy, sex workers like Eva Rosta retorted that 'all work involves selling some part of your body. You might sell your brain, you might sell your back, you might sell your fingers for typewriting. Whatever it is that you do you are selling on part of your body. I choose to sell my body the way I want to and I choose to sell my vagina.'[43] Defining prostitution as work and equating it with other forms of labour, sex workers highlighted the liberating aspects of the trade. As activist Priscilla Alexander pointed out, 'the average prostitute in this country [the US] can gross from about one hundred to two hundred dollars a day, or more, with a great deal of flexibility about hours and days of work'.[44] Seen in this context, sex work represents a choice, and one that pays better and proves more flexible to the needs of family than most 'traditional' women's labour. Rejecting the formulation of prostitution as exploitation, some sex workers argue instead that prostitution represented a positive and rational economic choice in a patriarchal world.

These 'sex wars' polarized the Anglo-American feminist community in the early 1990s, but some researchers have begun to move beyond the stark contrast between prostitution as the ultimate symbolic oppression, and prostitution as uniformly liberating. In their work on prostitution in contemporary Oslo, sociologists Cecilie Hoigard and Liv Finstad have addressed one concrete way in which prostitution can be seen as violence against women. They discovered that prostitutes use two mechanisms to distance themselves from their work. The first is to 'turn off' – to ignore what they are doing when they are doing it. One prostitute explained, 'Ugh, the whole thing is sick. I close my eyes and ears. I cut out everything to do with feelings. It's never, never okay. It would be totally different with a lover.'[45] Prostitutes also place certain parts of their bodies or certain kinds of touching (most often kissing) off limits to clients. An interviewed prostitute stated emphatically, 'He's not allowed to kiss or caress me. He's not allowed to touch my hair either. He's paying to stick his weanie in, and nothing more.'[46] While these strategies work to distance women from their bodies while they engage in prostitution, Hoigard and Finstad found that women have difficulty reconnecting their bodies in their intimate lives and thus have lost a crucial part of their 'private' self. Finally, they noticed that many women in prostitution admitted that they had lost the ability to have orgasms with their lovers. Hoigard and Finstad conclude that prostitution can be seen as violence against women because

> Prostitution tears feelings out of the women's bodies. The necessary emotional coldness from the public prostituted 'self' spreads and takes possession of large portions of the private 'self'. It is virtually impossible for the woman to have a love life while they're tricking. This effect can last for months, even years after prostitution itself is a thing of the past.[47]

Prostitution can be seen as violence against women because it alienates women from their bodies and their sexuality. In ceasing to feel their bodies and their sexual desires, prostitutes have lost one of the most essential and joyful parts of what it means to be human.

The sex wars, and particularly prostitutes' perspectives on the trade, have had a profound impact on the way historians have studied prostitution, forcing them to expand their focus from reformers, state policies, and the structures of the trade into a consideration of the balance between coercion and choice among prostitutes in the past. Historians seem to be better at these discussions than other academics, perhaps because we are so accustomed to studying people in the past who, from our early twenty-first-century perspective, had to choose between a range of appalling options. For example, we are used to describing the compromises slaves in the southern United States made between resistance and acquiescence. The choices they made are not the ones we would like to have, but they do represent a negotiation between agency and oppression, and as such reflect the human experience of history itself. No history of prostitution written in the wake of the sex wars can ignore the question of what prostitutes thought about themselves, their opportunities, and their world. Hemmed in less by ideological positions than by a paucity of primary sources that speak to this issue, historians like Luise White have uncovered both the voices of prostitutes and the moral and economic values of the working-class world most of them inhabited. White interviewed prostitutes in her work on Nairobi, which allowed her to create a particularly prostitute-centred narrative about the development of the trade in colonial Kenya. Those of us who study earlier periods where oral histories are impossible have to content ourselves with critically reading across the conflicting records of the courts, the prisons, and middle-class social workers to find the strident, resistant, and often wry commentary of prostitutes themselves. Feminism has completely remade the way that historians study prostitution, introducing new urgency into our attempts to evaluate the conflicting issues of prostitutes' agency and choice, and the larger economic, political, and societal factors that limit those choices. As Ruth Karras comments, the task for historians is to 'steer between the danger of portraying prostitutes as victims by concentrating too much on how others saw them and the danger of decontexualizing them by concentrating too much on their agency'.[48]

The theoretical debates of the sex wars continue to shape historians' understanding of prostitution and point us in a number of interesting directions for future research. Unlike many academics, sex workers themselves have consistently identified race and ethnicity as important factors in the experiences and structures of prostitution.[49] Their attention to the way that racial hierarchies continue to shape sex work needs to be taken up by historians, as does the counter claim that sex work itself shapes racial hierarchies and racialized sexual desires. Most historians of prostitution have commented on race, but few have really analysed the complicated way that sex, gender, race, and class combine in commercial sex, or the way that commercial sex itself both reflects and produces racial understandings, desires, and identities. One exception is Kevin Mumford's work on interracial sex districts in the early twentieth-century United States. Mumford argues that reformers' concerns over (legal) interracial sexuality led them to ignore black prostitution, an inattention which encouraged prostitution (by both white and black women) to concentrate in black neighbourhoods, even as white working-class communities saw prostitution driven from their boundaries.[50] Black neighbourhoods in Chicago and New York bore the burden of white desires for a sexual playground. Conceptions of race and sexuality literally shaped the geography of modern American cities, leading to the concentration of vice in black neighbourhoods and contributing to stereotypes of African-Americans as promiscuous and hypersexual.

Even in legal sex work, racial hierarchies continue to shape opportunities for women in ways that are patently illegal in the United States. The Lusty Lady peep show in San Francisco, for example, continued to classify women by skin colour (and breast size) in clear violation of US civil rights law in the late 1990s. While the theatre allowed women to call in sick, it required them to replace themselves with a dancer who had a lighter skin colour and bigger breasts. When employees brought their complaint to the California Labour Relations Board, the agency refused to hear their claim because it 'did not choose to waste the tax payers' resources on this class of workers'. What is it about sex work that allows employers to openly violate thirty years of civil rights law banning discrimination on the basis of race and sex (much less breast size)? Lusty Lady's management argued that they only supplied men with what they wanted, namely white women with large breasts. They even lauded themselves for trying to change the sexual tastes of American men by employing (in however a discriminatory fashion) African-American, Latina and Asian women. Such a position implies that American men do have racialized sexual desires, and that on the whole white women with large breasts represent a sexual ideal. Historians need to explore how race interacted with economy, gender, and social class in the past to construct the racism of certain sexual desires, sexual practices, and sexual economies that flourish today.

The flip side of these questions is of course how prostitution (and sexuality more generally) both interacted with and helped produce racial hierarchies and racial understandings. Maria Hohn's work on the immediate postwar period in Germany is an excellent exploration of these issues. She argues that prostitution (and other sexual activities) between African-American soldiers and German women provoked the ire of the German Christian conservatives who sought to reorder the postwar nation. The presence of African-American GIs allowed these leaders to blame the current materialism of German society and its attendant changes in sexual morality on racial outsiders. As Hohn explains, 'they depicted developments in Germany in the 1950s as a worse catastrophe than any others to confront the country, thus completely obliterating the country's murderous Nazi past'. She concludes that the obsession with the threat that racial outsiders posed to German morality suggests that 'racial hierarchies remained a powerful organizing principle by which Germans reformulated and expressed their nationality' in the postwar period.[51] Her arguments indicate the way that race, sexuality, and prostitution can support racial hierarchies.

Similarly, in Philippa Levine's recent work on the British Empire, prostitution emerges as a crucial lens through which we can see the racial arguments of imperialism itself. Prostitution and venereal disease directly threatened the health of British soldiers and colonial officials, but they could also corrupt their superior 'British' morals, the very values, attributes and practices that made England fit to rule the colonies in the first place. In addition, colonial officials often identified prostitution with 'native' practices, inscribing racial meanings onto sexual practices that they themselves participated in. As Levine argues, 'prostitution... could be represented as a throwback to primitivism. Colonial officials routinely argued that prostitution was normalized in non-white societies and held no stigma. This, they argued, was proof that subject peoples were less evolved.'[52] In this context, race and prostitution combined to support both British understandings of racial hierarchies, and Britain's mission to 'civilize' the savages under its care. Prostitution became one of many arguments to support colonization and the domination of 'white' Europeans over 'coloured' others.[53]

Another important issue that requires study is that of masculinity, men, and prostitution. Numerous historians have provided excellent studies of the intersections between prostitution and understandings and ideologies of femininity, but few have really addressed the issue of men as consumers or prostitutes. Timothy Gilfoyle's work on prostitution in New York City in the nineteenth century takes up the question of men as clients, painting a fascinating portrait of the place prostitution held in the creation of a new form of masculinity. The 'sporting man' he describes crossed class lines in his rejection of Victorian markers of middle-class and working-class male respectability and openly engaged the services of prostitutes as part of a new highly sexualized highly aggressive masculinity.[54] Since men make up the market for prostitution more work needs to be done to understand this market and how it interacts with and is shaped by questions of race, class, and performances and internalizations of male gender identity.

In their book on 1980s Oslo, Hoigard and Finstad also address what prostitution means to men as johns (clients) and pimps. Using both data from a national 'john' survey they conducted, and observations about the behaviour of men soliciting street walkers, they found that most men in Norway do not use prostitutes. The small percentage of men who do, view the decision to go to a prostitute, negotiating with her, and having sex to all be part of the same sexualized performance. This explains the large number of cars in street-walking districts. Most of the men present, Hoigard and Finstad found, are not actually looking for sex that night, but instead are engaging in a much more extended sexual fantasy that culminates in sexual intercourse but does not actually focus on it. This also sheds light on a behaviour of clients that has always baffled and amused prostitutes themselves, that is the tendency of men patronizing prostitutes to reach orgasm very quickly.[55]

Hoigard and Finstad also complicate both contemporary and historical understandings of 'pimping'. While a few pimps they met did in fact fit the stereotype of violent criminals directing the careers of several cowed women, they found that most were simply boyfriends or husbands who help their partners manage a difficult and dangerous job. Using their interviews with a lesbian who helped her partner prostitute more safely as a foil for this discussion, Hoigard and Finstad completely challenge our gendered understanding of the immorality of pimping. This poses the fascinating question of whether a lesbian can really be a pimp. Modern and past societies tended to view pimping with hostility because it violates the intertwined cultural assumptions that 'good men' support themselves and their families, and protect their wives' and daughters' bodies, virtue, and reputation. Hoigard and Finstad's conversations with the lesbian 'pimp' and their survey of prostitutes' attitudes toward their male 'pimps' reveal that, in Oslo at least, most pimping should really be seen as a form of job and family support rather than as the ultimate patriarchal exploitation of women's sexuality.[56]

In addition to being clients and pimps, men can also be prostitutes. Several historians of homosexuality now argue that male prostitution has an ambiguous and complicated relationship to gay male identity and sexual practice. Jeffrey Weeks, for example, suggests that the most important paradigm for understanding late nineteenth- and early twentieth-century sexualities is of the schism between acts (what one does) and identities (what one is). As Weeks argues, historians

> have failed to fit everyone who behaves in a homosexual manner within the definition of 'the homosexual' as a unitary type. Even those categorized as 'homosexuals' have had great difficulty in accepting the label. If this is the case for the clients of male prostitutes... how much more true is it for the prostitute himself who must confront two stigmatized identities – that of the homosexual and that of the prostitute?[57]

How then, Weeks asks us, does male prostitution connect with other sexual acts and identities? In an era when male homosexuality had been criminalized the line between prostitution as an act and homosexuality as an identity could be both blurry and dangerous. Upper- and middle-class 'queers' who picked up working-class men, ran the risk of blackmail, but also of violence, if they assumed a common gay identity with the working-class men they paid for sex. But of course prostitution could also offer a sexual outlet for working-class or young men who had same-sex desires they did not want to acknowledge or who wanted to profit from sex they also enjoyed and that made up an important part of their identity.

George Chauncey's work on New York City answers Weeks' call to examine the relationship between prostitution and male homosexuality, and in so doing lays bare the foundations of our modern understandings of homosexuality and heterosexuality. Working-class fairies (many of whom prostituted), he argues, understood themselves as women. They saw their sexual desire for men as a logical extension of their femininity. In this formulation, homosexuality emerges as a symptom of gender identity. Similarly, many working-class 'normal' men approached sex with fairies in the same way they did sex with prostitutes. As long as they could play the active role in intercourse, sex with fairies (either for pay or for free) did not compromise their masculinity. As Chauncey argues, 'many men alternated between male and female sexual partners without believing that interest in one precluded interest in the other... they neither understood nor organized their sexual practices along a hetero-homosexual axis'.[58] Under Chauncey's keen analytic gaze, understanding male prostitution and its relationship to gender and class systems exposes an older and very different sex and gender system than the one we currently inhabit and see as natural.

Other historians like Matt Houlbrook have used male prostitution to explore the conflicted relationships between masculinity, class, and nationalism. In his work on the guardsmen of Britain, Houlbrook argues that the guardsmen's propensity for exchanging sex for money and favours with elite 'queers' destabilized important understandings of masculinity and nationhood. The guard both represented the ideal of British masculinity, and by extension, British nationhood, at the same time as he also existed as an object of queer desire. As Houlbrook explains, 'if the guardsman was a soldier hero, he could also be a rent boy, his brigade's military exploits matched by equally distinguished traditions of exchanging sex for money and consumerist pleasures with older, wealthier men'.[59] The debates around the guard, his masculinity, his class, and his sexuality, exposed important anxieties about the British nation. Male prostitution, particularly that of soldiers and sailors, shed light on the complex relationships between sexuality, sexual identity, gender, and nationhood. More work needs to be done to understand these overlapping constructions of personal and national masculinities.

Finally, historians of prostitution need to begin to grapple with the practical and symbolic importance of prostitution across national boundaries. The consistent relationship between prostitution and the military reminds us that as the nations, economies, and militaries of the

West expanded, they changed both their own sexual cultures and the cultures of the people they encountered and dominated. While Philippa Levine's work on the role of prostitution in the imperial expansion of the West in the nineteenth century provides an excellent and crucial model, historians must begin to address the global sex trade that emerged in the wake of the Second World War.

In particular, America's military and economic expansion has led to the development of an extensive international market in sex tourism, particularly in south-east Asia. Deliberately used by governments like Thailand and Vietnam to support economic development, sex work in Bangkok and Saigon brings much needed foreign currency to these economies, stimulating their rapid expansion. The benefits of this trade have rarely trickled down to the prostitutes and their families, and have come at a grave cost to those involved. Rates of HIV infection have skyrocketed and sexual slavery and child sexual abuse are rampant.[60] The sex industry today implicates the entire structure of global economic development and at times involves not just local institutions, but international organizations like the International Monetary Fund and the World Bank. More work needs to be done to expose the ways local and international economic practices, national and nationalistic priorities, and understandings of race, sexuality, and gender continue to shape prostitution today. Exploring these issues will in turn illuminate the way sex work continues to shape not just Europe and the United States, but the world.

Prostitution in the modern West has a long, conflicted, and ambiguous history. Often associated with modernity, its forms and organization have remained remarkably stable over time. While its legal and cultural definitions have become more precise, it continues to be an issue whose real meaning evades us. Prostitution may no longer simply be another term for 'promiscuity', as it was in medieval England, but women who engage in sex with many partners still run the risk of being called a 'whore'. Furthermore, even as modern sexual values have evolved to allow much more freedom of sexual expression, the exchange of sex for cash remains heavily stigmatized.[61] This stigma matters in economic terms. Women in the United States continue to earn on average 75 cents for every dollar a man earns. The negative connotations of prostitution keep many women from participating in work that would be both more profitable and more flexible to the demands of family. Defining prostitution in moral terms blinds us to the fact that it is still work, and well-paying work at that. It is also dangerous work that can cause physical and emotional damage. But many working-class occupations like steel making and coal mining threaten the health, safety, and often lives of the people who work in them. We need to persist in our efforts to uncover the history of prostitution because untangling these complexities in the past may help us separate out the threads of morality, money, gender and power in the present.

notes

1. 'Investigative Reports, 1913–14', Box 28, Committee of Fourteen Papers, Astor, Lenox and Tilden Collection, Rare Books and Manuscripts, New York Public Library, New York City [Hereafter CFP].
2. See Kathy Peiss, *Cheap Amusements: Working Women and Leisure in Turn-of-the-Century New York* (Philadelphia: Temple University Press, 1986), pp. 88–125; Elizabeth Alice Clement, *Trick or Treat: Prostitutes, Charity Girls, Courting Couples, and the Creation of Modern Heterosexuality* (Chapel Hill: University of North Carolina Press, 2005).
3. See Ruth Mazo Karras, *Common Women: Prostitution and Sexuality in Medieval England* (New York: Oxford University Press, 1996); Mary Perry, *Gender and Disorder in Early Modern Seville* (Princeton: Princeton University Press, 1990); Alain Corbin, *Women for Hire*, translated by Alan Sheridan (Cambridge: Harvard University Press, 1990).
4. Donna Marie Niles, 'Confessions of a Priestesstute', in Frederique Delacoste and Priscilla Alexander (eds.), *Sex Work: Writings By Women in the Sex Industry* (Pittsburgh: Cleis Press, 1987), p. 148.
5. Karras, *Common Women*, p. 17.
6. Judith Walkowitz, *Prostitution and Victorian Society: Women, Class, and the State* (Cambridge: Cambridge University Press, 1980), pp. 69–89.
7. Ruth Alexander, *The Girl Problem: Female Sexual Delinquency in New York, 1900–1930* (Ithaca: Cornell University Press, 1995), p. 50.
8. Joan Jacobs Brumberg, *The Body Project: An Intimate History of American Girls* (New York: Vintage Press, 1998), pp. 139–92.
9. Mary Odem, *Delinquent Daughters: Protecting and Policing Adolescent Female Sexuality in the United States, 1885–1920* (Chapel Hill: University of North Carolina Press, 1995), pp. 38–62.
10. Inmate 2486, Box 14, Series 14610–77B, Bedford Hill Reformatory, Inmate Case Files, New York State Archives, Rare Books and Manuscripts, Albany New York. (Hereafter referred to as Bedford Hills.)
11. Inmate 2486, Box 14, Bedford Hills.
12. See, for example, Katherine Bement Davis, 'A Study of Prostitutes Committed from New York City to the State Reformatory for Women at Bedford Hills', in George Kneeland, *Commercialized Prostitution in New York City* (New York: Century Company, 1913), pp. 178–88.
13. Client CT (white Catholic), Box 81, Women's Prison Association, Client Case Files, Astor, Lenox and Tilden Collection, Rare Books and Manuscripts, New York Public Library, New York City.
14. Inmate Number 2480, Box 14, Bedford Hills.

15. See Clement, *Trick or Treat*. See also Victoria Thompson, *The Virtuous Marketplace: Women, Men, Money and Politics in Paris, 1830–1870* (Baltimore: Johns Hopkins University Press, 2000).
16. Lewis J. Valentine, Police Commissioner City of New York, 'Common Problems in the Apprehension of Civilian Contacts as Reported on Forms 140', p. 33, Box 7, Entry 40, RG 215, National Archives, College Park, Maryland.
17. Corbin, *Women for Hire*, xvi.
18. Timothy Gilfoyle, 'Prostitutes in History: From Parables of Pornography to Metaphors of Modernity', *American Historical Review*, 104 (1999), 136.
19. Timothy Gilfoyle, *City of Eros: New York City, Prostitution, and the Commercialization of Sex* (New York: Norton, 1992), pp. 92–116. For England see Walkowitz, *Prostitution*, p. 22.
20. George Chauncey, *Gay New York: The Making of the Gay Male World, 1890–1940* (New York: Basic Books, 1994), pp. 76–86.
21. George Chauncey, 'Christian Brotherhood or Sexual Perversion? Homosexual Identities and the Construction of Sexual Boundaries in the World War One Era', *Journal of Social History*, 19 (1985), 189–211.
22. See Alice Kessler-Harris, *Out to Work: A History of Wage Earning Women in the United States* (New York: Oxford University Press, 1982), p. 100.
23. Ibid., p. 79.
24. Quoted in Gilfoyle, *City of Eros*, p. 60.
25. Walkowitz, *Prostitution*, p. 19. Elizabeth van Heyningen, 'The Social Evil in the Cape Colony, 1868–1902', *Journal of South African Studies*, 10, 2 (1984), 182.
26. Christine Stansell, *City of Women: Sex and Class in New York, 1789–1860* (Urbana and Chicago: University of Illinois Press, 1986), p. 177.
27. Ibid.
28. Luise White, *The Comforts of Home: Prostitution in Colonial Nairobi* (Chicago: University of Chicago Press, 1990), pp. 1–21.
29. Gilfoyle, *City of Eros*, pp. 57–9.
30. Stansell, *City of Women*, p. 173.
31. Quoted in Corbin, *Women for Hire*, p. 4.
32. Carroll Smith-Rosenberg, 'Beauty, the Beast, and the Militant Woman', in her *Disorderly Conduct* (New York: Oxford, 1985), p. 109.
33. Ibid., p. 113.
34. Ruth Rosen, *The Lost Sisterhood: Prostitution in America, 1900–1918* (Baltimore: Johns Hopkins University Press, 1982), pp. 14–37. Recent data suggest that rates of venereal disease began to decline in the mid-nineteenth century. Philippa Levine, *Prostitution, Race and Politics: Policing Venereal Disease in the British Empire* (New York: Routledge, 2003), p. 2.
35. See Allan Brandt, *No Magic Bullet: A Social History of Venereal Disease in the United States Since 1880* (New York: Oxford University Press, 1987), pp. 40–1.
36. 'IR--Restricted--G-R', Box 36, CFP.
37. 'General Correspondence--1917–2', Box 24, CFP.
38. Walkowitz, *Prostitution*, pp. 69–112.
39. Judith Walkowitz, 'Male Vice and Female Virtue', in Ann Snitow, Christine Stansell, and Sharon Thompson (eds.), *Powers of Desire* (New York: Monthly Review Press, 1983), p. 422.

40. Harold Stanning, 'Sex Models Strip', *Broadway Brevities*, 7 November 1932, 14.
41. Peggy Morgan, 'Living on the Edge', in Delacoste and Alexander, *Sex Work*, p. 25.
42. Catharine MacKinnon, *Toward a Feminist Theory of the State* (Cambridge: Harvard University of Press, 1989), p. 68.
43. Eva Rosta, in Gail Pheterson (ed.), *A Vindication of the Rights of Whores* (Seattle: Seal Press, 1989), p. 146.
44. Priscilla Alexander, 'Prostitutes are Being Scapegoated for Heterosexual AIDS', in Delacoste and Alexander, *Sex Work*, p. 206.
45. Quoted in Cecilie Hoigard and Liv Finstad, *Backstreets: Prostitution, Money, and Love* translated by Katherine Hanson, Nancy Sipe, and Barbara Wilson (University Park: Pennsylvania State University Press, 1986), p. 65.
46. Ibid., p. 66.
47. Ibid., p. 115.
48. Karras, *Common Women*, 9.
49. See Priscilla Alexander, 'Prostitution: *Still* a Difficult Issue for Feminists', in Delacoste and Alexander, *Sex Work*, p. 197.
50. Kevin Mumford, *Interzones: Black/White Sex Districts in Chicago and New York in the Early Twentieth Century* (New York: Columbia University Press, 1997), pp. 19–35.
51. Maria Hohn, *GIs and Frauleins: The German–American Encounter in 1950s West Germany* (Chapel Hill: University of North Carolina Press, 2002), pp. 109–10.
52. Levine, *Prostitution*, p. 8.
53. Ibid., pp. 177–98.
54. Gilfoyle, *City of Eros*, pp. 92–116.
55. Hoigard and Finstad, *Backstreets*, pp. 25–39, 90–105.
56. Ibid., pp. 133–72.
57. Jeffrey Weeks, *Essays on History, Sexuality and Identity* (London: Rivers Oram Press, 1991), p. 48.
58. Chauncey, *Gay New York*, p. 65.
59. Matt Houlbrook, 'Soldier Heroes and Rent Boys: Homosex, Masculinities and Britishness in the Brigade of Guards, c.1900–1960', *Journal of British Studies*, 42, 3 (2003), 353.
60. Jeremy Seabrook, *Travels in the Skin Trade: Tourism and the Sex Industry* (Chicago: Pluto Press, 1996), pp. 1–17.
61. When I teach I ask my students which they think would be more difficult: coming out as gay to their parents, or coming out as a sex worker. Even in one of the most sexually conservative states in America (Utah, home of the Mormon Church), most of my students conclude that coming out as a prostitute would be harder.

10
childhood and youth

louise jackson

introduction

Histories of youth and sexuality have overwhelmingly examined processes of categorization and regulation by adults rather than the experiences of young people themselves. This is to a large extent a function of the types of record preserved for posterity. Archive collections mostly contain the papers of official institutions and notable individuals: the writings of adults rather than items produced by children. Constituted as legal dependants within the modern Western state, children have been positioned as a subaltern group; the historical record suggests they have been silenced and subjugated to a disciplinary regime. The nature of their being – and of 'appropriate' forms of education, training and development – has been defined through the written word of others, in particular those 'experts' who have made their indelible mark through 'the will to know'.[1]

The historical 'retrieval' of young people requires a refocusing on subjectivity and experience as well as a careful questioning of primary sources, research methods and organizing categories. Anna Davin has written: 'the question "What is a child?" must be followed by further questions – In whose eyes? When? Where? What are the implications?'[2] Rather than seeing childhood and youth as natural states of being, historians since the 1960s have tended to view them as socially and culturally constructed concepts, whose meanings have shifted and changed across time. Indeed the terms 'child' or 'infant', 'boy' or 'girl', 'lad' or lass' do not necessarily imply youth at all; rather they may be used to denote an individual's position as subordinate or even to denote intimacy.[3] Meaning depends on context. Furthermore, the moment when a child is deemed to become an adult depends on the criteria that are used to assess this. Within modern Western states, what it means to be a child has been defined through religion, law, medicine, parenting guides and education curricula. Each of these constructions may use different criteria although, as this chapter will suggest, they have often been inter-linked. Neither is a 'child' simply 'not an adult' since other terms have been used – 'juvenile' (nineteenth century), 'young person' or 'adolescent' (early twentieth century) and 'teenager' (late twentieth century) – to speak of an intermediate group. Nevertheless, as Carolyn Steedman argues, 'it is helpful to make an analytical separation between real children, living in the time and space of particular societies, and the ideational and figurative force of their existence'.[4]

The category of 'age' is now routinely added to those of class, gender, 'race', ethnicity, and sexuality as tools for analysing modern identity. Literary scholars and cultural historians have suggested that a modern sense of self came to be associated with a highly individualized and private inner being (or interiority) rather than a set of external reference points that shaped agency ('God' or 'the Devil').[5] This new sense of self was articulated through memory and personal history; identity was seen as a trajectory from youth to maturity. In relation to this emphasis on the autobiographical, childhood in general and one's own infancy in particular represented a 'golden age' or position of sexual innocence from which one had embarked on life's journey. The child was seen to some extent as the core essence of self but it was also that which was lost through adulthood; the desire to find the lost child is depicted by Carolyn Steedman as integral to the way in which Victorians thought about themselves.[6] Within Freudian psychology from the 1890s onwards the unconscious was associated with the child and childhood was analysed as the formative stage of psycho-sexual development. Thus concepts of childhood and youth have been crucial to the construction of modern sexualities.

This chapter will offer an overview of historical approaches to the study of childhood, youth and sexuality. I shall begin by examining the concept of innocence and its centrality in relation to definitions of the child, focusing on official regulatory frameworks of religion, medicine, and the law. I shall then consider the methodological problems that the historian encounters in seeking to find real young people and to analyse their experiences. A final section takes as its point of departure the contemporary preoccupation with child sexual abuse, considering the ways in which different narratives of sexual danger have constructed both 'abuser' and 'abused' across time and pinpointing the ambiguities that have informed interpretations of the child and childhood since the Enlightenment.

ages of innocence

Histories of youth have been profoundly influenced by the work of French demographer Philippe Ariès. Ariès argued in 1960 that 'the modern concept of childhood' had been constructed during the eighteenth century in relation to shifts in sensibility surrounding sexuality. He contrasted the Rabelaisian laughter that surrounded the infant Louis XIII's display of his genitals at the French court in 1604 with the invocation, made by St Jean-Baptiste de la Salle in *La Civilité Chrétienne* of 1713, that 'parents must teach their children to conceal their bodies from each other'.[7] An earlier 'immodest' encouragement of children's sexual interest was replaced with an emphasis on childhood as a state of pre-lapsarian innocence and 'a true reflection of divine purity'; children required careful protection and education so as not to become contaminated beings.[8]

Shaped by the writings of Rousseau and Wordsworth, the 'romantic' vision of a child redeemer' – derived from Christian frameworks – influenced nineteenth-century interventions.[9] Building on Ariès's work, social and cultural historians have emphasized the classed and racialized dynamics of the imperative to protect and educate. As Hugh Cunningham has demonstrated, the romantic vision was adopted as a middle-class ideal; the 'children of the poor' were cast, by social commentators and reformers, in sexual, spiritual and racial terms, as a corrupted, savage and heathen threat to the nation.[10] Whilst some historians have tended to assume that the urban poor described by nineteenth-century social commentators really were incestuous and debased, Cunningham's work on representation has suggested that the poor were constructed as an imaginary and sexualized 'other'. Similarly, historians influenced by post-colonialism have examined campaigns against child marriage in India to show that white Western writers created a distorted view of Hindu traditions as savage, uncivilized and effeminate.[11] The interest in cultural representations has been pursued further by James Kincaid, who has traced the origins of present-day concerns about paedophilia to the Victorian desire to enforce children's sexual innocence. He has argued that 'by insisting so loudly on the innocence, purity and asexuality of the child, we have created a subversive echo: experience, corruption, eroticism'.[12] The idealization of childhood innocence, arguably, led to its commodification and fetishization.

Michel Foucault's work also drew on Ariès's thesis in highlighting the 'pedagogization of children's sex' as one of the four strategic areas through which sexuality was defined, measured and managed from the eighteenth century onwards. Focusing on the medical construction of 'the masturbating child' as a figure of perversion, Foucault emphasized the ambiguity of nineteenth-century attempts to control children's sexual experimentation. On the one hand a child's sexual activity was recognized as an inevitability if left unchecked; on the other, the 'good' child did not entertain impure thoughts. Thus sexuality in children was both 'natural' or 'normal' and 'perverse' or 'contrary to nature'.[13] The British doctor William Acton argued that 'bad hereditary predisposition, bad companionship, or other evil influences' might lead to sexual disorders in children. Whilst Freud has often been credited with the 'discovery' of infantile sexuality from the 1890s onwards, this is to some extent to misunderstand earlier Victorian frameworks. Medics such as Acton recognized that 'children had sexual urges, even if they were pathologized'.[14] Nevertheless, medical discussions of stages of sexual development in young people were only fully articulated to a mass audience with the publication of G. Stanley Hall's *Adolescence* in 1904, which coined the term to describe the 'rapid spurt of growth in body, mind [and] feelings' that take place during puberty.[15] Thus the childhood/adulthood dichotomy – which contrasted a regulated innocence with sudden sexual maturity – was replaced during the late nineteenth century with assumptions about a natural process of growing sexual awareness. Such a shift can be linked to the development of psychological explanations (which sought to chart the relationship between mind and body) and their intersection with Darwinian evolutionary theories. The late nineteenth-century child study movement assumed that understanding of the child and his/her progression towards adulthood would lead to wider knowledge of mankind's relationship to other species in terms of self-consciousness and mental development.[16] For Freud, early childhood was crucial (although his ideas were not influential in Britain and the US until the mid-twentieth century). Freud delineated stages in psycho-sexual development, experienced during infancy, which he thought were integral to a mature heterosexual adulthood. Neurosis in adulthood (including sexual deviancies) was viewed as a result of childhood trauma.[17]

Whilst Foucault's *History of Sexuality* drew attention to the expert's creation of categories of perversion, his earlier study *Discipline and Punish* focused on the institutions of prison, reformatory and criminal justice system – as sites through which normative frameworks are constructed

– within the wider technologies of modern surveillance.[18] Increasing levels of intervention within the private lives of the working classes was also discussed by Jacques Donzelot in *The Policing of Families*. Foucault and Donzelot delineated the bourgeois attempt within the modern liberal state to regulate an increasing population by encouraging modes of self-regulation. Along with religion and medicine, the law and the criminal justice system have been depicted as important arenas in which ideas about childhood innocence and adult knowledge have been worked out.[19] If the ideal child was supposed to be innocent, what of its ugly twin: the juvenile delinquent? Cat Nilan's research on child criminality in the France of 1830–48 has shown how the concept of 'precocious perversity' influenced decision-making in the courtroom: 'either the child is proven not a criminal or the criminal is proven not a child'.[20] The child victim – particularly of sexual assault – was required to demonstrate moral status in terms of previous sexual innocence/knowledge when giving evidence in court. Those who used a vocabulary that was anything other than naive or childlike were assumed either to be precocious liars or to have been 'schooled' by others into making false allegations.[21]

Recent studies have shown that laws fixing an age of consent, whilst ostensibly seeking to protect, have demarcated those below it as lacking in sexual agency. They have also shown that ideas about sexual agency and innocence have been discussed and debated in gendered terms. Whilst adult women were subject to processes of infantilization, the figure of the child was increasingly viewed in terms of femininity during the course of the nineteenth century.[22] Both youth and femininity – because of their association with innocence and virtue – were positioned as 'endangered' within modern city space, which was increasingly constructed through 'narratives of sexual danger'.[23] The notion of a female age of consent – like that of childhood innocence itself – was not a solely modern phenomenon. An age of ten had been fixed as the statutory age of consent for females in England in 1576, although an older common law precedent of twelve was sometimes referenced. The late nineteenth and early twentieth centuries, however, saw the raising of the age of consent as reformers exposed 'the white slave trade' which made victims of female youth. A sensational newspaper exposé 'The Maiden Tribute of Modern Babylon', published by editor William Thomas Stead in the *Pall Mall Gazette* in 1885, fuelled legislative change on both sides of the Atlantic and led to extensive debate within British colonies. Stead exposed what he called 'the great workings of an organization of crime' which involved 'the sale and purchase and violation of children' on London's streets.[24] In Britain the age of consent for females was raised to thirteen in 1875 and to sixteen through the Criminal Law Amendment Act of 1885. US legislation (whilst varying across federal jurisdictions) pursued a similar trajectory. In New York City the female age of consent was raised from ten to sixteen in 1886 and to eighteen in 1916.[25]

This delineation of young women as sexually passive – as victims rather than agents – has led to feminist analyses of criminal justice as a system that has enforced the control of female sexuality.[26] A detailed examination of the business of the courts shows that ideas about who, exactly, was in need of protection, were contested, discussed and debated; vulnerability was tested rather than assumed. Under the British act of 1885 a male who had sexual intercourse with a female between the ages of thirteen and sixteen was guilty of a misdemeanour rather than a felony, invoking a less severe sentence if proven. Hence complainants in an intermediate category still faced extensive questioning that sought to elicit evidence of consent or resistance in order to prove a lesser charge of 'unlawful carnal knowledge' (rather than rape).[27] Similarly, in the New York courts the trial process created 'a distinction between adolescents and children': evidence of sexual knowledge or of previous sexual experience prompted juries to dismiss cases regardless of other forms of evidence.[28] The practice of criminal justice rejected a simple child/adult dichotomy, invoking notions of physical, moral and mental development. Ability to consent was tested and located in the 'precocity' of the individual rather than the absolute terms of the law.

Whilst the raising of the age of consent was seen by campaigners as an explicitly modern attempt to stamp out the vestiges of a brutal atavism, it should not be assumed that legislation was simply imposed upon British colonies as part of a civilizing mission. Late nineteenth-century debates about age of consent were complex and varied, with 'colonized' subjects occupying a range of positions.[29] In Bengal attempts to raise the age of consent for females from ten to twelve were fought by Hindu revivalist nationalists who sought to defend their tradition of child marriage against British rule. The tradition was said to involve the infant marriage of both parties (although in fact it was only requisite in females), with sexual intercourse taking place for the first time with the onset of menstruation. It was argued that hot climates led to earlier physical development in the colonies than in Britain and that menarche took place between the ages of ten and twelve. Intercourse was deemed necessary at this critical stage for religious reasons: to prevent offspring of the marriage from ancestral curses. It was argued that child marriage fostered a higher form of love that grew from infancy. Legislation against child marriage was supported by Hindu Reformists (seeking to modernize Hinduism),

Liberal Nationalists (wishing to make Indian self-determination more credible) and Liberal Anglophiles (who emphasized their difference as Parsees from other castes). The debate on Indian child marriage involved complex political and religious splits within the 'colonized' population. The eventual raising of the age of consent to twelve in 1891 resulted from compromise between Bengalis rather than a strategic attempt to impose imperial rule.[30]

Debates about differences between Western and colonial children's bodies focused on females. It was the girl child who was viewed as sexually vulnerable and in need of protection before the First World War. The outlawing of sexual acts between males (until 1967 in Britain) meant that an equivalent to 'age of consent' was constructed for homosex through reference to the age of criminal responsibility. In 1846 medico-legal expert Alfred Swaine Taylor noted that any case of sodomy involving a boy under fourteen (as well as its attempt) 'is felony in the agent only' and should be dealt with in a similar way to statutory rape of a girl under twelve.[31] Homosex was also prosecuted through a range of other charges, including the categories of indecent assault and (after 1885 in Britain) gross indecency. The totalizing effect of the legal prohibition meant that courts focused on the issue of criminal culpability (on *who* exactly was responsible for committing the act) and not the vulnerability of a minor (the protection of youth). Steven Maynard's research on urban Ontario, Canada, has demonstrated that acts appearing to involve coercion were often elided with those that were mutually negotiated in the late nineteenth and early twentieth centuries. Defence lawyers representing adult men in sex cases involving adolescents over the age of fourteen invariably attempted to demonstrate that youths were willing 'accomplices'. This made no difference in terms of the charge; it did, however, render the youth's evidence questionable and the case difficult to prove in the eyes of the court since a third-party witness was then required.[32] In 1928 this defence was successfully used to overturn the conviction of the superintendent of the Oshawa Children's Aid Society for the sexual assault of an adolescent boy in his care. As Maynard has argued, such 'legal technicalities' obscured 'the way sexual coercion was rooted in institutional relations of unequal power between men and boys'.[33] The evaluation of innocence in the public sphere depended on gendered stereotypes. Whilst the 'sexual precocity' of adolescent girls was constantly highlighted in the late nineteenth- and early twentieth-century courtroom, male youths tended to be depicted as pursuing material gain – seeking gifts/payment or resorting to blackmail – rather than sexual desire.[34] It was not until the interwar period that medical/

psychiatric discourse began to construct the sexual corruption of male youth as a social problem, leading to moral panics about the homosexual child molester and 'paedophile'.[35]

In the field of law the late nineteenth century also saw the appearance in Western states of legislation that sought to remove children 'in moral danger' from their parents and place them with foster parents or in reformatories and industrial schools. Precocious female sexuality was recast in terms of neglect by parents as well as individual delinquency; parents might also collude with authorities if they felt they were unable to control 'wayward' daughters. Girl victims of sexual abuse who were removed from parents were accommodated in separate homes from other children because their status as 'fallen' might corrupt others. The new institution of the juvenile courts – appearing in 1908 in Great Britain, and in 1912 in France and Canada – created, according to Donzelot, a 'tutelary complex' around young people which involved the intertwined mechanisms of welfare, education and the judicial.[36] Those who have examined the gendering of juvenile justice in the first half of the twentieth century have argued that sexual precocity was seen as particularly problematic in female youth. The process of 'reform' aimed to remodel working-class girls in line with bourgeois feminine respectability to perform a dutiful role as domestic servants, wives and mothers.[37] Whilst the city itself was sexualized and associated with corruption, nostalgia for a lost world of pre-lapsarian innocence was mapped onto the rural. The benefits of reform institutions that were located in countryside or in 'green' areas of a city were highlighted.

The early twentieth-century delineation of adolescence as a process of sexual development resulted in a move away from the depiction of teenage girls as sexual victims. Recategorized as 'problem' girls, perhaps suffering from 'feeble-mindedness' or 'moral deficiency', concerns were expressed through the language of eugenics that they would become the 'problem mothers' of 'problem families'. As social hygiene frameworks replaced social purity frameworks in the years after the First World War, sex education rather than the age of consent became the central focus of activists. Whilst Stead had argued that innocent female victims were abducted from London's streets in 1885, a construction of female sexuality as threat was evident in the British discussion of the 'problem' of amateur prostitution in the First and Second World Wars. The term 'amateur' was used to describe the heavily made-up and dressed-up adolescent who preyed on servicemen at railway stations and other public venues hoping for gifts and entertainment in return for sexual favours.[38]

Thus a diverse range of research – on medicine, psychology, law, and systems of penal welfare – has demonstrated the significance of gendered concerns about child sexuality in the development of modern policies and technologies. However, the study of regulatory frameworks needs to be balanced with an examination of the ways in which they have been internalized, resisted or avoided by young people. Research has demonstrated that ideas about childhood, youth and adolescence have been crucial to the construction of modern sexual identities. Yet the sexual identities and subjectivities of 'actual' children have remained elusive.

telling stories

To what extent does autobiography provide evidence of youthful experience? Analysing French and German 'lower-class' autobiographies, Mary Jo Maynes has argued that an open and picaresque discussion of sexual matters voiced by eighteenth-century male writers was replaced with 'discretion' and 'delicacy' amongst nineteenth-century authors, both men and women.[39] In the memoirs of lower-class women in particular, sexual assault – by fathers, stepfathers and employers – are common events that are used to stress the sexual innocence of the writer and to condemn the poverty in which they were raised. Angelina Bardin, whose unmarried mother abandoned her at birth (c.1901), 'prided herself on her sexual purity' despite the shame of illegitimacy and the experience of sexual harassment. When she was sixteen she refused to follow the advice of a female friend who suggested she sleep with a wealthier boy (whose mother disapproved of the match) in order to get pregnant. Although surrounded by forms of sexual knowledge, these female writers emphasized their 'innocence' and 'purity' as a personal choice in adolescence. The middle-class autobiography of Annie Besant suggests that 'innocence' was more a function of ignorance for young women of privilege: 'Many an unhappy marriage dates from its very beginnings to the terrible shock to a young girl's sense of modesty and pride, her helpless bewilderment and fear.'[40] Maynes's work suggests that both the concept of childhood innocence and the rhetoric of respectability were increasingly significant within peasant and working-class cultures as well as in the shaping of bourgeois *mentalités* and that these frameworks cannot be reduced to 'social control' or 'trickle-down' processes.

Autobiographies demonstrate the importance that was attached to decisions about sexuality during youth. Yet they are also problematic sources because they reveal thoughts and feelings of adults writing retrospectively rather than the thoughts and feelings of youth itself.

Autobiography, as a genre, is concerned with a quest to find the maturity and meaning associated with adulthood. It is a form of writing whose emergence has been associated with the delineation of a 'modern self'. It is concerned with the construction of adult identity and is driven by a desire to describe and explain the process of 'becoming' a grown-up rather than simply 'being' a child. Besant's description of the horror of innocence is described from a later position of 'knowing'. Bardin's delineation of the importance of respectability and purity in her adolescence can be linked to her own social mobility as she moved from 'being a foundling and farmworker to a nurse'.[41] As Joan Scott has suggested, historians need to distinguish between events and the ways in which they are remembered, retold and reconstituted as 'experiences' through the interpretative medium of language.[42] The 'experience' described by Besant and Bardin has been constituted through the passing of time and the trajectory from 'childhood' to 'adulthood'.

The diary of Anne Frank, whilst describing the extraordinary story of a Jewish family in hiding during the Nazi occupation of Amsterdam in the Second World War, also reveals the mental world of an 'ordinary' fourteen-year-old girl. Anne recorded her growing feelings for seventeen-year-old Peter, which are discussed in terms of both romantic love and sexual desire. She voices her frustration with adults who were 'so peculiar when it comes to sex', passing on small amounts of half-information about marriage or menstruation but veiling it in secrecy and mystery: 'if mothers don't tell their children everything, they hear it in bits and pieces, and that can't be right'.[43] As she acquires information about sexual reproduction – from books and discussions with friends – she also discusses the gendered ambivalence surrounding desire itself: 'Is it right for me to yield so soon, for me to be so passionate, to be filled with such passion and desire as Peter? Can I, a girl, allow myself to go that far?'[44] Her frustration at adult attempts to cover sex with secrecy and shame is overtaken by concerns about propriety. Warned by her father that it is a woman's responsibility to exercise restraint, she avoids spending time alone with Peter following their initial experimentation with kissing. The descriptions of her sexual experiences were censored when the diary was first published in 1947 to protect young readers from the knowledge that Anne herself had only gradually accumulated. Given the dearth of children's diaries, letters and autobiographies that have been preserved, are there other types of document that incorporate the testimony of children?

In August 1963, fifteen-year-old Christine was thrown out of the 'Sovereign' coffee bar in Manchester, England, for fighting with another girl. She was taken to the police station where it emerged that she had been reported missing from home by her mother three days previously. In a detailed statement, taken by a policewoman, Christine described the background to the incident:

> I used to go with another girl to the Amusement Arcade, Oxford Road, Manchester. The Manager there banned me because of my bad language and for larking about with the teddy boys in there. I have known a lot of lads, and I have been going out with them since I was thirteen. I have gone out with 'John', he was fifteen when I first met him, and 'Barry' he's nineteen. Also 'Jimmy', he was fifteen... I've forgotten the names of half the lads, I've been out with so many. When I was thirteen and going out with Michael we were down an entry one night and we were kissing. He put his hand under my bust, and he pulled my knickers down to my knees... I kicked him and we had a fight... I punched him and he fell onto the floor and I ran away... I don't know what I do these things for, I'm not happy at home, I don't get on with my Mam, because I don't do as I'm told. I don't want to go back home.[45]

Christine revealed that Manchester's all-night coffee bars and 'beat' clubs had provided shelter for her and that her intention had been to move in with another boyfriend, who was renting rooms in a private house. She was referred to the juvenile court as in need of 'care or protection'. Her case demonstrates police anxieties about urban leisure and entertainment venues associated with youth subcultures, which were linked with precocious and dangerous sexualities because they were spaces outside of adult surveillance/morality. The Sovereign club was one amongst many that was regularly visited by police officers as part of a wider preventative strategy against juvenile delinquency. In August 1963 Christine was participating in a specific form of youth culture articulated through styles of music and dress. The police and popular press were voicing concerns about the use of amphetamines for recreational purposes and police files identified the Sovereign as a place where drugs could be acquired.

Christine's case also tells us a great deal about the surveillance of adolescent sexuality and her statement was profoundly shaped by police questioning. She was clearly asked whether she had been 'in trouble' before, whether she had 'gone out' with young men, and if so, how many. She was also asked whether these encounters had been sexual and, possibly, whether she had resisted the boys' advances. Finally, she was asked what motivated her. Yet the text also provides glimpses of one fifteen-year-old's life in 1963 and it can be interpreted in terms of Christine's determination not to be labelled as victim. Her story can be seen as one of agency, which is demonstrated through her deployment of the tactics of resistance – in relation to older boys, to 'Mam', and others in authority – as well as her desire for excitement, transgression and consumerist pleasure. In her study of the experiences of 'runaway' girls in Toronto, Canada, Tamara Myers has shown that the anonymity associated with the city – as well as its cheap accommodation and employment opportunities – provided an escape from unhappy home lives.[46] A few decades later, Christine was using clubs such as the 'Sovereign' as a resource: for company, refreshment and shelter at night.

It is possible to read statements like Christine's 'against the grain' of the official purpose for which they were intended, looking for moments of resistance and subversion; glimpses of an internal world are manifest. Yet statements like Christine's – made before judges, police and social workers – were used to inquire into the illicit, the deviant and the sexual. They are personal 'confessions' of intimate private encounters brought to public attention. If modern autobiography approached sexuality with 'delicacy', the legally constructed statement provides blunt descriptions of acts and bodies. However, as Foucault has suggested, the aetiological question 'why?' was increasingly central to the penal/welfare process. The statement made by a child or adolescent before a court cannot, ultimately, reveal their 'being'. It, like other narrative forms, is deliberately organized through chronology – that is, through the passing of time – as the child's interrogator asks 'What happened *next*?' The legal statement is always a constructed history (of a set of events) and it is part of the process through which 'what actually happened' is remembered as experience. Christine was asked to structure her description of the Sovereign Coffee Bar episode in relation to previous moments of 'bad behaviour' and sexual activity. She was then asked to reflect on the meaning of 'these things', on 'why?' The policewoman who questioned her made reference to preconceived notions of the causes and effects of delinquency as she asked Christine to frame her story as a trajectory: as a process of 'becoming' (delinquent).

If the category of 'experience' – so widely used in social history – cannot reveal children's subjectivities because it is constituted through the passage of time, is it possible for the historian to uncover the transitory or fleeting, the precise moment of 'being' rather than 'becoming'? Are primary sources always 'afterwords' to the moment of 'being' a child? If spoken and written language is taught by adults and its acquisition involves the child's entry into the (adult) symbolic order, other 'purer' forms of evidence that are non-linear – the gestures and structures of child's play or children's drawings and paintings – may provide useful points of departure. The analysis of children's art in terms of historical subjectivity has been pioneered by Nicholas Stargardt, in his work on the 4,000 drawings produced by the children of the Jewish ghetto at Theresienstadt (known by its Czech name of Terezin after liberation in May 1945). Stargardt has argued that 'we need to think about subjectivity in a synchronic and collective sense, rather than in the diachronic terms of individual biography – as the frozen moments of a social history lived in a very particular time and location'.[47] Through the identification of detail, patterns of association, and moments when the artist simply 'gets it wrong', Stargardt aims to reveal the thinking of children as historical subjects. He shows that children's paintings do not portray violence. Rather, images of food and home, 'which offer the general prospect of comfort', predominate. This can be viewed as an indication of trauma or, alternatively, as a coping strategy. It could also be that the children of Theresienstadt were unaware of what was happening around them. It remains unclear, ultimately, how children's art can be interpreted precisely because it involves our own adult mediations. Moreover, the recording of children's drawings on paper is a very recent form (replacing the chalk and slate of the nineteenth century). The very questions that Stargardt raises about trauma or its lack reflect yet again the historian's interest in cause, effect and the passing of time – in producing a linear trajectory – which it proves difficult to escape. One is left asking whether a purely synchronic approach would, in fact, constitute 'history' since it would require a move away from an analysis of continuity/change that has become enshrined as the purpose of the discipline.

The search for the 'pure' source through which children's subjectivity can be studied ontologically is, of course, a futile exercise since children are not and cannot be positioned outside of adult culture. As Anne Frank's diary makes clear, 'growing up' is in part the process through which children and young people negotiate adult frameworks. Anne gradually pieces together her knowledge of human reproduction. She also expresses feelings of anger and resentment against the adult world. Furthermore, she is aware, in writing her diary, that she is recording the passing of time and her own relationship to it. The themes of 'being' a child and of 'becoming' an adult are present throughout her diary: 'I've changed quite drastically, everything about me is different…'; 'Am I really only fourteen? Am I really only a silly schoolgirl?'[48] The search for 'pure' or unmediated sources is a general problem for historical practice. The study of childhood sexuality, however, is positioned within a double problematic: not only are texts constructed in relation to adult notions of selfhood, but the realm of the sexual is always elusive precisely because it has been coded as private and hidden.

Ultimately, then it is impossible to separate children's subjectivities from the regulatory frameworks that have sought to shape them. Rather, the relationship between the two is a key area of study as is the relationship between subcultures and wider popular cultures. Recent research on queer and male youth cultures has cross-referenced and critically interrogated a wide range of sources (including autobiography and court records) in order to reconstruct the meanings of homosex for young men in the early twentieth century. These studies have argued that, within popular culture, 'homosexuality' and 'heterosexuality' were not viewed as mutually exclusive categories until the 1950s. Within the 'moral economy' of street life, working-class male youths traded sex for material resources (food, shelter, money and access to leisure or entertainment venues).[49] This was not simply a function of material desire as official narratives tended to suggest; rather, relationships with men offered sensual pleasure – as well as potential dangers – for male youths who did not see themselves as 'perverts or prostitutes'.[50] Involvement in homosex – with peers as well as older youths or men – can be interpreted as a life-cycle phase within communities in which there was a strong homosocial culture in the early twentieth century. Indeed, Matt Houlbrook has argued that a range of factors – including the emergence of heterosexual leisure practices based around coffee bars and dance halls (rather than a masculine world of pubs and clubs), greater affluence, and wider availability of contraception – led to a reorientation of desire and the association of youthful masculinity with heterosexuality after the Second World War.[51]

monsters and villains

The inequalities between adults and young people are physical and material as well as structural and cultural. Children are born into the world in a position of total dependency on adults for warmth and sustenance; they are socialized into adult cultures in which they occupy a position as subordinate or 'subaltern'. Adults can abuse children's trust and physical weakness; this abuse is glimpsed in the historical record when cases involving violence and other forms of coercion have led to court proceedings. However, as Maynard has argued, we need to examine the ways in which power was negotiated between adults and youths carefully – in relation to the axes of gender, class, and ethnicity as well as age – rather than making assumptions about total inequality.[52] The Victorian investment in youth rendered it desirable and, therefore, erotic.

It also meant that children and adolescents possessed something that adults could never have because of its ephemerality.[53] Adolescents might attempt to use their youth as a bargaining tool in the negotiation of sexual relationships with adult men; legal sanctions and other methods of blackmail could be invoked against those who 'reneged on their promises'.[54] Debates around sexual responsibility in Britain still focus on specific sexual acts in relation to specific ages rather than the rights of subjects to self-determination.[55] The tension between the desire to protect children from abuse by constructing them as vulnerable and the need to recognize the self-determination of young people has not been resolved. This is not to suggest, as Kincaid ultimately does, that all regulatory legislation must be lifted; rather that the dominant legal frameworks for thinking about children can be reworked.[56]

The final section of this chapter will explore why and how the wish for childhood innocence and the fear of its contamination have formed a constant thread within modern discourse. Whilst constructions of 'sexual abuse' are historically and geographically specific, I shall suggest that there are striking similarities as well as differences in the ways that the corruption of youth has been represented.[57] I shall argue that it is a significant theme in the genres of melodrama (which presents good and evil as clear opposites) and the gothic (in which evil is always unspeakable, hidden or unclear) and that both have played an important role in structuring the modern cultural imaginary. Whilst focusing on narratives of sexual danger – representations of abuse – I shall argue that these constructions have had a 'real' effect in terms of their impact on criminal justice and welfare policies.

The nineteenth-century 'myth' of the 'white slave trade' – which linked together youth, femininity and sexual danger – originated in response to the emancipation of slaves within the British Empire; if black slaves were now free, it was viewed as despicable that white women and children should be sexually victimized. A gendered concept of slavery was used in Chartist rhetoric of the 1840s to link economic and sexual exploitation as an expression of class politics: 'Our sons are the Rich Man's Serfs by day/ and our Daughters his Slaves by night'.[58] From the late 1830s onwards, middle-class philanthropists also expressed concerns about a 'white slave trade' which involved the abduction of country girls in their teens who, lured to London with promises of work in domestic service, were drugged and trapped in brothels. These myths were reactivated in the 1870s by feminist and social purity movements who were concerned about the moral state of the nation. They identified what they saw as a European traffic involving the decoying of English girls to Brussels and Paris, shifting the location of danger and associating it with continental decadence. In 1885, however, the focus returned to England as Stead 'revealed' what he presented as the scandalous incidence of child prostitution on the streets of the capital. Stead's description of the assault on Lily – a thirteen-year-old Londoner who had been ostensibly 'purchased' for £5 – ends with the highly sensational veiling of the scene of horror as the girl is drugged into oblivion: 'There was a brief silence. And then there was a wild piteous cry – not a loud shriek but a helpless, startled scream like the bleat of a frightened lamb. And the child's voice was heard crying, in accents of terror, "There's a man in the room! Take me home! Oh take me home!"'[59] The 'white slave' narrative used the melodramatic framework to emphasize the vulnerability of a working-class victim – 'a frightened lamb' – and the wickedness and violence of an evil wealthy villain.[60]

The relationship between the 'cultural myth' of 'white slavery' and the actual incidence of trafficking involving women, adolescents and children has been a subject of considerable debate – amongst both contemporary commentators and present day historians. In 1912 the feminist Teresa Billington Greig argued that white slave stories both 'strained credulity' and problematically depicted women as 'impotent and imbecile weaklings'.[61] Whilst Mark Connelly has viewed the American phenomenon of 'white slavery' in terms of 'moral panic' that distorts reality, the historian Ruth Rosen argues that it reflects the element of coercion that structured many young women's involvement in prostitution.[62] Judith Walkowitz has argued that most girls who became involved in prostitution in Britain did so at the age of fifteen or sixteen (rather than twelve or thirteen)[63] whilst Jane Jordan's biography of Josephine Butler has highlighted evidence that girls were involved at an earlier stage.[64] By positioning the white slave trade as a 'myth' it is not my intention to suggest that it was an entirely fictional or imaginary phenomenon. I use the term 'myth' to refer to the ways in which events are described, interpreted and made sense of as a result of cultural and symbolic processes. As Vicki Bell tells us, 'myths' form 'networks of talk and practice'.[65] The terminology of the 'white slave trade' functioned historically as a metaphor or euphemism to describe both the abuse of minors and a range of activities that were viewed in terms of the 'sexual exploitation' of young women (including the 'seduction' of unmarried girls). Hence the term (like trials for homosex) elided coercion and consent, obscuring the agency of young people as well as sensationalizing real abuse.

In 1937 Inspector Mildred White of Birmingham City Police produced a set of notes to accompany her training lecture on the taking of statements from adolescent girls aged thirteen to sixteen, in relation to cases of 'unlawful sexual intercourse':

> See the witness alone. You will already have learned from the mother whether or not there is a pregnancy. The mother will probably tell you it happened just once and that her daughter did not know the man. There may be some lurid tale of DRAGGING and DRUGGING. I have been a policewoman for nearly 20 years and have worked in three different cities, but not once, in all that time, have I met with a case in which the victim of an assault was either DRAGGED or DRUGGED! 'Enticed or gently led' into an entry, not DRAGGED. 'Offered a port or two half pints of ale', but not DRUGGED. So, unless something of this kind happens soon, I shall retire without having used either of those two verbs in my statements.[66]

White firmly rejected what she identified as lurid hyperbole, re-positioning the sexual encounters of underage girls within a model of 'courtship-gone-wrong': as everyday rather than monstrous encounters. White's suggestion is that the narrative of 'dragging' and 'drugging' was commonly used by young women to describe sexual assault to those in authority (to mothers or police officers) because of its familiarity and the way in which it assigned blame. In constructing themselves as victims, White suggests, adolescents adopted a narrative that they assumed others wanted to hear. As the dominant narrative of abuse within tabloid newspapers and popular literature, 'dragging and drugging' was perhaps also the only one that young women could draw on to appropriately convey their sense of the trauma of the event. However the adoption of this trope meant that they were increasingly less likely to be believed.

Why did the concept of 'white slavery' endure and continue to hold resonance? Depending on the emphasis, it offered confusion to fuel moral panic as well as different types of solution. The white slave narrative contained melodramatic components: the sensationalism of decoying and drugging and the stereotyping of characters. Good and evil were clearly ascribed and located. Stead's articles offered an interpretation of the threat in class terms: as the despoliation of the working class by a corrupt aristocracy. Yet the 'Maiden Tribute' series also contained a more amorphous delineation of a spectral monster which can be identified as a 'gothic' ambiguity involving secrecy and the hidden.[67] Through the semi-pornographic tone of various passages as well as the real-life drama of Stead's court trial, the separation of rescuer and monster – of writer and villain – was by no means clear-cut.[68] Similarly, the sexual 'beast' that had to be banished in suffragette texts was one that was in all men, not conveniently confined to a particular aristocratic group.[69]

The gothic, like the melodramatic, functioned as 'an imaginative mode and philosophical system' resonating beyond the literary text. The gothic, the law and criminal justice were intimately connected since its tropes were apparent in jurisprudence and criminology, which were 'locations par excellence of production of ideas of evil, particularly in the context of violence and criminal acts'.[70] Concepts of the sacred and the profane provided frameworks for the early nineteenth-century discussion of rape within medical and other forms of jurisprudence. Percival's *Medical Ethics* argued that: 'In all civil countries the honour and chastity of the [young] female are guarded from violence by the severest sanctions of the law... It is consonant to humanity that weakness should be secured against the attacks of brutal strength; it is just that the most sacred of all personal property should be preserved from invasion.'[71] Despite the apparent profanity of rape, medical jurisprudence also warned of central ambiguities in identifying the innocent. Sir Matthew Hale had famously argued that although rape 'is a most detestable crime', it is 'an accusation easily to be made and hard to be proved, and harder to be defended by the party accused though never so innocent'.[72] It was argued that 'thousands of innocent men must have been murdered' before rape was taken off the list of capital offences (in 1861 in Britain).[73] There had been considerable debate as to whether it was possible to rape an adult woman unless she had been 'overcome by drugs'. Adolescent girls, whilst technically under the age of consent, were still required to demonstrate resistance in order to prove their status as victims; similarly the testimony of younger children would not be accepted if deemed precocious. Thus the melodramatic narrative of 'dragging and drugging' was a significant device within (medical) jurisprudence as the ultimate proof of innocence/vulnerability. It was a clear black and white response – centring on the culpability of the victim rather than the accused – to the ambiguity regarding rape in jurisprudence.

White slave narratives evoked the monstrous, the phantasmagoric, and the horror of the grotesque: 'the maelstrom of the damnable and hideous traffic in human flesh'.[74] Similarly, the gothic motif of chasing the hidden beast from its lair, detailed in the 'Maiden Tribute' articles, resonated through descriptions of the streets, alleys, dives and underworlds of great cities as well as in the pursuit of traffickers from continent to continent. The aristocratic seduction narrative was often replaced with other anxieties about the relationship between abuse and social class: 'Satan is claiming our best, our VERY best girls of education, refinement, advantages and religious training...'[75] David Punter has recently argued that the central figure of the gothic is 'the haunting of the present by its own past'.[76] If melodrama is concerned with a nostalgia for a better past, the gothic is concerned with the fear of the past and its implications for the present. 'White slave' narratives are distinctly 'modern' texts, conveying concerns about the continued existence of barbarity, paganism and excess within civilized Western nations as signs of atavism and degeneration. They also gave voice to concerns about the rapid extension of communications and transport systems, the increasing pace of global migration and the need for international legal initiatives. The spectral and fluid nature of the monster was invoked by William Coote, secretary of the National Vigilance Association: 'It has no geographical boundaries, but in every clime, this hideous monster of vice seeks its victims, with a relentless and human ferocity.'[77] The myth could also be used to side-step the ambiguity of the 'beast in all men', by depicting it in clear racial terms. In 1910, Chicago attorney Edward Sims stressed that 'many of these white slave traders are recruited from the scum of the criminal classes of Europe'.[78] Thus the symbolic meaning of white slavery motifs was subject to constant realignment and adaptation in relation to other social anxieties.

During the interwar period the 'white slavery' narrative was gradually replaced with psychological categories of perversion. The construction of 'the paedophile' – through the work of sexologists Krafft-Ebing, Havelock Ellis and Alfred Moll – entered popular discourse as newspapers warned parents of the dangers of 'the park pervert'.[79] This model once again located abuse outside the home, viewing the abuser as an outsider or 'other' who was mentally deficient as a result of disease. As the work of Linda Gordon has shown, victims of abuse themselves were frequently pigeon-holed as psychologically retarded or mentally deficient.[80] Whilst the 'white slavery' narrative had focused on female victims, the model of 'paedophilia' incorporated discussions of homosexual abuse, which was linked to anxieties about male prostitution.[81] Moll wrote that 'there are certain homosexual adult males whose impulse is specially directed towards boys still possessing the milk-white face of the child... It is clear, too, that boys upon whom such relationships are imposed will sometimes tend to grow up as male prostitutes.'[82] The fetishization of childhood innocence – now viewed in terms of innocent masculinity rather than femininity – was seen as a specific attraction for the paedophile who was viewed as a predatory homosexual. Despite its initial genesis as a medical category, late twentieth-century constructions of the paedophile child molester continued to draw on the older repertoire of monstrosity as well as conspiracy theories; fears of a network of slave traders was replaced with fears of the paedophile ring (from the 1980s onwards). Recent criticisms of the creation of sex offenders registers in Britain and the US have argued that the labelling of a deviant and outcast group is unhelpful since it simply gives an 'illusion of safety'.[83] Furthermore, current stereotypes continue to invoke the innocence, vulnerability and passivity of the melodramatic victim. Within contemporary media coverage 'the abused child is represented by an anonymous figure sitting limp and despairing with her head in her hands... or sometimes, simply by a broken doll'.[84]

Despite feminist attempts to recast narratives by reclaiming 'victims' as survivors, the reality of abuse has not displaced an obsession with gothic monstrosity within popular imagination. Moreover, as David Punter has argued, the plot line of the late twentieth-century crime thriller and horror movie has reconfigured the narrative of sexual danger so that abuser and abused merge: the villain or monster is the man who was himself abused and is tormented by his past, whilst the culture of therapy and social work are critiqued, attacked, and themselves constructed as abusive.[85] The ambiguity surrounding youth – as innocent/desired/ perverse – is once again highlighted and, ultimately unresolved. The 'white slave' narrative had offered a simple explanatory framework that reflected the modern belief in progress, a positivist faith in the law, and an unproblematic delineation of the monster as 'other'. It sought to defend innocent whilst very few real 'victims' fitted the frame.

Narratives of sexual danger – which seek to position the innocent and the monster or victim and perpetrator – are constructions or representations that offer particular interpretations of social problems. They are not simply rhetorical flourishes. Rather, they have informed the writing of legal codes and their enforcement through modern penal-welfare systems. They shape the ways in which individual testimonies are received in the courtroom as well as the ways in which testimonies are presented; they have served to assign or deny agency and as such are constitutive of experience.

conclusions

I have argued that the concepts of childhood, youth and adolescence have underpinned the construction of modern sexualities: through their positioning as formative stages in the growth of sexual and self awareness as well as their construction as periods of susceptibility to sexual danger. The modern Western concept of 'childhood' is a moral and legal one, which denies sexual agency in those it invokes. It was developed and deployed in relation to ideologies associated with class, caste, gender and the colonial encounter. The 'innocence' of childhood has been central to the modern condition – despite Freudian challenges and interventions – because of its fixed legal status. If the 'normal' modern sexual subject has been positioned as an adult who can consent as sexual actor/agent from a position of knowledge, then legal discourses have consistently located the young child in terms of lack: as victim/object who is unable to consent because of innocence/ignorance. The clear black and white rubric of responsibility versus vulnerability has found it difficult, historically, to deal with those in an intermediate position. Thus the 'young person' (whether boy or girl) has fallen outside of both categories: as neither truly innocent nor truly knowing. Indeed the labelling of adolescence as a developmental stage – promoted through psychological study – was not reflected in frameworks that accorded legal responsibility. As a result, the continued obsession with innocence has functioned to marginalize the voices of young people by labelling sexual experiences in terms of deviancy, precocity and 'mental deficiency'.

'Innocence' as a sexual category has been gendered in different ways across time. Associated with femininity during the nineteenth century, few attempts were made to regulate or protect male youth until the 1930s when the 'monster' who despoiled young girls was recast in terms of homosexuality. As the homosexual was vilified, so 'normal' sexual development in the adolescent was constructed as heterosexual through psychiatric discourse. The 'paedophile' is viewed as doubly monstrous: for both assaulting the innocent and rejecting normative heterosexualities. The idea of 'innocence' has functioned as a focal point for a range of anxieties about social and sexual interaction: as that which is both desired as infinitely pure and that which is always threatened with contamination. As Kitzinger has argued, the rhetoric of 'vulnerability' and 'protection' is not necessarily helpful to children or young people; the attempt to replace it with a vocabulary of 'rights' and 'empowerment' has yet to be implemented.[86] In terms of the practice of history, we can at least aim to offer a more nuanced reading of our sources that seeks to interrogate the power dynamics that have shaped the negotiation of sexual relationships in the historical past and which seeks to deconstruct the categories that have shaped the experiences of children and young people.

notes

1. Michel Foucault, *The History of Sexuality. Volume 1. An Introduction* (London: Allen Lane, 1979), first published in French as *La Volonté de Savoir* or 'the will to know' in 1976.

2. Anna Davin, 'What is a Child?' in Anthony Fletcher and Steve Hussey (eds.), *Childhood in Question: Children, Parents and the State* (Manchester: Manchester University Press, 1999), p. 33.
3. Carolyn Steedman, *Strange Dislocations. Childhood and the Idea of Human Interiority 1780–1930* (London: Virago, 1995), p. 7.
4. Ibid., p. 5.
5. Charles Taylor, *Sources of the Self. The Making of Modern Identity* (Cambridge: Cambridge University Press, 1989).
6. Steedman, *Strange Dislocations.*
7. Philippe Ariès, *Centuries of Childhood* (London: Pimlico, 1996), p. 113.
8. Ibid., p. 111.
9. Peter Coveney, *The Image of Childhood. The Individual and Society: A Study of the Theme in English Literature* (Harmondsworth: Penguin, 1967).
10. Hugh Cunningham, *The Children of the Poor: Representations of Childhood Since the Seventeenth Century* (Oxford: Blackwell, 1991).
11. Mrinalini Sinha, *Colonial Masculinity: The 'Manly Englishman' and the 'Effeminate Bengali' in the late nineteenth Century* (Manchester: Manchester University Press, 1995).
12. James Kincaid, *Child-Loving. The Erotic Child and Victorian Culture* (London: Routledge, 1992), p. 4.
13. Foucault, *History of Sexuality. Volume 1*, p. 104.
14. Ivan Crozier, '"Rough Winds Do Shake the Darling Buds of May": A Note on William Acton and the Sexuality of the Male Child', *Journal of Family History*, 26, 3 (2001), 411–20.
15. Cited in Stephen Robertson, 'Age of Consent Law and the Making of Modern Childhood in New York City, 1886–1921', *Journal of Social History* (2002), 798.
16. Steedman, *Strange Dislocations*, pp. 77–95; Roger Cooter (ed.), *In the Name of the Child: Health and Welfare 1880–1940* (London: Routledge, 1992).
17. Freud's *The Aetiology of Hysteria*, published in Germany in 1896, linked neurosis with sexual abuse in childhood. For a discussion of why Freud allegedly abandoned this model for a theory of sexual phantasy linked to the Oedipal complex see J.M. Masson, *The Assault on Truth: Freud's Suppression of the Seduction Theory* (Harmondsworth: Penguin, 1985).
18. Michel Foucault, *Discipline and Punish* (London: Allen Lane, 1977).
19. Pamela Cox and Heather Shore (eds.), *Becoming Delinquent: British and European Youth, 1650–1950* (Aldershot: Ashgate, 2002).
20. Cat Nilan, 'Hapless Innocence and Precocious Perversity in the Courtroom Melodrama: Representations of the Child Criminal in a Paris Legal Journal, 1830–1848', *Journal of Family History*, 22, 3 (1997), 251–85.
21. Louise A. Jackson, *Child Sexual Abuse in Victorian England* (London: Routledge, 2000).
22. Steedman, *Strange Dislocations*, p. 5.
23. Judith Walkowitz, *City of Dreadful Delight. Narratives of Sexual Danger in Late Victorian England* (London: Virago, 1992).
24. *Pall Mall Gazette*, 6 July 1885.
25. Robertson, 'Age of Consent Law'.

26. For example, Mary Odem, *Delinquent Daughters: Protecting and Policing Adolescent Female Sexuality in the United States, 1885–1920* (Chapel Hill: University of North Carolina Press, 1995).
27. Jackson, *Child Sexual Abuse*.
28. Robertson, 'Age of Consent Law', p. 790.
29. Richard Phillips, 'Imperialism and the Regulation of Sexuality: Colonial Legislation on Contagious Diseases and Ages of Consent', *Historical Geography*, 28, 3 (2002), 339–62.
30. Tanika Sardar, 'Rhetoric Against Age of Consent. Resisting Colonial Reason and Death of a Child-Wife', *Economic and Political Weekly*, September (1993), 1869–78.
31. A.S. Taylor, *Elements of Medical Jurisprudence* (London: 1846), p. 561.
32. Steven Maynard, '"Horrible Temptations": Sex, Men and Working-Class Male Youth in Urban Ontario, 1890–1935', *Canadian Historical Review*, 78, 2 (1997), 192–235.
33. Ibid., 226.
34. Jackson, *Child Sexual Abuse*, pp. 102–6.
35. George Chauncey, 'The Postwar Sex Crime Panic', in William Graebner (ed.), *True Stories from the American Past* (New York: McGraw-Hill, 1993); Matt Houlbrook, *Queer London: Perils and Pleasures in the Sexual Metropolis, 1918–57* (Chicago: University of Chicago Press, 2005).
36. Jacques Donzelot, *The Policing of Families* (Baltimore: Johns Hopkins University Press, 1997).
37. Pam Cox, *Gender, Justice and Welfare. Bad Girls in Britain, 1900–1950* (Basingstoke: Macmillan, 2003); Odem, *Delinquent Daughters*; C. Strange, *Toronto's Girl Problem: The Perils and Pleasures of the City, 1880–1930* (Toronto: Toronto University Press, 1995).
38. Angela Woollacott, '"Khaki fever" and its Control: Gender, Class, Age and Sexual Morality on the British Homefront in the First World War', *Journal of Contemporary History*, 29, 2 (1994); Lesley Hall, '"The Reserved Occupation"? Prostitution in the Second World War', *Women's History Magazine*, 41 (2002), 4–9.
39. Mary Jo Maynes, 'Adolescent Sexuality and Social Identity in French and German Lower-Class Autobiography', *Journal of Family History*, 17, 4 (1992), 397–418.
40. Annie Besant, *An Autobiography* (London: T. Fisher Unwin, 1893), p. 71.
41. Maynes, 'Adolescent Sexuality', 410.
42. Joan W. Scott, 'The Evidence of Experience', *Critical Inquiry*, 17, 3 (1991), 773–97.
43. Anne Frank, *The Diary of a Young Girl* (London: Penguin, 1997), pp. 221–2.
44. Ibid., p. 273.
45. Greater Manchester Police Museum, Policewomen's Department: Box File on 'Clubs', Sovereign Coffee Bar.
46. Tamara Myers, 'Deserting Daughters: Runways and the Red-Light District of Montreal before 1945', in Jon Lawrence and Pat Starkey (eds.), *Child Welfare and Social Action in the Nineteenth and Twentieth Centuries* (Liverpool: Liverpool University Press, 2001), pp. 15–35.
47. Nicholas Stargardt, 'Children of the Holocaust', *Past and Present*, 161 (1998), 192–235.

48. Frank, *Diary*, pp. 235, 274.
49. Kevin Porter and Jeffrey Weeks (eds.), *Between the Acts: Lives of Homosexual Men 1885–1967* (London: Rivers Oram Press, 1991); Maynard, 'Horrible Temptations'; Houlbrook, *Queer London*.
50. Maynard, 'Horrible Temptations', p. 197.
51. Houlbrook, *Queer London*.
52. Maynard, 'Horrible Temptations'.
53. Carol Mavor, *Pleasures Taken: Performances of Sexuality and Loss in Photographs* (London: I.B. Tauris, 1996).
54. Maynard, 'Horrible Temptations', p. 197.
55. For detailed discussion of the current inconsistency between the age of consent to heterosex (sixteen for females) and homosex (twenty-one for males since 1967), see Matthew Waites, 'Equality at Last? Homosexuality, Heterosexuality and the Age of Consent in the United Kingdom', *Sociology*, 37, 4 (2003), 637–55.
56. Kincaid, *Child-Loving*.
57. The term 'sexually abused' appears in an 1864 translation of a work on forensic medicine. See Jackson, *Child Sexual Abuse* , p. 3.
58. Gerald Massey, *Poems and Ballads* (1854), quoted in Anna Clark *The Struggle for the Breeches* (Los Angeles: University of California Press, 1994), p. 222.
59. *Pall Mall Gazette*, 6 July 1885.
60. Walkowitz, *City of Dreadful Delight*.
61. T. Billington Greig , 'The Truth about White Slavery', *Englishwomen's Review*, 14 (1913), quoted in Lucy Bland, *Banishing the Beast. English Feminism and Sexual Morality 1885–1914* (London: Penguin, 1995), p. 299.
62. Mark Thomas Connelly, *The Response to Prostitution in the Progressive Era* (Chapel Hill: University of North Carolina Press, 1980); Ruth Rosen, *The Lost Sisterhood: Prostitution in America, 1900–1918* (Baltimore: Johns Hopkins University Press, 1982).
63. Judith Walkowitz, *Prostitution and Victorian Society* (Cambridge: Cambridge University Press), p. 17.
64. Jane Jordan, *Josephine Butler* (London: John Murray Publishers, 2002).
65. Vikki Bell, *Interrogating Incest. Feminism, Foucault and the Law* (London: Routledge, 1993), p. 178.
66. Metropolitan Police Museum, Papers of Miss K.M. Hill: First Conference of Provincial Policewomen, Leicester 5–6 March 1937.
67. Steedman, *Strange Dislocations*, p. 168.
68. For Stead's trial for abduction and indecent assault, see Walkowitz, *City of Dreadful Delight*.
69. Bland, *Banishing the Beast*.
70. Leslie Moran, 'Law and the Gothic Imagination', in F. Botting (ed.), *The Gothic* (Cambridge: D.S. Brewer, 2001), pp. 87–110.
71. Thomas Percival, *Medical Ethics* (Manchester: S. Russell, 1803), pp. 113 and 123.
72. Quoted in V.A.C. Gatrell, *The Hanging Tree. Execution and the English People, 1770–1868* (Oxford: Oxford University Press, 1994), p. 471.
73. Lawson Tait, 'An Analysis of the Evidence in Seventy Consecutive Cases of Charges Made Under the New Criminal Law Amendment Act', *Provincial Medical Journal*, 1 May 1894, 226.

74. Anon., *Startling Truths on the White Slave Traffic* (London: Success Publishing, c.1912), p. 3.
75. Ernest Bell, *Fighting the Traffic in Young Girls* (Chicago: G.S. Ball, 1910), p. 100.
76. David Punter, *The Modern Gothic* (London: Longman, 1996), p. 217.
77. W.A. Coote, 'The Suppression of the White Slave Traffic', in Bell, *Fighting the Traffic*, p. 31.
78. E.W. Sims, 'Introduction', in Bell, *Fighting the Traffic*, p. 17.
79. Alfred Moll, *The Sexual Life of the Child* (London: George Allen, 1912).
80. Linda Gordon, *Heroes of Their Own Lives* (London: Virago, 1989).
81. Chauncey, 'The Post-War Sex Crime Panic'.
82. Moll, *Sexual Life*, p. 197.
83. Deborah Jacobs, 'Why Sex Offender Notification Won't Keep Our Children Safe', *Corrections Today*, 65, 1 (2003), 22–3.
84. Jenny Kitzinger, 'Defending Innocence: Ideologies of Childhood', *Feminist Review*, 28 (1988), 77.
85. Punter, *Modern Gothic* cites the work of Stephen King and the 1991 movie *Freddy's Dead*.
86. Kitzinger, 'Defending Innocence', 83.

11
cross-dressing and transgender

alison oram

Introduction

In December 1954, Vincent (Violet) Jones and Joan Lee were each fined £25 at the local magistrates court, following their church wedding three months earlier in Catford, an ordinary working-class district of south London. Vincent's cross-dressing as a man followed a long Western tradition of 'female husbands', but what marked it as peculiarly 1950s was not only the white wedding dress and elaborate wedding cake, but the competing interpretations of their behaviour put forward by the couple themselves, the presiding magistrate and the popular press. Vincent Jones claimed through her solicitor that '[i]t seemed ridiculous for her to be a female'. She had attempted to obtain medical treatment and had 'written to Denmark after hearing about the girl doctor who changed from a female and later married her housekeeper'.[1] The magistrate refused to accept Jones' assertion of her innate male gender and her medicalized justification of what would soon be labelled transsexual identity, and condemned both young women for their immoral lesbian desires: 'The fact remains that you made a grave false statement to cover your unnatural passions with a false air of respectability.'[2]

As this example illustrates, cross-dressing, gender dissidence and unconventional sexuality have a longstanding and complex interrelationship. While they have tended to be intertwined historically, in that cross-dressing or passing was often seen as integral to assuming the sexual behaviour and role of another gender, more recently they have seemed to diverge, as it becomes increasingly possible to actually transform the physical body through hormone treatment and surgery. Passing as another gender is now no longer merely a tactic employed in order to assume the privileges or sensibilities of that gender, neither is it, as it has often been in the past, an assumed reflection of perverse desire or 'inverted' sexuality. Instead, viewed through the lens of modern psychiatry, the cross-dresser becomes the transvestite, a settled identity with little relevance to sexual preference. In addition, through the agency of the gender-crossing individual themselves, as in the example above, and via the clinical lens of psychology, cross-dressing frequently becomes a stage in the physical transformation of the body. The cross-dresser, viewed in this way, is on the way to transsexuality – the physical reassignment of sex through reconstructive surgery. Defining cross-dressing and transgender, in the present as in the past, is therefore fraught with difficulty and uncertainty

Even the definition of cross-dressing itself contains historical ambiguities. Cross-dressing can refer to a range of gender-crossing behaviours, from adopting elements of opposite-sex clothing and gesture to completely passing as the other sex. Similarly, the term 'masquerade' has also been central historically. It was frequently used in the past, as well as by historians today, to describe activities ranging from entertainment (drag balls for example) to an individual's disguise. Depending on the historical and social context, the implications of both terms range from the playful to the deceptive and potentially criminal. 'Masquerade' has also gained more particular meanings in relation to postmodern cultural theory, of which more below.

The word transgender, in contrast, belongs to a different order of language. From the 1950s onwards, the term transsexual was used to define those undergoing sex change operations. However, since then, transgender has increasingly supplanted it and taken on a specific meaning. Transgender was primarily a political term developed by queer activists during the 1990s to describe the deliberate disruption of gender as a fixed binary opposition by exposing it as a fiction.[3] Thus it includes not only the transsexual transition from one sex/gender norm to the other, but also the provocative adoption of social, technological or performance practices to maintain a subject position in the fluid space between genders.[4] However, more ambiguities reside here, since not all those who undergo sex-reassignment surgery embrace the notion of transgender and its political implications. Many of these men and women prefer merely to assert, along with much of medical science, that they are simply assuming their 'correct' anatomical sex, and realigning their bodies with their psychology.

In the early years of lesbian and gay history in the 1970s and 1980s, gender-crossing was researched as one archetype of gay identity. Thus the passing woman or female husband was seen as one means of expressing desire between women before lesbian identity was established, while male effeminacy and cross-dressing was subsumed within a parallel story as one strand of the historical construction of gay male identity.[5] There was also a further debate between feminist and lesbian historians over whether cross-dressing could even be interpreted as an expression of sexuality or whether it should be seen simply as a logical response to women's constrained economic and social position in patriarchy.[6] Following these debates, the Foucauldian turn in the history of sexuality from the 1980s onwards focused attention on the discursive formation of different sexual identities, particularly by late nineteenth-century sexual science or sexology.[7] The different ways in which cross-dressing was categorized as inversion, homosexuality, Eonism (so named after the celebrated eighteenth-century cross-dressing aristocrat the Chevalier D'Eon), transvestism and later transsexuality influenced first professional and later popular understandings of gender and sexuality.

From the early 1990s, increased interest in gender-crossing by cultural theorists, especially Judith Butler and Marjorie Garber, contributed a further postmodern conceptual apparatus with which some historians have experimented. In Butler's writings in particular, cross-dressing and drag assumed a particular importance. For Butler, drag, with its exaggerated parody of gender, is a symbol of the fact that gender inheres in a series of acts, rather than in the sexed body. Rather than seeing drag as an authentic impersonation of another gender, Butler sees it as a parody of the idea of gender itself. Gender, Butler suggests, is continually enacted in a series of inherited cultural and bodily rituals and practices, which together make up the process of becoming a human subject. This, of course, raises the possibility of 'borrowing' the gestures and manners of another gender in a more thorough manner, and of enacting some of the practices and rituals of that gender. Gender, in this sense, is performative, that is, only visible in the process of enaction, and drag draws attention to this fact, hence its symbolic, if not actual everyday importance to gender politics.

Butler's work suggested new ways to examine the disruptive effects of gender-crossing through the sex/gender dissonance of the cross-dresser, whether passing in everyday life or performing on stage. Garber, on the other hand, argues that the cross-dresser is always ambiguous, and cannot be reduced to some hidden inner motivation, to sexual identity, instrumental 'passing', or to transsexuality – an innate, psychological identification with, and desire to become, another gender. Instead the cross-dresser disrupts gender since he/she is never one gender or the other, but an 'or and' who puts in question the very nature of gender itself.[8] Queer theorists have used these ideas to emphasise the contingency and changing nature of gender. In attempting to historicize queer, that is to identify historical subjects who have resisted gender identification, individual cross-gender identification has been sought through the past and across cultures, in the role of the North American berdache or expressions of female masculinity. In the 1980s cross-dressers may have been claimed as lesbian or gay; from the 1990s they are likely to be interpreted as transgender.[9]

Historians of sexuality have engaged with a number of interrelated debates on cross-dressing. A key overarching question is this one: what does the reaction to cross-dressing tell us about how gender and sexuality is understood by contemporaries in particular historical periods? The history of cross-dressing approached in this way can therefore shed light on the workings of dominant (hetero)sexual and gender norms. Cross-dressing may be seen as connected to same-sex desire, or as a completely unrelated activity. In the past sexuality may have been read as reflecting a person's gender presentation, or in another era their sexual identity deemed to determine their gendered behaviour.

Over the past 250 years, in British, north American and European societies, gender-crossing in everyday life has been understood at different times as a deliberate adoption of disguise, the expression of a person's physiological nature, or a demonstration of their interior psychological state. These different views are of course determined by the historically-specific notions of gender in operation at the time, that is, whether it is viewed as a social role, as inalienably rooted in biological sex, or as a psychic sense of self. For most historians, gender, in this context is conceptualized as a distinct and opposing binary of feminine and masculine, or as a set of characteristics which may or may not overlap or be attached to sexed bodies. That is, gender as a social role and as anatomical sex has been considered malleable in the past, not just in the present, and has not always been isomorphic with the nature of the physical body. Cross-gender behaviour helps us to understand and demonstrate this fact, and to illuminate the ruling interpretations of gender.

Recent theoretical debates surrounding the work of Butler have encouraged the idea that gender-crossing is a transgressive activity which disrupts sex/gender systems and fields of knowledge. For historians, these debates centre on the question of whether the challenge of cross-dressing automatically threatens established ideas about gender and sexuality and thereby provokes punishment. This in turn begs the further question of how cross-dressing has been contained or normalized via regulatory regimes, for example by the state through the criminal justice system, or through the regulatory fictions of medical categories. This dynamic process works at the discursive level in the presentation and re-working of cultural knowledge about gender transgression through newspaper stories and through entertainment.

The slippage between the stage performance and the street performance of gender has given historians a useful range of tools in analysing a range of cross-dressing behaviours. The idea of the carnivalesque is sometimes invoked in order to analyse this debate about the effects of gender-crossing. Popular forms like the drag ball, female/male impersonation on the stage or the masquerade appear momentarily to invert the social and gender order, and to suspend the rule of conventional morality. However, these carnivalesque moments can also act as a safety valve; within these confined spaces opposition to the gender order can be expressed and thereby defused. Popular entertainments like male or female impersonation often seem to suggest that this is the case, especially given the theatrical convention of returning at the end of the act in 'appropriate' clothes, thereby revealing the temporary nature of the subversion. However these performances have often acted historically as a means to encourage or celebrate sexual dissidence rather than foreclosing it. Lawrence Senelick has shown that female impersonation in the theatre has had a long relationship with male homosexuality.[10] Male actors who impersonated women on the stage were often involved in homosexual subcultures, while a favourite euphemism for homosexual in the early twentieth century was 'theatrical', frequently combined with 'musical'.[11] In addition to these more obvious examples, it was common for famous actresses who specialized in male impersonation, such as the Victorian music hall artist Vesta Tilley, to receive admiring letters and flowers from her female fans, although these 'mash notes' have a much more ambiguous relationship to homosexuality, as I explain more fully below.

A final question centres on the subjectivity of the gender-crosser – their own reasons for their cross-dressing and sense of self. This has often been framed within present-day perspectives and the search for a usable past, leading to ahistorical debates about whether cross-gender identified individuals in the nineteenth century were 'truly' lesbian, gay or transsexual. Alternatively we can conceptualize cross-dressers as adopting an available, historically-specific social role. The evidence for individual self-fashioning is often particularly hard to retrieve, and is of course framed within contemporary discourses of what appeared possible at the time.[12] It is also important to remember that the degree of autonomy and agency available to women has generally been considerably smaller than that of their male counterparts. Gender-crossing women had fewer choices and probably less access to sexual knowledge than men. It is important to recall that male-to-female and female-to-male gender-crossing are not two sides of the same coin in modern Western societies where gender difference is over-determined by unequal power relations.

As this section suggests, it is often difficult to disentangle cross-dressing or cross-gender behaviour such as passing from its association with sexuality and identity. Although they are intimately linked, and in the past were frequently discussed together, we need to bear in mind the specific historical meanings given not only to gender, but also to the association of cross-dressing, gender dissidence, sexuality and gender identity. The best way to disentangle some of the above themes and questions is to approach them as a series of chronological phases, which is the method adopted below.

female husbands, warrior women and disguise in the long eighteenth century

The long eighteenth century in Britain – which stretched from the late seventeenth to well into the mid-nineteenth century as far as debates about cross-dressing are concerned – was a significant period for the establishment of modern ideas about gender and its relationship to sexuality. For much of the century there was a wide cultural appreciation of the pleasures of gender masquerade, which figured strongly in elite culture. Terry Castle, for instance, argues that masquerade was celebrated as the very essence of modernity.[13] Following this earlier period of greater fluidity, historians suggest that a 'gender panic' set in at the end of the century, leading to the cementing of gender as a dualism of opposing categories, at the same time that a masculine model of heterosexual penetration came to predominate, as a norm, over more expansive forms of sexual behaviour.[14] A homosexual role – the effeminate 'molly' – started to be identified and homosexual behaviour more closely policed. It was also increasingly associated with gender-crossing. Effeminate behaviour began to be observed among organized networks of men in northwestern European cities from the 1690s onwards. These social networks were centred on taverns, in which cross-dressing, the adoption of women's names and playing out aspects of the female role, including parody births and marriages, took place. Whether a parallel pattern of gender-crossing developed for 'sapphists' at the end of the century, suggesting the origins of a lesbian identity, is, however, open to question.[15]

Female cross-dressing took place in a distinctly different cultural and social context to the male molly subculture. For instance, it was less likely to draw public censure and could even elicit admiration. The warrior woman who disguises herself to serve as a soldier or sailor was a flourishing archetype in Anglo-American ballads of the eighteenth and early nineteenth centuries. In these standardized narratives she defies the authority of her parents, puts on men's clothes to follow her (male) lover, proves herself ambitious and brave in war, and is rewarded with public recognition of her heroism and a happy marriage.[16] While these songs are framed by the rules of patriarchal heterosexuality, Dianne Dugaw argues that they also subvert the gender order. The female soldier is admired for both her manly heroism and her womanly steadfastness in love. Gender systems are destabilized not only by revealing masculinity and femininity as performative rather than natural, but also as capable of being enacted by a single person.[17] Gender cannot be transparent and uncomplicated – biological identity and social gender (playing the part) are represented in these stories and songs as separately operating systems. Many ballads enthusiastically feature the homoerotic implications of gender disguise as both men and women fall in love with the female warrior, showing that gender-based attraction is a fragile construction. This mid-eighteenth-century fascination with masquerade had an exploratory and a playful quality. Ambivalence around gender and sexuality was not feared, nor were these forms simply a momentary carnivalesque challenge to normal hierarchies.[18] Any individual woman could potentially transcend gender boundaries and be applauded for the virtues of both.

Indeed the songs sometimes inspired women to emulate these heroines; and in turn they were frequently commemorated by the balladeers. But did 'real life' cross-dressing women provoke a similarly positive response? Historians have debated the motives of passing women, and have asked whether it could be seen as a lesbian sexual choice, or whether contemporaries recognized such a role. In her feminist analysis of women's military cross-dressing, Julie Wheelwright downplayed the evidence that female soldiers and sailors flirted with women, suggesting that passing women were obliged to behave like men in every way they could, including in their sexual behaviour.[19] Emma Donoghue, however, has developed a more strongly lesbian reading of these potentially erotic encounters between women, while a comprehensive study of female cross-dressing in the Netherlands and Germany between 1550 and 1839 argued that female husbands did have an erotic interest in other women, and dressed as men because they could only imagine their love and desire in terms of the existing heterosexual paradigm.[20]

Recent work has re-examined the meanings ascribed to different forms of cross-dressing, making a distinction between women who imitated the 'sexed body' of a man and adopted masculine work, and those who pursued a masculine sexual role as a male 'sexual body' and lived as female husbands.[21] Both cross-dressing women workers in civilian life and women warriors were tolerated as industrious individuals playing an appropriate part in the social order. Working women were accustomed to rough and heavy work in the eighteenth and early nineteenth centuries, but had an uncertain position in the gendered labour market, excluded from most skilled work and earning half of the typical male wage. It was easily understood that passing as a soldier, sailor or male worker gave women autonomy, liberty and economic independence and was a better option than prostitution or the workhouse. This was a recognized tradition at the time and since.[22]

The imitation of the *sexual*, not simply sexed male body by female husbands was another matter however. In contrast to the titillating acceptance of same-sex flirtation in ballads, real life passing women were likely to be mocked and criminalized if they took on masculine sexual rights. After 1746 and the case of Charles/Mary Hamilton, who had used 'vile and deceitful Practices, not fit to be mention'd' in convincing his bride of his masculinity, greater attention was paid to the mechanics of sexuality in such liaisons. Magistrates sometimes used the language of sodomy when considering these cases, and press reports might allude to sexual deviance. Despite the absence of a legal structure for prosecuting female homosexual behaviour, such female husbands were viewed as disrupting proper gender hierarchies, as criminal and disorderly, and were charged with related crimes such as fraud where possible. In some cases they were quite severely punished, with imprisonment or the pillory, where they were open to the hostility of the community.[23]

Lesbian passion was generally explained by male authors as the result of a particular anatomy until the eighteenth century. The early-modern idea of the 'tribade' assumed that having a large clitoris caused a woman's same-sex desire, as well as giving her the ability to assume a male, penetrative role in sex. The tribade's body therefore approximated the male, and determined the nature of her desire.[24] A variety of other explanations later amplified this interpretation and by the beginning of the nineteenth century the passing woman was more likely to be explained in instrumental or psychological rather than anatomical terms. Female husbands were held to have criminally pursued financial gain and sexual desire, without the justifications of necessity and the admiration of daring which might be attached to passing women workers. Instead, the female husband was increasingly a figure of sexual deviance.[25]

It has been argued that after the early nineteenth century, the incidence of female cross-dressing, as well as popular representations of the practice, declined as new ideals of female domesticity took hold. While this may have been the case for women passing as soldiers and sailors, as military systems became more rigorous in mid-century, civilian female husbands continued to be reported throughout the nineteenth and twentieth centuries. There is insufficient historical research to clearly trace changing responses to women's cross-dressing, however. Warrior women ballads remained popular into the early decades of the nineteenth century but thereafter went into decline. The songs show increasing unease and anxiety about the heroine's disguise as a man, and she is depicted as more delicate and womanly, or, by mid-century, she often becomes a figure of parody.[26]

Stories of women who dressed as men for work continued to circulate in popular culture during the 1830s and 1840s and into the mid-century.[27] But the development of bourgeois gender roles made passing women more dangerously transgressive. Yet any hints of lesbian sexual wrongdoing rapidly disappear. The story of James Allen, well-documented in ballads, newspapers and medical texts, provides an example where sexual behaviour is the focus of obsessive interest, but female same-sex agency seen as impossible. Accepted as an industrious male breadwinner by his workmates and neighbours for twenty-one years, Allen was discovered to be a biological female after his death in 1829 in an industrial accident while working as a carpenter. Subsequent ballads explored the intimate scenarios of his long married life at length.

> From his bride he turn'd and twisted,
> Then she to herself did say,
> My Husband is a Hermaphrodite,
> A wager I would lay [...]
>
> If women all could do the same,
> And keep their virgin knot,
> Why the King and all his subjects,
> Would quickly go to pot.
>
> So now my song is ended,
> I hope it's pleased you all,
> This poor woman had a husband,
> That had nothing at all [...][28]

Whatever passed between the female husband and his wife was regarded as an impossible sexual relationship. The humorous tone of the ballad serves as a form of social control of their behaviour and as a warning to others who might be disguised as a husband, or deceived as wife. James Allen is derided for his inability to play male sexuality – he lacks the capacity to make his wife pregnant, while the wife is commiserated with as an ignorant fool. Yet behind the jokes in the ballad, the female husband might potentially challenge the institutions of marriage and heterosexuality, the gender order, and national stability.

Gender ideologies of feminine maternalism, passivity and relative physical weakness also became incorporated into ideas of working-class respectability, as a case from Victorian London illustrates. Sarah Geals, aka William Smith, lived as a man in the 1850s and 1860s, and had been a female husband for more than ten years to her ostensible wife Caroline. When Caroline married Sarah/William's master, the spurned female husband tried to shoot him and was sentenced to five years' penal servitude. Camilla Townsend shows that the response to the case varied according to class. While establishment newspapers were patronizing and critical, the harshest condemnation came from the papers read by the aspirant lower middle-class. However there was some sympathy from the local working-class community in London's East End regarding her jealous and conflicted relationship with Caroline's husband, coupled with admiration for her achievement of respectability as a skilled worker and breadwinner.

Any notion of the female husband's lesbian desire seems to have disappeared from view or become unspeakable by the mid-nineteenth century in popular culture, and also largely in medical writing, at least in Britain. Women's sexuality was widely held to be completely passive, and unthinkable without the arousing agency of a man. The female husband's performance of the male body could not therefore extend to the phallus, and thus sexual pleasure was deemed to be unachievable for either partner. It may be the case that the female husband was reframed as a hermaphrodite and her sexual potential marginalized in this way, but this can only be speculative in the absence of more comprehensive research. It is notable that she was also displaced into a form of entertainment, a parodic figure of fun. Although the evidence for lesbian meanings may be limited, this sexual knowledge may have been preserved in a muted form. Martha Vicinus maintains that female masculinity *was* associated with same-sex desire throughout the nineteenth century, arguing that more was known about lesbianism than is recorded in the extant sources.[29]

The recognition and regulation of men's cross-dressing was of a different order. Susceptible to arrest and imprisonment under the laws against sodomy and vagrancy, effeminate and cross-dressing men were always found among the growing numbers of men tried for sodomy during the nineteenth century.[30] Whether individual men loitering in the London streets and parks, or as groups in molly houses and pub back rooms, they were perceived by police and magistrates as linked to sodomitical activities. However, an element of indeterminacy did creep back into the interpretation of these cases in the nineteenth century. Male cross-dressing or effeminacy was not necessarily synonymous with homosexual desire in any straightforward way. Instead, as H.G. Cocks points out, we should try and reconstruct the wider Victorian understandings of disguise and impersonation. At that time, the association of homosexual desire and secrecy was epitomized by the apparently 'disguised' cross-dressing man. He was often assumed to have put on women's clothes not because of an inherent sexual desire, but as a form of passing; not to advertise, but to conceal, as one magistrate put it, 'crime of the foulest character'. In these cases, we see the older language of passing for specific reasons merging with newer accounts of urban depravity and sexual deviance. The cross-dressing sodomite was 'in disguise', but at the same time he was associated with 'unnatural desire'. However, it was generally assumed that his disguise was adopted in order to allow him to entrap unwary men or to pass unnoticed as a female prostitute. At that time, the idea of the 'sodomite' as an equivocal figure, an impersonator whose nature is always concealed, and whose natural condition was secrecy and 'disguise' of all kinds, was given clarity in the popular mind partly through the publicity given to cross-dressing men.

As these cases show, gender-crossing changed dramatically during the eighteenth century as it became detached from anatomical explanations of perverse desire. By the nineteenth century it began to be stigmatized in new ways that reflected more coercive gender norms. The interpretation of gender-crossing behaviour also varied according to gender. By the nineteenth century a new pattern was emerging. For men, cross-dressing was clearly a practice with sexual objectives shared with others, and practised through networks of men on the city streets and organized private gatherings such as drag balls. For women, cross-dressing was more likely to be an act of solitary self-fashioning, possibly a secret shared with a female partner, but not within a subculture. Nevertheless, female husbandry and passing was an established, iterated tradition, continued knowledge of which was passed on through popular culture and later the mass circulation press.

on the streets and on the stage: impersonation, theatricality and modernity, c.1880–1920

Although it might be assumed that gender impersonation began to be indelibly marked by sexual deviance in the late nineteenth century, it also retained some of its earlier indeterminacy. On the one hand, it became associated with homosexuality among wider sections of the public. On the other, it was more strongly aligned with theatricality. The popular theatre, especially the British music hall, was a place of harmless fun and fantasy, though it was also a cultural location entangled with disreputable sexuality as a site of heterosexual prostitution and homosexual soliciting. A tradition of cross-dressing roles was already established in mainstream theatre, but a huge expansion of female and especially male impersonators accompanied the development of music hall as popular entertainment from the mid-nineteenth century onwards. These varied meanings of cross-dressing overlapped in late nineteenth-century discourses.

The trial in 1871 of two cross-dressing men, Frederick Park and Ernest Boulton (aka 'Fanny' and 'Stella'), for 'conspiracy to commit sodomy' opens up the range of readings of cross-dressing in this period. Despite initial evidence that Boulton and Park were part of a widespread network of cross-dressing men frequently appearing on central London streets and that, like some of their associates, they were engaged both in public attempts to flirt with and pick up men in shopping arcades and theatres, and in private same-sex relationships with domestic and emotional weight, the two men were acquitted.[31] The court seemed to want to avoid publicizing the flagrant and widespread transgression of gender norms by an assertive subculture of middle-class as well as working-class men. Charles Upchurch argues that this silencing served to distance middle-class men and patriarchal ideology from what was otherwise represented as the criminal practices of sodomites and urban low-life. British society as a whole, and in particular the widespread theatrical practice of cross-dressing, could thereby remain ostensibly untainted by its street-level counterpart.

Upchurch suggests that the police had intended to demarcate the limits on cross-dressing in the London West End and warn other 'mary-annes' to contain their behaviour. Boulton and Park's risible defence, that they were simply extending their hobby of drawing-room theatricals to the city streets for a mere 'lark', could, in these circumstances, remain culturally convincing. Yet the trial had also clarified the association between cross-dressing, effeminacy and the practices of sodomitical sexualities in mid-Victorian cities. This particular meaning was location-specific: whereas the Victorian mania for theatrical cross-dressing and impersonation was perfectly respectable in the private home or on the stage (two of Boulton and Park's usual venues), on city streets it was readily associated with criminality and sexual immorality. Although their acquittal meant that Boulton and Park's impersonations were ostensibly rendered innocent, their trial was one step towards the re-association of cross-dressing and effeminacy with homosexual desire.

However, if Boulton and Park's impersonations were not automatic evidence of an inner homosexuality in 1871, does this mean that cross-dressing on stage was insulated from such connotations? Did the carnivalesque imitation of masculinity or femininity disrupt the gender order and the presumption of heterosexuality, as Marjorie Garber suggests? Or was the popular theatre a safe and controlled space, allowing pleasure in a brief challenge to social hierarchies before reconsolidating gender difference? Theatre historian J.S. Bratton draws attention to the wide range of gender politics being played out on the British music hall stage at the end of the nineteenth century. She argues that the appeal of the male impersonator on the popular stage and the meanings attached to her were far more varied than either same-sex desire or a populist feminism. By the heyday of male impersonation in the halls in the 1890s, there was a range of acts, admired for their skill. Some offered a fantasy of female participation in masculine pleasures such as betting, drinking and, tacitly, sex, while others mocked particular male types – the swell, the over-dressed gentleman, the narcissistic clerk, the pretensions of the soldier – or indeed, burlesqued the costumes of the New Woman. There is little doubt that the female audience's pleasure in the parodying of masculinity was fuelled by class resentment as well as gender solidarity. Bratton suggests that despite their framing within the safely commercial world of variety, the 'distorted, mocking, exaggerated images of masculinity' projected by these women from the stage should be read as carnivalesque, as frequently provocative and at times threatening, often causing disquiet among reviewers.[32] Sexual transgression was certainly an element of this, but much innuendo was derived from heterosexual suggestiveness or the sexual appeal of the female body on display. It is by no means certain which sections of the audience would read male impersonation as a sign of lesbian desire.

There is some evidence that individual male impersonators, between the 1890s and the 1910s, presented themselves in a butch, manly way and may well have had some sort of lesbian appeal and popular following.[33] Clearly there was a wide fan base for these performers, as is demonstrated by the huge numbers of picture postcards of them circulating throughout the Edwardian period and into the First World War. Male impersonators were wooed and propositioned by admiring women. The British actress Vesta Tilley wrote of her obsessive female fans: 'Girls of all ages would wait in crowds to see me enter or leave the theatre, and each post brought piles of letters, varying from an impassioned declaration of undying love to a request for... a piece of ribbon I had worn.'[34] There is also evidence of a working-class lesbian audience in the 1900s in some major American cities, as the unease of New York reviewers shows, but it is unclear whether a similarly identified network existed at popular level in Britain before the First World War.[35] For women in more elite and bohemian circles, Martha Vicinus argues that theatrical transvestism was one source of modern lesbian identity and style. For some like Radclyffe Hall, this involved a very serious, austere style of masculine dress, while for others like Natalie Barney in her Parisian salon, wearing men's clothes took on a more playful and ironic tone.[36]

Historians have explored the multiple readings of male impersonation available to the music hall audience – according to their age, gender, and sophistication – of which lesbian desire was just one thread. In analysing the interplay of control and licence here and in other forms of popular culture, the idea of 'knowingness' is useful. Peter Bailey uses this term to suggest that although music hall songs may have seemed innocuous on paper, it was in their delivery that any challenges to social and gender hierarchies inhered. He describes how the British music hall performer, such as the comic singer and gender impersonator enacted, through a familiar repertoire of nods, winks, gestures and catchphrases, a kind of collusion with the audience to create a shared sense of defying respectability and overturning hierarchies of authority. Sexual suggestiveness and double entendre was created and enjoyed by the audience at various levels of sophistication.[37]

The theatre, then, continued to be a space of indeterminacy where cross-dressing was concerned, even though impersonation in other contexts was becoming visible as a phenomenon associated with perverse desire, especially for men. By the end of the nineteenth century, the connections between homosexuality and gender-crossing behaviour began to be theorized in new ways which drew a direct link between gender-crossing, sexuality and anatomy.

courtrooms, newspapers and sexual science

The dominant nineteenth-century view of cross-dressing as masquerade or impersonation focused on the act itself, which was interpreted as a deliberate attempt to disguise. In contrast, European sexual science developed a rather different conceptual approach between the 1880s and the 1920s, examining the innate qualities or biological markers of gender-crossing individuals to determine the *types* of person who would behave in this way. These interpretations reflected the overall methodology of the sexologists, which, as Chris Waters explains in this volume, tried to align gender, psychology and sexuality. The overall result was to challenge a long tradition of passing and to interpret gender-crossing as a symptom of an internal psychological state which belonged only to certain types of people who suffered from the inner 'inversion' of their outward gender.

The physical body was also scrutinized by sexologists for the signs and explanations of gender. A parallel development in sexual medicine which informed gender-crossing was a new approach to the treatment of hermaphrodites. In his discussion of the case of Herculine Barbin, who, in 1860 and much against her will was defined by doctors as a man, Michel Foucault has argued that there was an intense moral and medical anxiety about hermaphrodites in late nineteenth-century France.[38] While there was less concern and a variety of treatment regimes in other countries, the power to decipher and determine the 'true sex' of intersexed individuals now resided in the doctor's expertise.[39] Nineteenth-century science believed that the biological nature of sex produced appropriate heterosexual desire for the opposite sex. Sexologists developing the category of inversion therefore reasoned that sexual inverts might have some anatomical defect, possibly physical hermaphroditic traits.

Existing practices of gender-crossing had informed sexual scientists' categorization of homosexual desire as an 'inverted' form of normal sexuality. Gender inversion – evidenced by the effeminate man or masculine woman – was now linked to homosexual behaviour in a new way. Their deviant sexuality was an effect of their congenital condition – their behaviour was inborn, a consequence of their heredity. 'Inversion' was a complex and confused, yet powerful concept, merging as it did the idea of cross-gender identification or behaviour with that of (same-sex) sexual object choice. In short, the male 'invert' had the body of a man, but the sexual desires of a woman, and vice versa. As Alan Sinfield puts it, the sexologists, far from clarifying the situation, 'persistently tangle together transgender and homosexual desire'.[40] Using the lens of inversion, they could see all gender-crossing behaviour as a symptom of an inverted psychology or physiology.

Some researchers, including Havelock Ellis in Britain and Magnus Hirschfeld in Germany, believed that inverts were normally physically developed, on the whole. But they were still drawn back to the possibility that there were physical signs of inversion. Havelock Ellis argued that inverted men were not necessarily effeminate and were generally masculine, indistinguishable from other men except in their same-sex desires. But he hypothesized that female inverts were likely to exhibit cross-gender attributes and went to some length to consider the shape of the larynx, distribution of body hair and social gender role: '[T]here are all sorts of instinctive gestures and habits which may suggest to female acquaintances the remark that such a person "ought to have been a man".'[41]

However, inversion was not necessarily a conservative notion that fixed gender, sexuality and anatomy in new ways. Some, like the British socialist Edward Carpenter, seized on the idea and adapted it to their own purposes. Carpenter argued that homosexual men and women were a third or 'intermediate' sex, who existed at the mid-point of a continuum between the polar opposites of physical and psychological masculinity and femininity. As such, they were endowed with all the virtues of both sexes and could therefore play a valuable social role in an era of changing gender relations.[42]

The invert – the mannish lesbian and the effeminate man, so defined by their biology and psychology – was an influential idea. But how influential was it, and how quickly was it taken up by doctors and psychiatrists, judges and magistrates, social commentators and reformers, and in popular culture? Did it influence interpretations of and responses to cross-dressing over the early decades of the twentieth century? One way of answering this question is to look at how popular sources, such as newspapers, dealt with cases of gender-crossing. Lisa Duggan, for example, dates the emergence of the mannish lesbian in American mass culture to the 1890s (quite early compared to the UK), demonstrating the interdependent relationship between sexology, sensational newspaper stories of lesbian murder and American modernity.

In her book *Sapphic Slashers: Sex, Violence and American Modernity* (2000), Duggan describes the 1892 'love murder' of Freda Ward by Alice Mitchell in Memphis. This case, she suggests, was the first to involve medical experts and was reported in the press as an example of a morbid and perverse sexuality, expressed by Mitchell's masculine identification, and her plans to cross-dress and then elope with her lover Freda. Duggan interprets this as the beginning of a process whereby the twin models of romantic friend and female husband merge and develop into a modern lesbian identity.[43] Other reports of 'abnormal affection' among middle-class girls were similarly structured around the themes of male identity, impersonation and same-sex passion. Most of these newspaper stories had tragic endings, painting a picture of sexual passion between women as hopeless, insane and violent. The term 'lesbian' was not yet used, but the mannish invert was represented as a threat to the white bourgeois family from which she had sprung. Drawing on early medical discussions of homosexuality, these newspaper reports in turn fuelled the development of sexology into the 1920s.[44]

If the mannish female invert was recognizable in north American turn of the century culture, she was less apparent in Britain. There were signs, though, in the 1920s and 1930s that a lesbian identity was cohering around masculine styles and fashions. Historians have often assumed, with hindsight, that the typical Eton crop and masculine-style clothing of interwar women's fashions was synonymous with lesbianism after the advent of sexology. In contrast, Laura Doan has argued that this was not read as such by contemporaries. Very severe masculine-cut clothes and short hair were feminine high fashion in the 1920s, and worn by respectable married women. It was only after the 1928 trial for obscenity of the lesbian novel *The Well of Loneliness* that images of its author Radclyffe Hall wearing this modern masculine style circulated widely in the press and began to symbolize lesbianism or female inversion.[45]

For men on the other hand, Matt Houlbrook argues that the process by which gender (effeminacy) increasingly stood in for sexuality (male same-sex desire) was nearly complete by the 1930s. But this was less an effect of sexology than of changes in the media, in particular, the use of more explicit language in newspaper court reports, and the continuing significance of organized urban gay communities. A series of trials of groups of men arrested at drag balls or queer clubs in UK cities during the 1930s revealed a well-developed subculture which articulated a strong sense of identity and resistance to the authority of police and courts.

Analysing the 1933 trial of thirty-three men who called themselves 'Lady Austin's Camp Boys', arrested at a drag ball they had organized in West London, Houlbrook shows that sexuality was understood in working-class, metropolitan circles as a product of gender identity. It was the effeminate queenies who were perceived as homosexual, rather than their partners (kings) who presented themselves as normal men. Effeminate identity was articulated by these men as part of an innate sense of self. Similarly in interwar New York, the idea of identity based on sexuality did not yet hold, and men were not divided into homosexual or heterosexual categories. The effeminate man was visible and named as a fairy, but the masculine man who had sex with him or other men was not considered an invert or homosexual, so long as he remained within conventional gender boundaries.[46]

While the Lady Austin case might show that gender-crossing and sexual deviance were increasingly associated in Britain, another trial, that of Austin Hull in 1931, illustrates the increasing medicalization of gender deviance. In addition it shows the beginnings of differentiation in forensic medicine between the categories of homosexuality and transvestism. Hull was charged with procuring a man for an act of gross indecency, after passing as a woman and pursuing a six month common-law marriage with an unemployed man named George Burrows. The latter, for his part, swore in court that he believed Hull was a woman throughout their relationship. Doctors were called as expert witnesses in the case and argued that there was little or no physical evidence that homosexual acts had taken place; indeed they saw Hull as asexual, and one, using the language of sexology, argued that Hull was a true congenital invert not an immoral pervert. Nevertheless Hull was given a severe sentence of eighteen months' hard labour. On the face of it, this might indicate the lack of leverage for medical discourses in the courtroom. But sex reformers generated a campaign for Hull's release, arguing he needed clinical treatment rather than punishment, and influenced the authorities into sending Hull for psychotherapy at the Tavistock Clinic. Angus McLaren has argued that this outcome turned Hull from a prisoner into a patient and was a victory for psychiatry rather than for Hull himself. McLaren also points out that while sexologists and psychologists called for greater understanding of sexual deviance, they were themselves adopting a pathological approach which laid the responsibility for the condition with the individual, and that this process served the interests of the psychiatric professions rather than inverts themselves.[47]

However, another prominent interwar case shows that psychiatry did not have it all its own way in understanding gender-crossing behaviour. The case of Valerie Arkell-Smith, who spent much of the 1920s successfully masquerading as the British war hero, boxer, sometime fascist and husband 'Colonel Barker', demonstrates that medical or sexological readings of such behaviour were not always influential. Where women's cross-dressing was concerned, the suggestion of homosexual desire remained muted. Barker is in the grand tradition of the female husband and the passing woman, but by the twentieth century there were a number of existing ideas which could be used to understand her behaviour. Was she a transvestite, an invert, a lesbian, or some combination of all three?

James Vernon has sought to challenge the kind of historical interpretations which claim Barker for any of these identities and which seek to fix him/her within them. He examines the discourses emanating from the courtroom and press, and shows that, although positioned by a variety of new sexological interpretations, Barker was hard to fix into any of them. For instance, Vernon suggests that Barker's passing as a man might be understood by some as sexual inversion, even though Barker himself refused such a label. While there was no legal context to explain cross-dressing by women as homosexual behaviour, contemporary books about gender masquerade increasingly drew on medical and psychological explanations. But the press, and the public, still used masquerade to mean a disguise which hid a deeper reality – of biological sex – without reference to inversion, intersexuality or other medical knowledge. The idea of masquerade thus contained within it a range of different kinds of explanation. While the press did not explicitly discuss lesbianism they extensively interviewed Barker and his wife and girlfriends. Popular understandings of who he 'really' was included a variety of accounts. Some years later in 1937, when Barker worked as a sideshow exhibit in a seaside resort, the gawping public were flummoxed still further, suggesting he was one of those 'women who like women', a 'sex change' or a hermaphrodite. 'I don't know, it's a mystery', one observer said, 'I can't tell what he is, I call him Gene.'[48]

These two court cases seem to represent turning points in recognition and treatment of transvestism and inversion in a medical framework. But it is worth making a comparison between women and men. Medical discourses were more frequently deployed and increasingly multi-faceted in the case of men passing as women. For men, a distinction was beginning to be made between homosexuality and transvestism in medico-legal approaches. Hull won public sympathy because his case was covered by the newspapers as a medical condition rather than as an example of homosexual depravity.[49] Women faced far less judicial attention, and little in the way of sexological or psychiatrically-informed comment until after the Second World War.[50] Debating the question of masquerading as the opposite sex in 1937–38, professional legal opinion noted that men dressing as women were liable to be prosecuted for soliciting for immoral purposes. Since the press still tended to avoid reporting the actual charge in homosexual offences, people widely assumed that cross-dressing itself was illegal. But women's cross-dressing was not seen as in any way parallel. Indeed the sexual potential of female masquerading was not even mentioned in this debate; female cross-dressing was an 'innocent foible'.[51]

The 1929 trial of Col. Barker has been a rich site of historical debate. However, the unusually well-developed sexological knowledge of the judge in this case and the widespread newspaper interest were anomalous, and obscure the continuing popularity of stories about gender-crossing women in the twentieth-century press and the ways in which they were treated. Dozens of other stories of cross-dressing women appeared in the popular press between the wars, many of them involving female husbands. But they were generally presented as light entertainment, following common narrative conventions including the disclosure of 'true sex', some kind of economic or social explanation, jokes at the expense of the employer, wife or authority figures and wonderment at the skill and success of the masquerade. While some readers might have 'knowingly' interpreted further sexual innuendo into these accounts, as audiences at the variety theatre may or may not have done for the male impersonator figure, it was not until the late 1940s that any reference to lesbian sexual motives ('unnatural passion') began to creep into these stories.[52]

How did the cross-gendered individuals caught up in this mesh of legal, medical and media discussion see themselves? Vernon uses Judith Butler's theory of performativity to stress Col. Barker's limited agency and choice in his self-representation. He was decidedly not the playful, freely self-fashioning gender outlaw who might be imagined by queer theorists.[53] He sold his life story to the press several times for economic reasons; the press in turn presented it using particular narrative conventions. By retaining the more fluid interwar notion of masquerade, however, Barker was able, within the limitations of the discourses available to him, to reject the essentialist identities of first, the mannish invert, and later after the Second World War, the newer identity of the transsexual. Ruth Ford finds similar complexity in the Australian case of Harcourt Payne who passed as a man to marry her woman friend in 1911. Same-sex love was clearly part of her motivation and Payne may have been following the tradition of female marriage as the only economically and socially possible way for two women to set up home together. But she clearly also had a strong cross-gender identification, being proud of her mannish appearance and ability to work as a breadwinner. Ford argues that as well as it being ahistorical to try to fit individuals such as Payne into the identity categories of lesbian or transgender, it is important to recognize that there is likely to be a spectrum of motivations for the gender-crossing individual which change over their lifetime.[54] Ford also suggests that Payne's adoption of masculinity reinforced gender conventions in interwar Australia rather than subverting them, as did the action of the authorities in punitively confining her in a women's mental hospital after her sex was revealed in 1939.

Through attending to the traces left by such individuals, historians have contested the significance of sexological discourses in shaping identity and begun to map out alternative subjectivities within twentieth-century sexual politics. One person who might well be understood as transgendered today, but who in his/her own time understood his/her sense of self in spiritual and political terms, was the British feminist Thomas Baty, who preferred to be known as Irene Clyde. With a small group of radical women, Baty edited and promoted the privately published journal *Urania* (1916–40) which provided a substantially different perspective on cross-dressing, sexuality and gender. The journal aimed to abolish both sex and gender, and welcomed all anthropological, scientific and political findings which not only showed the social construction of gender but also unsettled the biological basis of sex difference: 'sex is an accident' was its maxim. It published reports of sex change in animals and humans, examples of cross-dressing from across different cultures and time periods, and idealized same-sex love between women. The feminist Theosophical beliefs of Baty and fellow editors, a kind of spiritual androgyny flavoured with Carpenterian notions of the intermediate sex, were the source of their campaign 'to discard sex', aiming for the dissolution of gender boundaries and the rejection of heterosexuality.[55]

Baty's sense of self – he wrote that he 'longed passionately to be a lady' – raises questions about the enthusiasm of some cultural theorists and transgender historians to generate a transgender identity across time.[56] Despite many similarities to a late twentieth-century transgender politics, Baty constructed a sense of identity which was historically specific and has important differences from those identities formed after change of sex was medically possible. The existence of *Urania* alongside the trials of Col. Barker and Austin Hull also demonstrates how very diverse sets of meanings can attach to gender-crossing at any moment, despite historians' desires to corral these expressions into identities and discourses which shift at identifiable points in the past.

transsexual identity and history

Although Thomas Baty aspired to collapse sex/gender categories as a sham, they were at the very same time being reified into the new socio-medical identity of transsexuality. The relationship between professional interests, popular knowledge and individual self-fashioning is particularly contested in accounts of the development of transsexual (TS) identity in the mid to late twentieth century. Strongly freighted with present day gender and queer politics, recent work also lays bare contrasting extremes in the debate about the ontology of identity. Was TS – the desire to alter biological sex to fit gender identity – an innate and pre-existing subjectivity, on the basis of which individuals demanded social and medical recognition? Or was TS a category developed through the coalescing of various interest groups, including the development of medical technology, the mediation of medical knowledge by the press in advertising 'sex change', and the agency of cross-gender-identified people increasingly organized as individuals and groups?

As we have seen, the sexological idea of inversion was replete with confusions and possibilities around both sexual desire and gender identification. The medical category of transvestism was described by Ellis and Hirschfeld by the 1910s. The idea of TS came rather later but was formed out of debates which examined the question of whether gender was innate and which themselves grew out of developing studies of inversion and intersex.

From the late nineteenth century, doctors sought to determine the 'true sex' of hermaphrodites from the evidence of their bodies, especially the dominant reproductive organs – 'the truth of the gonads'.[57] The idea that sex and gender identity lay in the body and 'glands' became a widespread cultural concept in the first part of the twentieth century. Of course, the science of endocrinology was shaped by existing cultural assumptions about the sharp biological differentiation between 'male' and 'female' and the 'natural' social roles which this determined.[58] While modern scientific ideas about glands and hormones enabled a further shift towards the idea of an essential or innate gender and sexual identity, it was the rising success rate and reputation of plastic surgery as a medical craft which was essential to the idea that medical 'sex change' was possible. Bernice Hausman argues that the availability of technology was crucial. She suggests that 'the emergence of TS in the mid-twentieth century depended on developments in endocrinology and plastic surgery as technological and discursive practices'.[59]

Medical treatment of intersexuality or hermaphrodism increasingly bordered the territory of what would become TS identity during the 1930s. With their new technologies, doctors (at different rates in different countries) increasingly moved towards deciding the 'best' biological sex for their intersexed patients, based on the social gender into which they had been most successfully socialized or had claimed for themselves.[60] In the British popular press in the 1930s, a number of 'sex change' operations were reported, mainly female to male, including the best-known case of Mary-Mark Weston, a former athlete, in 1936. These were reported as heroic successes of modern medicine in correcting 'nature's mistakes'; probably most were treatments of anatomically intersexed people, but the manner of press reporting emphasized the innate cross-gender identification of these individuals. In these progress narratives, the binary contrast of gender definition and its connection to normative heterosexuality was emphasized by approving reports of potential romantic attachments between these newly made men and their girlfriends.[61]

Hausman argues that TS identity depends on a relationship between the medical establishment and those who identify as TS, since their cross-gender identification can only be addressed by scientific technologies. Yet while TS identity depended on the development of endocrinology and plastic surgery, it was not the invention of doctors as an interest group seeking to legitimate and extend their medical control of bodies.[62] The demand for sex change in fact came from TS subjects themselves at an early date. In Germany in 1930, Einar Wegener/Lili Elbe may have been the first person to make a transition via surgery from a physiological male to a female sexed body. While Wegener/Elbe's case was reported in some contemporary medical literature in such a way as to suggest intersexuality, it seems rather that her's was the first recorded instance of a TS demand for surgical treatment on the basis of psychic gender identity, or what is now medically diagnosed as 'gender dysphoria'. A handful of other European examples preceded the widely publicized sex-change operation of Christine Jorgensen, a former soldier, in the US in 1952.[63]

TS identity tries to effect the 'correct' alignment of body, social gender and sexual desire and at times has been criticized for a consequent tendency to embrace conventional notions of gender. For instance, this apparent adherence to social convention marked transsexuals out in the 1960s as 'the Uncle Toms of the sexual revolution'.[64] As the idea of psychic gender became more widely subscribed to by both psychiatrists and the wider public, TS identity was often seen as a more authentic choice, as a legitimate medical condition, than the heavily stigmatized identity of homosexuality which was the alternative cultural reading. Some have argued that the number of transsexuals grew in the postwar period as this social knowledge was generated and legitimated.[65] Most transsexuals in the 1950s to the 1970s insisted on their distinctiveness from homosexuality: theirs was a pathology of gender identity which could be medically corrected, not an immoral sexual deviance.[66]

As with the circulation of the inverted homosexual figure (the mannish lesbian or effeminate pansy) earlier in the century, the idea that sex change was possible was fostered by the mass circulation press and its sensational headlines following rapidly upon one another during the 1950s. The Jorgensen case, for instance, rapidly became a popular headline: 'Ex-GI Becomes Blonde Beauty.'[67] In the UK it meant that gender dysphoria could be claimed by female husbands such as Vincent Jones as an explanation for their actions as early as 1954 and represented sympathetically by the popular press, if not by magistrates.[68] While sex change surgery was hardly available to all who demanded it on the newly established National Health Service, it was perceived as being possible to secure somewhere in Europe or north Africa if one had sufficient money. In the US the legal position of doctors who performed sex change surgery was unclear until later in the 1950s, leading to a small but influential lobbying community of transsexuals mutually demanding this treatment in concert with individual specialists, most notably Harry Benjamin. Joanne Meyerowitz traces the growing agency of the emerging TS community in the US, inspired by reports of overseas sex change in both the tabloid and sex reform press, in creating TS identity in medical and popular discourse in the 1950s and 60s.[69]

Some cultural theorists have been concerned to assert the integrity and longevity of a TS tradition. In rejecting the argument that medical technologies were key to late twentieth-century TS subjectivity, Jay Prosser posits a more dominant role for TS agency and indeed comes close to asserting a transhistorical identity for the trans-person.[70] This argument depends upon reading the confused category of the early twentieth-century invert as evidence of a past TS subject. However, this has to be qualified by recalling the interdependent relationship between sexologists' construction of gender/sexual inversion and patterns of same-sex desire and gender-crossing. In their work they were unable, in spite of their intention, to untangle the connections between inversion, sexuality and hermaphrodism. Nevertheless, TS historians suggest that cross-gender identification, in the form of a profound desire to become the opposite sex, 'the sense of wrong embodiment' was a subjectivity which preceded sexology, and contributed to the theory of inversion.[71] Prosser further argues that the autobiographies and self-descriptions of nineteenth- and early twentieth-century individuals who he would include in TS history are remarkably similar to their late twentieth-century counterparts.[72] Nineteenth-century individuals' 'commitment to cross-gender living and/or identification... cannot be explained without recognising transgender as identity, one irreducible to homosexuality', he suggests.[73] The confusion between cross-gender identification and same-sex desire is, not surprisingly, repeated in post-sexological narratives of inversion, including Radclyffe Hall's novel *The Well of Loneliness* (1928). Should the fictional Stephen Gordon be read as a mannish lesbian figure, as transgendered (as Prosser argues), or as representing a less determined expression of female masculinity?[74]

Judith Halberstam brings a more nuanced interpretation to this particular debate. She discusses the varying degrees of cross-gender fantasy and masculine self-fashioning among interwar inverts such as Radclyffe Hall and her contemporaries, stressing the importance of communities built around sexual and gender identifications.[75] Like the historians, she points out that there are many moments in the past when gender deviance and sexual transgression are hard to disentangle. As many of the cases examined here suggests, drawing definite boundaries is frequently awkward, and often does not fit the self-presentation of the individual concerned or their life experience. It is also sometimes fraught with the difficulties associated with polemic.

conclusion

One characteristic of modernity since the eighteenth century is an attempt to classify and demarcate. Sexology, medical science, psychiatry, the criminal law and a variety of other institutions all attempt to render a chaotic world intelligible, orderly, and subject to systematic scrutiny. One consequence of this is that personal identity is increasingly asked to fit such categories. The history of cross-gender behaviour and transsexuality/transgender would seem to fit this pattern. As modernity has progressed, the 'gender play' of the eighteenth century seems to have given way to order, system and identity. It would appear that, in the nineteenth century this fluidity was overtaken by scientific categories that demarcated experience and sought to identify gender deviance according to its apparently pathological nature. Thus the ambiguous female husband gave way to the lesbian, the molly to the homosexual, while the passing woman became the transvestite, and the hermaphrodite or intersex suffered the reassignment of gender through often arbitrary medical decisions. Moreover, those unhappy in their own sexed bodies were, in the medical gaze, held to suffer from a medical syndrome known as gender dysphoria. It is often argued that such people have always existed, but in the past were unable to physically alter their bodies, and were only able to change their appearance. It is assumed that only now can the 'real' nature of such syndromes – past and present – be glimpsed

However, although the twentieth century saw the rise of these forms of knowledge, and many of the medico-scientific identities proposed were grasped eagerly by many men and women eager to change sex or explain their behaviour to themselves, it is still the case that cross-dressing, sexual identity, transsexuality and transvestism retain links with each other that are difficult to disentangle. The rise of transgender, as a way of refusing gender identity itself and reclaiming the intersexual space between, perhaps retains and reasserts the older fluidity of meaning ascribed to cross-gendered behaviour. Whether such notions are inherently radical, as some writers maintain, is another question. At any rate, it is clear that gender and sexual identity, either through surgery or hormones, can be dependent upon technology and medical expertise as never before. These technologies encourage the fantasy that personal identity, even to the extent of the physical body, can always be the outcome of individual choice, without dealing with the sedimented weight of history or culture or the limits of corporeality. That is where the allure of the female husband and the surviving attraction of her daring continues to lie.

notes

1. *Daily Herald*, 14 December 1954. My warm thanks to H.G. Cocks, Anna Clark, Lucy Bland and Lesley Hall for their very helpful comments on an earlier version of this essay. Any errors and omissions remain my own.
2. *News of the World*, 19 December 1954, p. 2.
3. The term transgender is often supposed to have been coined by Leslie Feinberg, in *Transgender Liberation: A Movement Whose Time has Come* (New York: WorldView Forum, 1992).
4. On this see, for example, Zachary Nataf, *Lesbians Talk Transgender* (London: Scarlet, 1996); Della Grace Volcano and Judith Halberstam, *The Drag King Book* (London: Serpent's Tail, 1999).
5. See, for instance, Lillian Faderman, *Passing the Love of Men: Romantic Friendship and Love Between Women from the Renaissance to the Present* (London: Women's Press, 1985); and Jeffrey Weeks, *Coming Out: Homosexual Politics in Britain, from the Nineteenth Century to the Present* (London: Quartet Books, 1977); Jonathan Ned Katz, *Gay American History*, revised edn. (New York: Meridian, 1992).
6. See, for example, Julie Wheelwright, *Amazons and Military Maids: Women Who Cross-Dressed in Pursuit of Life, Liberty and Happiness* (London: Pandora, 1989); Emma Donoghue, *Passions Between Women: British Lesbian Culture 1688–1801* (London: Scarlet, 1993).
7. See Chris Waters' chapter in this volume.
8. Judith Butler, *Gender Trouble: Feminism and the Subversion of Identity* (New York: Routledge, 1989); Marjorie Garber, *Vested Interests: Cross Dressing and Cultural Anxiety* (London: Penguin, 1992), p. 10.
9. Judith Halberstam, *Female Masculinity* (Durham, NC: Duke University Press, 1998); Holly Devor, *Gender Blending: Confronting the Limits of Duality* (Bloomington: Indiana University Press, 1989); Jay Prosser, *Second Skins: The Body Narratives of Transsexuality* (New York: Columbia University Press, 1998); Leslie Feinburg, *Transgender Warriors* (Boston: Beacon Press, 1996).
10. Lawrence Senelick, *The Changing Room: Varieties of Theatrical Cross Dressing* (London: Routledge, 2000).

11. H.G. Cocks, '"Sporty Girls" and "Artistic" Boys: Friendship, Illicit Sex and the British Companionship Advertisement, c 1910–1929', *Journal of the History of Sexuality*, 11, 3 (2002), 457–82.
12. James Vernon, '"For Some Queer Reason": The Trials and Tribulations of Colonel Barker's Masquerade in Interwar Britain', *Signs*, 26, 1 (2000), 37–62.
13. Terry Castle, *Masquerade and Civilization: The Carnivalesque in Eighteenth Century English Culture and Fiction* (London: Methuen, 1986), p. 4.
14. For this argument see Tim Hitchcock, *English Sexualities, 1700–1800* (Basingstoke: Macmillan, 1997). On gender fluidity see Castle, *Masquerade and Civilization*; on gender panic see Dror Wahrman, 'Percy's Prologue: From Gender Play to Gender Panic in Eighteenth Century England', *Past and Present*, 159 (1998), 113–60.
15. On this see Randolph Trumbach, 'London's Sapphists: From Three Sexes to Four Genders in the Making of Modern Culture', in Gilbert Herdt (ed.), *Third Sex, Third Gender: Beyond Sexual Dimorphism in Culture and History* (New York: Zone Books, 1994), pp. 111–36; Emma Donoghue, *Passions Between Women: British Lesbian Culture 1668–1801* (London: Scarlet Press, 1993), pp. 20–1, 89–90; Martha Vicinus, *Intimate Friends: Women Who Loved Women, 1777–1928* (Chicago: University of Chicago Press, 2004), introduction and ch. 1.
16. Dianne Dugaw, *Warrior Women and Popular Balladry, 1650–1850* (Cambridge: Cambridge University Press, 1989).
17. Ibid., pp. 193–4.
18. Ibid., pp. 132, 143–60.
19. Wheelwright, *Amazons and Military Maids*.
20. Donoghue, *Passions Between Women*, chs 2 and 3. Rudolf Dekker and Lottie Van der Pol, *The Tradition of Female Transvestism in Early Modern Europe* (London: Macmillan, 1989).
21. Fraser Easton, 'Gender's Two Bodies: Women Warriors, Female Husbands and Plebeian Life', *Past and Present*, 180 (2003), 131–74.
22. See, for instance, Easton, 'Gender's Two Bodies'; Dugaw, *Warrior Women*; Wheelwright, *Amazons and Military Maids*.
23. Easton, 'Gender's Two Bodies', pp. 154, 157, 160–1.
24. On the tribade see Donoghue, *Passions Between Women*; Valerie Traub, 'The Psychomorphology of the Clitoris', *GLQ: Journal of Lesbian and Gay Studies*, 2 (1995), 81–113; and 'The Perversion of "Lesbian" Desire', *History Workshop Journal*, 41 (1996) 19–50.
25. Easton, 'Gender's Two Bodies', p. 173; Donoghue, *Passions Between Women*.
26. Dugaw, *Warrior Women*, pp. 51–2, 73.
27. Camilla Townsend, 'I Am the Woman For Spirit: A Working Woman's Gender Transgression in Victorian London', *Victorian Studies*, 36, 3 (1993), 293–314.
28. 'The Female Husband', Street ballad c.1838; M. Ryan, *A Manual of Medical Jurisprudence* (London: Sherwood, Gilbert and Piper, 1836), pp. 227–9 quoting *The Times*, 1829. Both reprinted in Alison Oram and Annmarie Turnbull, *The Lesbian History Sourcebook: Love and Sex between Women in Britain from 1780 to 1970* (London: Routledge, 2001), pp. 20–3.
29. Vicinus, *Intimate Friends*. It should be noted that her discussion is of middle-class letters and diaries, not popular culture.

30. H.G. Cocks, *Nameless Offences: Homosexual Desire in the Nineteenth Century* (London: I.B. Tauris, 2003), p. 101.
31. See on this, Charles Upchurch, 'Forgetting the Unthinkable: Cross Dressers in British Society in the Case of Queen v Boulton and Others', *Gender and History*, 12, 1 (2000), 127–57; Cocks, *Nameless Offences*, pp. 105–13.
32. J.S. Bratton, 'Irrational Dress', in Viv Gardner and Susan Rutherford (eds.), *The New Woman and Her Sisters: Feminism and Theatre 1850–1914* (London: Harvester Wheatsheaf, 1992), pp. 77–91, p. 89.
33. Bratton, 'Irrational Dress', pp. 79–81. Martha Vicinus, 'Turn-of-the-Century Male Impersonation: Rewriting the Romance Plot', in Andrew Miller and James Eli Adams (eds.), *Sexualities in Victorian Britain* (Bloomington: Indiana University Press, 1996), pp. 187–213.
34. Lady V. de Frece, *Recollections of Vesta Tilley* (London: Hutchinson, 1934), p. 233.
35. J.S. Bratton, 'Beating the Bounds: Gender Play and Role Reversal in the Edwardian Music Hall', in Michael Booth and Joel Caplan (eds.), *The Edwardian Theatre: Essays on Performance and the Stage* (Cambridge: Cambridge University Press, 1996), pp. 86–110.
36. Vicinus, 'Male Impersonation'. And see Bratton, 'Beating the Bounds', p. 78.
37. Peter Bailey, 'Conspiracies of Meaning: Music Hall and the Knowingness of Popular Culture', *Past and Present*, 144 (1994), 138–70.
38. Michel Foucault, 'Introduction' to *Herculine Barbin, Being the Recently Discovered Memoirs of a Nineteenth-Century French Hermaphrodite* (Brighton: Harvester Press, 1980).
39. Alice Domurat Dreger, 'Hermaphrodites in Love: The Truth of the Gonads', in Vernon Rosario (ed.), *Science and Homosexualities* (New York: Routledge, 1997), pp. 46–66.
40. Alan Sinfield, 'Transgender and les/bi/gay identities', in D. Alderson and L. Anderson (eds.), *Territories of Desire in Queer Culture* (Manchester: Manchester University Press, 2000), p. 156.
41. Havelock Ellis, *Studies in the Psychology of Sex, Vol. 1, Sexual Inversion* (London: The University Press, 1897), pp. 94–7.
42. Lucy Bland and Laura Doan (eds.), *Sexology Uncensored: The Documents of Sexual Science* (Cambridge: Polity Press, 1998). Also see H.G. Cocks in this volume.
43. Lisa Duggan, *Sapphic Slashers: Sex, Violence and American Modernity* (Durham, NC: Duke University Press, 2000). Lisa Duggan, 'The Trials of Alice Mitchell: Sensationalism, Sexology and the Lesbian Subject in Turn-of-the-Century America', *Signs*, 18, 4 (1993), 791–814.
44. Duggan, *Sapphic Slashers*.
45. Laura Doan, *Fashioning Sapphism: The Origins of Modern English Lesbian Culture* (New York: Columbia University Press, 2001).
46. Matt Houlbrook, '"Lady Austin's Camp Boys": Constituting the Queer Subject in 1930s London', *Gender and History*, 14, 1 (2002), 31–61; George Chauncey, *Gay New York: The Making of the Gay Male World, 1890–1940* (London: Flamingo, 1995), chs 2 and 3.
47. Angus McLaren, *The Trials of Masculinity: Policing Sexual Boundaries 1870–1930* (Chicago: University of Chicago Press, 1997), pp. 213, 223–6. Also see Chris Waters, 'Havelock Ellis, Sigmund Freud and the State: Discourses of

Homosexual Identity in Interwar Britain', in Lucy Bland and Laura Doan (eds.), *Sexology in Culture: Labelling Bodies and Desires* (Cambridge: Polity Press, 1998), pp. 165–79 for the influence of medical ideas on the criminal justice system in this period.

48. Peter Gurney, '"Intersex" and "Dirty Girls": Mass-Observation and Working-Class Sexuality in England in the 1930s', *Journal of the History of Sexuality*, 8, 2 (1997), 256–90, 284–6; Vernon, 'For Some Queer Reason', 54.
49. McLaren, *Trials of Masculinity*, p. 228.
50. Alison Oram, '"A Sudden Orgy of Decadence": Writing about Sex between Women in the Interwar Popular Press', in Laura Doan and Jane Garrity (eds.), *Sapphic Modernities: Sexuality, Women and Modern English Culture* (London: Palgrave Macmillan, 2005).
51. *Justice of the Peace and Local Government Review*, 102, 26 (1938), 136, quoted in Vernon, 'For Some Queer Reason', 45.
52. Oram, 'A Sudden Orgy of Decadence'; Alison Oram, *'Her Husband Was A Woman!' Women's Gender-Crossing and Twentieth Century British Popular Culture* (London: Routledge, forthcoming 2007). Ruth Ford finds a similar absence of lesbian sexuality in the reports on the 1920 Fellini murder case in Australia, in contrast to Duggan's research on the US; Ruth Ford, 'The Man-Woman Murderer: Sex, Fraud an the Unmentionable Article in 1920s Australia', *Gender and History*, 12, 1 (2000), 158–96.
53. Vernon, 'For Some Queer Reason', 39.
54. Ruth Ford, '"And Merrily Rang the Bells": Gender-Crossing and Same-Sex Marriage in Australia, 1900–1940', in David Phillips and Graham Willett (eds.), *Australia's Homosexual Histories* (Sydney: Melbourne: Australian Lesbian and Gay Archives, 2000).
55. Alison Oram, 'Feminism, Androgyny and Love Between Women in *Urania*, 1916–40', *Media History*, 7, 1 (2001), 57–70; Joy Dixon, 'Sexology and the Occult: Sexuality and Subjectivity in Theosophy's New Age', *Journal of the History of Sexuality*, 7 (1997), 409–33; Barbara Brothers, 'Fantasy and Identity: The Double Life of a Victorian Sexual Radical', in Angela Ingram and Daphne Patai (eds.), *Rediscovering Forgotten Radicals* (Chapel Hill: University of North Carolina Press, 1993).
56. Thomas Baty, *Alone in Japan: The Reminiscences of an International Jurist Resident in Japan, 1916–1954* (Tokyo: Maruzen, 1959), p. 185.
57. Alice Domurat Dreger, *Doubtful Sex: Hermaphrodites and the Medical Invention of Sex* (Cambridge, MA: Harvard University Press, 1998).
58. Nelly Oudshoorn, *Beyond the Natural Body: An Archaeology of Sex Hormones* (London: Routledge, 1994).
59. Bernice Hausman, *Changing Sex: Transsexualism, Technology, and the Idea of Gender* (Durham, NC: Duke University Press, 1995), p. 2.
60. Ibid., ch. 3.
61. Oram, *'Her Husband Was A Woman!'*
62. Dwight Billings and Thomas Urban, 'The Socio-Medical Construction of Transsexualism: An Interpretation and Critique', in Richard Ekins and Dave King (eds.), *Blending Genders: Social Aspects of Cross-Dressing and Sex-Changing* (London: Routledge, 1995), pp. 99–117.
63. Hausman, *Changing Sex*, pp. 15–19. Dave King, 'Gender Blending: Medical Perspectives and Technology', in Ekins and King, *Blending Genders*, p. 85.

Zachary Nataf argues there were earlier examples: Nataf, *Lesbians Talk Transgender*, p. 10l; See Joanne Meyerowitz, *How Sex Changed: A History of Transsexuality in the United States* (Cambridge, MA: Harvard University Press, 2002), pp. 49–98.

64. Meyerowitz, *How Sex Changed*, p. 259.
65. See King, 'Gender Blending', pp. 75–7.
66. Hausman, *Changing Sex*, pp. 6, 18, ch. 3.
67. Meyerowitz, *How Sex Changed*, illustration 6.
68. See example in the introduction to this chapter.
69. Meyerowitz, *How Sex Changed*, chs 4 and 5. And Joanne Meyerowitz, 'Sex Change and the Popular Press: Historical Notes on Transsexuality in the United States, 1930–1955', *GLQ*, 4, 2 (1998), 159–87.
70. Jay Prosser, 'Transsexuals and the Transsexologists: Inversion and the Emergence of Transsexual Subjectivity', in Bland and Doan, *Sexology in Culture*, pp. 116–31; Prosser, *Second Skins*, p. 133.
71. Jay Prosser and Merl Storr, 'Transsexuality and Bisexuality', in Bland and Doan, *Sexology Uncensored*, p. 76.
72. Prosser, *Second Skins*, ch. 3.
73. Prosser and Storr, 'Transsexuality', p. 76.
74. Prosser, *Second Skins*, ch. 4.
75. Halberstam, *Female Masculinity*, ch. 3.

select bibliography

introduction

Boswell, John. 'Revolutions, Universals, and Sexual Categories', in George Chauncey, Martin Duberman and Martha Vicinus (eds.), *Hidden From History: Reclaiming the Gay and Lesbian Past* (Harmondsworth: Penguin, 1991).

D'Emilio, John and Freedman, Estelle. *Intimate Matters: A History of Sexuality in America* (Chicago: Chicago University Press, 1997).

Foucault, Michel. *The History of Sexuality, Vol. 1. An Introduction*, trans. Robert Hurley (Harmondsworth: Penguin, 1990).

Jagose, Annamarie. *Queer Theory* (Carlton South: Melbourne University Press, 1996).

McNay, Lois. *Foucault: A Critical Introduction* (Cambridge: Polity Press, 1994).

Sedgwick, Eve Kosofsky. *Epistemology of the Closet* (Harmondsworth: Penguin, 1994).

Stein, Ed (ed.). *Forms of Desire: Sexual Orientation and the Social Constructionist Controversy* (New York: Garland, 1990).

demography

Cook, Hera. *The Long Sexual Revolution: English Women, Sex and Contraception 1800–1975* (Oxford: Oxford University Press, 2004).

Gay, Peter. *Education of the Senses: The Bourgeois Experience, Victoria to Freud* (Oxford: Oxford University Press, 1984).

Gillis, John, Levine, David and Tilly, Louise (eds.). *The European Experience of Declining Fertility: A Quiet Revolution 1850–1970* (Oxford: Blackwell, 1992).

Reher, D.S. and Schofield, R.S. (eds.). *Old and New Methods in Historical Demography* (Oxford: Clarendon Press, 1993)

Szreter, Simon. 'The Idea of the Demographic Transition and the Study of Fertility Change: A Critical Intellectual History', *Population and Development Review*, 19, 4 (1993), 659–701.

Szreter, Simon. *Fertility, Class and Gender in Britain, 1860–1940* (Cambridge: Cambridge University Press, 1996).

Wrigley, E.A. and Schofield, R.S. *The Population History of England, 1541–1871* (London: Edward Arnold, 1981).

Wrigley, E.A., Oeppen, J.E., Schofield, R.S. and Davies, R.S. *English Population History from Family Reconstitution, 1580–1837* (Cambridge: Cambridge University Press, 1997).

sexology

Bland, Lucy and Doan, Laura (eds.). *Sexology in Culture: Labelling Bodies and Desires* (Cambridge: Polity Press, 1998).

Bristow, Joseph. *Sexuality* (London: Routledge, 1997).

Bullough, Vern. *Science in the Bedroom: A History of Sex Research* (New York: Basic Books, 1994).

Davidson, Arnold. *The Emergence of Sexuality: Historical Epistemology and the Formation of Concepts* (Cambridge, MA: Harvard University Press, 2001).

Eder, Franz et al. (eds.). *Sexual Cultures in Europe: National Histories* (Manchester: Manchester University Press, 1999).

Irvine, Janice. *Disorders of Desire: Sex and Gender in Modern American Sexology* (Philadelphia: Temple University Press, 1990).

Mort, Frank. *Dangerous Sexualities: Medico-Moral Panics in England since 1830*, 2nd edition (London: Routledge, 2000).

Oosterhuis, Harry. *Stepchildren of Nature: Krafft-Ebing, Psychiatry, and the Making of Sexual Identity* (Chicago: University of Chicago Press, 2000).

Porter, Roy and Teich, Mikuláš. *Sexual Knowledge, Sexual Science: The History of Attitudes to Sexuality* (Cambridge: Cambridge University Press, 1994).

law

Cocks, H.G. *Nameless Offences : Homosexual Desire in the Nineteenth Century* (London: I.B. Tauris, 2003).

Cook, Matt. *London and the Culture of Homosexuality* (Cambridge: Cambridge University Press, 2003).

Knafla, Louis and Binnie, Susan. *Law, Society and the State: Essays in Modern Legal History* (Toronto: University of Toronto Press, 1995).

Moran, Leslie. *The Homosexual(ity) of Law* (London: Routledge, 1996).

Moran, Leslie, Monk, Daniel and Beresford, Sarah (eds.). *Legal Queries: Lesbian, Gay and Transgender Legal Studies* (London: Cassell, 1998).

Sangster, Joan. *Regulating Girls and Women: Sexuality, Family and the Law in Ontario 1920–1960* (Oxford: Oxford University Press, 2001).

Sinfield, Alan. *The Wilde Century: Effeminacy, Oscar Wilde and the Queer Moment* (London: Cassell, 1992).

Stychin, Carl and Herman, Didi. *Sexuality in the Legal Arena* (London: Athlone, 2000).

Sugarman, David (ed.). *Law in History: Histories of Law and Society* (Aldershot: Dartmouth, 1996).

marriage

Echols, Alice. *Daring to be Bad: Radical Feminism in America, 1967–75* (Minneapolis: University of Minnesota Press, 1989).

Gillis, John. *For Better, For Worse: British Marriages, 1600 to the Present* (New York: Oxford University Press, 1985).

Lystra, Karen. *Searching the Heart: Women, Men, and Romantic Love in Nineteenth-Century America* (New York: Oxford University Press, 1989).
Soloway, Richard. *Demography and Degeneration: Eugenics and the Declining Birthrate in Twentieth-Century Britain* (Chapel Hill: University of North Carolina Press, 1995).
Stone, Lawrence. *The Family, Sex and Marriage in England, 1500–1800* (London: Weidenfeld and Nicolson, 1977).
Sullivan, Andrew. *Same-Sex Marriage: Pro and Con* (New York: Vintage, 1997).
Warner, Michael. *The Trouble with Normal: Sex, Politics and the Ethics of Queer Life* (New York: The Free Press, 1999).

race and empire

Ballantyne, Tony and Burton, Antoinette (eds.). *Bodies in Contact: Rethinking Colonial Encounters in World History* (Durham: Duke University Press, 2005).
Cooper, Frederick and Stoler, Ann Laura. *Tensions of Empire: Colonial Cultures in a Bourgeois World* (Berkeley: University of California Press, 1997).
Hall, Catherine (ed.). *Cultures of Empire: Colonizers in Britain and the Empire in the Nineteenth and Twentieth Centuries* (Manchester: Manchester University Press, 2000).
Hall, Catherine. *Civilising Subjects: Metropole and Colony in the English Imagination 1830–1867* (London: Polity, 2002).
Hyam, Ronald. *Empire and Sexuality* (Manchester: Manchester University Press, 1990).
Koven, Seth. *Slumming: Sexual and Social Politics in Victorian London* (Princeton: Princeton University Press, 2004)
Mumford, Kevin. *Interzones: Black/White Sex Districts in Chicago and New York in the Early Twentieth Century* (New York: Columbia University Press, 1997).
Stoler, Ann Laura. *Race and the Education of Desire: Foucault's History of Sexuality and the Colonial Order of Things* (Durham: Duke University Press, 1995).
Stoler, Ann Laura. *Carnal Knowledge and Imperial Power: Race and the Intimate in Colonial Rule* (Berkeley: University of California Press, 2002).
Somerville, Siobhan. *Queering the Color Line: Race and the Invention of Homosexuality in American Culture* (Durham and London: Duke University Press, 2000).

sex and the city

Chauncey, George. *Gay New York: The Making of the Gay Male World, 1890–1940* (London: Flamingo, 1995).
Houlbrook, Matt. *Queer London: Perils and Pleasures in the Sexual Metropolis, 1918–57* (Chicago: Chicago University Press, 2005).
Howard, John. *Men Like That: A Southern Queer History* (Chicago: Chicago University Press, 1999).
Hubbard, Philip. *Sex and the City: Geographies of Prostitution in the Urban West* (Aldershot: Ashgate, 1999), p. 103.
Laumann, Edward. *The Sexual Organization of the City* (Chicago: University of Chicago Press, 2004).

Mort, Frank and Nead, Lynda. 'Introduction: Sexual Geographies', *New Formations*, 37 (1999), 6.

Walkowitz, Judith. *City of Dreadful Delight: Narratives of Sexual Danger in Late-Victorian London* (London: Virago, 1992).

Wilson, Elizabeth. *The Sphinx in the City: Urban Life, the Control of Disorder and Women* (Berkeley: University of California Press, 1991).

religion and spirituality

Alderson, David. *Mansex Fine: Religion, Manliness and Imperialism in Nineteenth Century British Culture* (Manchester: Manchester University Press, 1998).

Dixon, Joy. 'Sexology and the Occult: Sexuality and Subjectivity in Theosophy's New Age', *Journal of the History of Sexuality*, 7 (1997), 409–33.

Elfenbein, Andrew. *Romantic Genius: The Prehistory of a Homosexual Role* (New York: Columbia University Press, 1999).

Foster, Lawrence. *Women, Family and Utopia: Communal Experiments of the Shakers, The Oneida Community, The Mormons* (Syracuse: Syracuse University Press, 1991).

Hanson, Ellis. *Decadence and Catholicism* (Cambridge, MA: Harvard University Press, 1997).

Maynard, John. *Victorian Discourses on Sexuality and Religion* (Cambridge: Cambridge University Press, 1993).

Roden, Frederick. *Same Sex Desire in Victorian Religious Culture* (Basingstoke: Palgrave Macmillan, 2002).

Savile, Julia. *A Queer Chivalry: The Homoerotic Aestheticism of Gerard Manley Hopkins* (Charlottesville: University of Virginia Press, 2000).

pornography and obscenity

Dean, Carolyn. *The Frail Social Body: Pornography, Homosexuality and Other Fantasies of Interwar France* (Berkeley: University of California Press, 2000).

Goulemot, Jean Marie. *Forbidden Texts: Erotic Literature and its Readers in Eighteenth-Century France*, trans. James Simpson (Cambridge: Polity Press, 1994).

Hunt, Lynn (ed.). *The Invention of Pornography: Obscenity and the Origins of Modernity, 1500–1800* (New York: Zone Books, 1993).

Kendrick, Walter. *The Secret Museum: Pornography in Modern Culture* (New York: Viking Press, 1987).

Laqueur, Thomas. *Making Sex: Body and Gender from the Greeks to Freud* (Cambridge: Cambridge University Press, 1990).

MacKinnon, Catharine. *Only Words* (Cambridge, MA: Harvard University Press, 1996).

Moulton, Ian Frederick. *Before Pornography: Erotic Writing in Early Modern England* (Oxford: Oxford University Press, 2000).

Strossen, Nadine. *Defending Pornography: Free Speech, Sex, and the Fight for Women's Rights* (New York: New York University Press, 2000).

Williams, Linda. *Hard Core: Power, Pleasure, and the 'Frenzy of the Visible'* (Berkeley: University of California Press, 1989).

prostitution

Alexander, Ruth. *The Girl Problem: Female Sexual Delinquency in New York, 1900–1930* (Ithaca: Cornell University Press, 1995).

Clement, Elizabeth Alice. *Trick or Treat: Prostitutes, Charity Girls, Courting Couples, and the Creation of Modern Heterosexuality* (Chapel Hill: University of North Carolina Press, 2005).

Gilfoyle, Timothy. *City of Eros: New York City, Prostitution and the Commercialization of Sex, 1790–1820* (New York: Norton, 1992).

Hohn, Maria. *GIs and Frauleins: The German–American Encounter in 1950s West Germany* (Chapel Hill: University of North Carolina Press, 2002).

Karras, Ruth Mazo. *Common Women: Prostitution and Sexuality in Medieval England* (New York: Oxford University Press, 1996).

Levine, Phillipa. *Prostitution, Race and Politics: Policing Venereal Disease in the British Empire* (New York: Routledge, 2003).

Mumford, Kevin. *Interzones: Black/White Sex Districts in Chicago and New York in the Early Twentieth Century* (New York: Columbia University Press, 1997).

White, Luise. *The Comforts of Home: Prostitution in Colonial Nairobi* (Chicago: University of Chicago Press, 1990).

cross-dressing and transgender

Butler, Judith. *Gender Trouble: Feminism and the Subversion of Identity* (New York: Routledge, 1989).

Doan, Laura. *Fashioning Sapphism: The Origins of Modern English Lesbian Culture* (New York: Columbia University Press, 2001).

Duggan, Lisa. *Sapphic Slashers: Sex, Violence and American Modernity* (Durham: Duke University Press, 2000).

Garber, Marjorie. *Vested Interests: Cross Dressing and Cultural Anxiety* (London: Penguin, 1992).

Halberstam, Judith. *Female Masculinity* (Durham: Duke University Press, 1998).

Meyerowitz, Joanne. *How Sex Changed: A History of Transsexuality in the United States* (Cambridge, MA: Harvard University Press, 2002).

Senelick, Lawrence. *The Changing Room: Varieties of Theatrical Cross Dressing* (London: Routledge, 2000).

Upchurch, Charles. 'Forgetting the Unthinkable: Cross Dressers in British Society in the Case of Queen v Boulton and Others', *Gender and History*, 12, 1 (2000), 127–57.

Vernon, James. '"For Some Queer Reason": The Trials and Tribulations of Colonel Barker's Masquerade in Interwar Britain', *Signs*, 26, 1 (2000), 37–62.

childhood and youth

Ariès, Philippe. *Centuries of Childhood* (London: Pimlico, 1996).

Cox, Pam. *Gender, Justice and Welfare. Bad Girls in Britain, 1900–1950* (Basingstoke: Macmillan, 2003).

Jackson, Louise. *Child Sexual Abuse in Victorian England* (London: Routledge, 2000).

Kincaid, James. *Child-Loving. The Erotic Child and Victorian Culture* (London: Routledge, 1992).

Maynard, Steven. '"Horrible Temptations": Sex, Men and Working-Class Male Youth in Urban Ontario, 1890–1935', *Canadian Historical Review*, 78, 2 (1997), 192–235.

Nilan, Cat. 'Hapless Innocence and Precocious Perversity in the Courtroom Melodrama: Representations of the Child Criminal in a Paris Legal Journal, 1830–1848', *Journal of Family History*, 22, 3 (1997), 251–85.

Odem, Mary. *Delinquent Daughters: Protecting and Policing Adolescent Female Sexuality in the United States, 1885–1920* (Chapel Hill: University of North Carolina Press, 1995).

Steedman, Carolyn. *Strange Dislocations. Childhood and the Idea of Human Interiority 1780–1930* (London: Virago, 1995).

Strange, Carolyn. *Toronto's Girl Problem: The Perils and Pleasures of the City, 1880–1930* (Toronto: Toronto University Press, 1995).

index

Breinigsville, PA USA
06 January 2011

252813BV00004B/1/P

DISCARDED